Wetlands

Wetlands

GENERAL EDITORS

Max Finlayson and Michael Moser

INTERNATIONAL WATERFOWL AND WETLANDS RESEARCH BUREAU

IWRB

Facts On File

Oxford • *New York*

To Luc Hoffmann
For his inestimable contribution to
the conservation of wetlands

Wetlands

Facts On File Limited
Collins Street
Oxford OX4 1XJ
UK

Facts On File, Inc.
460 Park Avenue South
New York NY10016
USA

A British CIP Catalogue record for this book is available from the British Library.
U. S. Library of Congress CIP data is available from the Publisher's New York Office.
ISBN 0-8160-2556-8

Facts On File books are available at special discounts when purchased in bulk quantities
for businesses, associations, institutions or sales promotions.
Please contact the Special Sales Department of our Oxford office on 0865 728399
or our New York office on 212/683-2244 (dial 800/322-8755 except in NY, Ak or HI).

Title-page picture: Stromatolites are a special feature of the wetlands in Hamelin Pool, Shark Bay, Australia.

Edited and designed by Toucan Books Limited, London
Glossary and index by Isabell von Oertzen
Printed in Hong Kong
10 9 8 7 6 5 4 3 2 1
This book is printed on acid-free paper.

DISCLAIMER

The designations of geographical entities in this book, and the presentation of the material, do not imply the
expression of any opinion whatsoever on the part of IWRB, concerning the legal status of any country, territory
or area, or of its authorities, or concerning the delimitation of its frontiers or boundaries. The interpretations and
conclusions in this book are those of the contributors and do not necessarily represent the view of IWRB.

Contents

Contributors

PATRICK DENNY is a senior lecturer at the University of London and Director of the Centre for Research in Aquatic Biology at Queen Mary and Westfield College. His main research interest is in African waterplants and wetlands. He serves on the Wetland Programme Advisory Committee of IUCN, the Wetland Management Group of the IWRB and the Council of Management of the Asian Wetland Bureau. He is a Fellow of the Linnean Society and of the Institute of Biology and was awarded a DSc from the University of St Andrews for his contribution to tropical ecology.

MAX FINLAYSON is Assistant Director and Head of the Wetland Division of the IWRB. From 1983 to 1989 he worked on the wetlands of Kakadu National Park, Australia. He is a wetland plant ecologist with experience in temperate and tropical Australia. His work with the IWRB focusses on the conservation and management of internationally important wetlands.

TED HOLLIS is a hydrologist at the Department of Geography, University College, London, as well as the Chief Executive of the Biological Station at Tour du Valat in the Camargue, France. He is a member of the IUCN Wetland Programme Advisory Committee, co-ordinator of the IWRB's Wetland Management Group, and has worked extensively on the hydrology and conservation of wetlands in Europe and the Mediterranean Basin.

TIM JONES graduated from the Department of Geography at Durham University, UK. He has worked subsequently for the Wildfowl and Wetlands Trust, the Ramsar Convention Bureau and the International Waterfowl and Wetlands Research Bureau, where he is currently responsible for coordinating IWRB's technical support to the Ramsar Convention. He was a co-author of *Important Bird Areas in Europe*, published in 1989, and is a keen ornithologist.

JOSEPH LARSON is Professor of Wildlife Biology and Director of the Environmental Institute, University of Massachusetts, USA. He is a member of the IUCN Wetland Programme Advisory Committee, Executive Chairman of the National Wetlands Technical Council, USA, and founding Chairman of the US National Ramsar Committee. In 1990 he received the Chevron Conservation Award for his leadership of the team that developed the first models for functional assessment of freshwater wetlands. He acts in an advisory capacity to the US Congress on its policies for the management and protection of wetlands.

EDWARD MALTBY is a lecturer in geography at the University of Exeter, UK. He is a member of the IUCN Wetland Programme Advisory Committee and has researched extensively on wetlands in the USA, UK, Canada, Fiji, India and the Falkland Islands.

MICHAEL MOSER has been Director of the International Waterfowl and Wetlands Research Bureau since 1988, and was previously with the British Trust for Ornithology. He researched the ecology of herons in the Camargue, France, for his doctoral thesis. Population ecology of waterbirds is his main research interest.

DEREK SCOTT gained his doctorate at the University of Oxford, UK. He has worked extensively in Asia and the Neotropics, and has been responsible for the compilation of wetland directories covering Europe, North Africa, the Neotropics, Asia, Oceania and Australasia.

Editorial Note

The destruction of tropical rainforests, mainly in developing countries, has received spectacular media and public attention in the developed world. Ironically, a comparable rate of destruction of wetlands, under the very eyes of that same media and public, has proceeded, until recently, almost unopposed and unpublicized. Today, wetlands - the dynamic, highly productive and valuable interface between land and water - have joined the tropical forests at the top of the list of threatened habitats.

Why are wetlands so threatened? The answer is simple: these habitats have characteristics - be it flat land, rich alluvial soils, water, commercially exploitable species or recreational potential - which make them prime candidates for exploitation. Particularly during the last 50 years, the incessant demand for economic growth has provided incentives for small numbers of individuals to make substantial profits from the non-sustainable exploitation of these resources. This has been without regard for the long-term environmental consequences to society. This is the crux of the wetland conservation issue.

Today we are at a watershed for wetland conservation. While rural communities have long recognized the value of wetlands in providing food, water, transport and building materials, the more economically ambitious world has seen them as wastelands to be filled and drained. However, there is room for some optimism that these days are over: the Ramsar Convention on the conservation of wetlands is thriving; environmental groups are increasingly winning campaigns to save threatened wetlands; and as water becomes a more and more valuable resource, wetlands are gaining increasing public attention. Such measures have come too late for many wetlands.

We hope that this book will make people more aware of wetlands and the urgent need to conserve those that have escaped destruction, and to restore those that have been degraded. It is only by raising awareness across a broad spectrum of society that the political and economic will to conserve wetlands can become strong enough to stem further losses of this priceless resource. If we fail to tip the balance in favour of wetlands, the losses will continue with unimaginable consequences for the global environment and for society.

About the book

Wetlands represents the culmination of more than 20 years' work to document the status of the world's major wetlands, through a programme of regional wetland directories. These are detailed reference texts, which have received only limited circulation, distributed largely to conservation administrators in governmental and non-governmental organizations. One aim of this book has therefore been to make available this and other information to a wider audience.

There is little agreement among scientists on what constitutes a wetland, and to circumvent this endless and spirited debate, we have adopted the very broad definition agreed by the nations which have signed the Ramsar Convention on wetlands. Similarly, there is no universally agreed classification of wetland types, and these vary greatly in both form and nomenclature between regions. The authors have therefore adopted regionally appropriate classifications and nomenclature. Potential confusion over the use of common names of plants and animals has been eliminated where possible by the use of the exclusive taxonomic name for each species.

Current knowledge of wetlands varies greatly across the globe. For example, detailed inventories have not yet been made for large parts of Australasia and Oceania, the Middle East or the USSR. Together with the major geographical, political and environmental disparities between the regions, this has led to unavoidable differences in the level of information presented in each chapter. For example, it is extremely difficult to compare the tiny wetlands of the Oceanic islands with those of Asia on maps of the same scale. However, such wetlands may be of great importance to the ecology and economy of these small islands.

Acknowledgements

The book draws on the results of a number of regional wetland directories which have been coordinated by the IWRB and other organizations. We particularly wish to thank our major international partners in these projects: the Asian Wetland Bureau, the International Council for Bird Preservation (ICBP), the Ramsar Bureau, the World Conservation Union (IUCN), and the World Wide Fund for Nature (WWF). Derek Scott, the contributor of two chapters of this book, has played a leading role in several of these projects, and we thank him for his outstanding contribution to our knowledge of the wetlands of the world.

We owe our sincere thanks to the contributors of the individual chapters - Patrick Denny, Max Finlayson, Ted Hollis, Tim Jones, Joseph Larson, Edward Maltby and Derek Scott - all of whom are well-travelled, experienced and busy wetland conservationists. This brought production challenges both to the authors and to the editors and publishers, with communication between IWRB headquarters in England and fieldwork sites scattered across the globe.

We are also grateful to our publishers, Facts On File, and the editorial and design team at Toucan Books, for giving us the stimulus, opportunity and very necessary support during the preparation of this book. We would also like to thank Isabell von Oertzen for her editorial assistance in checking the text and compiling the glossary and index.

Finally, we acknowledge the thousands of wetland and waterbird conservationists around the world who have contributed to the work of IWRB and many other organizations. Without their efforts, the prospects for wetlands would be bleak indeed.

MAX FINLAYSON AND MICHAEL MOSER (EDITORS)
International Waterfowl and Wetlands Research Bureau (IWRB)
Slimbridge, Gloucester GL2 7BX, UK.

CONTRIBUTOR: E. MALTBY

Wetlands and their Values

WETLANDS have played a crucial role in human history. Major stages in the evolution of life itself probably took place in nutrient-rich coastal waters. Some of the first prehistoric cultures, such as those of the early Mesolithic settlements around the post-glacial lake margins and coasts of Europe and those of the coastal Indian communities in North America, depended on wetlands for food and materials for building, shelter and clothing.

Excavated archaeological sites such as the one at Star Carr in North Yorkshire, England show how strong the association was between these prehistoric cultures and wetlands. Some 10,000 years ago the occupants of the wetland margins of what used to be Lake Pickering probably selected a beaver (*Castor fiber*) clearing for their settlement. Evidence abounds of the importance in their daily lives of the lake and its associated wetlands: a birchwood paddle, for instance, and large numbers of waterbird bones, showing the dependence of this community on the wetland food chain.

Elsewhere in Europe and especially from the later Mesolithic period, shell middens and the remains of barbs and fish spears are evidence of a strong dependence of communities on the rich fishing resources of coastal lagoons, estuaries and other shallow bodies of water.

The regular inundation of the fertile floodplains of the Nile, Tigris and Euphrates Rivers was an important factor in releasing the peoples of these regions from the necessity of daily food collection and in enabling them to develop rich civilizations. There is still an important link between many wetlands and the health, welfare and safety of inhabitants of wetlands and their margins. The connection is particularly close in developing countries where many communities depend on wetlands for the maintenance of traditional subsistence activities, including livestock herding, hunting, fishing and farming. The dependence is now less direct, but no less important, for communities in the more economically developed countries. For example, two-thirds of the fish we eat depend on wetlands at some stage in their life cycle; in the Gulf of Mexico alone, 90 per cent of the fish harvested are wetland-dependent species.

Wetlands perform a wide range of functions that are essential for supporting plant and animal life and for maintaining the quality of the environment. These functions include: flood control; shoreline stabilization; sediment, nutrient and toxicant retention; and food chain support. The abuse of wetlands means a reduction in their ability to supply useful services and, in many cases, valuable products.

The destruction and degradation of wetlands has been particularly commonplace throughout the industrialized world. The results can be seen all too vividly in an ever-greater scarcity of wildlife and, for example, increased prices for wetland products such as fish and game, the need for water purification plants and concrete flood-protection structures. Hardest hit are developing countries for whom the expense of replacing these lost functions is an unwelcome, often impossible burden.

People are realizing more and more the true value of wetland goods and services, which are provided free of financial or environmental cost if used wisely. They are increasingly aware of the serious consequences of wetland transformation and the resulting losses not only for wildlife, but also for the well-being of human communities.

WHAT ARE WETLANDS?

Wetlands occupy the transitional zone between permanently wet and generally dry environments. They share characteristics of both environments, yet cannot be classified exclusively as either aquatic or terrestrial.

Classification of wetlands is fraught with controversy and problems, partly because of the enormous variety of wetland types and their highly dynamic character, and partly because of difficulties in defining their boundaries with any precision. Where, for example, does a wetland end and a deep-water aquatic habitat start? For how long and how

8

intensely does an area have to be flooded, or in any other way saturated with water, for it to be a wetland rather than a terrestrial ecosystem? There are no universally accepted or scientifically precise answers to these questions. The difficulties are compounded by changes over time by which some wetlands may evolve through various stages to become dryland areas.

Certain features, nonetheless, are obvious. It is the predominance of water for some significant period of time which characterizes and drives the development of wetlands. Surface-water flooding or high water tables result in conditions that require significant adaptation by plant and animal life and contribute to the development and the properties of the soil.

Whilst lacking scientific exactness the Ramsar Convention on Wetlands of International Importance Especially as Waterfowl Habitat uses a definition which conveys much of the essential character of wetlands, as well as implying the complexity involved. It defines them as: 'areas of marsh, fen, peatland or water, whether natural or artificial, permanent or temporary, with water that is static or flowing, fresh, brackish or salt including areas of marine water, the depth of which at low tide does not exceed 6 m [just over 19 ft].'

Wetlands exhibit enormous diversity according to their genesis, geographical location, water regime and chemistry, dominant plants, and soil or sediment characteristics. There may be considerable variation within a single wetland area, due to the importance of even subtle differences in flooding. Many different types of wetland may be found in close proximity, forming not just different ecosystems, but wholly distinctive landscapes.

The dynamics of water supply and loss are fundamental to the development, maintenance and functioning of wetlands. The hydrology of a wetland is defined by three factors: how much water enters it, how much water leaves it and how much water the wetland is able to store. Whilst the inflow-outflow balance is influenced primarily by climate and catchment configuration, storage is controlled more by local geomorphology (that is, the configuration of

the land) and geological characteristics.

Hydrology, in turn, influences the physical and chemical characteristics of the wetland - salinity, oxygen and other gas diffusion rates, the reduction-oxidation (redox) state of ecologically important nutrients, chemical reactions and nutrient solubility - which have major implications for both flora and fauna, as well as for ecosystem dynamics. The composition and diversity of species in the wetland influences the way in which nutrients and pollutants are cycled in the wetland ecosystem - all these are influenced by the hydrological regime.

Marshes

Marshes have a number of specific characteristics. They are usually dominated by reeds, rushes, grasses and sedges, that are commonly referred to as emergents since they grow with their stems partly in and partly out of the water. Marshes are sustained by water sources other than direct rainfall, and vary considerably in response to what are often no more than subtle hydrological and chemical differences. They include some of the most productive ecosystems in the world. There are three major groups: freshwater marshes, tidal salt marshes and tidal freshwater marshes.

Freshwater marshes account for a large proportion of the world's temperate wetlands; they comprise, for example, over 90 per cent of the wetland area of the United States of America (excluding Alaska and Hawaii). They are found in all latitudes in places where ground water, surface springs, streams or lakes cause frequent flooding. They typically occur in shallow water along the edges of lakes or rivers and especially in the abandoned sections of river channels, such as oxbow lakes. In the Okavango Delta of Botswana, reeds (especially *Phragmites*) and sedges form a distinctive marsh community along the channels separating swamp areas from the so-called flats in the middle parts of the delta which are less frequently flooded than the rest of the region. Depressions in floodplains or other similar landscape features, such as the Prairie Potholes of North

THE RAMSAR CONVENTION

The Convention on Wetlands of International Importance Especially as Waterfowl Habitat, often known as the Ramsar Convention from its place of adoption in Iran in 1971, is an intergovernmental treaty which provides the framework for international cooperation for the conservation of wetlands.

By 1991, more than 60 countries had joined the Convention, thereby agreeing to accept a number of obligations, including the following:
(i) to designate wetlands of international importance for inclusion in a list of so-called 'Ramsar sites'
(ii) to maintain the ecological character of their listed Ramsar sites

(iii) to organize their planning so as to achieve the wise use of all of the wetlands on their territory
(iv) to designate wetlands as nature reserves.

Already, more than 500 wetland sites have been added to the Ramsar List, covering more than 30 million hectares (74 million acres) of wetland habitat.

America, also enable the development of freshwater marshes, often through a process of ecological succession.

Dominant plants in most freshwater marshes include species of reeds (*Phragmites*), reedmace (*Typha*), club rush (*Scirpus*), sedges (*Carex*), spike rushes (*Eleocharis*), sawgrass (*Cladium*), cockspurs (*Panicum*), rushes (*Juncus*) and papyrus (*Cyperus papyrus*). The precise nature of the vegetation, however, varies geographically and with the hydrology of the marsh. Where water depth is greater than 50 cm (19 1/2 in), for example, emergent vegetation generally gives way to floating and submerged water plants which often form attractive mosaics of different colours and textures, as, for example, in the complex of sawgrass marshes and broad channels of the Florida Everglades.

Tidal salt marshes are typical of temperate sheltered shorelines, and dominate large areas of the Arctic and Atlantic seaboards of North America, the Gulf of Mexico and coastal Europe. They often develop in complex zones, reflecting tidal fluctuations and differences in salinity and period of inundation. They are often dissected by tidal creeks which provide the vital pathways that allow the exchange of water, nutrients, organic matter and biota. These are also the routes by which salt marsh, estuary and open sea are linked, enabling the salt marsh to play a vital role in

ECOLOGICAL SUCCESSION

Succession is at work in wetlands throughout the world and underlines not only their dynamic character but also their highly changeable nature, making them vulnerable to both man-induced as well as environmental changes.

The distinct zones of different vegetation that surround the edge of a water body provide the clue to the fate of many shallow lakes and ponds. It is a fate which may result eventually in the complete elimination of the wetland - an ecosystem self-destruct process in which successive plant communities alter environmental conditions in a way that makes the habitat less favourable for its own survival, though more favourable for the development of a different community.

Water plants such as species of duckweeds (*Lemna*), pondweeds (*Potamogeton*), water lilies (*Nymphaea*),

bladderworts, *Salvinia* or *Trapa* may be the first flowering plants to colonize the open water of a shallow lake or pond. These produce organic detritus which accumulates along with other sediment that is washed into the system. The result is that the lake gradually fills from the margins to the centre. This process can be very slow and is strongly influenced by organic decomposition rates and hydrological flushing, for example.

As the water becomes shallower the emergent species - rushes, sedges, reeds and grasses - establish themselves. They do three things: impede water movement, trap more sediment and shade out the floating water plants. The result is that the basin simply fills up. This may in due course mean that the lake or pond is unable to store enough water to last the whole year. The evapotranspiration rates of the

more terrestrial plants may accelerate the whole process of drying out. The lake or pond is transformed progressively into a marsh. Or it may become a fen - a fen forms where the infill is primarily organic, resulting in a peaty substrate; it also depends on a nutrient-rich water flow. The diversity of species in a fen is often a good guide to the chemistry of the water supplying it.

Trees such as species of alder or willow may establish themselves in temperate regions. The result is 'carr woodland' or 'fen carr'. Continued drying out of the site by tree growth allows more massive species such as oak to occupy the site. Domination of the area by these trees culminates in the final transformation of the original wetland into a terrestrial woodland ecosystem.

The process of succession does not always take this turn. If, for example, the peat continues to accumulate above the nutrient-rich ground water or if waterlogging at the site is maintained largely by rainfall, the marsh or fen stage may lead instead to the formation of a bog. This will be dominated by acid-loving plant species such as bog mosses, cotton grasses and bog asphodel - or, in the Southern Hemisphere, additional species such as *Astelia*.

As the vegetation changes, and as the character and wetness of the substrate are transformed, so too the kinds of animal populating the wetland will change. Fish and other aquatic organisms that normally dominate permanent water bodies and that support fish-eating and diving birds will eventually give way to new groups of terrestrial animal species. What happens in between the two extremes of aquatic and terrestrial is what makes wetlands such special habitats.

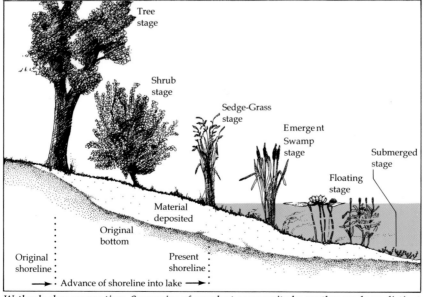

Wetlands change over time. Succession of one plant community by another produces distinct zonation of vegetation and habitat around open water bodies.

Cypress (Taxodium distinctum) *swamp in Louisiana, USA, with duckweed covering the standing water.*

supporting the spawning, nursery and feeding requirements of many marine organisms.

Salt marshes are characterized by a range of highly adaptive salt-tolerant plant species, such as cord grass (*Spartina*), glasswort (*Salicornia*), sea blite (*Suaeda*), sea purslane (*Halimione*), sea-lavender (*Limonium*) and perennial glasswort (*Arthrocnemum*). Farther inland, these give way to species more adapted to brackish, then to freshwater conditions.

Tidal freshwater marshes are found farther inland than salt marshes, at the heads of tides. Although influenced by the rise and fall of tides, they are not exposed to high levels of salinity. Plant life is more diverse than that of salt marshes and often includes a wide range of vividly coloured flowering plants such as those found in the Maryland marshes of the United States.

Swamps

Swamps are often confused with marshes. They are, however, very different. Swamps generally have saturated soils or are flooded for most, if not all, of the growing season. They are often dominated by a single emergent herb species, or are forested. The reed *Phragmites australis* dominates large temperate swamps (reed swamps) and was once a characteristic feature of the Fenland landscape of eastern England. It still covers extensive tracts in areas such as Hokkaido (northern Japan) and the Danube and Volga Deltas which have so far avoided large-scale drainage. Members of the Restionaceae family such as *Empodisma*, along with grasses (for example, species of *Sporobolus*), dominate swamps in the low latitudes of the Southern Hemisphere.

The form of many large tropical African lakes -

such as Lakes Chad, Bangweulu (Zambia), George (Uganda), Naivasha (Kenya), Malombi (Malawi) and Chilwa (Malawi and Mozambique) - favours marginal swamp development. These swamps tend to be dominated by tropical species of reed and reedmace (or cattail) as well as papyrus.

American authors generally consider swamps to be frequently flooded wetlands which are dominated by woody plants. This still encompasses an enormous diversity, from the swamps of the northeast of North America dominated by red maple (*Acer rubrum*) to the residual tracts of bald cypress (*Taxodium distichum*) and tupelo (species of *Nyssa*) swamps that were once so much more extensive in the south and southeast.

In the Caribbean, royal palm (*Roystonea princeps*) may dominate locally, whilst in the tropical valleys of Amazonia the swamp forest or igapo is much more species-diverse.

Peatlands

Peatlands are estimated to cover 500 million hectares (1,236 million acres), or possibly more, of the world's land surface; they occur on all continents.

Peat is formed when decomposition fails to keep pace with the production of organic matter. This is a result of waterlogging, a lack of oxygen or of nutrients, high acidity or low temperatures. Peat can be found in many types of wetland, including marshes, swamps, floodplains and coastal wetlands such as mangroves. Where the peat deposits are deeper than 300-400 mm (12-15 in), they create various distinctive wetland ecosystems such as bogs and fens. These are known collectively as mires to distinguish them from other wetland systems which may simply accumulate some organic matter or peat.

Peatlands or mires are complex ecosystems both in their physical structure and in the relationships that develop among the plants and animals which depend on them. Their maintenance relies on particular hydrological regimes, vegetation cover and in some cases, forms of grazing. Many peatlands are so delicately balanced that only very slight changes are sufficient to cause substantial alteration or degradation.

Bogs form where a high water table, fed directly by rain and snow, results in waterlogged soil with reduced levels of oxygen. Rainfall leaches out nutrients in the soil, and the slow fermentation of organic matter produces acids. Bogs are characterized by acid-loving vegetation such as cotton grasses (*Eriophorum*), purple moor grass (*Molinia caerulea*), rushes (*Schoenus*), sedge (*Carex rostrata*), horsetails (*Equisetum*) and mosses (*Sphagnum*). Of particular importance are the *Sphagnum* bog mosses which can, sponge-like, hold more than ten times their dry weight of water. In the taiga (the vast coniferous forest of sub-Arctic North America and Eurasia), larch (*Larix decidua*), black spruce (*Picea mariana*), pine (*Pinus*), birch (*Betula*), alder (*Alnus*) and sallows (*Salix caprea*) may grow on the bog surface. Extreme waterlogging in the summer causes many tall trees to lean, producing spectacular 'drunken forests'.

There are two principal types of bog: blanket bogs and raised bogs. Where the peat covers wide tracts of terrain independent of the details in relief the formation is called blanket bog. In such cases, the peat may have expanded beyond the original confines of a lake or pond basin. These bogs are typical of coastal and upland areas of western Europe, the Kamchatka Peninsula in the Soviet Union, southern Chile, southwestern New Zealand, the sub-Antarctic islands, and parts of the tundra (the treeless zone between the Arctic icecap and the northern timber line) and the taiga of the Northern Hemisphere.

Peat may continue to grow upwards to form a raised bog. This has a distinctive dome-shaped form, and as a result its own peculiar hydrological system. Eventually, the bog may grow to the point where it is no longer possible for a permanently high water table to be maintained. Trees or shrubs can then establish themselves on the drier surface, provided that climate and human activities allow. This has happened, for example, at Shapwick Heath in the Somerset Levels, England, where deciduous woodland has established itself over a raised bog, and in Switzerland, where forests of mountain pines (*Pinus montana*) rise over mountain bogs.

Raised bogs are found in Europe, the Soviet Union, Japan and North America. Similar peat masses also occur in the tropical lowlands of Indonesia, Malaysia and Brazil and in the temperate regions of Chile, Argentina, New Zealand and the sub-Antarctic islands.

In Britain, the vegetation of an actively growing raised bog is dominated by heather-clad or cotton grass hummocks and *Sphagnum*-carpeted hollows or open water pools. But other plants often vary the pattern - the insectivorous species of sundew (*Drosera*), bog asphodel (*Narthecium ossifragum*), cranberry (*Oxycoccus palustris*), bog rosemary (*Andromeda polifolia*), white beak sedge (*Rhynchospora alba*) and the rarer cloudberry (*Rubus chamaemorus*).

The depth of peat in raised bogs - generally 4-12 m (13-39 $^1/_2$ ft) - has made them prime candidates for exploitation in places such as the British Isles, Finland and the Netherlands for energy or horticultural uses. Concern is growing that a similar fate may be in store for the tropical peatlands of Southeast Asia and South America.

Strange bog patterns have developed in regions of permafrost and frequent frost action. These include the remarkable geometry of frost-wedge polygons. Other interesting formations are palsa bogs (mounds or hills covered in peat which is, in turn, covered with cotton grass, sedges, mosses and sometimes shrubs) and string or aapa bogs where the influence of ice movement and waterlogging forms complex mosaics of ridges and hollows.

Fens which are fed by ground water or by interior drainage into hollows - rather than by precipitation - produce wetlands higher in nutrient content than bogs, but still able to accumulate peat. The combination of more nutrients and lower acidity results in fens supporting a very different vegetation, often a luxuriant and species-rich cover of reeds, sedges and herbs. Frequently fed by alkaline ground water, springs or hillside flushes, they are common throughout Europe, parts of North America, low latitude mountains and parts of Australia and New Zealand. Attractive broadleaved herbs often grow in association with these wetlands.

One final form of peatland, peculiar to North America, is the pocosin. This term derives from an Algonquin North American Indian word and describes a special type of wetland - also known as 'swamp-on-a-hill' - dominated by evergreen shrubs of bays (such as *Myrica gale*), hollies (*Ilex verlicillata*) and pond pine (*Pinus serotina*). They occupy the broad, flat regions of higher land between two rivers that are characteristic of parts of the coastal plain from Virginia to the Carolinas. Despite their warm location they have accumulated extensive and deep tracts of acidic peat. Akin to bogs in genesis they are extremely difficult to penetrate because of dense growths of often spiny vegetation and the waterlogged terrain. They are an important place of refuge for insectivorous plants such as the pitcher plant (*Sarracenia minor*) and animals such as the black bear (*Ursus americanus*) and bobcat (*Felis rufus*).

Floodplain Wetlands

Floodplains - the flat land bordering rivers that is subject to periodic flooding - tend, naturally, to be most expansive along the lower reaches of rivers. In many areas, floodplains are associated with coastal lowlands and often end in estuaries or deltas. In other cases, however, floodplains may spread out into large deltas at a considerable distance from the coast, as for example in the vast inland deltas of the Niger in Mali, the Pantanal in South America and the Okavango in Botswana.

The natural configuration of the land controls the depth, timing and duration of flooding. In some places the terrain is so flat that seasonal rainfall can produce flooding over large areas. Extensive sheet-flooding of this kind occurs, for example, in the basin of the Chari-Lagone River in southern Chad. In all areas subject to flooding, permanent or semi-permanent areas of standing water may be left in oxbows and other depressions after the floodwaters have receded. These waters are often shallow, but nevertheless, can be vital dry season refuges for fish and other wildlife. The floodplain grasses in areas that have seen sheet-flooding can sustain large populations of grazing animals, including domestic livestock.

Some of the largest sheet-flood regions are in South America. The Gran Pantanal of the Paraguay River comprises a vast area of shallow interconnecting lakes and wetland complexes, which in some years can cover 10 million hectares (24.7 million acres); the Apure-Aranca tributaries of the Orinoco in Venezuela flow through a floodplain of 7 million hectares (17.3 million acres).

Distinctive wetland forests have developed over floodplains throughout the world, particularly those of larger rivers. Remnants of these forests can be seen, although on a tiny scale, in the lines of trees that follow the banks of even small river channels but never extend inland onto farmed or built-over land, where unconfined flooding has long since been regulated. Generally speaking, only small areas of these floodplain forests remain in Europe. One of the largest to have survived is the Hainburg Forest near Vienna, Austria. Regularly flooded by snow-melt waters, it supports a rich fauna and flora including three-quarters of the tree species found in Europe, over 200 species of breeding and migratory birds (including

sea eagles, storks and spoonbills), over 40 species of fish as well as tree frogs, tortoises and otters.

The scale of the Hainburg is dwarfed, however, when compared with the floodplain forest of the Lower Mekong of Indochina where the Tonle Sap (Great Lake) in Cambodia changes in area from 2,500 km² (965 sq miles) in the dry season to 11,000 km² (4,250 sq miles) when flooded. Equally impressive are the so-called bottomland hardwood forests which still dominate vast tracts of the valley of the Lower Mississippi River, USA.

Species composition in such forests reflects the flooding regime. Whilst true swamp species like bald cypress (*Taxodium distichum*) and water tupelo (*Nyssa aquatica*) occupy the wettest areas, black willow (*Salix nigra*), silver maple (*Acer saccharinum*) and cotton-wood (*Populus dettoides*) are most prominent in the semi-permanently inundated zones. Species of oak (*Quercus*), ash (*Fraxinus nigra*), elm (*Elmus*) and hickory (*Carya aquatica*) are more characteristic of the seasonally flooded margins.

Mangroves, Nipa and Tidal Freshwater Swamp Forest

Mangrove forests are, in fact, diverse collections of trees which include many unrelated genera and species that share the ability to grow in salty, tropical environments.

Extensive cable roots of the pioneering red mangrove in the Black River, Jamaica.

The world's mangrove forests cover at least 14 million hectares (34.6 million acres) and are most common on the coasts of some of the poorest nations on Earth. The greatest concentration is in the Indian Ocean-West Pacific region; about 20 per cent of the world's total area of mangroves borders the Sunda Shelf region enclosed by Vietnam, Thailand, Malaysia, Sumatra, Java and Borneo. Two of the largest single mangrove forests are the Sundarbans forest in Bangladesh which covers nearly 1 million hectares (1.47 million acres) and, on the west side of Africa, the Niger Delta which covers 700,000 hectares (1.73 million acres).

Mangroves, which are mostly limited to within 25° North and South of the Equator, are the tropical and subtropical equivalents of the tidal salt marsh of mid and high latitudes, and like salt marshes are highly adapted to the stresses of flooding and salinity. Adaptations include specialized root-cell membranes which prevent or reduce entry of salt, salt secretion and loss from leaf fall. Other adaptations are the ability to exchange gas more efficiently through lenticels (small gaps in the bark where the cells fit loosely, leaving air gaps that link with air spaces in the trunk) or even more elaborate tube-like breathing structures called pneumatophores, which grow vertically upwards from the roots, often in dense arrays as in the black mangrove (*Avicennia germinans*). Prop roots and floating seedlings all help the various plants of the mangrove forests to survive in hostile coastal environments.

There are an estimated 80 species of mangrove tree and shrub. They are extremely varied and provide habitat for a rich array of dependent organisms (the whole assemblage - trees, shrubs and dependent organisms - being called mangal). Closed forests of red mangrove (*Rhizophora mangle*) and black mangrove grow 40-50 m (130-165 ft) high in parts of Brazil, Colombia, Equador and Venezuela. In Asia and Oceania, the plants form tangled, almost impenetrable closed forests. On more arid coasts and near the extremes of the climatic range for mangroves (such as in Florida, Louisiana and the Japanese Pacific islands) stunted shrubs less than 1 m (3 1/2 ft) high form communities, often with discrete and widely separated clumps.

Mangrove forests frequently show distinct zonation. Red mangrove is often a pioneer, growing up in the zone that is more continually flooded, with seedlings and small trees sprouting even below low water. These give way first to full-grown *Rhizophora* species with prop roots, and then, towards the high tide zone, come the taller black mangroves.

Once established, the network of horizontal or cable roots anchors the trees to the soft mud and traps more sediment. Indeed, mangrove wetlands can advance out to sea at a rate of more than 100 m (328 ft) a year. Palenbang in Indonesia provides an interesting illustration of this process in action. It was once a thriving port on the north coast of Sumatra; it was visited by Marco Polo in the thirteenth century. Today it lies 50 km (31 miles) inland.

Various other kinds of wetland forest develop farther inland. On river banks in areas that are periodically inundated, freshwater nipa palm (*Nypa fruticans*) becomes prominent and is often associated with dense growths of the fern *Acrostichum aureum*. Together they may cover extensive areas separating mangrove from freshwater swamp forest. Beyond the influence of saltwater, a rich variety of Dipterocarp species abound in floodplains where standing water persists for significant periods, often to a depth of 1 m (3 1/2 ft) or more.

The waterlogged substrate of these swamp forest regions is highly productive. In particular, it frequently leads to the accumulation of deep peat deposits. These can exceed 10 m (33 ft) in parts of Southeast Asia such as Sumatra, but are more often limited to 1-3 m (3 1/2-10 ft). The swamp forests of South America and Southeast Asia are also rich in tree species, many of which are commercially important for timber. The swamps forests of North Selangor, Malaysia, for example, are a rich source of meranti bakan (*Shorea uliginosa*), biritangor (*Calophyllum ferrugineum*), mertaf (*Cteriolophon parvifolius*), ramin melawis (*Gonystylus bancanus*), geronggang (*Cratoxylon arborescens*), terentang (*Campriosperma coriaceum*) and terap (*Parartocarpus ridleyi*).

Paper barks (*Melaleuca* species) are often dominant and are particularly common as secondary growth on the edge of floodplains and permanent waterholes. They are frequently successful in colonizing areas where attempts to clear and drain peat swamps have been abandoned. Palms such as sago palm (*Metroxylon sagu*), on which large numbers of people in Irian Jaya (the Indonesian part of New Guinea) subsist, and pandans (*Pandanus*) are frequent understorey trees in the swamp forests of Indonesia which cover over 17 million hectares (42 million acres). In Africa, *Ficus* and *Syzigium* species and borassus palms are characteristic elements of comparable forests.

Lakes

Standing bodies of water occupying either large basins or small depressions in the landscape give rise to a huge variety of wetlands. These bodies of water range from full-scale lakes, usually with deep water in

Prespa Lake, north Greece, with artificial islands to encourage breeding of Dalmatian pelicans.

which temperature changes with depth, to ponds, which are small, generally shallow and with water of more uniform temperature; they may be of natural or man-made origin. Wetlands form in the shallow margins of these lakes or ponds; how exactly they develop depends on differences in shoreline orientation, gradient and water depth.

A basic distinction can be made between exoreic lake systems in which there is a more-or-less balanced throughflow of water and endoreic lakes which are the focus of internal drainage. In the latter case, water leaves the lake usually by evaporation only, which results in the progressive accumulation of mineral salts and hence the formation of a salt lake. This contrasts with exoreic lakes where throughflow is generally sufficient to flush out salts and maintain freshwater conditions. Exoreic lakes are the largest, oldest and most permanent. They include Lake Baykal in the USSR and the lakes of the East African Rift Valley, such as Lake Tanganyika. The turnover of water in these large exoreic lakes is measured in thousands of years, which explains, in part, the high degree of species endemism that is a characteristic of so many of them.

Compared with, for example, rivers, lakes tend to offer a relatively more stable environment. River-transported sediment settles out in the lake water, and the amount of light that penetrates the water increases. This allows a suspended community of phytoplankton (various kinds of minute, floating aquatic plants) to develop and by the process of photosynthesis they bring about the production of organic nutrients and oxygen; this community, together with submerged plants growing in the lake, serves as the food base for the lake ecosystem.

The growth of the phytoplankton and other plants that provide the food base is controlled not only by light penetration and temperature, but also by nitrogen and phosphorus availability. For this reason the character of the drainage basin - its geology, soils, vegetation and land use - is extremely important in determining the processes and development that characterize the lake as well as its marginal wetlands.

Two processes resulting from human activities have brought about major changes in the character of lakes. The first, eutrophication, is due, paradoxically, to an excess of nutrients. These arrive in the lake in fertilizer run-off and organic waste from, for example, sewage, animal effluent and fish farms. The results include increased phytoplankton and aquatic plant growth. This in turn may mean that submerged water plants disappear through competition from phytoplankton as the water clarity declines. The phytoplankton may produce toxins in quantities harmful to humans as well as to fish and other wildlife. The high levels of organic matter arising from increased phytoplankton production may cause massive deoxygenation of the lake water, with severe loss of aquatic animal life.

The second process is called acidification. Many lakes, ponds and upland headwaters running off hard, resistent bedrock or bogs in the high latitudes of the Northern Hemisphere are naturally poor in nutrients; they rely on the scant supply of nutrients provided by rainwater to support the effective functioning of their ecosystems. This has positive consequences. The characteristic clarity of such waters, for instance, not only reflects limited phytoplankton production, but also high levels of oxygen saturation, which is what makes them ideal for fish spawning.

On the other hand, these water bodies have little resistance to acidity from atmospheric sources or upland drainage, and the results can be catastrophic. Associated high aluminium and heavy metal concentrations cause a major reduction in the diversity of the lake community. Fish, in particular, suffer - fish eggs fail to hatch; fry fail to develop normally and gills are damaged.

Waters that have been especially badly affected by acidification include many of the shallow lakes of southern Canada and Scandinavia - for example, Baby, Alice, Swan and Clearwater Lakes adjacent to the Sudbury smelters in Ontario, Canada.

Endoreic lakes are often ephemeral and seasonal - dry saltpans in the summer and shallow flooded areas in the wet period. Their animal and plant life is limited to just a few species, although around their margins a salt marsh community may establish itself.

Endoreic lake water is often more concentrated than seawater, but nevertheless may be capable of high levels of productivity. In Lake Nakuru, Kenya, to take just one example, the blue green alga *Spirulina platensis* supports over 1 million lesser flamingos (*Phoeniconaias minor*) which, in turn, play their important part in the life of the lake by filtering the algae from the water.

In other similar lakes large numbers of brine shrimp, such as *Artemia salina*, occur. These are also to be found in artificial saltpans, where shorebirds (waders) and flamingos feed on them.

Estuaries and Lagoons

Estuaries and lagoons are complex environments supporting a range of wetland types, including inter-tidal mud and sandflats, salt marshes, mangroves (in the tropics), beaches and rocky shores as well as shallow water bodies. Their character and ecological stability, however, cannot be divorced from processes and events upstream.

River mouths are commonly funnel-shaped, widening as they meet the sea. The modern form of these estuaries was caused by a general rise in sea level since the end of the last Ice Age, some 10,000 years ago. Estuaries provide important zones of contact between freshwater and marine environ-ments; they benefit from nutrient inputs that arrive from at least three different directions: the river that enters the sea through the estuary, the open sea itself and adjacent marshes. The combination of shelter, food supply and suitable physical habitat makes estuaries of great importance to wildlife: for example, many species of marine fish use estuaries as spawning, feeding and nursery areas, while millions

of shorebirds gather on estuaries to feed and roost both during the winter and on migration.

The precise form and productivity of an estuary varies according to geology, geomorphology, climate and hydrology. In sheltered estuaries the rates of sedimentation will be high. Estuary outlets and delta channels may be more or less completely blocked by sandbars, sandspits or sand dunes, resulting in the formation of lagoons which may be closed or with limited access to the sea. Lagoons are a key morphological feature of many depositional environments, such as in the Mediterranean Basin.

Artificial Wetlands

These may include anything from rice paddies, fish ponds and reservoirs to extraction pits, waterways and saltpans. Some wetlands are an unintended result of human intervention; an example is the extensive blanket peats of upland Britain whose development owes much to prehistoric forest clearance. The origin of others was not always known - for example, the flooded medieval peat diggings which now form the Norfolk Broads in England and similar areas in the Netherlands.

On the one hand, rice paddies provide the largest single food base for the world's population; on the other, they may also be one of the largest sources of methane in the world and thus be a major contributor to global warming.

Aquaculture ponds throughout the tropics are undoubtedly one of the greatest threats to the natural wetland ecosystems of the coastal zone, yet they usually play an important part in local village economies. The ability to create artificial wetlands has led developers to argue that it should be acceptable to

Intensive shrimp ponds are now being built in areas of mangrove in southern Thailand.

Alligators, such as those in the Everglades, USA, are relics from the age of dinosaurs when many large reptiles roamed the earth.

destroy a natural wetland if it is replaced with an identical or equally valuable system elsewhere, or if the damaged wetland is later restored. Such a 'mitigation' concept assumes that the processes and resulting functions and benefits of the natural wetland can be adequately replaced or mimicked. Scientists and engineers are still a long way from being able to ensure this, even though artificial wetlands often superficially *look like* natural areas.

ANIMAL AND PLANT ADAPTATIONS

Many plants and animals have evolved special life styles and strategies to survive or make best use of wetland environments. A wide range of so-called carnivorous plants, such as sundews and pitcher plants, supplement their needs for nitrogen, not easily available from acid peatland soils, by trapping insects which they then dissolve to absorb the proteins. The bladderworts (*Utricularia*) have air bladders which trap insects and larvae in the water - very important in nutrient-poor wetlands such as the Okavango and Everglades.

Large aquatic and emergent wetland plants are generally porous and contain tissue with large intercellular spaces called Aerenchyma, allowing growth in oxygen-poor environments that would be lethal to terrestrial plants. Some of these plants can convert nutrients into plant material in the absence of oxygen, a chemical process resulting in the accumulation of ethyl alcohol which they, unlike dryland species, are able to tolerate.

Rabbits show some fascinating adaptations to wetland life. In North America, the swamp rabbit (*Sylvilagus aquaticus*) has splayed feet which allow it to move with ease over wet soil; it is an excellent swimmer and can escape predators by remaining submerged with only the tip of its nose exposed. If flooding occurs during the breeding season its relative the marsh rabbit (*Sylvilagus palustris*) can re-absorb a developing embryo into the placenta, thus helping to ensure survival of newborn offspring.

The lechwe (*Kobus leche*) is an African antelope which is able to graze while standing in water up to 500 mm (20 in) deep. Lechwe have elongated hooves for moving through thick reed beds and soft mud; they can actually run faster through shallow water than on dry land. Their breeding period is timed to coincide with the flooding pattern: in the Okavango Delta, for instance, the young are born just after the floods recede in September when rich new growth on the floodplains is there for them to graze.

Alligators have also made interesting adaptations. In the Everglades, for example, they often excavate their own depressional wetlands ('gator holes') to ensure a permanent water body through the dry season and a concentration of fish to serve as an instant supply of food. These places of refuge attract other wildlife as well, particularly fish-eating birds, such as egrets and herons.

It is, perhaps, the migratory waterbirds which have evolved the most spectacular adaptations to take advantage of the productivity of wetlands. Millions of migratory swans, ducks, geese, shorebirds and other species arrive each spring on the vast Arctic wetlands of North America and Eurasia. Here, in the brief summer they rely on the productivity of these wetlands to enable them to breed successfully before they migrate once more to spend the non-breeding season on inland and coastal wetlands many thousands of kilometres to the south. Some of these birds travel as far south as Australasia, South Africa and South America, making use of a whole network of wetlands as vital refuelling stops. Clearly, such migrations depend on the integrity of these networks being maintained.

A number of the parasites that cause so much human misery have also adapted their life history to the dynamics of wetland habitats. Malaria, schistosomiasis, filariasis (river blindness), yellow fever, encephalitis, trypanosomiasis and numerous lung and liver flukes, all are transmitted by wetland animals. The malaria parasite *Plasmodium* is carried by some 60 of the 400 or more species of *Anopheles* mosquito. *Anopheles* generally lay their eggs in still, shallow water. In natural wetlands the larvae may be an important element in the food chain - in the tropics and subtropics they are preyed on by mosquito fish (*Gambusia*). Drainage and replacement of the wetland

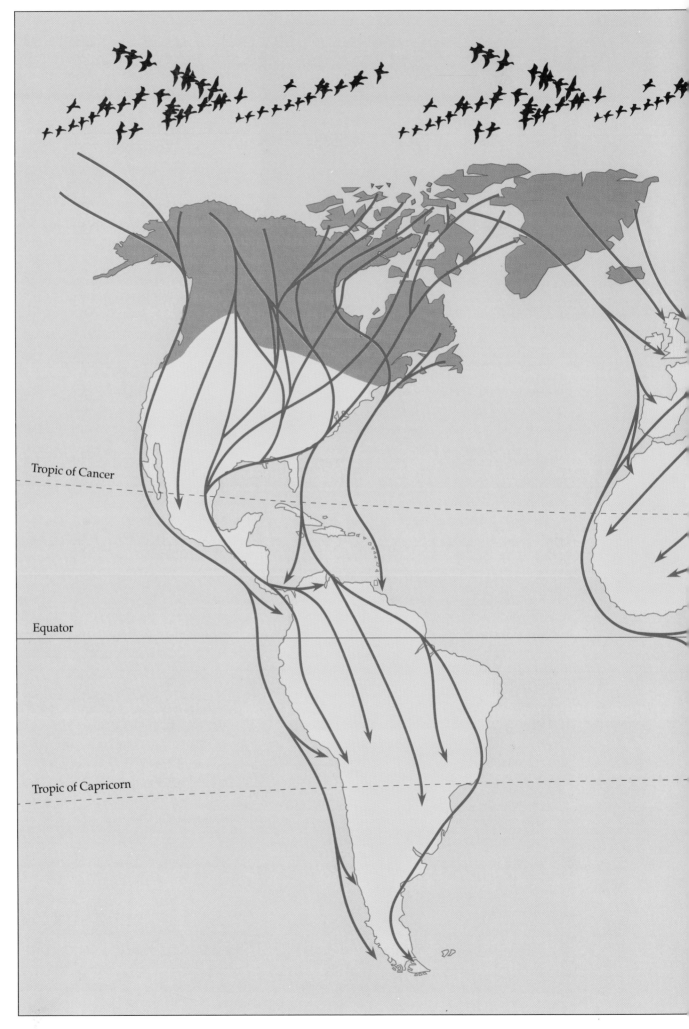

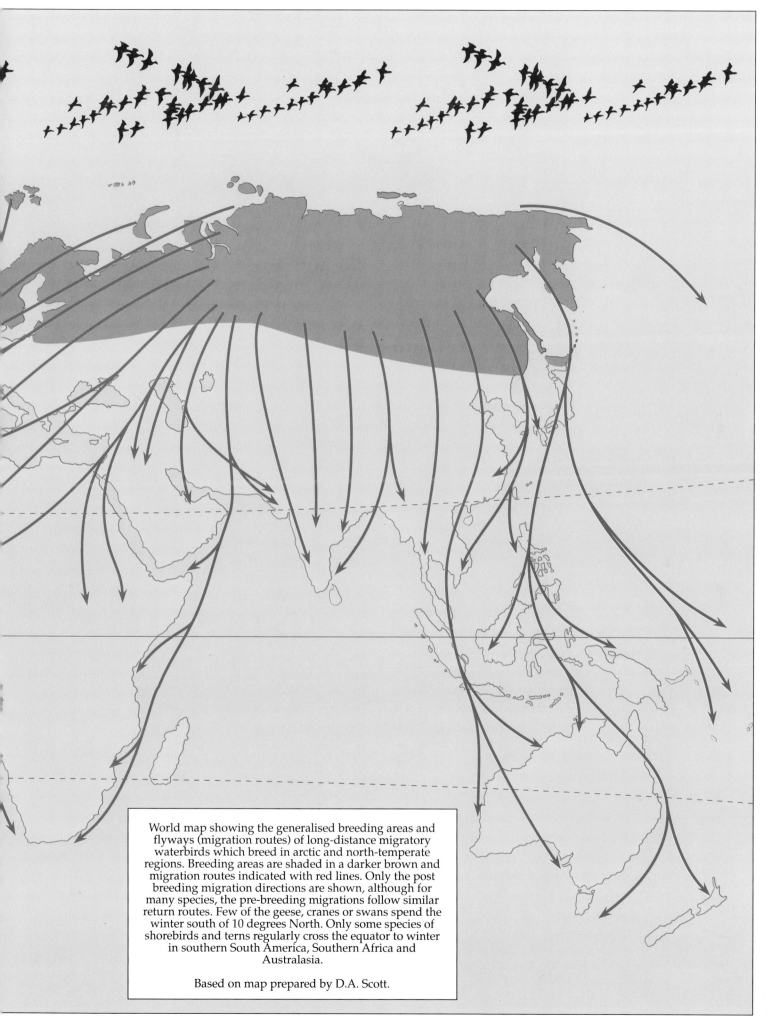

World map showing the generalised breeding areas and flyways (migration routes) of long-distance migratory waterbirds which breed in arctic and north-temperate regions. Breeding areas are shaded in a darker brown and migration routes indicated with red lines. Only the post breeding migration directions are shown, although for many species, the pre-breeding migrations follow similar return routes. Few of the geese, cranes or swans spend the winter south of 10 degrees North. Only some species of shorebirds and terns regularly cross the equator to winter in southern South America, Southern Africa and Australasia.

Based on map prepared by D.A. Scott.

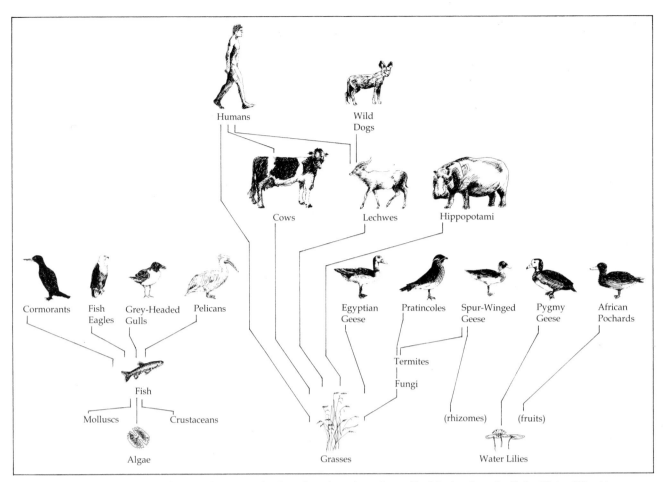

Human communites are frequently dependent on wetland goods and services. Generalized food web on the Kafue Flats of Zambia.

with irrigated agricultural land and shallow canals may actually create better breeding conditions for the mosquitoes, and an environment where they are at less risk from predators, than the original marsh or swamp.

Wetland plant communities, especially those of marshes and swamps, are among the most productive in the world; they are comparable to tropical rain forest. The reasons include: the regular supply of nutrients and water; advantageous microclimatic conditions; the physical impact of water flow which removes old tissue and maintains vigorous growth; an ability to grow under oxygen-deficient conditions and to deal with potentially toxic by-products.

Like all ecosystems, wetlands are maintained by an energy flow. The process starts with the production of living matter by green plants and incorporation of nutrients and essential trace elements from the soil, sediment or water.

This production forms the basis of the energy flow through the ecosystem. The energy flow can run in two main directions. In the 'grazing food chain', herbivores consume living plants and in turn provide the food supply for carnivores often in a complex food web. In the 'detrital food chain', dead organic matter provides the energy for a wide range of decomposers such as bacteria and fungi. The decomposers break

down the organic material, and important mineral elements, such as nitrogen, phosphorus and potassium, are released back into the environment. In most wetlands, the two food chains are interlinked and support an array of plants and animals. All these organisms have mechanisms to ensure survival in the wetlands, whether fresh or saline, dry or flooded.

WETLANDS ARE VALUABLE

Among the many vital functions of wetlands, flood control is one of the most important. Wetlands act like sponges, storing and slowly releasing rainfall and run-off, thus reducing flood peaks. This can reduce the need for expensive dams and other engineering structures. In Wisconsin, for instance, it has been shown that water catchment zones with 15 per cent of their area composed of wetlands and lakes have flood peaks 60-65 per cent lower than those without them. Wetlands on the Charles River (Massachusetts, USA) have been preserved as natural flood defences because this was a cheaper option than filling them and then being obliged to build an artificial flood-defence scheme. This placed a flood prevention value of some US$13,500 per hectare (US$5,465 per acre) on the intact wetland area. The lesson here has been registered elsewhere in the world. Recent opposition to a wetland drainage programme in the Dong Thap province of the Mekong Delta, Vietnam was based partly on the flood-storage argument.

The binding effect of their vegetation is another important aspect of wetlands; it helps in the stabilization of banks and shores. Not only that - in some cases it helps in the accretion of sediment, thus counteracting forces of erosion, subsidence and sea level rise. Both these are vital functions. Coastal salt marshes reduce the cost of sea wall defences by an important amount in, for instance, eastern England. Mangroves help to build up and retain sediment along tropical coastlines. The value of this protection from tidal surges has been recognized by the government of Bangladesh, in particular, and it is actively promoting the planting of mangroves on freshly deposited sediment.

Wetlands have a further key role to play in what is known as 'ground water recharge and discharge'. Recharge occurs when water moves from the wetland into the underground aquifer - rock, such as sandstone, which holds water. The wetland acts as a filter for certain kinds of waste and soluble contaminants. The process is important for controlling storm water run-off, for replenishing supplies of water for human consumption, and also in maintaining the flow of ground water which may support other wetlands at the point of discharge. A large proportion of the historic Florida Everglades, now impounded as so-called Water Conservation Areas, serves to recharge the limestone aquifer of South Florida, which is used not only to supply water for domestic and agricultural purposes but also to prevent saltwater intrusion. In Massachusetts, 750,000 people derive their water from wells drilled in or near wetlands.

Many wetlands exist because of discharges from springs. This source of water may be especially important to maintain stream-flow, particularly in drought periods or in highly seasonal climates. The wetland ecosystem itself benefits from the relatively constant supply and temperature of the water. It is no accident that wetlands along spring lines and other areas of water emergence commonly support luxuriant and diverse plant communities. Discharge of wetland-stored ground water may be important in sustaining the agricultural production of surrounding land, as is the case with the peat swamps in Malaysia which release water essential for the maintenance of rice paddies during the dry season. Disruption of the biological linkage between wetland and agricultural land reduces the value of both.

Regular deposition of nutrient-rich silt contributed to the success of agriculture along large rivers such as the Nile. But sediment is also vital for maintaining aquatic fertility and the physical stability of floodplains and deltas. Thus the Aswan High Dam, by preventing silt from passing down the Nile has destroyed, among other things, the sardine fishery of the eastern Mediterranean, resulting in the closure of canning factories. The delta is receding at a rate of up to 30 m (98 ft) per year as sharply reduced sedimentation fails to offset continued subsidence, on the one hand, and sea level rise, on the other.

The Mississippi Delta has suffered similarly. In its case, upstream structures have reduced by half the amount of sediment carried by the river. Levee (bank) construction to reduce floods has so diminished the historic supply of sediment to the delta marshes that wetland loss is running at 0.5 per cent per year.

Tampering with wetlands can also damage their ability to deal with various contaminants and nutrients. Biological, chemical and physical processes in wetlands are often able to immobilize and transform a wide range of environmental contaminants and nutrients, which, in excess, would cause severe eutrophication and pollution.

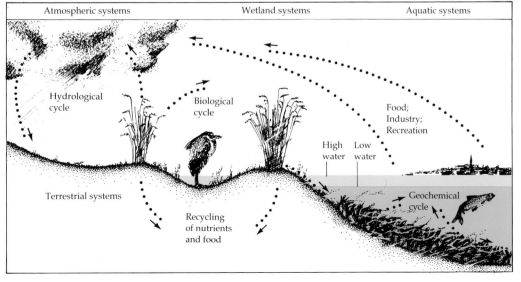

Water, nutrients, organisms, sediment and contaminants move between aquatic, atmospheric and terrestrial systems. Wetlands are at the interface of these systems and the way in which they cycle material is of vital importance to the environment.

Heavy metals, pesticides and industrial wastes, for instance, can be bound to soil and sediment particles, and there be rendered more or less inert.

Wetlands can act as a 'sink', preventing nitrate build-up which could lead to eutrophication. Nitrate run-off from fertilized agricultural areas can be recycled to harmless nitrogen gas by this mechanism, but where wetlands along river margins have been drained and incorporated into agricultural land the ecosystem, which could once have buffered against influx into stream water, has been lost.

Wetlands prevent nitrates from reaching freshwater streams and lakes. Their destruction removes this benefit, a fact that is being increasingly brought home as nitrate levels in streams and ground waters rise throughout Europe and North America. An environment rich in wetlands can reduce the potentially harmful impacts of fertilizer use on the landscape. Recent estimates from Sweden indicate that a wetland area of 2 km² (³/₄ sq mile) would reduce the amount of nitrogen leaking into adjacent waters by nearly 2,000 tonnes (1,968 tons) a year. The value of this service alone may be worth more than US$200,000 per hectare (US$80,940 per acre).

There is now a lot of interest in reconstructing wetlands or rehabilitating degraded ecosystems to restore their ability to retain nutrients and contaminants. Both capital and maintenance costs may be substantially less than for the artificial systems that would be required to achieve the same thing. Considerably more scientific research is needed, however, to establish the optimum environmental conditions. A proposal to use Florida's cypress swamps as natural treatment centres for domestic waste water found that 98 per cent of all nitrogen and 97 per cent of all phosphorus was removed before waste water entered the ground water. Findings elsewhere suggest that such levels of efficiency may be only short-lived and nowhere near attainable in other types of wetland.

In any event, in the developed world at least, few significant areas of expendable natural wetlands exist near centres of population, which would remain ecologically resilient and could be used for these purposes. On the other hand, the situation may be quite different in developing countries where disturbing the plant community composition of wetlands would probably be a small ecological price to pay for a 'fail-safe' system of water purification.

Aquatic plants such as water hyacinth (*Eichornia crassipes*) are particularly effective in absorbing contaminants and nutrients. Although the plant itself can become a nuisance - because it spreads rapidly over open water, restricts navigation and reduces dissolved oxygen levels - current research is aimed at ancillary benefits: the fertilizers, bio-gas and animal feed which could, for example, be obtained from its harvest.

Wetlands may also act as a source of both nutrients and contaminants. Nutrients absorbed by living vegetation may become available again when the plants are decomposed at the end of the growing season. Especially in wetlands where water flow is rapid, these nutrients are readily transported and may be an important input into the aquatic food chain. Some nutrients and contaminants previously tightly bound to mineral particles can be released to flow out with drainage water. This may occur with phosphorus and may happen with some pesticides and industrial waste products. In other words, it requires careful attention to the character of the hydrological regime and soil processes before wetlands are incorporated into waste-water treatment projects.

Peatlands occupy just 3 per cent of the world's land area, yet they store almost 20 per cent of the globe's soil carbon pool. The storage of organic matter in wetlands represents a carbon resource without which there could be dramatically higher levels of atmospheric carbon dioxide. Under their naturally waterlogged regime wetlands may also release methane, hydrogen sulphide and dinitrogen oxide. Methane and dinitrogen oxide belong to the group of so-called greenhouse gases. These gases absorb infra-red energy, and changes in their concentration in the atmosphere may influence the earth's radiation balance and the global climate.

A significant shift may occur in the balance of

Water hyacinth is efficient at absorbing nutrients, but also a nuisance that clogs waterways and may substantially reduce productivity and wildlife habitat in wetlands.

Drainage of Lake Karla, Greece, has destroyed one of Europe's important migratory bird habitats and an important fishery. It has also created enormous water pollution problems.

carbon movement between wetlands and the atmosphere as a result of human intervention, particularly drainage for agriculture. Oxidation of previously accumulated organic carbon is accelerated by peat extraction for fuel and horticultural use, and in the peat mangrove swamps of the tropics by excavation for aquaculture ponds. A recent study found some areas of the world were already storing less carbon while others had actually become net sources of carbon. By 1980 the amount of carbon stored in Finland and the USSR had fallen by 21-33 per cent, in western Europe by almost half, whilst in central Europe carbon resources had been lost completely. This situation could be exacerbated in Finland with the opening, in 1990, of the world's largest peat-fired power station.

WETLANDS ARE VULNERABLE

Wetlands are highly sensitive to disruption by human activities. Since medieval times, at least, these natural ecosystems have been purposefully transformed throughout what is now known as the developed world to provide land for non-wetland uses. Technology has provided the means, but the twin driving forces have been population and economic growth, aided by inadequately informed public opinion and government policy.

Much of Europe's wetland heritage was lost well before the modern period, largely to wholesale agricultural drainage enterprises. It is perhaps hardly surprising that generations of Dutch engineers, inspired by the need to create dry land in their own country for sheer survival, would continue to take polder and drainage technology to wet areas wherever they existed - from the fens of Europe to the

tropical peatlands of Indonesia. Over half the wetland area that existed in the United States at the time of European settlement has now been lost, more than 80 per cent of it to agriculture. The rate of loss in the United States, despite major legislation and regulation, still exceeds 125,000 hectares (308,875 acres) a year. It is estimated that over 900 million hectares (2,224 million acres) of wetlands worldwide could still be developed in similar fashion for agricultural or other uses.

The scale of human impact on wetlands varies from transient or temporary to irreversible. Those actions which alter hydrology or substrate are generally more permanent than those which influence only the animal and plant life, although in extreme cases this may lead to extinction of species.

The threats to wetlands are various, though one common link in many cases is government backing. Lake Karla in Greece once supported an important fishery. Drainage has converted it directly to agricultural production, but this only occurred with major government subsidies.

Pressures for wetland alteration and loss are now increasing in the tropics and developing nations, despite growing awareness of their important life and environmental support functions. Potentially enormous losses threaten the floodplains of Africa and South America, mangroves in South America and especially in Southeast Asia, and coastal zone wetlands throughout the tropics. Already, in Africa, large areas of natural floodplain grazing and important fisheries have been lost due to regulated river flow and large-scale irrigation projects; in the Senegal River Delta, for example, 2,400 hectares (5,930 acres) of floodplain have been dyked in a recent

The extremely important Doñana wetlands in Spain are threatened by a lowering of ground water levels.

irrigation scheme, which has not only failed as an irrigation scheme, but also reduced the capacity of the wetland to carry out important functions. Nearly 20 per cent of the wetlands rated as internationally important in Central and South America are threatened by direct drainage for farming or ranching.

Areas of natural mangrove are being converted to shrimp and fish ponds, to rice paddies and for various non-wetland uses at an unprecedented rate. Less than a quarter of Puerto Rico's original mangrove fringe survives; Thailand has probably lost more than a quarter of its mangroves since the early 1970s. Dramatic losses of intact mangrove and peat swamp forest have occurred throughout Indonesia, usually as a result, direct or indirect, of development and other projects. Conversion of tropical peatlands to agriculture or aquaculture has led to major environmental problems because the oxidation of potential acid sulphate materials has released sulphuric acid and reduced pH to levels that are toxic to both aquatic plants and animals. Loss of mangroves has severely reduced the habitat for fry essential to stock artificial ponds in many parts of South America and Southeast Asia.

However, the greatest threats often originate a considerable distance from individual wetlands, due to excessive demand for finite water resources. Over-exploitation of the ground water aquifer supporting many Mediterranean wetlands is a common problem. The important Spanish wetland of the Tablas de Daimiel is almost completely desiccated as a result of the lowering of the ground water table. It is unlikely to recover its former condition despite efforts to redirect water flow from other sources. The Doñana wetlands, also in Spain, are threatened with a similar fate because of the increasing demands for ground water for adjacent tourist developments and for the irrigation of strawberries higher up the catchment.

Examples pile up. Plans to divert the flow of the Akheloos River in western Greece in order to provide more irrigation water for Thessaly and the Lake Karla region are likely to cause major alteration of the coastal wetlands of Messolonghi (Mesolongion). Reduced freshwater flows in Lake Ichkeul, Tunisia, caused by damming of headwaters, have resulted in large salinity changes and loss of biological diversity.

Major changes are occurring currently in the Everglades marshes (Florida, USA) as a result of nutrient inputs from agricultural areas upstream. In parts of the Everglades closest to the source of the nutrient-laden run-off, a cattail (*Typha domingensis*) monoculture is expanding rapidly at the expense of a natural diversity of sawgrass, floating aquatics and open water 'sloughs' (channels). Some estimates put the rate of expansion at 2 hectares (4.9 acres) a day.

The result is loss of habitat for a wide range of wading birds, fishes and alligators. Organic matter builds up at an accelerated rate, reducing water quality. The assemblage of algae, bacteria and other micro-organisms which are a major component at the base of the Everglades food chain is altered to include more pollution-tolerant species. The detrimental effects of nutrient enrichment are transmitted over 50 km (31 miles) south and across the boundary of Everglades National Park.

Whilst the consequences of such ecological imbalance have yet to be fully elaborated, the example serves as a dramatic illustration of the progressive impact of human activities, the location of which may be quite distant from the area affected. The flow of water is not only the lifeblood of wetlands, it is also a potent source of contamination and degradation, especially if it has been carelessly altered.

A New Conservation Era

Human beings have lived in close contact with wetlands for millennia - that balance still exists in numerous developing communities, but it is constantly under siege. Societies in the developed world have detached themselves from this direct association and have done so in the name of economic progress with various levels of success over the last 200 years.

Early conservation action focused on the dramatic direct effects on wildlife of species over-exploitation and the loss of wetland habitats.

For some time it has been recognized that there is a linkage between wetland habitat and the ability of migratory birds to maintain essential connections along transcontinental flyways. The ease with which just small breaks in the chain can lead to serious disruption has also been realized. All this led to the development of the Ramsar Convention, which has done much to raise awareness and promote international cooperation in wetland conservation. But the Convention still has only just over 60 contracting parties (members) - in other words, no more than a third of all nations, with many absentee names from the developing world.

Despite the general obligation on contracting parties to include wetland conservation as part of their general strategies for national land-use planning, the destruction and alteration of wetlands has continued. Only now is the Convention beginning to attract stronger membership from the developing world.

The traditional conservation ethic based on

The emergent cattail has expanded to cover a mosaic of wetland habitats in the Everlades, USA.

maintaining species and populations, and putting a special emphasis on preserving rarity, uniqueness and model examples of ecosystems, has by and large failed to compete successfully with issues, such as employment opportunity, standard of living and economic development. It has limited appeal to communities whose prime concern tends to focus on where the next meal is coming from. However, a wider approach has now begun to have some impact on decision-makers. Assessment of the full values of wetlands to communities and to society as a whole, and the real costs, social as well as economic, of their destruction or inappropriate utilization, provides the basis for competing more effectively with assessments based on alternative economic uses. Sadly, these values have often become apparent only when the wetlands have been irreparably altered - thus, in an example already cited, the Aswan High Dam gave gains for electricity generation and water supply, but resulted in the loss of the eastern Mediterranean sardine fishery and is causing accelerated land loss from the Nile Delta.

Underpinning the current thinking on wetland conservation is a recognition of the importance of, on the one hand, allowing wetlands to function naturally and yet, on the other, of managing them so as to optimize the resulting benefits. This recognition was implicit in the development of a sophisticated regulatory mechanism for wetland protection in the United States of America. Permits are required for activities likely to have an impact on wetlands and are administered by the United States Army Corps of Engineers in cooperation with the Environmental Protection Agency through section 404 of the Clean Water Act. President George Bush has built on earlier Executive Orders from President Carter by establishing a National Policy of 'no net loss of wetlands'.

Nowhere else in the world is there such overt support for wetland conservation - yet even with this legislation, what might seem to be the most protected of the nation's wetlands, the Everglades, is threatened by continued degradation because of activities elsewhere in the drainage basin. Resolving the problem of competing demands from inherently incompatible land-use activities in a way that is acceptable within democratic societies is neither easy nor cheap. In 1988 the US federal government filed a law suit against the South Florida Water Management

District over continued degradation of, and resulting ecological imbalance in, the Loxahatchee National Wildlife Refuge as well as the Everglades National Park. The state agency had spent nearly US$6 million on lawyers' fees alone up to 1991 in contesting the suit. Some estimates of the total cost of the legal action are as high as US$20 million. The cost of restoration may be as high as US$500 million. Such use of taxpayers' money is inconceivable in any other country and clearly beyond the capacity of developing nations.

The situation in the Everglades is an important reminder of the potential costs of rectifying damage. It also shows the limited benefit to wetland management and conservation of the 'protected area' approach, by which nature reserves, Ramsar sites and National Parks are set up. A very different strategy, one that takes into account all the various requirements of wetland catchment areas, needs to be developed. Otherwise, the few remaining, and highly vulnerable, areas of wetland in the industrialized nations will continue to be degraded. Such an approach is even more essential to the conservation and wise use of wetlands in developing countries.

The final objective of wetland conservation will, of course, be the same for all wetlands throughout the world. That objective should be that they are protected and managed in order to maintain the optimum range of sustainable benefits for humankind and wildlife for environmental quality.

Recent initiatives by the World Conservation Union (IUCN) Wetlands Programme, the World Wide Fund for Nature (WWF), IWRB and other non-governmental organizations have been strengthened by action from the European Community, US Treasury, World Bank and other agencies that are involved worldwide in funding projects likely to have an impact on wetlands. The arguments are not for a 'return to Mother Nature', but for the valuable natural resources of wetlands to be used in order to realize their fullest economic return, whilst at the same time retaining their ecological and environmental integrity. All this is being urged to avoid converting them to some other use, not necessarily sustainable, which would result in irretrievable habitat losses.

Source for diagram on page 20: adapted from Handlos 1982 in Drijver and Marchand 1985.

CONTRIBUTORS: G.E. HOLLIS AND T.A. JONES

Europe and the Mediterranean Basin

EUROPE and the Mediterranean Basin encompass a huge variety of landscapes, climates and patterns of human, animal and plant life. The region extends from the Arctic seacoasts in the north to the Sahara Desert in the south, and from southwest Ireland and Cape Finisterre in the west to the Ural Mountains in the east.

Just as the region as a whole is so varied, so are the wetlands and the means by which they receive their water. In the north the wetlands are fed by water melted from permanent ice; those on the Atlantic fringes receive their water from over 2 m (6 ft) of rainfall, whilst the resurgence of fossil water can sustain oases in the south where there is less than 100 mm (4 in) of rainfall. The deeply indented coastline, the region's semi-closed and closed seas, and its many islands also have a significant influence on the types of wetland and their distribution.

During the last 1,000 years, humans have increasingly acquired the ability to transform wetlands - a process that has accelerated particularly in this century and especially since 1945. As a result, many wetlands of Europe and the Mediterranean Basin have been destroyed. The ecological character of the wetlands that have survived is also influenced to some degree by human activity; in effect, there are few entirely natural wetlands left. The remaining large wetlands, notably those in North Africa and central and northern Europe, are of great importance and still in danger of degradation by continued human pressure. Even those with the highest level of statutory protection are liable to ecological change and conversion to non-wetland use.

There are, however, many signs that the tide of wetland destruction in Europe and the Mediterranean Basin may be slowing or even turning in some countries. Most countries of the region have now joined the Ramsar Convention.

GEOGRAPHIC SETTING

An intimate relationship between sea and land is to be found in many parts of the region because of the large number of semi-closed seas and gulfs. The Baltic Sea and the White Sea bring marine influences to bear on continental Russia and Finland. The North Sea includes on its southeast shore the shallow inter-tidal and estuarine area of the Wadden Sea.

The Mediterranean, meanwhile, is connected to the Atlantic only by the Strait of Gibraltar. The Black Sea joins the Mediterranean through the twin constrictions of the Dardanelles and the Bosporus. Within the Black Sea itself the Sea of Azov is an almost closed gulf. In the extreme east of the region is the Caspian Sea, an entirely closed sea.

These land-locked seas have an important influence on the character of the coastal wetlands of the region. Tides, for example, are subdued in the Baltic, minimal in most of the Mediterranean and largely unknown in the Black Sea. The northern parts of the Baltic Sea freeze over each winter. On another front, the Black Sea and Sea of Azov, so far removed from the open ocean, contain brackish rather than saline water.

The relatively jagged coastline and the series of mountain chains across Europe mean that there are few large rivers. Typically, rivers rise in hills or mountains and flow directly, and over comparatively short distances, to the sea. Exceptions to this are the Volga and the Danube.

Many European wetlands derive to a large extent from the repeated glaciations of the Pleistocene era when ice sheets spread south to southwest England and Kiev in Russia. The movement of the ice scraped some areas, such as parts of the Scottish Highlands, clear of soil, whilst in other areas, large sweeps of soft glacial boulder clay were laid down. In some areas the ice pushed up linear hillocks of depositional material such as the moraines of the north German Plain. In other areas, such as northern England, small depressions, called 'kettleholes', were formed when ice, trapped in the sediments eventually melted allowing the deposits to subside. In yet other areas, such as Denmark and parts of Poland, the glaciers released large volumes of water heavily charged with sediment which formed extensive sandy plains and hillocks.

SELECTED MAJOR WETLANDS
IN EUROPE & THE
MEDITERRANEAN

1 Ria Formosa
2 Sado Estuary
3 Tejo (Tagus) Estuary
4 Ria Aveiro
5 Marismas del Odiel
6 Marismas del Guadalquivir
     (including Doñana National
     Park)
7 Lagunas de Fuentadepiedra
8 Las Tablas de Daimiel
9 Albufera de Valencia
10 Delta del Ebro
11 El Kala – Annaba complex
12 Lac Ichkeul
13 Bassin d'Arcachon et Banc
     d'Arguin
14 Marais de l'Ouest
15 Marais de Brière; Estuaire de
     la Loire
16 Golfe du Morbihan
17 Baie du Mont-St-Michel
18 Baie de la Somme; Marais
     de Balançon
19 La Brenne
20 Etangs du Roussillon
21 Rhône Delta (including
     La Camargue)
22 La Dombes
23 Lac Léman (Lake of Geneva)
24 Essex estuaries
25 The Wash
26 Humber Estuary
27 Flow Country
28 Solway
29 Morecambe Bay
30 Alt Estuary
31 Dee and Mersey Estuaries
32 Severn Estuary
33 Strangford Lough
34 Lough Neagh & Lough Beg
35 Lough Erne
36 Lough Swilly
37 Blacksod Bay
38 Lough Corrib

Wetlands

0 km   200   400

39 Inner Galway Bay	119 River Sura floodplain
40 Shannon and Fergus Estuaries	120 Rybinsk Reservoir
41 Castlemaine Harbour	121 Dubna marches
42 Myvatn-Laxá	122 Moskovskoye Morye
43 Thjórsárver	123 Zavidovo reserve
44 Arnarvatnsheidi-Tvidægra	124 Karachevskoye marsh
45 Breidafjördur	125 Obol, Polotsk, Shumilino
46 Vlaamse Banken	126 River Cepkeliai marshes
47 Rhine and Meuse Deltas	127 Lake Zuvintas
48 IJsselmeer	128 Kursiu Bay
49 De Wieden & De Weeribben	129 Nemunas delta
50 Diepholzer Moorniederung	130 Teicu Bog, Jekabpils &
51 Wadden Sea	Madona
52 Elbe Estuary	131 Lake Ilmen
53 Fjords, shallow coastal waters	132 Sources of River Oredezh
of Denmark, Germany, Poland	133 Lake Vvalye
54 Odra valley, Lake Dabie	134 Lake Chudsko-Pskov
55 Koszalin & Slupsk coastal areas	135 River Emajogi mouth
56 Slowinski National Park	136 Muraka marsh
57 Vistula Lagoon (Zalew	137 Narva reservoir
Wislany)	138 Koporski Bay
58 Mazurian Lakes	139 Svir Bay
59 Biebrza Valley	140 Kilpola Island
60 Bug & Liwiec valleys	141 Vyborg Bay
61 Narew & Vistula valleys	142 Matsalu Zaliv
62 Milicz fishpond complex	143 Vilsandi Archipelago
63 Middle Warta valley	144 Vaygach Island
64 Obra marches	145 Varandeyskaya Lapta
65 Lac de Neuchâtel	Peninsula
66 Boddensee	146 Khaaypudyrskaya Bay
67 Trebonsko Protected	147 Lakes Vashutkiny,
Landscape Area	Padimeyskiye, Khargeyskive
68 Donau-March-Thaya Auen	148 River Chernaya
69 Záhorské marches	149 Russki Zavorot Peninsula
70 Neusiedlersee/Fertö	150 Kanin Peninsula
(including Seewinkel)	151 Solovetski Archipelago
71 Podunají	152 Onega Bay
72 Lake Balaton	153 Lakes of northern Karelia
73 East Slovakia marshes	154 Kandalaksha Bay
74 Hortobágy	155 Strelna/Varzuga watershed
75 Pusztaszer	156 River Ponoy middle reaches
76 Kopacki rit	157 Iokanga/Ponoy watershed
77 River Sava alluvial wetlands	158 Chalmny-Varre, Lovozero
78 Obedska bara	159 Lapland, Monchegorsk
79 Mostistea wetlands	160 Koitilaiskaira
80 Danube Delta	161 Varangerfjord
81 Soviet Union Black Sea	162 Sammuttijänkä
wetlands	163 Lätäsenol
82 Primorsko-Akhtarsk/	164 Taavavuoma
Grivenskaya area salt lakes	165 Sjaunja
83 Veselovskoye Reservoir	166 Lake Tjålmejaure-Laisdalen
84 E. Manych, Ozero (Lake),	Valley
Manych-Gudilo	167 Mountains of Vindelfjällen
85 Volga delta	168 Lake Ånnsjon
86 Kizihrmak & Yesihrmak deltas	169 Forramyrene
87 Sultan marshes	170 Froan
88 Cukurova (incl. Ceyhan,	171 Smola Archipelago
Seyhan & Tarsus deltas)	172 Dovrefjell
89 Göksu delta	173 Hardangervidda
90 Karapinar Ovasi	174 River Dalälven:
91 Hotamis Sazligi	Färnebofjärden
92 Tuz Gölü	175 Liminganlahti-
93 Beysehir Golu	Lumijoenselkä
94 Burdur Golu	176 Valsörarna-Björkögrunden
95 Acigol & Calti Golu	177 Signilskär
96 Egirdir Golu & Hoyran Golu	178 Southern archipelagic seas:
97 Aksehir Gölü & Eber Gölü	Föglö-Dragsfjärd
98 Iznik Golu	179 Lake Åsnen
99 Apolyont Golu	180 Oland coastal areas
100 Kocacay delta	181 Azraq Oasis
101 Manyas Golu	182 Dead Sea
102 Buyük Menderes delta	183 Sea of Galilee
103 Evros/Meric delta	184 Lake Bardawil
104 Lake Vistonis, Porto Lagos	185 Great Bitter Lake
Lagoons	186 Nile Delta
105 Nestos Delta	187 Bahiret el Biban
106 Lakes Volvi and Langada	188 Chott Djerid
107 Lake Kerkini	189 Chott el Fedjaj, Sebkhet
108 Axios-Loudias-Aliakmon delta	el Hamma
109 Messolonghi	190 Kneiss Islands & Mudflats
110 Amvrakikos Gulf	191 Sebkhet Sidi Mansour
111 Lakes Vegoritis and Petron	192 Sebkhet Sidi el Hani
112 Lakes Mikri Prespa, Megali	193 Sebkhet Sidi el Kelbia
Prespa	194 Tunis complex
113 Lake Skadar	195 Constantine complex
114 Neretva delta	196 Marais de la Macta
115 Lakes Lesina & Varano	197 Grande Sebkha d'Oran
116 Lago Trasimeno	198 Sologne
117 Northern Adriatic coast	199 Etangs de Lorraine
lagoon complexes	200 Etangs du Forez
118 Po Delta wetland complex	

CLIMATE

The climate of Europe is influenced greatly by the Gulf Stream and the prevailing moist westerly winds. As a result the difference between summer and winter temperatures in Western Europe averages 12°C (54°F). Eastern Europe, with a more continental climate, experiences an annual temperature range of around 24°C (75°F). The Mediterranean climate is different again. In winter, depressions from the Atlantic pass through the Mediterranean bringing mild and humid conditions and plenty of rain. In summer, the depressions pass farther north so that the Mediterranean has hot dry weather.

The northern parts of Scandinavia, Finland and Russia have a Boreal climate that merges into an Arctic climate in the mountains of Scandinavia and the lands bordering the Arctic Ocean. The Boreal winters are cold with temperatures below -7°C (19°F). Summers can be relatively warm with temperatures of 15°C (59°F). Rainfall tends to be low and the growing season is usually less than 100 days. In the Arctic zone, with summer periods of continuous daylight, the temperature rarely exceeds 10°C (50°F); the subsoil remains frozen as a permafrost zone. The severe winters have modest precipitation which falls mostly as snow.

The climatic elements that are of most direct relevance to wetlands are precipitation and evapotranspiration, since these determine the amount of water available to the wetlands and its distribution through the year. The highest precipitation, in excess of 1,500 mm (59 in) per year, is found in western Ireland, Wales and Scotland, on the west-facing mountains of southern Norway and on the higher parts of the Alps. Significant rainfall peaks also occur on the northwestern tip of Spain and on the mountains of Yugoslavia. Much of the rest of the region has between 500 and 1,000 mm (20 and 39 in) annual rainfall.

The regions with less than 500 mm (20 in) annual rainfall are found in central and eastern Spain, parts of Sweden in the lee of the Norwegian mountains, the Arctic north of Scandinavia and Russia and the lands north and east of the Black Sea and central Turkey. The North African coast, from central Tunisia to southern Israel and inland through Jordan, is the driest part of the region with less than 250 mm (10 in) of rain and often substantially less. The rate of evaporation decreases with latitude and is highest in June and July and lowest in winter.

The amount of water from rainfall which remains on the Earth's surface after evapotranspiration is very variable across Europe. On the Arctic slopes, over 55 per cent of the run-off occurs with the snow-melt in May and June; winter run-off is minimal. In western Europe there is a more even distribution of run-off through the year. In the rivers of the southern Soviet Union that drain into the Black Sea, over 70 per cent of the run-off comes in April, at the time of snow-melt in central and nothern Russia; by autumn, however, many streams have dried up completely. In North Africa almost all of the rivers dry up in the late summer; the peak flows are in January and February.

WETLANDS

Europe and the Mediterranean are so densely populated and have had such long histories of both civilization and industrialization that few, if any, entirely natural wetlands remain. Indeed, the three most common natural wetland types are 'lost', 'degraded' and 'threatened' wetlands. Areas where direct human interference has been less severe include parts of Iceland and the northern European taiga and tundra. Elsewhere, the catalogue of wetland destruction is remarkable.

The only relatively bright spot is in the creation of artificial wetlands. There have been some notable gains in wetland area throughout the European and Mediterranean region as a result of the creation of reservoirs, fishponds, gravel pits and the like. In France, in the 1980s, for instance, the rate of growth of artificial wetlands has been estimated at around 3,000 hectares (7,400 acres) per year. In Tunisia, at least 12 per cent of the country's wetlands are water-storage reservoirs. The total area of open water created there is 22,400 hectares (55,350 acres) compared to the loss of natural wetlands, since 1881, of 19,034 hectares (47,033 acres).

The Arctic, Scandinavia and Iceland

The lowlands of Arctic Russia, northern Finland and Spitsbergen have extensive tundra wetlands, characterized by permafrost, but with seasonal thawing of a thin surface layer giving rise to vast expanses of boggy ground interspersed with innumerable pools and meltwater channels. During the brief northern summer, long hours of daylight provide the stimulus for an explosion of plant and insect life, which in turn attracts huge numbers of nesting waterbirds that have spent the winter elsewhere in Europe, around the Mediterranean and in Africa.

Amongst the many internationally important sites in the region are the Kongsfjorden bird sanctuary on Spitsbergen, and Kandalaksha Bay, on the eastern side of the White Sea, which has been designated as a Ramsar site because of its breeding waterbirds; it also sustains a substantial fishery.

Part of the extensive Myvatn-Laxa area in Iceland which has been designated a Ramsar site.

Iceland is an island of ice and fire, with glaciers, volcanoes and hot springs. Whilst many lowland wetlands have been degraded, many bogs, marshes, lakes and rivers, together with shallow offshore waters and inter-tidal areas around the deeply indented coastline, still remain. The many freshwater lakes, originating from tectonic and glacial activity, are especially varied. Icelandic wetlands provide staging posts for waterbirds migrating between breeding grounds in the Canadian Arctic and Greenland, and wintering areas as far away as west Africa. Scandinavia has a great variety of wetlands; western areas benefit from a generally mild, wet climate controlled by the Gulf Stream, whilst the region's highly indented coastline, with countless fjords, islands, rivers, lakes and mires, provides extensive breeding, moulting and roosting areas for waterbirds. The rivers and lakes of the coastal zone are also rich in fish.

Scandinavia holds vast expanses of peatlands, though some areas are under threat from moves to increase timber production, to safeguard agricultural land by wetland drainage and to excavate peat for horticulture and for fuel. On the other hand, the picture is not all bleak. The long period of study that has gone into planning the restoration of Lake Hornborga in Sweden has been one of the landmarks of wetland conservation in Europe. Thanks to its small human population and the inaccessible nature of much of the country, the huge areas of Finnish wetlands are amongst the least threatened in Europe. Denmark has taken the lead in a number of areas of wetlands conservation including the evaluation of government policies for their sustainability, the banning of the use of lead shot for hunting in Ramsar sites and an imaginative pace-setting restoration scheme for the Skjern River. Historically, however, 89 per cent of wetlands have been affected, to some extent, by land reclamation or drainage or both.

European Soviet Union

The Arctic coastal zone of the Soviet Union includes extensive tundra wetlands which merge with the vast expanse of the taiga, dominated by coniferous forest. However, tree cover in the taiga is not continuous, being interspersed with open areas and containing numerous wetlands, which support large populations of nesting waterbirds, including many shorebirds (waders).

The huge plain that comprises Russia, the Ukraine, Moldavia and the Baltic republics drains slowly

KANDALAKSHA BAY, SOVIET UNION

A substantial, 180 km (112 mile) stretch of wetlands lies at the head of Kandalaksha Bay on the White Sea in Arctic Russia. It consists of open sea, over 860 rocky islands and parts of the coastal strip. The coastal vegetation is predominantly coniferous forest; the narrow shoreline is mainly pebble and sand but is rich in invertebrates, including many species of mollusc. Eel grass (species of *Zostera*) grows on the shallow sandy sea bed. There is a commercial fishery in the bay and shipping passes by, but the area is mainly noted for the breeding of waterbirds, of which eiders are the most numerous.

This important wetland habitat has suffered a great deal. The atmospheric testing of nuclear weapons at Novaya Zemlya certainly increased the background radiation and this may have affected the marine associations which ultimately provide the food for sea ducks. Oil spills have killed many hundreds of ducks in recent decades and a gradual build-up of pollution at the constricted head of the bay is threatening the typical marine ecosystems of the area. Intensive hunting in the 1920s led to the disappearance of breeding colonies of eider in many areas of the White Sea. Since hunting in the northern part of the archipelago was banned in 1932 this problem has diminished.

Large areas of the bay are State Reserves with strict controls. Since the first designation of the northern archipelago as a reserve and a subsequent designation in the south of the bay, six further reserves have been created. The whole site was listed as a wetland of international importance under the Ramsar Convention in 1976.

FLOW COUNTRY, UNITED KINGDOM

The far northeastern corner of Scotland has Britain's largest continuous expanse of blanket peat bog (365,310 hectares - 902,681 acres), known as the Flow Country. The area is one of the most intact expanses of blanket bog in the world and exhibits special surface features, including the occurrence of numerous small lakes or 'lochans'.

Conditions for peat formation are optimal in basins or on flat ground underlain by clay or impermeable bedrock, in areas of acidic rocks covered with fibrous vegetation, and where there is a climate with high, evenly distributed rainfall and relatively low temperatures. The particularly fine development of blanket bog in the Flow Country results from the combination of all three of these circumstances.

The vegetation of these peatlands is characterized by *Sphagnum* mosses and species such as cross-leaved heath, ling, purple moorgrass, together with sedges and rushes. The nutrient-poor conditions favour the occurrence of insect-trapping plants such as the sticky round-leaved sundew and common butterwort.

The Flow Country supports significant fractions of the total European breeding populations of certain bird species and is especially important in the context of the European Community. Notable breeding birds include black-throated diver (*Gavia arctica*), red-throated diver (*Gavia stellata*), common scoter (*Melanitta nigra*) and greenshank (*Tringa nebularia*).

By 1987, 17 per cent of the original peatland area had been planted or programmed for planting with coniferous forest - all this with the encouragement of government subsidies for upland afforestation. While public pressure has led to an acknowledgement that environmental concerns must be taken into account, there is no guarantee yet that what remains of the Flow Country is safe.

southeastwards via the Dnieper, Don and Volga Rivers. While there are extensive marshy areas inland, especially east of Moscow and north of Kiev, and many large reservoirs, particularly on the Volga and its tributary the Kama, the wetlands of international importance are generally along the coasts of the Baltic, Black Sea, Sea of Azov and in the great delta of the Volga which discharges into the Caspian Sea.

Matsalu Bay in Estonia on the Baltic is a large coastal wetland around a shallow bay with rocky and shingle islands, shingle spits and a river delta and floodplain. The rich mosaic of wet meadows, marshes, reed beds, freshwater lakes, fens, coastal meadows and woodlands has been created by prolonged human activity; current conservation measures are maintaining both its biological diversity and human usage. There are many species of mammal, bird and fish to be found; the wetland is important for breeding, migrating and moulting waterbirds; for example, almost one million birds stop over during spring migration.

The 6,500 km² (2,510 sq miles) of the Volga Delta, the terminus of Europe's longest river, consist of flat alluvial islands, with some dense tree growth, separated by hundreds of channels fringed by marshland and a vast fore-delta of shallow, low-salinity water forming the northern edge of the Caspian. The scale of the delta, its productivity and its wildlife are astounding. Up to 7 million migratory waterbirds stop over in the delta and 230,000 pairs of waterbirds breed here including Dalmatian pelican (*Pelecanus crispus*), great white egret (*Egretta alba*) and glossy ibis (*Plegadis falcinellus*). The river and shallow offshore zones are vital to the life cycle of the Caspian sturgeon or beluga (*Huso huso*), so important to the Russian psyche and dining table.

British Isles

The British Isles have a great diversity of wetlands, though these have been massively reduced in area. They owe this wealth to a long coastline, high tidal amplitude, moist maritime climate, variable geology and a relatively long tradition of conservation.

The mainly igneous geology and mild, wet climate experienced by the deforested uplands of northern and western regions of Britain and Ireland has favoured the development of peatlands, including the famous blanket bogs of Ireland and the Flow Country in Scotland. Many of the region's peatlands are under threat; for instance, 60 per cent of the remaining, and already massively reduced, area of Britain's lowland raised bogs were lost or significantly damaged between 1948 and 1978 by afforestation, peat digging, reclamation or repeated burning.

The extensive inter-tidal zones are especially important as a refuge for migratory shorebirds. Some of the more notable sites include: Strangford Lough, the Solway Firth, Morecambe Bay, the Ribble, Dee and Severn Estuaries in the west, and the Moray Firth, Firth of Forth, Humber Estuary, Wash, Thames Estuary, and Chichester and Langstone Harbours in the east and south.

The lowland rivers, lakes and reservoirs are highly eutrophic and most carry substantial loads of sewage effluent or run-off from agricultural land, or both. Under more natural conditions, rich vegetation communities can still be found. However, eutrophication, has led to algal blooms that have impoverished the submerged and floating vegetation. The vigorous, introduced Canadian pondweed (*Elodea canadensis*) now dominates many eutrophic lakes and ponds to the detriment of other species.

There are considerable areas of wet pasture and coastal grazing marsh in east and southern Scotland,

Round-leaved sundews compensate for a lack of nutrients in peat bogs by ensnaring insects on their sticky leaves.

and in England. The landscape around East Anglia's Broadland lakes, created by peat digging in the Middle Ages, is especially notable for such grazing marsh wetlands.

Among the major natural lakes are Lough Neagh in Northern Ireland and Loch Leven in southeast Scotland; these too are highly eutrophic. The Lake District, in northwest England, owes its lakes and landscape to glaciation. Here, long deep lakes, such as Windermere, are interspersed with mountains, moors and bogs which make the region excessively popular as a tourist destination. There are also large numbers of drinking-water reservoirs in the Pennine hills of northern England, in Wales and, particularly, in and around London.

Northwest Continental Europe

Most of the major wetlands in this region are situated along the generally low-lying coastline. The Wadden Sea is undoubtedly the most significant of these wetlands, though the estuaries of several of the great rivers, notably the Elbe, Rhine, Schelde, Somme and Loire, are also of great importance.

The Wadden Sea is a muddy inter-tidal zone, which stretches from Den Helder in the Netherlands as far as Esbjerg in Denmark. It also includes the Friesian Islands. At certain times of year, the Wadden Sea is home to more than 10 per cent of the west European populations of certain shorebirds, such as dunlin (*Calidris alpina*). It is a vital spawning and nursery area for North Sea fish and also supports large numbers of common seals (*Phoca vitulina*), providing a nursery for the young pups. Since 1963, an area of 350 km² (135 sq miles) of the Wadden Sea has been embanked, and plans exist to embank a further 230 km² (89 sq miles).

The Netherlands was, to a large extent, built by the Dutch as they struggled against both floods and seawater. Recent policies have sought to conserve wetlands and there is very active management of the wetlands created by hydraulic engineering. An interesting case is the Flevoland polders in the Ijsselmeer, the freshwater lake created by the construction of a barrier across the old Zuyder Zee in 1932. Here, 6 km² (2 1/3 sq miles) of the lowest-lying land was designated for an industrial estate. However, before construction got under way, the area developed into a wetland paradise of open water, reed bed and willow forests. So many waterbirds and animals frequented the Oostvaardersplassen that it was declared a State Nature Monument in 1986 and a Ramsar site in 1989. Nevertheless, between 1979 and 1983, the Netherlands lost 29 km² (11 sq miles) of wetlands, including areas of wet heather, mudflats, marsh and swamp. This followed the previous loss of 55 per cent of Dutch wetlands since 1950. Belgium has also drained huge areas of peatland. Flooded pasture in Flanders once covered 35,000 hectares (86,485 acres), but it has now been reduced to 10 per cent of this.

The delta of the Rhine and Meuse suffered disastrous floods in 1953 because of storm surge tides in the North Sea. The ensuing Delta Plan envisaged shutting out the sea by permanent dams and sluices across all of the inlets in the delta. During the decades of construction, ideas changed. The largest opening, the Eastern Schelde, was provided with a remarkably expensive but moveable storm-surge barrier 9 km (5 2/3 miles) long. This barrier guarantees that most of the former tidal regime will be maintained for the benefit of the tidal marshes, shoals and mudflats, shallows, deep-water and submerged dykes of the estuary. This estuary is a vital element in the chain of wetlands along the Western Palaearctic migration route which links Arctic Siberia, Europe and west Africa. The Eastern Schelde regularly holds 47,000 ducks, geese and swans and 160,000 shorebirds. It is also important for breeding waterbirds, and for its fish and fishermen.

Europe has several notable large lakes, such as Lake Geneva, many reservoirs, and extensive river floodplains. These floodplains and their river channels have been much modified over the centuries. Today, they are a focus of increasing attention from conservationists. Lowland peat deposits are widespread in the Netherlands, Belgium and parts of France, while Switzerland has 21,000 km (13,049 miles) of water courses, 1,200 lakes and 11,000 other wetlands; however, these wetlands represent no more than 10 per cent of those existing a century ago.

The Loire is the only large French river not controlled by dams. The extensive floodplain is regularly inundated, though in summer the water level is so low that water resources are stretched to the limit. Large parts of the river have been reclaimed for industry, and the construction of nuclear power plants has added to the demands on the river's water. A large scheme to dam the headwaters and upper reaches was proposed as a means of eliminating floods and maintaining low flows. This scheme stimulated an outcry to protect France's last 'wild' river with all of its natural and ecological values. As a result, the government has recently decided to reconsider the plans for further dams on the Loire.

Freshwater meadows, bogs and woods once covered 1.3 million hectares (3.2 million acres) of France, but they are currently being lost at a rate of 10,000 hectares (24,710 acres) per year.

To the northeast, in inland Germany, the most common wetlands are freshwater marshes and, above all, lakes, whether natural, man-modified or artificial. The lower part of the Elbe floodplain, although threatened by Hamburg's industrialization, is important for migrating swans and geese. A large part of the Rhine floodplain near the Dutch border has been listed as a Ramsar site. The complex waterway of the Havel River near Magdeburg includes the shallow eutrophic lake, Gülper See, and floodplain delimited by dykes. The area is important for breeding and migratory waterbirds.

Other important wetlands include Lake Constance (Bodensee), at the head of the Rhine, the Ismaninger Reservoir near Munich, the lakes to the east and south of that city, and the reservoirs along the Inn Valley. The Berga-Kelbra flood-protection reservoir near Erfurt is the largest water area in the Thuringian Plain, while the reservoirs on the Ruhr and Mohne supply the Ruhr industrial complex but also provide winter quarters for large numbers of waterbirds.

On the north German plain the Dümmersee is a shallow lake associated with peat bogs, sand dunes and glacial moraines. The Diepholzer Marsh (Diepholzer Moorniederung) and peat bogs near Osnabrück have been much modified by peat digging, but the original peatland vegetation survives

LAKE BALATON, HUNGARY

Lake Balaton (596 km² - 230 sq miles) is the largest lake in central Europe. It is a shallow lake in western Hungary which drains into the River Danube. The large oscillations in depth that used to be one of its characteristics have been reduced to around 200 mm (7 3/4 in) by the enlargement of the outflow canal and careful sluice management. The level is maintained within narrow limits to assist navigation, coastal recreation and agriculture in the surrounding lands.

Reeds cover 2.5 per cent of the lake but their spread is limited by the violent waves on the southern shore and the steep slopes on parts of the northern shore. Some 2,000 species of algae have been identified in Lake Balaton. However, large nutrient inputs have caused eutrophication and excess production of algae. There are around 1,200 species of invertebrates and

512 species of fish in the lake.

Lake Balaton is a major wintering refuge for up to 70,000 geese, 30,000 ducks and 10,000 coot (*Fulica atra*). The commercial fish catch is 1,200 tonnes (1,181 tons) per year, of which 75 per cent is bream (*Abramis brama*) and 15 per cent pike-perch (*Stizostedion lucioperca*). Fish traps on the Sió Canal harvest over 100 tonnes (98 tons) of eels per year. Fishing permits were issued to 115,000 people in 1986 and these anglers caught a further 500 tonnes (492 tons) of fish.

Balaton is of enormous importance for water-based recreation in land-locked Hungary. The region's permanent population of 250,000 swells to 860,000 when the holiday-makers arrive.

From 1950 to 1975 there was a sixfold increase in the quantity of fertilizers used in the basin and a fourteenfold increase in the number of tourists.

The resulting massive increase in phosphorous has contributed to the eutrophication of the lake. There has been an active campaign for sewage treatment plants often with phosphorous removal facilities. Agricultural and river inputs are being controlled by the construction of detention reservoirs which remove over 50 per cent of the phosphorous. Similarly, soil conservation and anti-erosion measures are being implemented.

Around Lake Balaton there are five large landscape protection areas and six small nature reserves. In 1989, the lake became the world's first part-time Ramsar site, being included in the List only between 1 October and 30 April each year. The active promotion of the idea of the 'wise use' of wetlands by the Ramsar Convention may lead to full-time designation in the near future.

in some areas. Up to 500 cranes (*Grus grus*) stop over during migration. Between 1950 and 1985, there was a 57 per cent decline in wetland area, excluding marshes, in the Federal Republic of Germany.

Central and Eastern Europe

The catchment of Europe's largest river, the Danube, extends from southern Germany, through Austria, Czechoslovakia and Hungary to Yugoslavia, Bulgaria and Romania, until, at its delta, it also incorporates part of the Soviet Union. The Danube forms the main artery for wetlands throughout central Europe, providing a major route for fish, shipping and pollution. The river starts to be charged with sediment and pollutants downstream of Regensburg in Germany. Many towns and cities use it as an open drain into which they dump raw sewage, detergents, household waste and untreated industrial effluents. This pollution has been exacerbated by low river flows during the dry years since 1985. Each year the Danube discharges 1.8 million tonnes of nutrients, mostly from agricultural chemicals, into the Black Sea, causing algal blooms which have decimated fisheries.

The controversy over a plan to construct a hydro-electric power plant and associated works at the Hainburg Ramsar site in Austria marked the birth of the green movement in that country. The scheme was to harness the Danube to generate power, requiring a low dam and the raising of water levels upstream by around 16 m (52 ft). This would have destroyed some 800 hectares (1,977 acres) of prime riverine forest, as well as causing other environmental problems. Public outcry led to the cancellation of the scheme in 1986. However, an alternative dam site is now being developed upstream, in Vienna itself.

At the same time, substantial Austrian finance was committed to the Gabcikovo-Nagymaros hydro-power project on the Danube in Czechoslovakia and Hungary. This involves a lengthy concrete diversion for the river's entire flow, and raised international concern about the environmental impact of the scheme on the recharge of aquifers upon which 10 million people depend for their water supplies. Public protest in Hungary led to the shelving of the Nagymaros Dam in 1989.

Despite its problems, the Danube Basin retains some of Europe's greatest wetland assets. Lake Balaton, in Hungary, is one of the continent's largest lakes, supporting internationally important numbers of waterbirds in winter and acting as a major tourist resort in summer. Other important freshwater lakes include Srebarna in Bulgaria and Obedska Bara in Yugoslavia.

Poland is noted for its 9,300 lakes which, at 3,200 km² (1,235 sq miles), cover 1 per cent of the country and result mostly from glacial erosion or deposition. They are often enriched with nutrients and commonly have wide fringing belts of reeds (*Phragmites australis*) and wooded surrounds. The lakes are frozen for about four months of the year but are important for breeding and passage waterbirds. One of the most important wetland areas is the Mazurian Lakes complex, in the northeast of the country, which contains more than 4,000 separate water bodies. Poland's Baltic coastline includes many bays, lagoons and sandy spits, forming a vital staging area for migratory waterbirds.

Fish ponds are amongst the most important wetland habitats in many parts of eastern Europe, including Poland and Czechoslovakia. For example, the complex of carp ponds in the vicinity of Milicz in Poland provides an important economic resource and also supports large numbers of waterbirds. Other notable fish ponds include the 500 or so around Trebon in Czechoslovakia which contribute to one of the eight wetlands designated by Czechoslovakia in 1990, under the terms of the Ramsar Convention. The ponds are often eutrophic and provide significant yields of fish for local and regional markets. They are also an important recreational resource in many areas.

Iberian Peninsula, Mediterranean Basin and Black Sea

The wetlands of the Mediterranean Basin are predominantly at low altitudes and they are usually coastal. The region is notable for its river deltas: the Camargue at the mouth of the Rhône, the delta of the Po, the combined delta of the rivers Axios, Aliakmon and Loudias near Thessaloniki, the Evros Delta on the border of Greece and Turkey, the Danube and, of course, the enormous Nile Delta - to name but a few. These deltas tend to have complexes of lagoons, marshes, lakes, temporary pools, river channels, irrigated agriculture and shallow coastal zones.

The Danube Delta covers 5,000 km² (1,930 sq miles) in Romania and the USSR. It is the largest wetland in the region, noted for its huge populations of waterbirds. While most of the delta remains in a semi-natural and undeveloped state, 25 per cent of it has been converted to arable land, fishponds and poplar (*Populus*) plantations. A project dating from 1983 envisaged the conversion of another half of the delta, but a presidential decree in February 1990, following the political changes in Romania, sought to stop the conversion work; influence, however, is still being exerted by enterprises concerned with winning a quick economic return. The delta has been designated as a Biosphere Reserve and was listed under the Ramsar Convention in May 1991. To date, however, only 40,000 hectares (98,840 acres) have been given

Greater flamingos are found in large numbers in the Camargue, southern France.

protection as nature reserves under Romanian law.

The Camargue, the most notable wetland of France, is the 850 km² (328 sq mile) delta of the Rhône. Although originally created by the flooding of the Rhône, the delta is now completely protected by high banks, and the wetland's water is supplied only by irrigation canals, rainfall or seawater inflows. Much of the natural habitat of the Camargue has been transformed into extensive saltpans, rice fields, pastures and for tourist development. Temporary marshes are used for commercialized waterfowl hunting.

The significant wetlands of Portugal are all coastal and generally estuarine. The Tagus Estuary is a vast inter-tidal zone of mudflats bordered by salt marsh and rice fields. Industry has intruded into the wetland, but the area is still visited by over 50,000 shorebirds and several thousand ducks. The Ria Formosa complex of freshwater and brackish marshes, lagoons, mudflats, beaches, dunes and saltpans extends to the west of Faro in the south of Portugal. The mosaic of habitats here supports an abundance of bivalve molluscs, crustaceans and fish which are exploited by a large fishing community. The area hosts up to 20,000 shorebirds in winter and

has a diverse and significant population of breeding birds. Holiday homes, sewage, aircraft noise and hunting all threaten the integrity of the wetland. A Council of Europe survey found that 80 per cent of Portuguese salt marshes are threatened with reclamation.

Mediterranean freshwater marshes have been greatly affected by human activity and only limited areas remain. Some freshwater marshes in the Camargue are strictly protected and supplied with pumped water by national and private agencies. Almost all of the freshwater marshes have been drained around the north of the Adriatic, although freshwater marsh conditions have been restored to a reserve at the mouth of the Isonzo River in Italy. In Roman times, 10 per cent of Italy (3 million hectares - 7.4 million acres) was wetland. Only 764,000 hectares (1.89 million acres) remained by 1865, and by 1972 this had diminished to only 192,000 hectares (469,490 acres).

Wet meadow exists in the Prespa National Park in Greece and around the northern edge of the Amvrakikos Gulf in the west of the country. However, here too, reclamation, fish farm construction and altered flow regimes because of

PRESPA NATIONAL PARK, GREECE

The lakes Megali Prespa and Mikri Prespa and their associated reed beds and wet meadows lie on the borders of Greece, Yugoslavia and Albania. They are fed by seasonal torrents which have a peak flow in May, the time of snow-melt on the high mountains. Perhaps more importantly, since the lakes are in a largely closed basin, large volumes of water flow out from the lakes through fissures and caves in the limestone. So large is the underground flow from Megali Prespa, in particular, that fish have regularly swum up into the lake from Lake Ochrid which lies beyond the mountains surrounding Megali Prespa and at a lower level.

Both Megali and Mikri Prespa have their highest water levels in spring. Flooding of the wet meadows allows fish to spawn successfully and means that food is available for waterbirds.

Mikri Prespa is important for breeding waterbirds; large colonies use the marshlands and reed beds.

Especially important are the nesting Dalmatian pelicans and white pelicans (*Pelecanus onocrotalus*). The wide range of habitats means that over 200 bird species occur in the area, including cormorant (*Phalacrocorax carbo sinensis*), night heron (*Nycticorax nycticorax*), squacco heron (*Ardeola ralloides*), ferruginous duck (*Aythya nyroca*), spoonbill (*Platalea leucorodia*), black kite (*Milvus migrans*), little tern (*Sterna albifrons*) and white-tailed eagle (*Haliaeetus albicilla*). The rich biological diversity of the park is also reflected in the flora which includes over 1,200 species.

Probably the major threat to Prespa lies in the fact that the traditional harmony between people and nature has been largely lost. Efforts to address the area's social and economic problems have had adverse environmental impacts. An irrigation scheme involved heavy channelization of the streams, widespread clearance of mature trees and some loss of the upper part of the

wet meadow habitat. The European Community funded the construction of a fish breeding station which was located in a highly sensitive area of the wet meadows. To date, the station has not operated because of technical problems and concern over its possible effect on Mikri Prespa. Reed burning was traditional but its banning in 1974 has led to expansion of the reed beds, restricted access for the fish to their spawning grounds on the wet meadows and uncontrolled fires such as that in 1989 which wiped out a pelican colony.

In spite of being declared a National Park, Prespa has benefited from only minor conservation activities on the ground by the Greek government. The area has only recently had two part-time wardens appointed; other work has included the construction of car parks, observation towers and picnic places. However, a comprehensive manage-ment plan is nearing completion and there is a thriving Centre for Man and Nature.

---

upstream dams are serious threats. In Greece a 60 per cent loss of wetlands, mainly lakes and marshland, took place through two periods of land drainage for agriculture. From 1920 to 1940 there was a need for new agricultural land for immigrants, while since 1950, the push has been for more production and income.

Probably the largest remaining freshwater marsh in the entire Mediterranean is the 8,900 hectare (22,000 acre) Mekhada Marsh in the El Kala complex in northeast Algeria. Sadly, it too is being reclaimed around the margins and will soon have large dams on both rivers feeding it. The Mediterranean coast of Spain has a few small freshwater marshes, such as Prat de Cabanes-Torreblanca and many lagoons such as those of the Ebro Delta and Mar Menor.

Lagoons, usually separated from the Mediterranean by sandy spits or dunes, have their character determined by the proportions of freshwater and seawater which they contain. The northern Adriatic has many lagoons in the Po Delta and eastwards to Marano and Grado, as well as the world-famous Venice Lagoon. The Tunisian coast is lined with lagoons, from the hypersaline Bahiret el Biban on the Libyan border, to the Korba lagoons of Cap Bon, the much reclaimed and transformed Lake of Tunis and the large lagoons at Ghar El Melah at the mouth of the Medjerda River.

Most of the Mediterranean is tideless, but in the

Gulf of Gabes, off southern Tunisia, circumstances conspire to produce almost 1 m (just over 3 ft) of tide, which creates over 200 km^2 (77 sq miles) of inter-tidal mudflats. There is a rich fauna of invertebrates and this normally draws over 100,000 wintering shorebirds. The tidal salt marshes of the Atlantic coast of Spain, the Odiel Marshes at Huelva, the Doñana Marshes in the south and the Ortigueira and Santoña marshes on the north coast are all located at river mouths and are amongst the most important wetlands for waterbirds in the entire European and Mediterranean region.

Some 25 per cent of all Mediterranean coastal wetlands are in Egypt, but as the Egyptian Wildlife Service reports, 'there has been a sustained contraction of wetland areas due to continuous land reclamation'. Lake Burullus, now a Ramsar site, was reduced from 58,000 hectares (145,295 acres) in 1913 to 46,100 hectares (113,913 acres) by 1974.

Permanent and temporary salt lakes are common, particularly in the east and south of the Mediterranean. Permanent salt lakes such as the 94 km^2 (36 sq mile) Akrotiri salt lake in southern Cyprus can be fed by the sea; or, as in the case of Sidi El Hani in central Tunisia, they can draw water primarily from underground sources; or, as with the Dead Sea, be the terminal point of perennial rivers. Temporary salt lakes, such as those on the high plateau of Algeria, the enormous Chott Djerid in southern

GARAET EL ICHKEUL, TUNISIA

Ichkeul National Park is situated in northern Tunisia and comprises a lake of 8,900 hectares (22,000 acres), a limestone mountain of 1,363 hectares (3,368 acres) and 770 hectares (1,903 acres) of marshes. The wetland is fed by six rivers though the local rainfall is also a significant input. Ichkeul is the most important site in North Africa for breeding, migrating and wintering (up to 400,000) waterbirds. The park also supports significant populations of fish, mammals and birds of prey.

Around 120 families live in the park and graze their livestock on the marshes. The numbers of grazing animals are rising, with many herds brought into the park on a daily basis. The marshes are a significant local resource because they are used in an integrated way within a grazing system employing land in the uplands, marshes and harvested agricultural fields.

Ichkeul attracts many Tunisian and foreign visitors, particularly since the opening of a visitor centre in 1990.

The main threat to Ichkeul is from urban and irrigation demands for water, involving the damming of the six rivers feeding the lake. Two of the dams have been completed. Agricultural development on the plain outside the park has brought deep drainage canals and agro-chemicals to its boundaries; drainage canals cut across two of its freshwater marshes have become seriously degraded. Several large quarries exist on the mountain and the marshes are heavily overgrazed.

The site was the first in the world to be listed as a Ramsar site, Biosphere Reserve and World Heritage site. Ten years of planning, however, have not yet guaranteed its long-term safety. Nevertheless, efforts to find and implement long-term solutions have recently intensified, partly as a result of external reluctance to fund part of the water resources plan in view of what are likely to be its adverse environmental impacts.

Tunisia, and the Grande Sebkha d'Oran in western Algeria, generally derive their periodic inflows from flash-floods in the surrounding ephemeral streams.

Shallow inland saline lakes are common in the Ebro, Guadalquivir and Tagus Basins of Spain. They have a paucity of species but several are notable for their halobacteria communities. One of the best-known saline lakes is the Fuente de Piedra in Andalusia where greater flamingos (*Phoenicopterus ruber*) breed regularly.

The rivers of the Mediterranean Basin have been so dramatically transformed by human activity and engineering work that only the smallest streams in remoter corners retain both their natural regime and an unaltered channel. One such river is the Goksu of southeastern Turkey feeding a modest delta which has been much transformed to agricultural land. Similarly, most of the region's floodplains have been changed with dykes, drainage and pumping. In Italy's Po Delta, only at small Ramsar sites, such as the shallow Valle Santa flood-storage reservoir, do the last remnants of the once-extensive floodplain marshes remain.

Numerous freshwater lakes remain in the Mediterranean region. A series of mountain lakes in the middle Atlas of Morocco include habitat suitable for waterbirds, including the rare crested coot (*Fulica cristata*). The Italian Alpine lakes Como and Maggiore are known worldwide, but there are also smaller, but important, Alpine lakes such as Lago di Mezzola in the Como region. The mountainous Montenegro region of Yugoslavia has a beautiful lake in the

The view from a hide in the famous Doñana National Park of southwest Spain. The reed beds are home to many nesting birds including the rare purple gallinule (Porphyrio porphyrio).

The small brackish pool at Ghadira is Malta's only significant wetland. The area is important for endemic flora and fauna, migratory birds and conservation education.

Biogradska Gora National Park and there are many lakes in the impressive Durmitor Mountains.

Spain has very few large natural lakes because most of it was not glaciated. The two notable lakes are Banyolas - 110 hectares (272 acres) and 40 m (131 ft) deep - and Sanabria - 300 hectares (740 acres) and 50 m (164 ft) deep - which is glacial in origin. However, all of the major rivers, and most of the smaller streams, have been dammed to give the country a plethora of freshwater reservoirs. Permanent ponds and wet meadows are found in

glacially excavated hollows in the mountains above 1,500 m (4,920 ft). Shallow temporary ponds, generally with freshwater, comprise the majority of inland wetlands in Spain.

Important lakes elsewhere in the Mediterranean include the Sea of Galilee with Lake Hula upstream, in Israel, while the El Kala complex in Algeria boasts a freshwater lake in Lac Oubeira, a freshwater lake with emergent vegetation at Lac Tonga, the appropriately named Lac des Oiseaux and the 150 km² (58 sq miles) Lac Fetzara, which has recently been restored to something of its former glory. Lake Skadar (350 km² - 135 sq miles) is shared between Yugoslavia and Albania. The level of the lake rises significantly in winter and floods extensive marshes, meadows and woodlands. The lake supports a thriving fishing industry, augmented by thousands of sport fishermen, and is famed for its breeding and wintering waterbirds.

Oases characterize the more arid parts of the Mediterranean Basin. Azraq in Jordan is listed as a Ramsar site and six oases have been identified amongst Tunisia's 239 wetlands.

Saltpans are found all around the Mediterranean and in various degrees of operation. Those in the Camargue are thriving; the salt company at Messolonghi (Mesolongion) in Greece is hoping to diversify its operations to include a visitor centre for its enhanced breeding populations of birds. The saltpans at Ghadira on Malta closed long ago, leaving a diverse flora and fauna.

The heavy demand for water in the Mediterranean has meant that all of the countries of the region have constructed reservoirs. Irrigation is the purpose of many, such as the Kerkini Reservoir on the Strymon

AZRAQ, JORDAN

Azraq lies some 80 km (50 miles) from Amman, Jordan's capital city, at the heart of a shallow basin which receives storm run-off from a network of wadis. In times of high rainfall, a huge saline lake may develop at Azraq, which is also the location of two strong fresh-water springs. Until recently, these springs fed a lush oasis which for centuries had supported local people. As one of the few wetlands in this arid region, the oasis is of strategic importance for migratory birds. The reserve also has the only Jordanian communities of the marsh frog and the black water snake (*Tropidonotus tessalate*).

1980 marked the commencement of electrical pumping from the Azraq springs to meet an ever-increasing demand for freshwater in Amman.

The manufacture of salt is an important economic activity at Azraq oasis in Jordan. The raw product is taken from these evaporation basins to a nearby refinery.

In 1982, withdrawal of water from the springs was replaced by ground water extraction from a newly built government well field nearby. At the same time, withdrawals from private

wells also increased dramatically, so that by 1989 the natural spring discharge at Azraq was only one-fifth of its 1981 level, leading to the gradual drying-out of the oasis. Excessive exploitation of freshwater also led to the threat of salt water entering the well field, thus endangering one of Amman's most important sources of drinking water.

The Jordanian government has identified a 'safe' level of pumping which could maintain supplies to Amman and allow natural spring flow to continue (though at a reduced level). However, progress towards wise use of Azraq's resources has undoubtedly been disrupted by the conflict in the Gulf region and there is considerable social and political pressure for short-term (non-sustainable) exploitation.

DAIMIEL, SPAIN

The Daimiel National Park, 30 km (19 miles) northeast of Ciudad Real in central Spain, consists of extensive areas of state-owned marshland together with some private ponds and lakes. The marshland has formed at the confluence of the Río Cigüela and the Río Guadiana. In addition there were once strong springs within the marshes (or Tablas) which brought a continuous supply of calcium-rich ground water into the park.

The wetland includes large reed beds with reedmace and sawgrass fringing the water courses. The expanses of cut sedge (*Carex*) are the most extensive in Europe. *Chara hispida,* an important food supply for certain waterbirds, extends over almost the whole submerged surface. Small mammals such as otters (*Lutra lutra*), polecats (*Mustela putorius*), stoats (*Mustela erminea*), water voles (*Arvicola terrestris*) and hares (*Lepus capensis*) occur, along with increasing numbers of wild boar (*Sus scrofa*). Daimiel is also important for its large and diverse population of waterbirds, including large numbers of breeding ducks, among these over 1,000 pairs of red-crested pochard (*Netta rufina*). Many surface-feeding ducks use the wetland as a moulting refuge and large numbers of waterbirds spend the winter here.

The region was declared a National Park in 1973. The 1,812 hectare (4,453 acre) Ramsar site, within the National Park, was listed in 1982 and a visitor centre has been constructed. There have been considerable works within the park in relation to water management, including an outflow sluice and the reinstatement of some wetlands which had formerly been drained for agriculture.

In spite of these measures, however, dangers to the wetland abound. Local farmers began extensive irrigation in 1979, leading to drying of springs, marked reduction of the flow of the Guadiana and the rapid infiltration of the Cigüela into the aquifer. As a result, Daimiel was almost completely dry from 1982 to 1987, with fires in its organic soils in 1986 and 1987. Additional problems derive from the severe pollution of local watercourses and a new EC-funded dam on a tributary of the Guadiana.

Since 1988 a regeneration plan has been operating. This involves the release of water from the Tajo-Seguria irrigation transfer pipe into the Cigüela from February to May each year and the pumping of ground water from new emergency wells around Daimiel during the summer months. Sadly, the clearing of the Cigüela Channel, to speed the flow of at least a proportion of the released water, resulted in the destruction of riverine habitats, the desiccation of upstream lagoons and the destruction of sluices on other internationally important sites.

Whilst the regeneration plan has put water back into Daimiel, it has changed the wetland from an area of ground water discharge to one of ground water recharge; hence the support of the local farmers for the scheme. The water is of a different chemical composition to that which occurs naturally in the wetland and it is always moving downward rather than upward. This recharge has stabilized the water table about 1 m (just over 3 ft) below Daimiel, but beyond the park boundary the water table drops away rapidly and it is expected to fall further in the coming years. Within the park the plant communities have begun to change as a result of the changed water regime. Only one village has formed a committee to examine the over-exploitation of the aquifer. There has been no implementation of the Water Act's requirement for a community of users to be formed.

Recently, a plan has been developed to enlarge the restoration scheme by a further heavy dredging of the Cigüela Channel and the construction of dams on both the Cigüela and Zancara Rivers. These ideas are unlikely to benefit Daimiel, though they seem certain to damage the internationally important lagoons in the headwaters of the Cigüela, and they are probably promoted primarily by agricultural interests.

River in northern Greece. Others provide irrigation and potable supplies, such as the Mexa Dam at El Kala in Algeria and the Djoumine upstream of Lac Ichkeul in Tunisia. The multiple dams on the Rhône in France regulate the river but are mainly designed to generate hydroelectric power.

Over the last 100 years, 28 per cent of Tunisian wetlands have disappeared. The catchment of the Medjerda River has the largest loss of wetland area at 84 per cent. The most frequently destroyed wetland type here has been shallow freshwater inland marsh. The main causes of wetland loss have been drainage, urbanization, agricultural encroachment and dam construction.

FLORA

The present flora of the region reflects a wide range of inter-acting natural and anthropogenic factors. Amongst the most important of these are geology and topography; the influence of the Atlantic Ocean (especially of the Gulf Stream); the impact of Pleistocene glaciation; deforestation; and increasing human population density and agricultural intensification.

Truly aquatic vegetation communities show a broadly similar composition and structure throughout Europe and the Mediterranean Basin, in sharp contrast to the marked zonation (mainly climatic) which is found in semi-terrestrial communities (for example, tundra and peatland vegetation).

The word 'tundra' derives from the Finnish 'tunturi' meaning 'completely treeless heights', and has been widely adopted as the term for the treeless landscape bordering the Arctic Ocean and its islands and for the similar vegetation growing beyond the tree line in high mountain zones. Mosses and lichens dominate, whilst flowering plants are represented mainly by sedge (*Carex*) and cotton-grass (*Eriophorum*) species. Other important components of the tundra vegetation include grasses; dwarf birch (*Betula nana*) and birch (*Betual glandulosa*); members of the Ericaceae family, such as bilberries (*Vaccinium* species); alder (*Alnus glutinosa*) and willow (*Salix*) species.

Only mountain tundra occurs in Scandinavia.

Marsh marigolds (Caltha palustris) *are found in many shallow freshwater habitats.*

Cotton grasses are a major component of the vegetation of tundra and peat wetlands in northern Europe.

In much of the European Soviet Union, the Arctic coastal vegetation is typical of southerly tundra zones; in fact, it forms part of the tundra forest ecotone - the transition between true tundra and the taiga. Only on the Arctic islands such as Novaya Zemlya and Spitsbergen does the true 'polar desert' (with a discontinuous cover of mainly lichens and mosses) occur.

The extensive taiga of the Soviet Union and Scandinavia merges with birch forest and tundra to the north and with scattered mixed forest and drier steppe habitats to the south. Tree cover in the Boreal zone is far from continuous and the region contains innumerable wetlands in a mosaic of forest, peatland and open water habitats. Mires are characteristic; indeed they occupy more than 5 per cent of the European land surface.

The bog vegetation of much of western Norway, western Ireland and the uplands of the United Kingdom, is characterized by species such as cross-leaved heath (*Erica tetralix*), ling (*Calluna vulgaris*), purple moorgrass (*Molinia caerulea*) and mosses, notably *Sphagnum* species, together with members of the sedge family Cyperaceae such as common cotton-grass (*Eriophorum angustifolia*) and white beak-sedge (*Rhynchospora alba*), and rushes such as bulbous rush (*Juncus bulbosus*). Insect-trapping plants such as the sticky round-leaved sundew (*Drosera rotundifolia*) and common butterwort (*Pinguicula vulgaris*) are also commonly found in these areas.

Lowland peatlands are now rare in western Europe, but those that remain support some of the plants characteristic of upland acidic bogs. They are also notable for the occurrence of a much richer variety of sedges, including great fen sedge (*Cladium mariscus*), grasses such as common reed and, especially, broad-leaved herbs such as purple

loosestrife (*Lythrum salicaria*) and meadowsweet (*Filipendula ulmaria*). Rapid vegetational succession, especially the invasion of trees such as willow and alder, is characteristic of fens, so that intensive management is usually required to maintain these important habitats.

Eutrophic streams, rivers, ponds and lakes are the most common wetlands of much of lowland Europe and under natural conditions are typified by rich vegetation communities. The continuous flow of water in rivers is largely responsible for determining the aquatic vegetation, although the rate of flow, width and depth of the channel and pH of the water are amongst other important factors. Typical species of relatively fast-flowing, eutrophic rivers may include river water-crowfoot (*Ranunculus fluitans*) and fennel pondweed (*Potamogeton pectinatus*), with water forget-me-not (*Myosotis scorpioides*) and arrowhead (*Sagittaria sagittifolia*).

Fast-flowing, oligotrophic rivers and streams support a flora that is much less rich but includes species such as common water-crowfoot (*Ranunculus aquatilis*) and alternate water-milfoil (*Myriophyllum alterniflorum*), whilst marginal plants may include rushes (*Juncus*) and branched bur-reed (*Sparganium erectum*).

White water lilies are common in still, freshwater wetlands.

The eutrophic headwaters of the River Thames in southern England support a rich emergent vegetation.

Amongst the plants typical of slowly flowing water courses are canary reed-grass (*Phalaris arundinacea*), reed sweet-grass (*Phalaris maxima*), common reed and greater reedmace (*Typha latifolia*), with submerged or floating species including yellow water lily (*Nuphar lutea*).

Many of the plants mentioned above are widely distributed across the region, although wetlands in the Mediterranean Basin may support some different species; for example, great reed (*Arundo donax*), an introduced species, is now naturalized in southern Europe, where it colonizes shallow, slow-flowing waters and marshes.

The vegetation of the region's still waters is roughly similar throughout Europe and the Mediterranean. In deep eutrophic waters, the aquatic vegetation is likely to be dominated by pondweeds such as shining pondweed (*Potamogeton lucens*), spiked water-milfoil (*Myriophyllum spicatum*) and the introduced Canadian pondweed. Common reed is typical in waters of up to 500 mm (20 in) in depth. Among the more common species of still, mesotrophic waters in central Europe are water soldier (*Stratiotes aloides*) and frogbit (*Hydrocharis morsus-ranae*). Duckweeds (*Lemna*) are common and widespread free-floating surface plants. The water chestnut (*Trapa natans*) occurs only in the south of the region. Still-water communities dominated by water lilies are widespread in Europe, with white water lily (*Nymphaea alba*) being the commonest species.

Coastal regions of northwest Europe contain some major expanses of salt marsh vegetation, which have developed between the low and high tidemarks on flat, muddy or sandy substrates in areas protected from wave action, notably around the major estuaries. Typical species include common saltmarsh grass (*Puccinellia maritima*), glassworts (*Salicornia* species), sea club-rush (*Scirpus maritimus*), sea rush (*Juncus maritimus*), thrift (*Armeria maritima*), sea arrowgrass (*Triglochin maritima*), oraches (*Atriplex* species) and sea aster (*Aster tripolium*). In the British Isles, a new species, common cord-grass (*Spartina anglica*) has derived from a hybrid cord-grass which in its turn developed as a result of the introduction of the North American species, *Spartina alternifolia*. Common cord-grass is extremely vigorous and has colonized many formerly open areas of inter-tidal mud.

FAUNA

Invertebrates and Fish

European and Mediterranean wetlands support an enormous diversity of invertebrates, many of which form the staple diet of other wetland fauna, whilst others are economically important as food for human beings. Shellfish and crustaceans such as prawns and shrimps are harvested from many coastal wetlands, although contamination of shellfish with heavy metals, such as mercury, has become a serious problem in some areas.

Amongst the more spectacular wetland invertebrates are dragonflies and damselflies (Odonata), which are widespread in Europe and the Mediterranean, with only Iceland having no resident species. Although well over 100 species have been recorded, relatively few are endemic to the region; the composition of the Mediterranean Odonata, in particular, has strong African and Asian elements, the latter being more evident in the eastern part of the basin. At the opposite end of the region, the European tundra supports only a handful of species, but diversity increases rapidly to the south. A few species, such as *Coenagrion hylas*, found only in southeast Germany, are extremely restricted in their distribution, whilst others, such as the common blue damselfly (*Enallagma cyathigerum*) occur virtually throughout the region. Some damselflies and dragonflies, such as common darter (*Sympetrum striolatum*), travel long distances in search of wetlands suitable for colonization.

Throughout Europe and the Mediterranean Basin, fish provide important economic returns from wetlands - from both commercial and sport fisheries. Fish are also an essential element in wetland food chains; for example, they are a major component of the diet of many waterbirds such as herons, cormorants and pelicans.

The shallow waters of the region's coastal wetlands provide plenty of food and act as a vital spawning ground and nursery for commercially important fish species. For example, the Wadden Sea and other inter-tidal areas provide a nursery for plaice (*Pleuronectes platessa*), sole (*Solea solea*) and herring (*Clupea harengus*) prior to their dispersal into the North Sea. Some other species, such as the sea trout (*Salmo trutta*), spawn in freshwater rivers, using the Wadden Sea as a nursery and main feeding area.

Another economically important species is the salmon (*Salmo salar*), whose natural European distribution extends from the west coast of Portugal to the coastal waters of the Arctic Ocean as far as the White Sea. The adults live at sea but migrate upstream through estuaries and rivers to spawn in freshwater, where the immature fish grow and develop. Pollution of major rivers and the construction of dams and other impediments to salmon migration have caused serious declines in some parts of the species' range.

A pair of mating common darter dragonflies. Common darters are amongst the more numerous and widespread of the European dragonflies.

43

Eels (*Anguilla anguilla*) also undertake long migrations; for example, juvenile eels (or 'elvers') which migrate up the Severn Estuary in the southwest United Kingdom begin their lives in the Sargasso Sea on the opposite side of the Atlantic. Catches of elvers in the Severn, using low-intensity, traditional methods, have also fallen dramatically in recent years.

More than 150 species of fish are found in the freshwater wetlands of Europe, with oxygen content of the water (determined by such factors as flow-rate, temperature, turbidity and pollution) being a strong influence on the species present at a given site.

Tench (*Tinca tinca*) and carp (*Cyprinus carpio*) are amongst the species best able to cope with a low oxygen content and may tolerate levels of pollution which would kill most other fish.

Reptiles and Amphibians

The diversity and distribution of reptiles and amphibians in Europe and the Mediterranean Basin is markedly uneven, with the cooler, less sunny, northern parts of the region supporting only a handful of species. The Mediterranean climate is suitable for reptiles but marked seasonal aridity restricts the distribution of amphibians.

The fire salamander (*Salamandra salamandra*), which occurs in central and southwestern parts of the region, is the only widespread European salamander. It is rarely found far from water - mainly in forested streams in hilly or mountainous districts. Newts require still or slowly flowing water in which to breed but are terrestrial for much of the year. Among the more widely distributed of the eight European species are the warty newt (*Triturus cristatus*) and smooth newt (*Triturus vulgaris*), both of which occur throughout north-central parts of the region.

The common frog (*Rana temporaria*) occurs in almost any moist habitat throughout the region, except permanently frozen areas. It is often found at high altitudes, reaching as far as the snow line, especially in the south of its range, where it tends to avoid lowland habitats. Among other species are the marsh frog (*Rana ridibunda*) found in many types of wetlands in southwest France, Iberia and eastern Europe; the stream frog (*Rana graeca*) found in cool mountain streams in Italy and the Balkans; and the moor frog (*Rana arvalis*) found in damp fields, fens and sphagnum bogs in northeast Europe.

The common toad (*Bufo bufo*) is widespread in wetlands but also occurs in quite dry habitats. Other European toads, which are more restricted to wetland areas, include the fire-bellied toad (*Bombina bombina*) found in eastern Europe and yellow-bellied toad (*Bombina variegata*) found in central-southern Europe.

Common toads return annually to their traditional mating and spawning grounds.

Wintering Bewick's swans feeding on seasonally flooded grassland in the United Kingdom. These birds breed in the tundra wetlands of Siberia and migrate in family parties, reaching the UK in October or November.

Two species of terrapin occur in Europe; the European pond terrapin (*Emys orbicularis*), widespread in southern and eastern areas, is found in small wetlands with still or slowly flowing water and rich aquatic vegetation. The stripe-necked terrapin (*Mauremys capsica*), limited to Iberia and the Balkan peninsula, tends to inhabit larger, open waters, including major rivers.

Few of the region's reptiles are linked closely with wetland habitats. The viviparous lizard (*Lacerta vivipara*) occurs throughout central and northern parts, favouring moist habitats, especially in the south of its range where it is associated with marshes and wet ditches. The closely related meadow lizard (*Lacerta praticola*) occurs only in a few isolated areas of the Balkans and Caucasus but is also associated with wetland habitats including stream banks and marsh edges.

Most European snakes are found in dry habitats, although three species of the genus *Natrix* are found mainly in wetlands. The grass snake (*Natrix natrix*) is widespread, though it is absent from the far north and some islands. Although it occurs in a diversity of habitats, it is strongly associated with lakes, ponds and wet grassland where it feeds on invertebrates and, especially, on amphibians such as frogs and newts. Dice snakes (*Natrix tessellata*), which occur only in the southeast of the region, spend much of their lives in weedy ponds and rivers. The viperine snake (*Natrix maura*) occurs in French and Spanish wetlands.

Birds

Birds are the most spectacular of the European and Mediterranean wetland fauna, and many, such as herons, ducks, geese, swans, and shorebirds, are intimately linked to wetlands for their survival. These important groups contain over 150 species, among them some of the most striking and colourful in the region such as the elegant yet bizarre greater flamingo.

The importance of individual wetlands often varies greatly, reflecting seasonal movements of huge numbers of migratory birds. The need to maintain a network of wetland 'service stations' throughout their flyways to provide food and shelter is clearly vital.

The tundra wetlands are only habitable during the late spring and summer, but during this 'window of opportunity' huge numbers of migratory waterbirds arrive to breed, taking advantage of a super-abundance of insect food and round-the-clock daylight. Typical groups include divers (Gaviidae), wildfowl (Anatidae) - for example, long-tailed duck (*Clangula hyemalis*) and pink-footed goose (*Anser brachyrhynchus*) - and shorebirds such as dunlin, turnstone (*Arenaria interpres*) and phalaropes (*Phalaropus* species).

The extensive peatlands of northern and eastern Europe host a large number of breeding ducks, geese and shorebirds, including many species whose ranges do not extend into the Arctic tundra zone. The sheer vastness of the peatlands is the key to their importance, because the nutrient-poor wetlands have

Grey herons (Ardea cinerea) *are found in many wetland habitats. They nest in tree-top or reed bed colonies.*

45

Arctic terns (Sterna paradisaea) *nest in coastal wetlands of northern Europe. They are true long-distance migrants, flying south to spend the European winter in Antarctica.*

a low productivity and can only support correspondingly low densities of breeding birds, including species such as golden plover (*Pluvialis apricaria*) and wigeon (*Anas penelope*). General landscape conservation measures, such as the adoption of sensitive agricultural and forestry practices, are therefore of more importance than the protection or management of individual wetlands.

Peatlands elsewhere in the region are also of major importance for birds. For example, the bogs of Ireland support scattered wintering flocks of the vulnerable Greenland white-fronted goose (*Anser albifrons flavirostris*). The extensive and largely still-intact fens of the Biebrza Valley in Poland are home to thousands of nesting spotted crakes (*Porzana porzana*), corncrakes (*Crex crex*) and aquatic warblers (*Acrocephalus paludicola*) - all species which are scarce and declining in Europe.

The inter-tidal mudflats and estuaries of northern and western Europe are amongst the most productive ecosystems on Earth and are vital to the survival of millions of migratory waterbirds. Nowhere is this more clearly seen than in the Wadden Sea. The Netherlands section alone may support up to 290,000 wintering oystercatchers (*Haematopus ostralegus*), 93,000 bar-tailed godwits (*Limosa lapponica*) and 111,000 knot (*Calidris canutus*) amongst a multitude of other species. The world's largest concentration of

moulting shelducks (*Tadorna tadorna*) is found in the German Wadden Sea, where more than 100,000 adult birds gather to moult in late summer.

The high productivity of eutrophic freshwater lakes and marshes is reflected in an avifauna characterized by high density of individuals and high species diversity. Amongst the most typical birds of these habitats are the bitterns, herons and egrets (Ardeidae), many species of which nest in large, mixed tree-top or reed bed colonies. Other groups nesting typically in eutrophic freshwater habitats are grebes (Podicipedidae), cormorants (Phalacrocoracidae), two species of pelican (Pelecanidae), many species of wildfowl and rails (Rallidae). Some of these are globally threatened, such as the pygmy cormorant (*Phalacrocorax pygmeus*) and Dalmatian pelican (*Pelecanus crispus*), while others, such as the glossy ibis (*Plegadis falcinellus*), are declining in Europe as a result of habitat loss.

The rich emergent or marginal vegetation often associated with eutrophic freshwater lakes may support large populations of breeding passerines such as the reed warbler (*Acrocephalus scirpaceus*), bearded tit (*Panurus biarmicus*) and reed bunting (*Emberiza shoeniclus*), whilst reed beds are the favoured nesting habitat of the marsh harrier (*Circus aeruginosus*).

Freshwater lakes and marshes are also amongst the most important waterbird wintering areas in Europe and the Mediterranean. For example, the Bodensee, shared by Germany and Switzerland, holds huge numbers of wintering pochard (*Aythya ferina*) and tufted duck (*Aythya fuligula*) while Doñana National Park, in southwest Spain, supports tens of thousands of greylag geese (*Anser anser*), teal (*Anas crecca*), pintail (*Anas acuta*) and shoveler (*Anas clypeata*).

As natural sites continue to be destroyed and degraded, man-made freshwater wetlands such as reservoirs and gravel pits are becoming increasingly important areas for waterbirds, especially in parts of northern Europe where very high human population densities have resulted in especially high losses of natural wetlands.

Coastal inlets, lakes and lagoons are further rich habitats for birds, from the salinas and seasonal lagoons of the Mediterranean to the shallow fjord areas around the Baltic. The high productivity of these wetlands makes them important for breeding, passage and wintering birds alike, according to their geographical location and the time of year. Breeding species typical of Mediterranean wetlands, include the little egret (*Egretta garzetta*), purple heron (*Ardea purpurea*), greater flamingo, marsh harrier, black-winged stilt (*Himantopus himantopus*) and Kentish plover (*Charadrius alexandrinus*).

WHITE-HEADED DUCK

One of the region's most unusual ducks is the white-headed duck (*Oxyura leucocephala*), a member of the so-called 'stiff-tails' Oxyuridae. The world population is estimated to be no more than 15,000 individuals, occupying a restricted and fragmented range from southern Spain to the central Soviet Union. The vulnerability of this small population is exacerbated by loss of breeding habitat, and dependence during the winter months of nearly three-quarters of the world's white-headed ducks on a single lake, Burdur Golu, in Turkey.

The breeding range in Europe and the Mediterranean Basin has decreased markedly in the present century. White-headed ducks have stopped nesting altogether in ten countries, so that Spain is now the only country of the region where they breed regularly. Favoured nesting habitats here are in small, shallow freshwater or brackish wetlands, often in enclosed drainage basins. Many of these wetlands are semi-permanent, but all have abundant submerged vegetation, are rich in invertebrates, and are usually fringed by reed beds.

Such habitats are often vulnerable to drainage for agriculture, whilst water extraction or diversion for irrigation schemes is also a serious threat. Water pollution and hunting have been the principal problems at the Turkish wintering ground of Burdur Golu, but hunting at the lake was banned during the 1990/1991 winter as a direct consequence of a conservation action plan developed by the International Waterfowl and Wetlands Research Bureau (IWRB) and The Wildfowl and Wetlands Trust. Encouragingly, the annual IWRB International Waterfowl Census found record numbers of white-headed ducks on Burdur Golu in January 1991 and it must be hoped that sound conservation measures can ensure the future of this unusual species.

In the north of Europe, a different range of species is encountered; typical nesting birds may include eider (*Somateria mollissima*), ruff (*Philomachus pugnax*), black-headed gull (*Larus ridibundus*) and sandwich tern (*Sterna sandvicensis*), whilst migratory waterbirds arriving from yet farther to the north (notably swans, geese, ducks and shorebirds) spend the winter in the comparatively mild climate of the coasts of northwest Europe. The shallow offshore waters of the southern North Sea and western Baltic are especially important for wintering sea ducks such as common scoter (*Melanitta nigra*).

Mammals

There are approximately 170 native species of mammals in Europe, including the marine groups such as seals and dolphins. To this total can be added around 25 species which have been introduced, mainly from North America and Asia.

Only a few of the region's mammals, for instance European beaver (*Castor fiber*), are found exclusively in wetlands, although the distribution of around 20 per cent of species, including, for example, pipistrelle bat (*Pipistrellus pipistrellus*), can be linked closely, at least in part, with wetland habitats.

Mammals characteristic of the tundra wetlands of the far north include the Norway lemming (*Lemmus lemmus*), grey-sided vole (*Clethrionomys rufocanus*), Arctic fox (*Alopex lagopus*) and wolverine (*Gulo gulo*). Another essentially tundra mammal, although it also occurs in open woodland in Finland, is the reindeer (*Rangifer tarandus*). Reindeer feed on a variety of sedges and grasses during the brief summer, but specialize in lichens during the winter. Polar bears (*Thalarctos maritimus*) are limited to the coastal zones of the High Arctic tundra, whilst the distribution of brown bears (*Ursus arctos*) extends north onto the tundra from the forests of Scandinavia and the Soviet Union.

The innumerable forest wetlands in the northeast of the region support the majority of the surviving indigenous populations of European beaver (although re-introductions have been successful in parts of France, Germany and Austria). Elks (*Alces alces*) are found in areas with a mixture of forest and open ground, favouring, in particular, river valleys and lake shores. The European mink (*Mustela lutreola*) is now confined to the marshes, rivers and lakes of eastern Europe, except for an isolated population in western France.

The otter (*Lutra lutra*) was once distributed throughout the river systems of Europe, but it has declined in both population and range, as a result of water pollution, hunting and disturbance.

Among mammals which are still widely distributed in European wetland habitats are water shrew (*Neomys fodiens*), northern water vole (*Arvicola terrestris*) and common rat (*Rattus norvegicus*) - naturalized throughout the region for centuries, though originally introduced from Asia. Certain bats - such as the pond bat (*Myotis dasycneme*) and long-fingered bat (*Myotis capaccinii*) - are often found in close association with open water habitats, but their distributions are limited by climatic factors, showing a strong south to southeasterly bias.

Six species of seal breed in the region, but four of these are primarily marine. However, the common seal (*Phoca vitulina*) is found in shallow coastal waters and estuaries around the North Sea, western Baltic and Atlantic coasts of Britain, Scandinavia and Iceland, whilst the ringed seal (*Phoca hispida*) breeds in the High Arctic and the Baltic but also in the freshwater Lakes Saimaa (Finland) and Ladoga (Soviet Union).

Several introduced mammals occur in European wetlands. Some, such as the Canadian beaver (*Castor canadensis*), were introduced deliberately, whilst others, such as the American mink (*Mustela vison*), muskrat (*Ondatra zibethicus*) and coypu (*Myocastor coypus*), escaped from fur farms, rapidly establishing feral populations.

VALUES AND USES

There has long been a mistaken belief that wetlands are wastelands. A nineteenth-century view of the Somerset Levels in western England held that they 'must have been either a gloomy waste of waters, or still more hideous expanse of reeds and other aquatic plants, impassable by human foot and involved with an atmosphere pregnant with pestilence and death'. Michael Williams, the historical geographer, has shown that in reality the area was rich in pasture land, fish, timber and turf for fuel.

In recent decades, the value of European and Mediterranean wetlands for waterbirds has received considerable attention. Birdwatching is an increasingly popular leisure activity and many bird conservation organizations have become established, some of which are very large and influential. For example, the Royal Society for the Protection of Birds (RSPB) in Britain has almost one million members. There are also many well-organized hunting associations; hunting is a major pastime throughout the region, especially in Mediterranean countries. Birdwatchers and hunters cooperate in the annual mid-winter waterfowl census organized by the IWRB,

The small-scale cutting of peat for domestic fuel is an ancient and sustainable tradition in many parts of northern Europe. However, commercial peat 'mining' has permanently destroyed many delicate peatland habitats.

while the motivation of non-governmental organizations was crucial to the success of meetings which led to the drafting of the Ramsar Convention.

More recently, it has been appreciated that wetlands are much more than just 'restaurants and runways for birds', and that they perform a range of valuable functions which are of importance to humans. For example, traditional uses of wetland resources include peat-cutting and reed-harvesting.

There have been very few economic analyses of the values of wetlands in Europe and the Mediterranean. However, future arguments about the conservation of wetlands will have to be based, in part, on such material. The Ichkeul National Park in Tunisia has been subject to economic valuation and the analysis revealed that the goods and services rendered by the park were economically significant. It was also shown that it was more profitable to allocate water to the conservation of the wetland ecosystem than to use it for irrigation.

The recharge of ground water by wetlands acts as a vital regulator of the water cycle to provide water and river flow in dry periods. River floodplains, with their sponge-like layers of sands and silts, are recharged during floods and release the water slowly to the aquifer to maintain low flows in dry seasons. The floodplain of the Loire, like its similarly uncontrolled British equivalent the Severn, is a major regional aquifer.

Ground water discharge is a common phenomenon at low-lying wetlands. The S'Albufera de Mallorca, on the Mediterranean island of Majorca, is fed partially by river run-off channelled though upstream drainage canals. But within the wetland reserve there are also many powerful springs that play a vital role in keeping the extensive reed beds wet throughout the year. At Azraq in Jordan, springs used to maintain a rich freshwater marsh. However, heavy pumping has now almost desiccated these springs.

Flood storage is yet another vitally important function of wetlands. Where the ability of particular wetlands to carry out their flood-storage functions is impaired, the results can be very serious. Sebkhet Kelbia near Kairouan in Tunisia used to overflow only rarely to the sea because of its huge storage capacity. Heavy sedimentation has reduced its capacity by two-thirds since 1933. Consequently, the enormous floods of 1969 passed through the Sebkhet and cut the country's communication network.

The role of wetlands in anchoring shorelines and preventing erosion is normally associated with tropical, mangrove-dominated coastlines. In Europe and the Mediterranean, coastal wetlands occur mainly in areas of strong deposition where their role in

The harvesting of reeds is a long-established, sustainable use of wetland resources. Reed bed management is an essential element in wetland conservation.

preventing erosion is limited. Nevertheless, coastal salt marshes, such as those of Hamford Water, the Blackwater Estuary in southeast England and around the Loire Estuary at Nantes in France, certainly provide protection from approaching waves and there is some evidence that they can rapidly accumulate sediment. Trapping of sediment in wetlands can be economically important where it protects navigation channels from siltation and where it protects dams and reservoirs from sedimentation and adverse effects on water quality.

One of the functions of wetlands that is growing in importance most rapidly is their ability to retain nutrients from input water. Nutrients such as nitrogen and phosphorus, deriving from sewage effluent and fertilizers, are a growing problem since they cause the eutrophication of inland and coastal waters and, in the case of nitrates, problems with drinking water supplies. In Sweden, for instance, the Environmental Protection Board is re-establishing traditional water meadows on former arable land since they are very efficient at removing nutrients from the river water. In Israel, one of the justifications for re-establishing a reed bed dominated nature reserve in the former Lake Hula was that it would be an effective filter preventing dangerous nutrients from reaching the Sea of Galilee, the country's main water resource.

Coastal wetlands have a large role to play in sustaining marine fisheries. Young fish tagged in the Thames Estuary are caught all along the Channel coast of Britain and possibly off France too, while mullet (*Muletus surmuletus*) migrate into coastal lagoons all around the Mediterranean. The demand for eels in the Mediterranean has resulted in a thriving

trade in elvers taken from intact wetlands such as Ichkeul in Tunisia and the El Kala complex in Algeria. The trade is so great and the habitat for these eels is declining so quickly that there is a real fear that this once-ubiquitous species could soon be threatened in the Mediterranean.

Some years ago a Council of Europe survey showed that a high percentage of Europe's threatened plant species were confined to wetlands. *Acetous boryana*, a rush found in only 10 lakes in France and Spain, is, for example, on the verge of extinction. Lake Mikri Prespa in Greece is the only place in the world with the endemic fish *Barbus prespensis*. Sea turtles need special nesting beaches: those for loggerhead turtles (*Caretta caretta*) on the Greek island of Zakynthos are under particular pressure from tourist development, whilst in Turkey at Dalyan and Goksu the pressure seems likely to grow in the future.

Wetlands can provide diverse opportunities for active outdoor recreation but, if not carefully managed, there can be a serious degradation of other functions. Broadland in eastern England now has National Park status and an integrated management authority, but it still suffers from water quality problems, erosion and tourist pressure problems. The careful zonation of certain broads (shallow lakes) and the separation of some of them from the main river system has done much to reconcile the problems of nature conservation and heavy recreational use.

The peatlands of Europe and the Mediterranean have a considerable archaeological heritage value, since their chemical make-up preserves much that is buried in them. Detailed analysis of pollen grains in the peats of the Rocina Valley, near Doñana in Spain, has helped our understanding of the vegetational evolution of the area and the human role in that through fire and grazing.

THREATS

The high standard of living of the countries of northern and western Europe has, to a large extent, been bought at the expense of massive environmental change. The burgeoning population of the Mediterranean will continue to put wetlands under severe pressure because these are dry, or even arid, countries. The continued urbanization of the region, heralds demands for improved living standards and further pressure on the environment.

There are signs, however, in several of the more developed countries, and indications of future good intentions in many others, that the remaining wetlands may be retained; although the threat remains that their value to humans and wildlife will be damaged by a deterioration in the ecosystem.

A fundamental cause of wetland loss in the past has been, quite simply, that few people have demanded their conservation. This resulted from a lack of awareness of the true, multiple values of wetlands. This, in turn, meant a lack of political will to deal with the issue. There has also been a rather uncritical acceptance of schemes and policies which convert wetlands to other uses. Nowadays, lack of public awareness is no longer a serious threat to wetlands in the more developed countries of the region. The national campaign to conserve the wild character of the Loire in France, and the Soviet greens protesting about pollution of the Volga, are testimony to the power of the people. However, in most of the Mediterranean region, awareness of wetlands and the need to conserve them remains low.

Governmental reluctance to get involved in wetland conservation is often caused by intense pressure for economic development. Over-centralization of decision making and a mega-project mentality cause disrespect for local conditions and aspirations. Secrecy and the manipulation of information, the dominance of short-term private profit over long-term public benefit, deficient economic policy (such as that which regards water as a free good), and insecure or undocumented land tenure - all these cause wetland loss. Irregular financial practices are another major, if largely unseen, process.

External factors include the supra-national policies of organizations such as the European Community (EC), and development aid agencies. The Common

Agricultural Policy of the EC has been, and still is, a powerful force for wetland destruction. By the end of the 1970s 10 per cent of France's wetter lands, and 60 per cent of those of the United Kingdom and the Netherlands, had been drained. EC support was available at up to 70 per cent of the cost. Ostensibly, these schemes affect only agricultural land, but the need to deepen drainage channels and the general fall of ground water levels over wide areas always affects wetland reserves. The EC's Integrated Mediterranean Programme has also been severely criticized for its lack of attention to environmental effects. It is to be hoped that the failure of coordination between the various parts of the EC Commission, which has been a problem in the past, will not be a difficulty with the very substantial Structural Funds now being disbursed.

In Algeria, the World Bank is a major financier of the Mexa Dam being constructed in the El Kala National Park. Such dams take a long time to build and as ideas have developed, the planned operation of the dam and its environmental impact are now being reviewed. There is growing concern about threats to the wetlands in the area and fears that the dam may exacerbate these.

In the Mediterranean region it is widely acknowledged that laws and regulations are not enforced. Spain, for example, passed a new Water Law in 1986 which contained a host of modern ideas and some visionary principles. However, in the case of the Daimiel National Park the law's requirements about communities of users for over-exploited aquifers have received little attention.

Many conservationists believe that there is not enough international pressure for wetland conservation, and that where there is pressure, it does not always achieve its goal. The Ramsar Convention, being an international governmental treaty, can only exert moral pressure and has always operated on the basis of consensus. Designation as a Ramsar site cannot automatically guarantee the future of a given wetland without active implementation of 'wise use' principles.

Data for all the European and Mediterranean Ramsar sites, published with governmental approval, reveals that only 58 of the 318 wetlands (18 per cent) are definitely not threatened in some way. Only sparsely populated and affluent Finland, dominated as it is by lakes, forests and peatlands, is able to report that almost all of its Ramsar wetlands are without threat. But it was in Finland at Haapavesi that the world's largest peat power station, with the capcity to consume 2.5 million m³ (88 million cu ft) of peat annually, was opened in 1990.

Recreation and Pollution

Whilst disturbance may not threaten the loss of a wetland, the degradation that it brings to wetland values can be enormous. Recreational pressure can bring pollution by sewage; erosion of banks and destruction of plants by boats; breeding failure of birds frightened by visitors approaching; and visual and aural intrusion from the tourists and their cars.

Hunting is a traditional activity in many wetlands and the many million waterbird hunters in Europe and the Mediterranean can provide an important lobby for conservation. However, in some Mediterranean countries, hunting has led to severe degradation through the killing of excessive numbers of birds, disturbance, inappropriate habitat management and the use of lead shot which poisons waterbirds.

Pollution modifies the functioning of wetlands. Organic pollution can lead to the removal of all of the oxygen in the water, killing wetland flora and fauna and eventually producing stinking, black water. Sewage pollution has brought these conditions to parts of Molentargius Lagoons on Sardinia. Lake Vistonis in northwestern Greece smells very badly because it receives the raw sewage from more than 100,000 people. However, the pollution has not yet killed the fish and a thriving, but threatened, fishing industry continues.

Industrial pollution of wetlands can kill the flora or fauna directly, lead to a build-up of heavy metals in the food chain, or cause a modification to the ecosystem. The Odiel Marshes Ramsar site in southern Spain receives extremely acid water from pyrites mines in the surrounding mountains via the Ríos Tinto and Odiel. A large oil refinery, a cement works and a chemical works have discharged effluents rather freely into the estuary until recently and Huelva, a nearby city of around 200,000 people, has no sewage treatment at all. The fact that the inter-tidal marshes have retained internationally important numbers of waterbirds is testimony to the cleaning powers of estuarine systems. Fortunately, a project is now under way to deal with the immediate sources of pollution.

Agriculture

In western Europe, drainage of wetlands for arable land has been under way for centuries, but it probably reached its peak in the 1970s and early 80s. There are still substantial funds for drainage work in areas such as Northern Ireland. In the early 1980s, the Blackwater scheme, which received EC support, was heavily criticized because of its needless impact on channel habitats.

Hunters are being encouraged to use steel shot cartridges for their sport. Thousands of waterbirds die every year as a result of being poisoned by the ingestion of spent lead shot.

Drainage of peatlands can be especially hazardous, leading to the lowering of the land level as the peat gradually disappears. In the Fenland of eastern England, an iron column marking the previous peatland surface stands over 4 m (13 ft) above the present ground level. Increasingly efficient pumps have kept the land dry, but the cost has escalated as the land has sunk and there must be a question mark over the long-term value of these lands.

In Algeria a new market-oriented approach to agriculture has fostered a spirit of enterprise amongst farmers. Sadly, in the case of the Lac Oubeira Ramsar site, the extensive use of new private pumps for irrigation completely dried out the lake during the 1990 drought. Similar problems seem certain to grow in significance in the countries of eastern Europe as well, as their economies respond to market forces and development aid.

Water Resource Schemes

Human efforts to develop water resources and hydro-power have inevitably affected wetlands. Hydro-power dams are particularly disruptive because they produce river regimes that are related to the demand for electricity rather than to the natural seasonal cycle. Similarly, inter-basin transfers of water can cause problems both for the system which gives the water and that which receives it.

Major irrigation schemes also present problems. Admittedly, they can bring substantial short-term benefits even if they destroy wetlands in the process, but there is a growing list of examples where over-exploitation of ground water has caused difficulties.

Dams directly threaten 17 Ramsar sites in Europe and the Mediterranean but they are so widely employed for water resources development that they have probably affected wetlands from the Arctic to the Sahara. A Norwegian government proposal for another major hydro-power dam in Lapland generated such ferocious opposition that the project was dropped and a new national policy developed. The finishing of the Volgograd hydro-power station in the Soviet Union completed the Volga-Kama scheme of dams and produced a regime for the Volga River controlled by reservoirs. This reduced the volume and duration of large spring floods by 25 per cent and in dry years the dams absorbed the floods completely. Large floods used to inundate 90 per cent of the Volga Delta and the prolonged high water created ideal spawning conditions for fish. The reduced flood volume, the short flood peak and the occasional years without a flood have had an adverse effect on fish reproduction and resulting yields.

When dams are built across international rivers the results can be explosive. The Vadar River is dammed and extensively used for irrigation in southern Yugoslavia to the extent that in summer and autumn virtually no flow arrives in Greece where the river is called the Axios. This is a source of great resentment in Greece and every effort is seized to deny Yugoslavia water from other shared wetlands. Similarly, the completion of the large Ataturk Dam on the headwaters of the Euphrates in Turkey seems likely to be a further complicating factor in the turbulent relationships between Turkey, Syria and Iraq.

The canalization of the Rhine in the nineteenth century reduced its length by over 100 km (62 miles). This increased stream velocities by up to 30 per cent in some places, caused a fall in the water table of between 3 and 4 m (10 and 13 ft) over an area up to 3 km (2 miles) from the river and resulted in the river lowering its bed by 3 to 4 m. It has been estimated that in South Baden the drying out caused agricultural damage of US$139 million and damage to forestry of US$24 million; fisheries suffered by US$8 million. These disadvantages seriously detract from the economic advantages accruing to navigation interests from shortening the river.

The pressure to find renewable sources of power for electricity generation has renewed interest in estuarine tidal power schemes such as that established in the 1960s at La Rance in Brittany, France. Recent British interest, has focused on the huge funnel-shaped estuary of the Severn, which has one of the highest tidal ranges in the world, apparently ripe for exploitation as a source of electricity.

The estuary is, however, protected by national and international law. Conservationists fear that the barrage scheme could permanently submerge up to half of the mudflats upon which internationally important migratory shorebird populations rely for food. It is also feared that the barrage could cause a serious build-up of pollutants which are currently flushed out to sea by the tides.

Abstraction of ground water for irrigation is often attractive because the water can appear plentiful, cheap and of good quality. In the case of Garaet El Haouaria in Tunisia, the benefits were short lived. The problem was exacerbated by wetland drainage which removed water previously destined for underground recharge. This freshwater marsh was once used for sport hunting, grazing and some fishing. Drainage in the 1960s removed all of the surface water and wells drilled into the deep aquifer supplied local towns and tomato-processing plants. Most farmers constructed

The mudflats and salt marsh of the Severn Estuary (left) are home to internationally important numbers of migratory shorebirds. Many parts of the estuary have already been subject to development, such as this nuclear power station (right) at Oldbury.

The formerly rich oasis wetlands at Azraq in Jordan are gradually disappearing as a result of ground water extraction to supply the capital, Amman.

shallow wells to draw irrigation water from the surface aquifer. Ground water levels fell dramatically and many shallow wells have had to be abandoned, because the water has become too saline for irrigation.

Other Threats

There is still strong pressure for construction in and around wetlands, which provide attractive flat land, often adjacent to the sea. Tourism can be a serious factor in promoting wetland loss and degradation, especially around the Mediterranean. The filling in of wetlands in Languedoc, France, to provide land for low-grade mass tourism, the theme park planned for the Rainham Marshes near London, the pumping of freshwater from the coastal dunes of Doñana for the Matalascañas tourist complex in Spain, the planned ice rink for the winter Olympics at Akersvika in Norway, and the illegal construction of summer houses on the Louros sand bar at Messolonghi (Mesolongion) in Greece - all are examples of some of the adverse effects of tourism.

Fisheries activities, which are entirely compatible with the wise use of wetlands in so many situations, can threaten wetland functioning through intensive aquaculture schemes with fixed installations and polluting discharges, also through the introduction of exotic species which disturb ecosystem dynamics, and through overfishing. The salmon farms which have blossomed in Scottish sea-lochs and Norwegian fjords require substantial inputs of chemicals and pesticides and there is a fear that fish escaping from them will threaten the genetic variation of the wild stock.

On the shores of the Amvrakikos Gulf in Greece, extensive concrete fish ponds have been constructed in a protected area, and the dark green effluent

threatens to exacerbate the already serious eutrophication of the semi-closed gulf. The introduction of exotic grass carp (*Ctenopharyngodon idella*) to Lac Oubeira in Algeria in 1983 resulted in the quasi-disappearance of extensive beds of pondweeds (*Potamogeton*) and reedmace (*Typha*) species. At Lake Mikri Prespa in Greece the fall in catches of carp, which has been blamed on an outbreak of disease, seems to have been caused by overfishing. Scientific investigations, followed by intensive consultation with the fishermen, led to the acceptance of larger mesh nets and there are signs that the fishery is recovering and that the population of the small endemic *Barbus prespensis* is soaring.

One of the most threatening extractive industries for wetlands is peat-cutting. Whilst small-scale peat digging by hand has been going on for centuries, the modern mechanized operation can remove peat at an alarming rate. It is in Ireland where the threat is especially severe. The total area of intact bog has fallen from 311,000 hectares (768,000 acres) to 65,000 hectares (161,000 acres) in 1974 and 20,000 hectares (49,000 acres) in 1985. A survey of 200 Irish raised bogs showed that only 4 per cent still merited conservation activity and that all of these were likely to be damaged by 1992.

The construction of dykes can fragment wetlands, breaking many hydrological and ecological links. When the dykes surround the wetland they are usually located so as to reduce the area of periodic inundation. This results in the destruction of marsh habitat and a major reduction in shallow feeding zones for waterbirds and spawning areas for fish. Dyke construction also normally heralds land reclamation and wetland loss. A dramatic recent example of dyking in a Ramsar site was at the Leybucht coastal marshes on the German Wadden Sea. In order to drain agricultural land and to ensure navigation into the tiny harbour of Greetsiel, the local government has constructed new dykes around 740 hectares (1,829 acres) of the existing Ramsar site. Despite assurances that sedimentation outside the dykes will soon restore the ecological balance, international concern remains high.

Global warming and the related rise of sea level pose new threats to wetlands. Changes in the level of the sea relative to land have a strong impact on coastal ecosystems. Sea level rise is now between 1 and 2 mm ($^1/_{25}$ and $^2/_{25}$ in) per year and this is expected to increase to between 3 and 8 mm ($^1/_{10}$ and $^1/_3$ in) per year by 2030. Changes in the level of the land also affect the relative rate of sea level rise. In the Nile, Po and Rhône Deltas there is land subsidence and this will cause high rates of relative sea level rise. Sea level rise will threaten coastal wetlands through marine incursions, increased erosion and the need for strengthening of coastal defences.

The impact of global warming on wetlands in Europe and the Mediterranean will depend on the extent and location of the actual climatic changes. A study for North Africa showed that if the only change were the 1.5°C (2.7°F) average warming, then evaporation would increase and river flows would decrease. Increased erosion would be limited to the higher parts of the basin because rivers will not be able to carry the increased sediment to the sea. Downstream wetlands would suffer from these changes and from the necessarily increased demand for irrigation water. The study showed that a number of the internationally important fresh and brackish wetlands of the area would become saline sebhkas similar to those which are already common on the desert fringes.

Among other possible impacts of global warming, a warming of the Arctic tundra could be disastrous for the millions of waterbirds which breed there each spring. One scenario envisages a northward spread of the taiga which would rob these birds of their breeding grounds since only the Arctic Ocean lies to the north.

MANAGEMENT

Comprehensive management plans for wetland reserves to redress effects of human impacts are accepted as essential tools throughout the region. The integration of wetlands into regional and national planning has also become established with schemes for water resources and river basin development in some countries.

Probably the most exciting aspect of management in Europe and the Mediterranean at present is wetland restoration. Restoration schemes have already been completed at three Ramsar sites. Srebarna, Bulgaria's largest river lake, has recently had its connection with the Danube River restored. This now maintains its natural water depth of between 1.5 and 3 m (5 and 10 ft). The Spanish national parks at Doñana and Daimiel have had, respectively, water pumps installed to flood the marshes and substantial releases each winter from an inter-regional irrigation pipeline to compensate for reduced river and ground water flow.

Lac Fetzara in Algeria was drained in the 1930s, but has recently been restored as a lake. Local hydraulic engineers used it to store floodwater in an emergency and found that they had created a valuable source of irrigation water and grazing land. In the Netherlands a national conservation competition has resulted in the Ooievaar scheme to restore natural floodplain functions to the lower Rhine floodplain. The scheme seeks to remove some of the small summer dykes from the river to allow flooding between the permanent winter dykes. This area will be devoted to nature conservation and its flooding should improve both the quality of the river water and the flora and fauna dependent upon it.

The Swedish Government has decided that maximum effort must be put into managing existing wetlands rather than restoring those which have been degraded. Even so, there are at present four state restoration projects under consideration. One of these schemes concerns Lake Hornborga, a large shallow lake in central southern Sweden where it is anticipated that eventually US$161 million will be spent. From 1802 onwards, the water level was progressively lowered to facilitate agricultural drainage. As a result, the lake was almost completely overgrown with emergent vegetation and used to dry up completely in the 1940s and early 50s. Since then some dyking and experimental clearance of reed beds has restored a part of Hornborga's importance for waterbirds and intensive work has led to the formulation of a more extensive restoration scheme.

Denmark's largest river, the Skjern, flows into a delta at Ringkøbing Fjord on the country's west coast. There have been many efforts to control the river delta because of the dangers of flooding, and in 1961 the government approved a drainage scheme for the conversion of 4,000 hectares (9,900 acres) into arable land. The project was completed in 1969, but a few years later, farming in the delta and farther upstream resulted in excessive eutrophication, causing serious depletion of flora and fauna. However, in 1990 the government began implementation of a US$10 million restoration project that will reinstate natural nutrient filtration processes, thus allowing the ecosystem to recover its former productivity.

CONSERVATION

Within Europe and the Mediterranean region, most of the countries are Contracting Parties to the Ramsar Convention, the exceptions being Albania, Andorra, Cyprus, Israel, Lebanon, Libya, Liechtenstein, Luxembourg, Syria and Turkey. More than 300 wetlands have so far been listed in the region and some countries, such as Italy and the United Kingdom, have listed many sites of international importance. The largest Ramsar wetlands in the region are the Danube Delta in Romania and the Wadden Sea, where Denmark, Germany and the Netherlands have together designated five sites covering some 600,000 hectares (1.5 million acres).

The Ramsar Convention was largely born out of the efforts of European conservationists. European countries have always played a major role in the Convention. Today, many have policies for assisting developing countries in conservation and sustainable development. For instance, the Dutch government

Birds like this nestling marsh harrier (Circus aeruginosus) *depend on wetland conservation for their survival in many parts of Europe.*

has provided substantial support to the Ramsar Bureau's 'wise use' programme.

The Ramsar Bureau works closely with the officers of other international conventions. A Western Palearctic Waterfowl Agreement is currently being developed under the Bonn Convention on Migratory Species, aiming to provide an international framework for the conservation of the region's migratory waterbirds throughout their annual cycle.

The European Community does not have a wetlands policy as such, although certain conservation objectives are set out by various directives and these must be incorporated into the national law of member states. The 1979 Directive on the Conservation of Wild Birds requires protection of the sites used by certain species, whilst the new Habitats Directive may greatly strengthen protective measures for wetlands. Perhaps the EC's greatest contribution to wetlands conservation would be the removal of direct and indirect subsidies for wetland destruction, through, for example, the Common Agricultural Policy and Structural Funds Programme.

Multi-lateral and bi-lateral banks and international development agencies have, in the past, promoted many projects which have had adverse impacts on wetlands. However, the work of the United Nations 'Brundtland' Commission on Environment and Development has promoted the idea of sustainable development, and international funding agencies have grown to appreciate the importance of environmental considerations, including wetlands. 'Protecting the environment is a central concern of the World Bank and the European Investment Bank,' say their presidents in the introduction to their Environmental Programme for the Mediterranean. The World Bank, European Investment Bank and the Commission of the European Community have also launched the Mediterranean Environmental Technical Assistance Programme (METAP) which will give grants for environmental projects in the Mediterranean.

Almost all countries have laws which provide for some element of wetland protection. For instance, in Spain, the 1985 Water Law established three principles: the public character of terrestrial water; the planning of water according to the hydrological cycle; and the public administration of water in each river basin. Several additional measures refer to wetland inventories, wetland rehabilitation, environmental impact assessment, water quality control and respect for the Ramsar Convention. The 1988 Shore Act protected unaltered coastal areas including wetlands. In 1989, the Spanish Parliament passed an Act establishing the need for river basin planning to consider wetland conservation.

However, new laws are not always needed for effective conservation. In 1987 Greece's Supreme Administrative Court prohibited a new ship-scrapping yard in the Nestos Delta Ramsar site because it contravened the laws which implicitly implement the country's obligations under the Ramsar Convention. The judges added that the incompatibility of the development proposal and Ramsar status did not depend on experts' opinions, but was considered to be a matter of common sense and experience.

Strong non-governmental organizations (NGOs), with secure and independent funding from a large and well-informed membership base, are powerful forces for conservation. Such groups lobby for action, mount campaigns with strong support from their members, undertake independent research, promote awareness and information activities, buy or manage reserves (or both), and assist similar organizations in other countries. Britain's Royal Society for the Protection of Birds (RSPB) undertakes all of these activities and is becoming increasingly involved in European and other international issues. The Wildfowl and Wetlands Trust (WWT), also based in Britain, operates a number of regional visitor centres aimed at bringing people and wetland wildlife together in carefully managed habitats. The Trust's headquarters at Slimbridge, in southwest England, include an extensive visitor centre, part of the Upper Severn Estuary Ramsar site, and large research

department. WWT has hosted the headquarters of the International Waterfowl and Wetlands Research Bureau since 1969. The World Wide Fund for Nature (WWF) has both an international headquarters based in Switzerland and national organizations in most European and Mediterranean countries. WWF raises funds for conservation work and conducts major campaigns, as well as running a large number of conservation projects directly.

Many of the wetlands in Europe and the Mediterranean have been either destroyed or degraded, and a majority of those that remain are under threat. However, the future for wetlands in Europe is probably quite optimistic because of the social changes that have brought public pressure for 'greener' governmental policies with regard to agriculture and industry. It is likely that in addition to the enlargement of the extensive European network of wetland reserves, changes in national and EC policies will allow wetlands to be conserved because of the wider social and economic importance of their functions and values. The strong NGO movement in western Europe, the rapidly developing NGOs in the east, and the more environmentally aware policies being adopted by development banks and agencies can only enhance this optimistic assessment.

However, the rapidly increasing populations of the east and south of the Mediterranean, and the existing environmental problems of many of those countries, suggest that it will be more difficult to conserve the wetland jewels which still remain in this region.

CONTRIBUTOR: J.S. LARSON

North America

AN ASTRONAUT'S VIEW of North America reveals wetlands in all regions of the continent - extensive marshes on the south Atlantic and Gulf of Mexico coasts, more wetlands on the southern shore of the huge Arctic Hudson Bay, and a few wetlands scattered along the Pacific coast.

The view from space of the continent's interior shows broad bands of different landscapes sweeping east-west across its northern half, ranging from cold Arctic desert in the far north, through tundra and coniferous forest farther south, to moist prairies in the centre of the continent - these variations in landscape being the result of temperature differences and their effect on precipitation.

In the southern half of the continent, bands of different vegetation run north-south rather than east-west, reflecting the effects of mountain ranges on the rainfall brought by the prevailing westerly winds. A traveller from the west coast to the east would first cross forests on the Pacific coast, then the alpine vegetation of the western mountains, next deserts in the rain shadow east of these mountains, followed by grassland in the continent's centre and then, finally, temperate forest before reaching the east coast.

Flung across the northern patterns of vegetation is a host of lakes, from huge to small, and a web of large rivers flowing north to the Arctic Ocean. The view from space reveals relatively few lakes in the southern half of the continent. It does, on the other hand, show one of the world's largest river systems - that of the Mississippi - draining the continent south to the Gulf of Mexico.

Within all these bands of vegetation, on the shores of lakes, along the valleys of rivers and scattered over the land in between, lie the richly varied wetlands of the forests and plains of North America. Their sizes and shapes, and the kinds of vegetation and wildlife they attract, are influenced by the land, temperature and precipitation within the major regions seen from the imaginary space platform.

The native Americans, who occupied this continent before European settlement, trace their origin to peoples who crossed from Asia to modern Alaska. They were the first humans to use the North American wetlands for food, fibre and fuel. Significant European settlement started only in the late 1500s. While European people brought a different culture to the continent, they too used the wetlands as sources of hay for their cattle, of furs for trade and of fish and game for food. In time they applied technology to make vast changes to the wetlands in the southern half of the continent where, today, most of the 225 million North Americans live.

GEOGRAPHY AND CLIMATE

For the purposes of this chapter, North America is taken to consist of the United States (including Alaska), Canada, the French island possessions of St-Pierre and Miquelon off Canada's Atlantic coast, and Greenland (Denmark). It spreads upwards from a southern latitude close to the Tropic of Cancer, at about 24.5° North, to about 83° North, well above the Arctic Circle. It comprises a land mass of 24 million km² (9.3 million sq miles). Spanning such a wide range of latitude, North America, not surprisingly, possesses a startling diversity of wetlands, from High Arctic tundra to tropical mangroves.

This is a continent of climatic extremes. At its most northerly point, the average annual precipitation is less than 150 mm (6 in), while average January temperatures are lower than -30°C (-22°F) and average July temperatures are under 4°C (39°F). At its southernmost limit, the average annual rainfall is over 1,140 mm (45 in); average January temperatures are in excess of 24°C (75°F); and average August temperatures are over 28°C (82°F).

Most of the southern half of the continent drains south to the Gulf of Mexico by its longest river, the Mississippi. Most of the northern portion drains in three principal directions: northwest to the Bering Sea via the Yukon River; north to the Arctic Sea down the Mackenzie River; and into Hudson Bay via the Nelson River in central Canada. Southeastern Canada and the north-central part of the United States drain east to

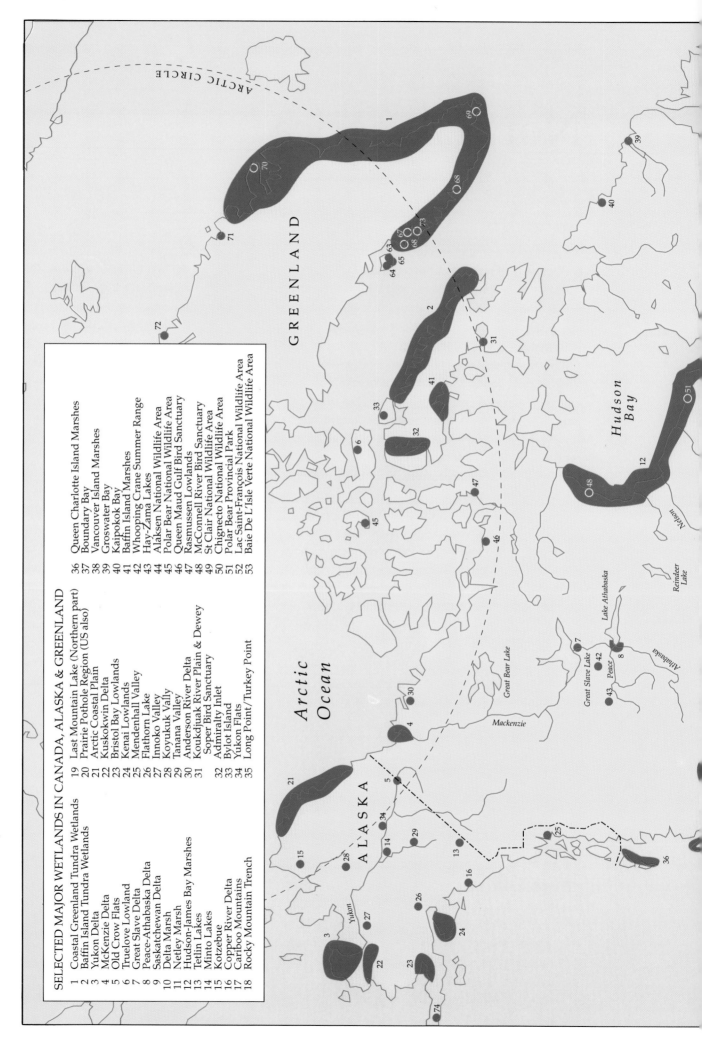

SELECTED MAJOR WETLANDS IN CANADA, ALASKA & GREENLAND

1	Coastal Greenland Tundra Wetlands	19	Last Mountain Lake (Northern part)	36	Queen Charlotte Island Marshes
2	Baffin Island Tundra Wetlands	20	Prairie Pothole Region (US also)	37	Boundary Bay
3	Yukon Delta	21	Arctic Coastal Plain	38	Vancouver Island Marshes
4	McKenzie Delta	22	Kuskokwin Delta	39	Groswater Bay
5	Old Crow Flats	23	Bristol Bay Lowlands	40	Kaipokok Bay
6	Truelove Lowland	24	Kenai Lowlands	41	Baffin Island Marshes
7	Great Slave Delta	25	Mendenhall Valley	42	Whooping Crane Summer Range
8	Peace–Athabaska Delta	26	Flathorn Lake	43	Hay–Zama Lakes
9	Saskatchewan Delta	27	Innoko Valley	44	Alaksen National Wildlife Area
10	Delta Marsh	28	Koyukuk Vally	45	Polar Bear National Wildlife Area
11	Netley Marsh	29	Tanana Valley	46	Queen Maud Gulf Bird Sanctuary
12	Hudson-James Bay Marshes	30	Anderson River Delta	47	Rasmussen Lowlands
13	Tetlin Lakes	31	Koukdjuak River Plain & Dewey	48	McConnell River Bird Sanctuary
14	Minto Lakes		Soper Bird Sanctuary	49	Soper Bird Sanctuary
15	Kotzebue	32	Admiralty Inlet	50	Chignecto National Wildlife Area
16	Copper River Delta	33	Bylot Island	51	Polar Bear Provincial Park
17	Cariboo Mountains	34	Yukon Flats	52	Lac Saint-François National Wildlife Area
18	Rocky Mountain Trench	35	Long Point/Turkey Point	53	Baie De L'Isle Verte National Wildlife Area

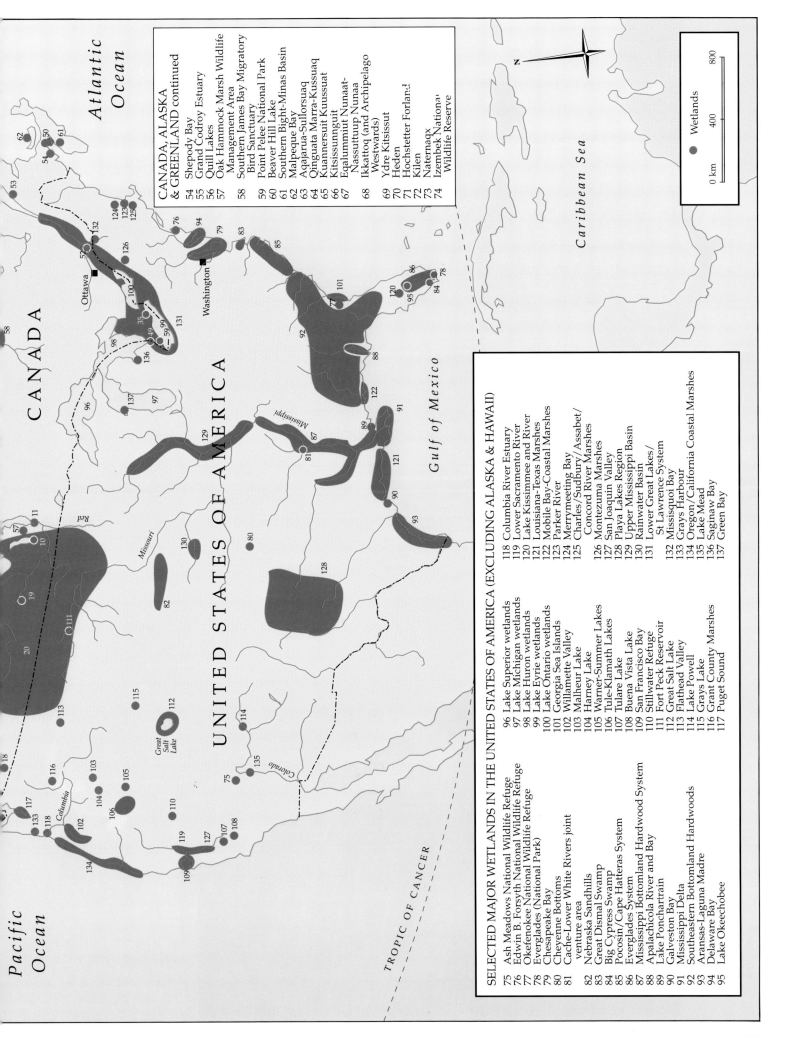

CANADA, ALASKA & GREENLAND continued
54 Shepody Bay
55 Grand Codroy Estuary
56 Quill Lakes
57 Oak Hammock Marsh Wildlife Management Area
58 Southern James Bay Migratory Bird Sanctuary
59 Point Pelee National Park
60 Beaver Hill Lake
61 Southern Bight-Minas Basin
62 Malpeque Bay
63 Aqajarua-Sullorsuaq
64 Qinguata Marra-Kussuaq
65 Kuannersuit Kuussuat
66 Kitsissunnguit
67 Eqalummiut Nunaat-Nassuttuup Nunaa
68 Ikkattoq (and Archipelago Westwards)
69 Ydre Kitsissut
70 Heden
71 Hochstetter Forland
72 Kilen
73 Natermaqx
74 Izembek National Wildlife Reserve

SELECTED MAJOR WETLANDS IN THE UNITED STATES OF AMERICA (EXCLUDING ALASKA & HAWAII)
75 Ash Meadows National Wildlife Refuge
76 Edwin B. Forsyth National Wildlife Refuge
77 Okefenokee National Wildlife Refuge
78 Everglades (National Park)
79 Chesapeake Bay
80 Cheyenne Bottoms
81 Cache-Lower White Rivers joint venture area
82 Nebraska Sandhills
83 Great Dismal Swamp
84 Big Cypress Swamp
85 Pocosin/Cape Hatteras System
86 Everglades System
87 Mississippi Bottomland Hardwood System
88 Apalachicola River and Bay
89 Lake Ponchartrain
90 Galveston Bay
91 Mississippi Delta
92 Southeastern Bottomland Hardwoods
93 Aransas-Laguna Madre
94 Delaware Bay
95 Lake Okeechobee
96 Lake Superior wetlands
97 Lake Michigan wetlands
98 Lake Huron wetlands
99 Lake Eyrie wetlands
100 Lake Ontario wetlands
101 Georgia Sea Islands
102 Willamette Valley
103 Malheur Lake
104 Harney Lake
105 Warner-Summer Lakes
106 Tule-Klamath Lakes
107 Tulare Lake
108 Buena Vista Lake
109 San Francisco Bay
110 Stillwater Refuge
111 Fort Peck Reservoir
112 Great Salt Lake
113 Flathead Valley
114 Lake Powell
115 Grays Lake
116 Grant County Marshes
117 Puget Sound
118 Columbia River Estuary
119 Lower Sacramento River
120 Lake Kissimmee and River
121 Louisiana-Texas Marshes
122 Mobile Bay-Coastal Marshes
123 Parker River
124 Merrymeeting Bay
125 Charles/Sudbury/Assabet/Concord River Marshes
126 Montezuma Marshes
127 San Joaquin Valley
128 Playa Lakes Region
129 Upper Mississippi Basin
130 Rainwater Basin
131 Lower Great Lakes/St Lawrence System
132 Mississquoi Bay
133 Grays Harbour
134 Oregon/California Coastal Marshes
135 Lake Mead
136 Saginaw Bay
137 Green Bay

• Wetlands

0 km   400   800

Pacific Ocean

Atlantic Ocean

Caribbean Sea

Gulf of Mexico

CANADA

UNITED STATES OF AMERICA

TROPIC OF CANCER

Ottawa

Washington

Great Salt Lake

Mississippi

Missouri

Red

Columbia

Colorado

the North Atlantic via the St Lawrence River.

In the northern half of the continent, a semi-circle of large lakes extends from northwestern Canada to the northeastern United States. These are the Great Bear, Great Slave, Athabaska, Reindeer and Winnipeg Lakes in Canada and the Great Lakes (Superior, Michigan, Huron, Erie and Ontario) along the United States/Canada border. As already stated, there are few large natural lakes in the southern half of North America. Those that do exist include the Great Salt Lake in the western United States, Lake Pontchartrain near the Gulf of Mexico and Lake Okeechobee on the Florida Peninsula. Large man-made reservoirs include Lake Mead, Lake Powell and Fort Peck Reservoir, all created on rivers of the western United States, and several large reservoirs on the Tennessee River, a tributary of the Mississippi, in the southwestern United States.

North America's terrain, like its climate, offers dramatic contrasts. The highest elevations - max. 6,193 m (20,318 ft) on Denali, Alaska - occur along the Rocky Mountain chain that runs north-south along the western side of the continent from Alaska to western Mexico; the low, eroded Appalachian Mountains run north-south along the continent's east side. The lowest point is in Death Valley, California, at 925 m (3,035 ft) below sea level. A vast region of tundra covers the northern extremes; coniferous and broadleaf forest is the major natural cover of the north-central, eastern and southeastern portions of the continent and the Pacific coast. The central regions of North America are dominated by grassland, while the southeast is characterized by desert and desert shrub.

Climate and the morphology of the land surface are the principal factors governing the natural formation of wetlands in North America: climate determines the amount, form and timing of precipitation received by each region; the morphology of the land surface guides the run-off and snow-melt into natural wetlands.

Between the Mexico/United States border and Canada's Arctic islands lies a vast spectrum of climate and landform, from the subtropical/tropical (monsoon) climate of southern Florida, through the desert and semi-arid conditions in the southwestern United States, and on to the continental weather patterns of cold winters and hot, dry summers in the grassland plains of both the United States and Canada.

The forested eastern half of the continent has a well-watered temperate climate. Across the northern latitudes cold Arctic and low rainfall conditions prevail. The western Rocky Mountain ranges rise to an alpine environment and cause the prevailing westerly winds to drop their moisture on the west side. This creates temperate rain forest conditions along the coasts of Oregon, Washington and British Columbia and dry mountain range environments in the eastern rain shadow of the Rockies.

The last glacier in North America created large wetland areas of blocked and slow drainage in the northern Canadian mainland and the northeastern United States. Erosion of the eastern Appalachian Mountains and the plains of the central United States developed extensive wetlands on sedimentary coastal deposits along the Atlantic and Gulf coasts in the south of the United States. The younger and more active mountain ranges on the west coast of the continent have not, however, developed extensive wetlands. And the low precipitation and temperatures

Poor drainage in the glaciated parts of North America creates complex patterns of open water, forested and floating-leaved wetland communities.

Only 5 per cent of the Arctic tundra is considered as wetland, such as this area on Prince Charles Island, in Foxe Basin, Canada.

of the Arctic islands of Canada produce an inhospitable and cold desert environment where, similarly, there are few wetland areas.

WETLANDS

Canada is estimated to hold 24 per cent of all the world's wetlands. These occupy over 127 million hectares (314 million acres) - 14 per cent of the country's territory. The original wetland area of the United States is difficult to estimate because of the greater degree of wetland alteration, but the most reliable estimate is 89 million hectares (220 million acres) - excluding Alaska - of which only approximately 47 per cent remain. Most of the Alaskan wetlands, on the other hand, are still in pristine condition; they cover an estimated 81 million hectares (200 million acres).

The wetlands of North America have different origins due to differences in climate and topography. Their relationships to local and regional hydrology are likewise varied and are therefore described on a regional basis.

Arctic and Boreal Wetlands

The treeless tundra region of North America, including the Canadian Arctic archipelago, was the last land mass to be exposed after the retreat of the glaciers. A large part of Greenland remains under perpetual ice and snow. Wetlands of this region were formed in a relatively warm period following glacial retreat. More recent climatic conditions have not been as favourable to the creation of wetlands, and today peat formation has virtually ceased in all but the southernmost part of the region.

In the summer, tundra has the appearance of a grey-green plain or of rolling countryside dotted with innumerable shallow lakes and ponds. In the High Arctic, continental tundra extends from Alaska's Seward Peninsula in the west right across to the eastern end of Pearyland in northern Greenland. Most of the eastern coast of Greenland, as well as its southwestern coast, is mat-forming tundra, especially at the mouths of streams. Altitudinal tundra occurs at elevations of over 515 m (1,690 ft) in Greenland and over 600 m (1,968 ft) in Newfoundland and on the Canadian mainland in Labrador.

On the islands of the Canadian High Arctic archipelago, tundra is limited to small areas of isolated coastal lowlands at or near sea level. Although the expanse of tundra is vast, only those portions that are waterlogged year-round are considered wetlands, and they occupy no more than about 5 per cent of the land area of the High Arctic. A tundra similar to that found in continental regions also occupies important areas on the Aleutian Islands and at the highest altitudes of the Rocky Mountains in

Mountain laurel (Kalmia latifolia) *and yellow water lily along the shore of a forested pool in Boreal northeastern North America.*

Alaska, Yukon Territory and British Columbia.

On the High Arctic islands, including the northern and northeastern part of Baffin Island and the Greenland tundra, the common wetlands are lowland polygon fens and peat-mound bogs. Fens occur on a mineral substrate fed by ground water and the polygon fens represent an early stage of wetland development. A polygon pattern of ridges, pushed up by ice, has created shallow angular bowls where melt-water accumulates and thin layers of peat develop. The peat-mound bogs are small peat-covered mounds that rise as high as 1 m (3 1/3 ft) above the surface of the surrounding wetland. A dome develops as the surface peat develops an insulating layer which allows cooler temperatures to develop at lower depths. Ice then forms, raising the surface.

Along the coast, and in low-lying areas, marshes and shallow-water wetlands are common. Because most of the region is polar desert, High Arctic wetlands are scarce.

The Mid Arctic section consists of the more southerly of Canada's Arctic islands and the northern and north-central part of the Canadian mainland northwest of Hudson Bay. Wetlands here are much like those of the High Arctic, but snowfall is higher, and where winds create snow banks, the snow-melt produces fens both in depressions and on slopes. Salt marshes are common along the coastal lowlands.

The Low Arctic stretches from the Aleutian Islands of the North Pacific Ocean, along the northern slopes of Alaska, down the Beaufort Sea coast of Canada, eastward across the area north of the tree line until it reaches upper Quebec, to the northeast of Hudson Bay. Here the most widespread wetlands are low-centre, lowland polygon fens and bogs. Floodplain marshes occur beside river channels, and willow (*Salix alaxensis*) swamps are found on river deltas. Large deltas like those of the Yukon in Alaska and the MacKenzie in the Northwest Territories of Canada contain important areas of wetland.

The Boreal region extends from central Alaska to Labrador. At its northernmost fringe some 6 per cent of its land area is wetland; this increases to about 50 per cent in the south. The northern, sub-Arctic section of this region consists of a sparsely treed band that stretches across Canada just below the tree line. South of the sub-Arctic region lies the vast Boreal coniferous forest extending from central Alaska and across Canada; similar forests grow at high elevations of the Rocky and Sierra Mountains.

Sub-Arctic wetlands occur in a landscape of open-canopied coniferous forests and intermingled patches of forest and tundra. The most common wetlands are fen and peat-plateau palsa bog complexes; there are also large areas of northern ribbed fens. Peat-plateau bogs are perennially frozen wetlands elevated about 1 m (3 1/3 ft) above the water table. Palsa bogs are mounds of peat with a permafrost core, often rising 1-7 m (3 1/3-23 ft) above the surrounding wetland. Ribbed fens are wetlands in low-gradient wide channels fed by surface water. Low, narrow peat ridges, sometimes called 'strings', cut in gentle arcs across the fens at right angles to the water movement.

Along the western coasts of Hudson Bay and James Bay is the longest stretch of shallow, emergent wetland shoreline in the world. Salt marshes cover 85-90 per cent of the coast of the Hudson Bay lowland.

The Boreal zone supports close-canopied, predominantly coniferous forests, that are frequent victims of fires. The common wetlands here are fens and bogs. Forested swamps are uncommon in the north. Those that exist tend to be coniferous, though some deciduous trees are found in wooded swamps towards the south. Delta marshes, some very extensive, occur where rivers discharge their waters into large lakes, such as the deltas of the Great Slave (Great Slave Lake), the Peace-Athabasca (Lake Athabaska), the Saskatchewan River (before drainage), the Delta Marsh at the southern end of Lake Manitoba and the Netley Marsh on the Red River at Lake Winnipeg.

Prairie Grasslands and Upper Mississippi Wetlands

This region consists of the temperate grasslands of the southern parts of the Canadian provinces of Alberta, Saskatchewan and Manitoba. In the United States, continental grasslands lie east of the Rocky Mountains, extending south to Texas and are bounded on the east by the temperate forests of the Great Lakes region and the Mississippi Basin. The extent of the wetlands in these regions varies according to precipitation. Less than 5 per cent of the land is wetland in the western and south-central portion, while in the central portion, 15 to 25 per cent may be wetland.

Wetlands are an important part of all the Canadian prairies. In the United States, wetlands are most significant in the northern prairie areas of eastern Montana, North and South Dakota, Minnesota, parts of Wisconsin, and the Sandhills and the Rainwater Basin, both in Nebraska. Wetlands are much less common in the central and southern portions of the grassland region. Today the moist eastern and north-central areas comprise the major 'grain basket' of North America. The more arid western grasslands are the most extensive grazing region of North America and modern agriculture has vastly modified both the natural grasslands and wetlands of the eastern and central parts of this region.

Most wetlands here tend to be around deep prairie lakes and in a myriad of depressions called 'potholes'. The potholes trace their origin to huge blocks of glacial ice deposited as the glacier retreated. As they melted the land surface slumped, creating depressions. While potholes occur as far east as New Jersey and west to Montana, they are most common in this region.

Where the grassland meets the Boreal region lies the Aspen Parkland whose wetlands differ from those of the main grasslands in that they have more than 15 per cent tree cover, primarily aspen (*Populus tremuloides*) and balsam-poplar (*Populus balsamifera*).

Rushes, sedges and grasses are the characteristic plant life of prairie wetlands. Few, if any, trees grow around their borders. The wetlands are generally near seasonally, semi-permanently and permanently flooded basins, ponds and lakes. The wetlands of the short-grass, low-precipitation western portion of the prairies tend to be more saline; the mixed-grass prairie wetlands include some saline lakes. Due to the

PRAIRIE POTHOLE WETLANDS

The millions of wetland depressions in the Prairie Pothole and Nebraska Sandhills region of the northern prairies led one writer to refer to the area as a 'Swiss cheese landscape'. It comprises some 776,000 km² (300,000 sq miles) and the density of pothole wetlands can be as high as 28 per km² (roughly 73 per sq mile).

These wetlands are typically closed basins, 0.1-10 hectares (0.2-25 acres) in size, with no surface inlets or outlets, receiving water from precipitation and loosing it by evaporation and transpiration through plants. Water in the wetlands fluctuates widely, both seasonally and annually, because of highly variable precipitation. Wetland plant communities occur around the potholes in concentric bands, reflecting how long the shoreline is flooded.

The potholes effectively receive more precipitation than does the surrounding land because dry, wind-driven snow collects in the wetland depressions, on protected slopes above the wetlands or is trapped in vegetation around the rim of the potholes.

A small prairie pothole wetland in June showing vegetation bands derived from different seasonal water levels.

The pothole region is also good grain land that is today tilled by machines. The presence of the pothole depressions makes tilling increasingly difficult as the tilling equipment has become too large to work around them. Farmers often run cultivating machinery right though the shallower potholes and in all but the most wet years they serve as good crop land. But, encouraged by government subsidies, farmers have drained larger potholes. The deeper potholes stay wet longer in most years, and the returns from farming them are often marginal.

One key to the future of these wetlands could be adjustments of farm subsidies to reward farmers for improving their best lands rather than ploughing up marginal potholes that are valuable to duck breeding.

extreme variations of the climate, vegetation in prairie wetlands is highly dynamic. That is to say, a wetland nearly covered with vegetation one year may be virtually all open water the next. Since most of the annual precipitation in the region comes as snow, the gradual summer drying of the wetland edges creates a series of different vegetation zones that spread out in concentric bands, each clearly visible to the eye, around each wetland.

The Nebraska Sandhills wetlands have formed in the valleys of the largest stabilized dune-field in the Western Hemisphere, extending over 51,800 km² (20,000 sq miles). Here, grassy wet meadows or marshes with algal, submerged and emergent plant communities border alkaline to slightly alkaline lakes. There are some shrubby wetland communities of false indigo (*Amorpha fruticosa*) and willow in the region, but few trees grow in these wetlands. The Rainwater Basin in south-central Nebraska covers about 11,000 km² (4,246 sq miles) of rolling plain. Originally, 4,000 marshes covering some 38,000 hectares (94,000 acres) occupied this area; now only 10 per cent of those remain.

Although individual prairie wetlands are small in size, their total area accounts for a substantial portion of the region north of the Sandhills. For example, wetlands occupy 6 to 15 per cent of the plains of North Dakota, and 7 to 14 per cent of the hummocky moraines in Manitoba.

Atlantic and Gulf Coast Wetlands

This region extends southwards from the coasts of the Canadian provinces of Nova Scotia and New Brunswick, down through the New England states and along the entire eastern seaboard of the United States, stretching inland as far as the Appalachian crest, south as far as the Louisiana Gulf coast and including the Florida Peninsula. Across the region the proportion of the land area in wetlands ranges from 5 to over 25 per cent.

In the part of the region that lies north of the mouth of the Hudson River, at New York City, glacial action has been a major force in forming widely distributed freshwater wetlands of various sizes. The coastal wetlands of this glaciated area are generally small and scattered on the northern Atlantic coast of Canada, but increase in size farther south towards the Hudson.

At the northern extreme of the region, in the maritime provinces of Canada, and the northern New England states, extensive peatlands containing bogs and fens are common. From central New England to the limit of glaciation, bogs are limited to higher elevations and fens are scattered. Forested swamps

are the single most common form of freshwater wetland, with marshes occurring around lakes and ponds and beside river courses. On the glaciated coast, freshwater tidal marshes are common in the lower portion of major streams, and salt marshes often lie behind coastal barrier beaches, spits and in protected bays.

Dominating significant portions of the mid-Atlantic states, the Gulf coast and the southern Florida Peninsula are coastal wetlands, frequently large and many behind barrier beaches. Unglaciated and more fertile freshwater wetlands are found predominantly along river courses with very few on the uplands.

South of the limit of the most recent glaciation, there are a few bogs - in the highest parts of the Appalachians south of Pennsylvania. Extensive forested swamps, 'bottomland hardwoods', are the commonest freshwater wetlands. They occupy the floodplains of river courses and large coastal basins, such as the Great Dismal Swamp (Virginia and North Carolina) and the Okefenokee Swamp (Georgia). In 1975 there were over 12 million hectares (30 million acres) of bottomland hardwoods in the southeastern United States alone.

Red mangrove, with well-developed prop roots, is found on the tidal marine shoreline of south Florida.

The lodge of beaver. Beavers are natural creators of wetlands in many forested areas of North America.

Evergreen shrub freshwater wetlands, called 'pocosins' and 'Carolina bays', are found along the coast of the mid-Atlantic states. Pocosins form on the flat, clay-based soils of shallow basins at the divides between ancient rivers and sounds. Their bog-like vegetation originally developed in response to waterlogging of soils due to a combination of a rise in the sea level and blocked freshwater drainage. Carolina bays have similar vegetation but tend to lie farther inland in elongated, elliptical depressions of unknown origin found in areas of clay-based and sandy soil.

On the glaciated coast, tidal salt marshes are highly developed in large drowned river valley estuaries such as the Delaware and Chesapeake Bays. Some hypersaline marshes have formed behind ocean barrier beaches; extensive salt marshes lie behind barrier beaches at Cape Hatteras and between the mainland and the sea islands of the Georgia coast.

The Gulf coast of northern Florida has important salt marsh complexes in bays and estuaries fed by rivers draining extensive forested wetlands in the interior. Where the tidal range is low, salt marshes develop on the open coast. In coastal Mississippi and Louisiana, huge marsh and forested wetlands have developed on the historical deltas of the Mississippi River. The Gulf coast of Texas boasts a major complex of saline lagoon marshes.

The south Florida Peninsula is particularly interesting: it is, in fact, unique in North America. Large freshwater flows originate north of Lake Okeechobee in central Florida and originally poured south in wide, flat, shallow basins through the Great Cypress Swamp and the Everglades, the largest freshwater marsh system in the United States. These flows go out through coastal mangroves, North America's only forested marine wetlands, into the Gulf of Mexico.

Freshwater wetlands on the Florida Peninsula have developed on marine sedimentary deposits that have interacted with the freshwater overland sheet-flow on the higher ground and with currents along the coast. On the upland, forested cypress (*Taxodium distichum*) wetlands occur as 'domes' around shallow pothole-like depressions, as open-canopy forests with wet-grass ground cover and as elongated strands paralleling surface waterflows. The depressions are formed by weak acids from decaying vegetation that slowly dissolve the limestone substrate. The name 'dome' comes from the visual effect created by the

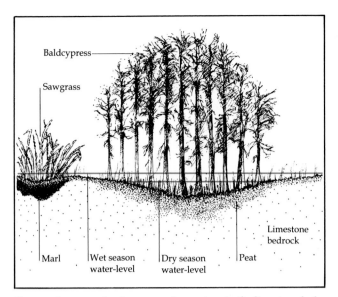

Baldcypress

Sawgrass

Limestone
bedrock

Marl   Wet season   Dry season   Peat
       water-level   water-level

Cypress domes, or heads, occupy depressions in the limestone bed-
rock of south Florida. They remain wet during the seasons when the
sawgrass Everglades dry up, and some provide shelter for alligators.

tallest cypress trees growing in the centre of the
depression and the shorter trees on the margin.

Wet prairies occur along the broad river sloughs,
as do communities dominated by species of sawgrass
(*Cladium jamaicense*), rushes (*Juncus*), maidencane
(*Panicum hemitomon*), flag and pickerel-weed (*Iris* and
Pontederia), and cattail (*Typha*).

This unique system has been significantly altered
by structures built north of the Everglades to control
and divert the water, in order to support agriculture
and to provide drinking water for the cities of the east
Florida coast.

Great Lakes and St Lawrence Basin Wetlands

This region includes the glaciated band of the United
States that lies immediately south of the Great Lakes,
extending from Lake Superior in the west to the
eastern end of Lake Huron. It then continues east-
wards through the sedimentary lowlands of the
St Lawrence River in southern Ontario and northern
New York, and after that down the St Lawrence River
Valley to Quebec City.

Glacial melt-water action and post-glacial shifts in
the drainage patterns of the Great Lakes have been
important factors in creating the freshwater wetlands
of this region. Forests covered most of the area before
European settlement. Although much was cleared for
agriculture, the poorest sites have now reverted to
forest. The land area in wetlands ranges from less
than 5 per cent to 15 per cent.

The wetlands of this region are bogs, fens, swamps,
marshes and associated shallow-water areas. Bogs
have formed in depressions, but most common are the
forested swamps that formed in standing waters, or
gently flowing surface waters, or over sub-surface

waterflows. Marshes with robust emergents and also
floating-leaved and submerged plants, occur on the
shores of water courses and in permanently
submerged areas of shallow water bodies.

Mississippi Basin Wetlands

This region occupies the bulk of the central portion of
the United States that lies south of the prairies and
between the Rockies and Appalachians. Much of the
northern part once consisted of large shallow
wetlands but these have long since been drained and
now support important agricultural activities.
Most parts of this region have less than 5 per cent of
their land area in wetlands, but this rises to over
15 per cent in the lower portion.

The remaining wetlands occur primarily on the
lowland floodplains of rivers and streams. There are
also some shrub swamps and a few sedge meadows.
The floodplain communities are highly dynamic,
thanks to the constant shifting of channels, islands and
bars. The forested communities are dry during low
water, while the aquatic communities are covered
with water for most of the year and support a variety
of emergent and submerged plants. Wetlands also
occur near small floodplain ponds and large oxbows or
cut-off meanders of large streams. A few shrub swamps
and wet meadows occur outside the floodplains.

West Coast Ranges Wetlands

This region comprises the Rocky Mountain cordillera
and the various Pacific coastal ranges that extend
from western Alaska in the north to Mexico in the
south. Included are the prairie basins that lie between
the mountains: those of southern British Columbia,
the Columbia River Basin, the Great Basin of Idaho,
Utah, Nevada and western California, and the
Colorado River Basin. Less than 5 per cent of the land
area is in wetlands.

In the Canadian inter-mountain, area wetlands occur
in two large valleys in southern British Columbia.
They have developed on a landscape of eroded
plateaus, hills, valleys and terraces, all overlain with a
mantle of glacial drift. The characteristic types are
floodplain, pothole, and shallow basin marshes.

In the Rocky Mountains, alpine environments
support wetlands on glacial lakes, on sideslopes and
on the alluvial landforms that lie by winding slow-
flowing streams in a number of U-shaped glaciated
valleys. On the vast Columbia Plateau - 38,600 km^2
(14,900 sq miles) - wetlands are largely restricted to
the river system, internal drainages, sinks, potholes
and steep-sided Coulee Lakes of the lower Columbia
catchment. Extensive marshes in the Harney (alkaline)
and Malheur (relatively fresh) Lakes make up one of

THE EVERGLADES

The Everglades wetland system of south Florida originally extended over 160 km (99 miles) from its source at Lake Kissimmee to Florida Bay. It consisted of several different wetland types: the grass and sedge Everglades community extending from the north to near the coast; the coastal mangroves; and the Big Cypress Swamp of the southwest section. A sheet of water 80 km (50 miles) wide and 150 mm (6 in) deep once flowed slowly from north to south through this system.

Today the Everglades community has been reduced to the southern half of the original system; the western edge of Big Cypress Swamp has been drained. Much of what remains is in a National Park, protected from filling, but still threatened by water diversion and pollution. Water flowing from Lake Okeechobee is impounded in large water conservation areas and then routed by canals to the east coast of

Everglades National Park. The scattered dwarf or pond cypress (Taxodium ascendens) *may be 100 years old, while the large bald cypress* (Taxodium distichum) *in the dome on the horizon are about 50 years old.*

Florida for drinking water and to protect city aquifers from salt water intrusion due to overpumping at municipal wells. The original wetlands south of Lake Okeechobee have been drained for farming and the run-off, especially from subsidized sugar-cane farms, is polluted with agricultural chemicals.

The plants and animals of this huge system are a blend of tropical and temperate species. Within the larger system is a complex mix of distinct ecosystems ranging from alligator holes, treed islands, cypress domes, sedge and grass marshes to coastal mangrove forest. At least four mammals, seventeen birds, and three reptiles and amphibians are listed as rare or endangered.

---

the most extensive inland marsh systems in the United States. Grays Lake in the upper catchment of the Colorado is, in fact, an 8,900 hectare (about 22,000 acre) marsh system.

In the Grant County section of Washington state, meadows and marshes are found in up to 1,000 permanent and temporary potholes. The Willamette Valley of Oregon and the Flathead Valley of Montana have significant wetlands in an important agricultural landscape. Wetlands on the Colorado Plateau - 50,190 km² (19,373 sq miles) - are sparse and are associated with perennial rivers, intermittent streams and some springs and seeps. In the Great Basin of Nevada, wetlands also occur by streams and at springs along fault lines. There are extensive lakeside wetlands on the shores of the Great Salt Lake. At Ash Meadows, wetlands are sustained by springs and seeps, some of them thermal. Here the naturalist can find the highest concentration of endemic plant and animal species in the whole of the continental United States. In the southern deserts of this region, small forested, shrub and marsh wetlands are found along streams.

North Pacific Coast Wetlands

This region runs from Prince William Sound in Alaska south to Seattle. Mean annual precipitation ranges from 1,044 mm (41 in) in the rain shadow of the island mountains to 2,117 mm (83 in) on the ocean coast that supports highly productive coniferous forests. Less than 5 per cent of the land area is in wetlands.

Wetlands include basin, shore, floating, slope,

flat and domed bogs that have formed on waterlogged soil. Forested swamps occur in basins, along meandering streams, on floodplain terraces and fans, and at high elevation springs. Fens are localized along flowing water and lake margins and on terraced slopes. Narrow salt marshes rim the deltas at the heads of fjords and large salt marshes occur on the deltas of large rivers.

In Alaska, the Copper River Delta, Stikine River Delta, Sitka Sound and the Mendenhall area have important coastal wetlands. In Canada, major coastal wetland areas are the Fraser River Delta, Boundary Bay and the southern mainland of British Columbia.

South Pacific Coast Wetlands

This region extends from Seattle in the state of Washington south to the Mexico/United States border and inland through the valleys behind the coast ranges as far as the Cascade Range. It is a coast of active tectonic and volcanic forces.

Most of the region has wet winters and dry summers. There is a high diversity of landforms with a variety of sedimentary deposits on the coast: deep clayey soils among the central and northern coast ranges; glacial and volcanic materials in the higher elevations of the north; and alluvium or thin rocky deposits in the interior of the central and southern parts of the region. Very large wetlands, now filled in or drained, used to fringe many of the region's large bays. Now less than 5 per cent of the land area remains as wetland.

In the Cascade Range, wetlands occur on narrow

floodplains, or in isolated alpine and sub-alpine meadows. Along the coast, tidal marshes fringe the rivers that flow into the Pacific Ocean. These wetlands historically extended well inland, but have long since been dyked for pastures. Another type of wetland has developed behind bars at the mouths of broad river valleys. The estuary of the Columbia River contains important tidal wetlands. Puget Sound in central Washington contains a complex of fjords and drowned valleys with a convoluted shoreline that includes many estuarine deltas. The small valleys of the Oregon and California coast ranges mostly contain seasonal wetlands.

The northern half of the central valley of California is drained towards the south by the Sacramento River while the southern half is drained to the north by the San Joaquin River. Along the lower half of the Sacramento, the floodplain supports isolated seasonal and perennial wetlands, and shallow lakeside and riverine wetlands. In the San Joaquin Valley, Tulare and Buena Vista Lakes formed on a blocked drainage; high rates of evaporation have resulted in both brackish and freshwater wetlands. The vast freshwater wetlands that once spread out at the confluence of the Sacramento and San Joaquin Rivers have been drained for agriculture and irrigation. The San Francisco Bay estuary, which receives the drainage from much of California, contains a large complex of freshwater, brackish and saline wetlands that have evolved from the sediments of the drainage system. Some 95 per cent of the Bay tidal marsh area that existed in 1850 has now been dyked for agriculture and salt production, filled by hydraulic mining debris or had freshwater flows diverted to meet irrigation and municipal needs.

Seasonal wetlands occur in the Sierra Nevada Range under snow-melt conditions in the alpine region; perennial wetlands, including bogs, and lakeside wetlands are restricted to hanging valleys and mid-elevation reservoirs. In southern California, coastal wetlands are small and confined to narrow river valleys separated by coastal hills and mountains. The lower Californian Peninsula has streams that terminate in small coastal lagoon wetlands, but the major wetland types here are inter-tidal flats and salt marshes. On the mountain summits in Lower California, vernal pool wetlands (seasonally wet and dry) have formed on impermeable substrate.

FLORA AND FAUNA
The North American wetlands are host to a rich variety of plants and animals. The regional patterns of the wetlands themselves influence how these plants and animals are distributed. The north-south orientation of the wetland patterns and river systems

Black spruce trees grow in the organic soils of Boreal wetlands.

in the central interior and of the Atlantic and Pacific coasts have a major influence on the flyways of migratory birds.

Arctic and Boreal Region
The dominant plants of the Arctic fens and peatlands are species of sedges (*Carex*), cotton grasses (*Eriophorum vinidi-carinatum*), lichens, *Sphagnum* moss, ericaceous shrubs and dwarf birch (*Betula glandulosa*). Low willows (*Salix*) are primarily restricted to river delta marshes.

Animal populations increase in variety and number from the High Arctic to the Mid and Low Arctic; many depend on the wetlands of this region for some part of their life cycle. The large mammals characteristic of the region are barren ground caribou (*Rangifer arcticus*) which graze in birch-willow shrubland and wetlands; musk ox (*Ovibus moschatus*) found in sedge-grass meadows; and polar bears (*Thalarctos maritimus*) which feed on seals, eider duck eggs, and summer grasses and roots along the sea coast. Other mammals include the Arctic fox (*Alopex lagopus*), Arctic hare (*Lepus arcticus*), lemmings (*Lemmus trimucronatus* and *Dicrostonyx hudsonius*), ground squirrels (*Citellus parryi*), voles (*Microtus pennsylvanicus*) and weasels (*Mustela erminea* and *Mustela rixosa*).

Many birds breed on the tundra. Geese, brants and swans are particularly common grazers: they include tundra swan (*Cygnus columbianus*), Canada goose (*Branta canadensis*), brants (*Branta bernicla* and *Branta nigricans*), emperor goose (*Philacte canagica*), snow goose (*Chen caerulescens*), white-fronted goose (*Anser albifrons*) and others. Many species of shorebirds (waders) and ducks breed here, with eiders being especially characteristic of the region: common eider (*Somateria mollissima*), king eider (*Somateria spectabilis*), spectacled eider (*Somateria fischeri*) and steller's eider (*Polysticta stelleri*). Characteristic loons are the yellow-billed and arctic loon (*Gavia adamsii* and *Gavia arctica*). Sandhill cranes (*Grus canadensis*) are found in some marshes, and of the six gulls that occur here the ivory (*Pagophila eburnea*), glaucous (*Larus hyperboreus*), Iceland (*Larus glaucoides*) and mew (*Larus canus*) gulls are particularly characteristic of the region.

The wetlands of the Boreal region provide several examples of how the source of water influences the kinds of plants that grow in each wetland. In the northern, sub-Arctic portion of the region, perennially frozen peat-plateau bogs support scattered black spruces (*Picea mariana*) with abundant lichen ground cover. *Sphagnum* moss occurs in the wetter depressions along with low shrubs of birch and Labrador tea (*Ledum decumbens*). Ridges in ribbed fens fed by flowing surface water support shrubs of birch, Labrador tea and leatherleaf (*Chamedaphne calyculata*), while the intervening depressions, called 'flarks', support sedges, cotton grass and mosses. The vast Hudson Bay tidal salt marshes are dominated by sedges, cinquefoil (*Puccinella phryganodes*) and *Potentilla* on the low tidal flats.

Many of the bogs in the southern portion of the Boreal region receive water only from precipitation;

Musk ox are the largest herbivores on the northernmost coastal wetlands in North America.

they support black spruce and tamarack (*Larix larcina*) with low shrubs of leatherleaf, Labrador tea, laurel (*Kalmia latifolia*), birch, willow, blueberry (*Vaccinium* species) and bog rosemary (*Andromeda polifolia*). The surface vegetation consists of *Sphagnum* moss or cotton grass, or both.

The fens are fed by ground water and support a different community of plants: tamarack with scattered black spruce, birch, buckthorn (*Rhamnus alnifolia*) and bayberry (*Myrica gale*). The herb layer components are species of bulrush (*Scirpus*), horsetail (*Equisetum fluviatile*), sedges and cotton grass, with several species of moss.

Floodplain forested swamps, subject to annual inundation by slow-moving streams and dominated by black ash (*Fraxinus nigra*), occur in the southern portions of the region. The vegetation of delta marshes is closely related to moisture conditions, which are, in turn, dictated by how often and how long the marshes are flooded by waters from rivers, lakes and in some cases wind tides. Horsetail, sedges, willows, cattail, grasses, bulrush, spike-rush (*Eleocharis palustris*), smartweed (*Polygonum amphibium*) and reed (*Phragmites australis*) are common plants here.

Characteristic large mammals that make seasonal use of these Boreal wetlands include woodland caribou (*Rangifer caribou*) in bogs, and moose (*Alces americana*), which in summer head for wetlands growing yellow and white water lilies (*Nuphar* and *Nymphaea* species), sedges, grasses, pondweeds (*Potomogeton* species), willow, alder (*Alnus rugosa*), aspen and some horsetail.

Many bird species make important use of the wetlands and their vegetation for food and shelter. When trees and shrubs invade the mats, warblers, sparrows and flycatchers nest there. Other breeding birds using the shallow water wetland complex are the common loon (*Gavia immer*), four kinds of grebe, the double-crested cormorant (*Phalacrocorax penicillatus*) and the Canada goose. Fifteen species of duck use the region for nesting. Great blue herons (*Ardea herodias*) breed in the southern part of the region, as do several species of shorebirds.

The most significant wetlands for wildlife are those of the marsh and shallow water complexes. The world's largest ranging herd of bison depends on the sedge meadows of the Athabasca Delta for grazing. Sedge and shrub wetlands in montane areas are essential for wapiti (*Cervus canadensis*), moose, wolf and coyote (*Canis latrans*).

Fens and bogs are important habitat for small mammals, while beaver (*Castor canadensis*) and muskrat are prime users of Boreal wetlands associated with swamps. Moose use the fens. Swamps and bogs are an essential part of the habitat of woodland caribou.

Marshy inlets, leading inland from large lake marshes in the prairie pothole region, are called 'passes' by waterfowl hunters because they are important local flight routes for ducks.

Prairie Grassland Region

Wet meadows, inundated for a few weeks in the spring, are common in the prairie grasslands and upper Mississippi River Basin. Plants growing in them tend to be low herbaceous grasses, sedges and forbs. The meadows in the Aspen Parkland include trees and woody shrubs.

Shallow marshes that are flooded from spring to mid-summer or early autumn have herbaceous grasses and coarse sedges. In the emergent deep marshes that are flooded from spring through to autumn, and frequently during the winter as well, tall cattails and bulrushes can be seen. The shallow, permanent, open-water wetlands that are flooded all the year round, except in years of severe drought, have submergent or floating aquatics. While in the alkali wetlands, both those with open water and those that are intermittently flooded, there may be either no vegetation at all or just some ditch-grass (*Ruppia maritima*).

The most widely recognized wildlife species using these wetlands are waterbirds. This is the single most important breeding habitat for most North American ducks. Some 50 to 80 per cent of the continent's ducks are raised here. The most common ducks of the region are mallard (*Anas platyrhynchos*), northern pintail (*Anas acuta*), gadwall (*Anas strepera*), blue-winged teal (*Anas discors*), northern shoveler (*Anas clypeata*), green-winged teal (*Anas carolinensis*), American wigeon (*Mareca americana*), canvasback (*Aythya valisineria*), the redhead (*Aythya americana*), lesser scaup (*Aythya affinis*), ring-necked duck (*Aythya collaris*) and the ruddy duck (*Oxyura jamaicensis*).

Beavers are regularly found in the Aspen Parkland wetlands but less so in the prairie wetlands farther south. Muskrats (*Ondatra zibethica*) use all types of wetlands in the region but survive best in deep-water wetlands that do not freeze to the bottom. Small mammals such as shrews (*Sorex* species), ground squirrels, voles and mice (*Peromyscus maniculatus*) are common. Large mammals in and around these wetlands include red fox (*Vulpes fulva*), raccoon (*Procyon lotor*), mink (*Mustela vison*) and white-tailed deer (*Odocoileus virginianus*).

Fathead minnows (*Pimephales promelas*) and brook sticklebacks (*Culaea inconstans*) are usually the only fishes to be found in wetlands less than 5 m (16 1/2 ft) deep. In deeper wetlands some landowners stock northern pike (*Esox lucius*) that may survive for a few years.

The Nebraska Sandhills and the Rainwater Basin, while in many ways similar to the main body of prairie wetlands, have significant differences. The soils are more permeable and it is the high-ground water table that supports wet sedge meadows. Where cattle trample the surface 'blow-out ponds' occur and wetland vegetation develops in windmill-tank overflow areas.

A wide variety of fish is found in most of the Sandhills wetlands, except for those areas that are highly alkaline. Amphibians and reptiles are more commonly found there than in the northern prairie wetlands and include the tiger salamander (*Ambystoma tigrinum*), seven species of frog and toad, four lizard species, six turtles and eight snakes.

Long-billed curlews (*Numenius americanus*) are a common species, as are bobolinks (*Dolichonyx orzivorus*). Many waterbirds, including shorebirds, nest here. Mallards, blue-winged teals, pintails and northern shovelers are the primary nesters. White pelicans (*Pelecanus erythrorhynchos*) are summer residents. The American avocet (*Recurvirostra americana*) makes special use of fairy shrimp (*Artemia*) and other invertebrate and insect fauna of the strongly alkaline lakes as a high-protein food source for its young.

Ninety per cent of the mid-continent's white-fronted geese make a stop in the wetlands of the Rainwater Basin each spring.

Atlantic and Gulf Coast Region

The plants in the wetlands of the northern, glaciated part of this region are similar to those of the Boreal region.

The more southerly forested swamps in the area that extends from central New England down as far as New Jersey may be either coniferous or deciduous. Common coniferous species are hemlock (*Tsuga canadensis*), tamarack and pine (*Pinus*). The scant ground cover may include holly (*Ilex verticillata*), alder, sensitive fern (*Onoclea sensibilis*), beggar-ticks (*Bidens*), touch-me-not (*Impatiens biflora*), *Eupatorium* and *Lobelia* in deciduous swamps, and elder (*Sambucus racemosa*), Virginia creeper (*Parthenocissus quinquefolia* and *vitacea*) and *Solanum* in coniferous swamps.

Deciduous forested swamps become more frequent towards the south where red maple (*Acer rubrum*), black and white ash (*Fraxinus nigra* and *Fraxinus americana*), pin and swamp white oak (*Quercus palustris* and *Quercus bicolor*) and black gum (*Nyssa sylvatica*) are common.

Tidal freshwater marshes in this region have a great variety of submerged, floating-leaved and emergent plant species. Their composition is largely influenced by elevation and by how often and how long the marshes are flooded.

Tides and salinity mean that the plant communities of the Atlantic and Gulf coast marshes are simple and dominated by no more than one or two species. The tall cordgrass (*Spartina alterniflora*) is the

Marconi Station, Cape Cod National Seashore, Massachusetts. *This forested wetland of Atlantic white cedar, with its ground cover of* Sphagnum *moss, is a remnant of what once was a major wetland type.*

characteristic species of the lower levels of the various tidal marine marshes that dot the eastern seaboard from the Canadian Maritime Provinces south as far as northern Florida. The short cordgrass (*Spartina patens*) and black grass (*Juncus gerardii*) are the common species of the upper salt marshes from Canada to New Jersey. From there on south, the dominant upper marsh species is the rush *Juncus roemerianus*. The smaller tidal range of the Gulf coast means that there is little difference between the plant life of upper and lower marshes.

NORTH ATLANTIC SALT MARSH DEVELOPMENT

Behind protective barrier islands and spits, on the northern Atlantic coast, salt marshes started their formation at sea levels lower than today. It started with a thin line of tall inter-tidal cordgrass that withstood high salinity and wave action. The cordgrass trapped sediment from the upland and sand on the waterside, and started to lay down a deposit of coarse peat.

As the sea level rose, due to melting of the polar ice caps, the land, freed from the weight of the glacier, also rose and the coarse cordgrass continued to lay down peat. Between the tall cordgrass and the upland there developed a zone reached only by the highest tides and favourable to the less salt-tolerant short cordgrass species. As these species became established

they began to deposit fine peat under the high marsh.

The combined action of the rise in the level of both sea and land, together with the effects of sediment trapping and peat formation by two plant species, has joined to extend the salt marsh both inland and on the waterside from the original point where cordgrass first started.

Pond cypress (Taxodium ascendens) *in sawgrass in the dwarf cypress area of Everglades National Park.*

The Gulf coast of Texas has a narrow band of marshland with a major concentration east of Galveston Bay. These marshes grade from saline to fresh and have a wide diversity of vegetation. West along the coast to the United States border with Mexico at the Rio Grande are a number of salt marshes fringing coastal lagoons behind long barrier beaches. In this area of low precipitation, little freshwater flows into the wetlands and evaporation rates are high. Some coastal lagoons are hypersaline and few plants can tolerate the salt concentration.

The freshwater wetlands of southern Florida are dominated by the grass *Muhlenbergia filipes* and forests of cypress. The wet grass marshes consist of sawgrass and rushes. Maidencane flats are dominated by *Panicum hemitomon,* and communities of flag, pickerelweed, cattail, *Thalia* and *Sagittaria* species.

Mangrove forest swamps replace cordgrass and rushes on the subtropical southern end of the Florida Peninsula. Red mangroves (*Rhizophora mangle*) dominate the small off-coast, overwash islands and the coastal fringe; they also share the river edges with some black and white mangroves (*Avicennia germinans* and *Laguncularia racemosa*). Black mangroves, mixed with some reds and whites, dominate high-salinity basins inland. Red mangroves are most common on the isolated, slightly raised inland tree-islands called 'hammocks', while the scattered dwarf mangroves on poor inland soils are both reds and blacks.

In the wooded wetlands of the north, many warblers, black duck (*Anas rubripes*) and wood duck (*Aix sponsa*) are common nesters, often taking advantage of ponds created by the beavers that have recently returned in strength to the region. White-tailed deer and black bears (*Ursus americanus*) use these wetlands as a winter habitat, as do snowshoe hares (*Lepus americanus*) in the most northern swamps.

The wooded wetlands of the southern portion of the region are important migratory resting areas and winter habitat for many species of duck and other waterbirds, including 2.5 million mallards and nearly 4 million wood ducks. Coastal Texas is the sole breeding site in the United States for fulvous tree ducks (*Dendrocygna bicolor*) and black-bellied tree ducks (*Dendrocygna autumnalis*).

Up to 53 species from at least 20 families of fish spawn or feed, or both, in the forested wetlands (bottomland hardwoods) of the floodplains of the southern rivers. The catfish (Ictaluridae), sunfish (Cetrarchidae), gar (Lepisosteidae), perch (Percidae) and sucker (Catostomidae) families are particularly dependent on this system. Reptiles and amphibians are common, including the American alligator (*Alligator mississippiensis*) and the cottonmouth moccasin snake (*Agkistrodon piscivorus*). Crayfish (*Procambarus*) are an important crustacean and food source in this area.

Tidal freshwater marshes are rich in wildlife. Anadromous fish - fish that migrate from the sea up rivers in order to breed - pass through them in spawning runs; striped bass (*Morone saxatilis*) and blue crabs (*Callinectes sapidus*) spawn in their fresh waters. The different kinds of vegetation support a large and diverse population of nesting birds. Ducks, herons, egrets, rails and shorebirds, birds of prey, gulls, terns, kingfishers, crows, arboreal birds, ground and shrub nesters - up to 280 species in all - have been reported in tidal freshwater marshes. In addition, over 100 species of amphibians and reptiles frequent the marshes, as do many mammals. Marsh rabbit (*Sylvilagus palustris*) and marsh rice rat (*Oryzomys palustris*) are both characteristic of these wetlands.

A mollusc reef wetland with oysters, typical of those found on North American coasts.

Muskrats and raccoons are found in the low-salinity parts of the tidal marshes.

Northern tidal salt marshes are important breeding grounds for waterbirds. Herons, egrets, rails, marsh hawks, ospreys and marsh sparrows are year-round residents. Black duck, mallard and wigeon are important breeders. Many fish and shellfish feed along the marsh edges and follow the tides on to the marshes. Coastal salt marshes from the mid-Atlantic states south into Florida and along the Gulf of Mexico are major resting and wintering grounds for waterbirds that breed on the wetlands of the northern regions of North America. These marshes also provide habitat and food sources for soft-shelled clams, oysters, shrimp and many fin-fish.

In the freshwater wetlands of the Florida Peninsula crayfish and prawns (Palaeomonetes) are common invertebrates. Also abundant are fishes of the Centrarchidae (bluegills) and Cyprinodontidae (topminnow) families and the livebearers, Poecilidae, which include the mosquito fish (*Gambusia affinis*). Amphibians and reptiles abound too, including the alligator and American crocodile (*Crocodylus acutus*).

Birds are the most numerous vertebrates - there are over 200 species of them. Of particular interest are the herons, white ibis (*Eudocimus albus*), wood stork (*Mycteria americana*), roseate spoonbill (*Ajaia ajaja*), Everglades kite (*Rostrhamus sociabilis*), brown pelican (*Pelecanus occidentalis*) and Florida sandhill crane. The mammals of special interest in the south Florida freshwater wetlands include the mangrove fox squirrel (*Sciurus niger*), the Florida cougar (*Felis concolor coryi*), the manatee (*Trichechus manatus*), the seminole sub-species of the white-tailed deer and the round-tailed muskrat (*Neofiber alleni*).

In the mangrove forest swamps, oysters (*Crassostrea virginica*) attach themselves to the mangroves' stems and prop roots, while crabs find cover among the prop roots and sediments. Alligators, American crocodiles, turtles, bears, bobcat (*Lynx rufus*) and Florida panther (*Felis concolor*) are also to be seen.

Great Lakes and St Lawrence Region
The vegetation in the bogs and fens of this region is similar to that of the bogs and fens of the Boreal region. The forested coniferous and deciduous swamps are much like those of the northern Atlantic region.

Common lakeshore marsh emergents are bur-reed (*Sparganium*), arrow-head, cattail, bulrush, flowering rush (*Butomis*), spike rush, sweet flag (*Acorus calamus*) and wild rice (*Zizania lacustris*). Floating species include duckweed (*Lemna* and *Spirodela* species), and common submerged species in marshes are spike rush, water-weed (*Anacharis*), water celery (*Vallisneria americana*), mud-plantain (*Heteranthea*), water milfoil

A small shallow, permanently flooded wetland with flowering white water lily (Nymphaea odorata).

(*Myriophyllum*) and coontail (*Ceratophyllum demersum*).

The large mammals that breed and feed in these wetlands are generally similar to those of the Boreal wetland region. Migratory birds make much use of the wetlands, and mallards, blue- and green-winged teals, black ducks, wood ducks and Canada geese breed here. The Lake St Clair and Lake Erie marshes are important staging grounds for migratory ducks and geese. Other birds dependent on the wetlands include mute swan (*Cygnus olor*), gadwall, pintail, wigeon, shoveler, redhead, ring-necked and ruddy duck, hooded merganser (*Lophodytes cucullatus*), king rail (*Rallus elegans*), coot, grebes, great blue heron, egrets, bitterns, gallinule (*Gallinula chloropus*), terns and long-billed marsh wren (*Telmatodytes palustris*).

The marshes and swamps also provide spawning grounds for important freshwater fish species including northern pike, muskellunge (*Esox masquinongy*), largemouth bass (*Micropertus salmoides*), yellow perch (*Perca flavescens*), brown bullhead (*Ictalurus melas*) and pumpkinseed (*Lepomus gibbosus*). Six turtles are dependent on these wetlands, as are two snakes and several amphibians.

Mississippi Basin Region

The major tree species found in the wooded floodplain wetlands are willow, aspen (*Populus*), maple (*Acer*), ash (*Fraxinus*) and elm (*Ulmus*) in the north. Farther south, oak, hickory (*Carya*), black gum

(*Nyssa*), sweet gum (*Liquidambar*), cypress and persimmon (*Diospyros virginiana*) become common.

Marsh rice rat, cotton mouse (*Peromyscus gossypinus*), swamp rabbit, muskrat, nutria (*Myocastor coypus*), raccoon (*Procyon lotor*) and white-tailed deer are mammals found here.

This region serves as the most important wintering area for ducks and geese in the whole of the central part of the continent and provides staging and resting areas on the single most important waterbird flyway in North America. Eighty-seven per cent of the continent's wintering gadwalls, 77 per cent of the blue-winged and cinnamon teal, 60 per cent of the green-winged teal, 57 per cent of the ring-necked ducks and a high proportion of the scaups, American wigeon, geese and other species use these wetlands. Wood duck, mallard, hooded merganser, black and yellow-crowned night heron (*Nycticorax nycticorax* and *Nyctanassa violacea*) also use them. Cormorants, herons, water turkeys (*Anhinga anhinga*) and egrets nest in the region's full-grown cypress wetlands.

West Coast Range Region

Pothole wetlands in the Rocky Mountains and western river basins support rush-sedge meadows, bullrush and cattail marshes and submerged aquatic plants. The dominant tree of the riverine wetlands is cottonwood, while the springs and seeps support ferns, herb and mosses. The sparse southern desert wetlands support cottonwood, mesquite, willows, tamarisk, sycamore (*Platanus*), arrow-weed and sedges.

The sparse wetlands of the west coast ranges act as oases in a predominantly arid environment for many forms of wildlife. The large wetland mammals of the region include muskrat, river otter (*Lutra canadensis*), mink (*Mustela vison*), bobcat (*Lynx rufus*), white-tailed deer and moose. Beaver and trout (*Salmo*) compete for habitat in high altitude stream-side forested wetlands.

The few large marshes in this region are important breeding and migratory areas for waterbirds. Breeding densities of ducks in the British Columbia basins may be as high as 4-8 per km² (roughly 10-20 per sq mile). A large proportion of the world's population of Barrow's goldeneye (*Bucephala islandica*) is concentrated in the inter-mountain prairies of Canada. The Malheur, Tule-Klamath and Summer Lake areas of Oregon and the Great Salt Lake area in Utah may produce over 200,000 ducklings annually. Trumpeter swans (*Cygnus buccinator*) now breed in a few wetlands in the region. Tundra swans winter on the Great Salt Lake, while Canada geese breed throughout the scattered wetlands of the northern part of the region, as do about 20 species of duck, five species of grebe, white-faced ibis (*Plegadis chihi*) and a number of other wading birds, shorebirds and gulls.

North Pacific Coast Region

In the small basin bogs of the North Pacific region *Sphagnum* moss is the main ground cover. Coniferous bogs have pine and hemlock in the tree canopy, and a shrub layer in the understorey. *Sphagnum* bogs occur as floating and shore bogs at the margins of small lakes and on slopes in the upland, while slope bogs may have trees and shrubs. On the coast, major plants found in the low salt marshes include species of *Spergularia, Triglochin, Salicornia, Distichlis, Plantago, Cotula* and *Atriplex*. The high marsh supports *Hordeum, Elymus, Aster, Achillea* and *Rumex* species.

Roughly the same birds and mammals are to be found in the inland wetlands here as in similar areas of the Rocky Mountain region. Few mammals, however, use the coastal wetlands. Birds that breed in wetlands along the Pacific coast include the Canada goose, bald eagle (*Haliaeetus leucocephalus*), osprey (*Pandion haliaetus*) and short-eared owl (*Asio flammeus*). The coastal wetlands of south and south-central Alaska support an important breeding population of trumpeter swans. Coastal wetlands provide important wintering grounds for various grebes, goldeneyes, the common loon, greater scaup (*Aytha marila*), common merganser (*Mergus merganser*), Canada goose and double-breasted cormorant.

Moving down the coast to the low tidal marshes of the northern part of the southern Pacific region, pickleweed (*Salicornia virginica*) becomes the most characteristic plant. Grasses and rushes are common on both high and low marshes. In the estuaries the principal species is eelgrass (*Zostera marina*). Tidal marshes of the San Francisco Bay area and southern California have Pacific cordgrass (*Spartina foliosa*) and pickleweed as their most common species.

Freshwater wetlands occur as lakes, marshes and bogs and as alpine meadow wetlands of sedge, grass and willow species. On sub-alpine sites rushes and forbs mix with sedges.

The most common mammals in the northern part of this region are muskrat, nutria, beaver, river otter, mink, raccoon, bobcat and white-tailed deer. The use by mammals of the wetlands in the southern portion is limited.

The freshwater wetlands of the river basins and agricultural areas are important wintering areas for dabbling and diving ducks, some geese, and swans. Herons, some rails, wood duck and some dabbling ducks breed here. Coastal wetlands are also important wintering areas for sea ducks, some diving ducks, shorebirds, brants, pelicans and some gulls and terns. Breeding birds that use the coastal wetlands of the region include herons, clapper rails (*Rallus longirostris*), gulls, terns, American avocets, black-necked stilts (*Himantopus mexicanus*) and certain passerines, including the savanna sparrow (*Sterna antillarum browni*).

California is the major duck and goose wintering

Arctic loons (Gavia arctica) breed in the freshwater wetlands of Alaska and Canada.

The bleached antlers of two male caribou which drowned while locked in mortal combat symbolize the wild and pristine nature of much of the Arctic region.

area of the Pacific coast of the United States and most of these birds use the Central Valley wetlands. Significant species are the tundra swan, trumpeter swan, Ross's goose (*Chen rossii*), lesser Canada goose, cackling Canada goose, mallard, pintail, shoveler, American wigeon, scoter (*Melanitta* species), bufflehead (*Bucephala albeola*) and ruddy duck.

VALUES AND USES

Arctic and Boreal Wetlands

High Arctic wetlands are important oases for wildlife in an otherwise arid environment. Their role as breeding grounds for migratory waterbirds has international significance. The wet lowlands of the Great Plain of the Koukdjuak in the southwest corner of Baffin Island, for example, support over a million nesting birds annually, including up to 50 per cent of North America's greater snow goose population. This region is, then, a producer of resources whose value is also realized in other parts of the continent.

There are other examples to show the importance of the region's wetlands. Its sedge wetlands are essential winter habitat for musk ox. The salt marshes of the Arctic are indispensable to the survival and reproduction of many species of freshwater and marine fish of important commercial value. These wetlands are also a key component in the traditional harvest of local resources carried out by some 50,000 resident Eskimos and Inuits; they are, too, a vital support system for northern recreation and tourism. The value to Canada of fur trapping, from all regions, can be as much as Can$69 million (approximately US$61 million) and the economic benefit of the waterbird resources to Canada is about Can$118 million (some US$104 million).

The chief value of the wetlands in the sub-Arctic sector of the Boreal region is their wildlife. Peat resources are vast, but since a large part is perennially frozen, mining would be most difficult. The Mackenzie River Delta, Old Crow Flats and the coastal areas of Hudson Bay are particularly productive for waterbirds and fur-bearing mammals. The latter two areas are also major staging grounds for migrating waterbirds.

In some areas within the main Boreal region, the wetlands are important for the forests they contain. As much as 80 per cent of the black spruce harvest in parts of the province of Ontario is from wetlands.

Wild rice is harvested for human food from the shallow littoral zone of Boreal lakes. In 1983, 750,000 kg (1.65 million lb) were produced in Canada, mostly in the Boreal regions. The value of the annual harvest can be as much as Can$7 million (about US$6 million).

In Alaska and Canada, residents of native communities owe as much as 75-80 per cent of their total fat, protein and vegetable intake to the hunting, fishing and trapping of animals and other ways of harvesting wild resources. The ways of life of most such communities are adapted to coastal or riverine areas, and are closely associated with wetlands. The products of natural wetlands provide a source of food and are an essential component in a complex integration of economic, social and cultural factors that make up the subsistence economies of the rural communities of the vast Arctic and Boreal regions of the continent.

Prairie Wetlands

While the value of the prairie wetlands as wildlife habitat is well known, their other important functions are less widely recognized. The problem is that they occur in a region that is highly valuable for agriculture. Competition over the fate of these wetlands between agricultural and wildlife interests is high.

Grain production is the dominant agricultural use - the grains produced ranging from corn and beans in the south to canola (rape) and barley in the north.

Over one half of the original 8 million hectares (20 million acres) of pothole wetlands has been drained for conversion to agricultural use. The drains are often connected to highway ditches with outlets on streams. In this way the natural capacity of the wetlands to retain water is defeated, and higher streamflows and downstream flooding often result.

The Nebraska Sandhills are also valuable for agriculture, predominantly cattle ranching, and maintenance of wet meadows in order to water livestock and as a source of native hay for winter forage is economically important.

Atlantic and Gulf Wetlands

Because the wetlands of the Atlantic and Gulf coasts occur in the most populated region of North America, their values as sources of water, wood and fish rank as high or, in some areas, higher than their values as havens for wildlife. The northeastern states of this region were the first to enact laws that regulated the alteration of privately owned wetlands, laws that have since been emulated in the Canadian province of Ontario and that have been followed, in the United States, by a national system of wetland regulation.

Where people live near wetlands, the hydrological values to humans, such as flood control, sediment trapping and maintenance of water quality may equal

A warm reef wetland colonized by a species of reef worm (Sabellaria) *is typical of the tropical coast of southern Florida.*

WETLAND LOSSES IN THE MISSISSIPPI RIVER DELTA

At the mouth of the Mississippi River, as with the mouths of all the major rivers of the world, lies a huge delta built with sediments transported by the river. From the barrier islands along the coast, and reaching 16-97 km (10-60 miles) inland, lies a 2.6 million hectare (6.5 million acre) wetland complex estimated to account for 40 per cent of the marsh ecosystem of the United States. The existence of this system is threatened from a number of directions.

To keep the Mississippi from flooding over its natural plain, the banks of the river have been lined with dykes. River sediments that once settled on the plains are now carried to the mouth of the river. In former times, the mouth of the river would shift many kilometres east and west every few years as sediments built up and were washed away by coastal currents and storms. In order to maintain a constant open shipping channel sediments are dredged and the dykes have been run out on the delta to stabilize the shifting river mouth.

Today the river sediments flow far out into the Gulf of Mexico where they drop into deep water and no longer settle out on the delta wetland communities. The old sediments of the delta are subsiding due to natural compression and organic decay. The sea level is rising. Canals opened into the marshes to provide access for oil drilling rigs have not been refilled and their banks are eroding. The end result is that this huge system is losing as much as 100 km² (39 sq miles) of wetland each year.

Half of the fur harvest and one-third of the seafood of the United States comes from this region and both are dependent on the wetland system. The annual harvest of fish for bait and fertilizer alone is valued at US$80 million, the shrimp harvest at US$50 million, oysters at US$3-4 million; the state of Louisiana collects between US$175 and $200 million in hunting, fishing and trapping licences annually. Restoration and preservation of this wetland system has become a high national priority in the United States.

or exceed other values. About two-thirds of the commercial shellfish and fin-fish harvested in the United States are dependent on the coastal wetlands of this region for nursery and breeding sites or are dependent for food on forage fish that breed here. This is particularly true of the south Atlantic and Gulf coast wetlands. Some forested and marsh wetlands are beginning to be used, on a trial basis, as places to provide biological treatment of effluent from sewage plants in small non-industrial communities.

The bottomland hardwood wetlands contain important forest resources that can be harvested using appropriate techniques. Specialized high-value crops grow on certain other wetlands, though intensively managed commercial bogs retain little resemblance to a natural bog: blueberries grow on the northern organic bog and shrub wetlands in a more or less natural environment; cranberries (*Vaccinium macrocarpon*) are a highly valuable wetland crop; and horticultural peat is dug in some

Pickerelweed (Pontederis cordata), *right, and water plantain* (Alisma *species*) *left, are common wetland plants of North America.*

wetlands of the northern part of the region.

Tidal freshwater marshes provide the source of a significant portion of the fur harvest of the mid-Atlantic states. The tidal fresh and salt marsh complex of the Chesapeake Bay produces about 90 per cent of the harvest of striped bass, a highly valuable commerical and sport species.

The commercial harvest of shrimp, fish and shellfish in the bays and off the shore of the Gulf coast is closely tied to coastal wetlands. Water flowing through the south Florida cypress, Everglades and mangrove complex flushes nutrients from the floodplains in support of a major fin-fish and shellfish industry.

Great Lakes, St Lawrence and Mississippi Wetlands

The wetlands of the Great Lakes region and St Lawrence River Basin are important as a key habitat for fish and other wildlife; the wetlands here are again much used by humans. They provide goods and services that are important to health, welfare and safety, including the regional economy. In Ontario alone, fur trapping provides over Can$10 million (about US$9 million) annually. Hunting, fishing and trapping provide Ontario and Quebec each about

Can$60 million (about US$53 million) annually. Timber, wild rice and peat are other commercial wetland products, with wild rice harvested in Ontario valued at near Can$1 million (about US$0.9 million) annually. Some wetlands produce horticultural peat, and in Quebec certain wetlands are used to produce market garden crops valued at over Can$50 million (about US$44 million) a year.

The wetlands of the Mississippi River Basin are located primarily on the floodplains of rivers. They provide important wildlife habitats and migratory resting and wintering areas for waterbirds, as well as being crucial for flood control and forestry. The wetlands of this region once served as major sediment traps and temporary flood-storage areas in the Mississippi drainage. While various navigation and flood-control devices have reduced this role, to the detriment of the Mississippi Delta wetlands, the remaining areas continue to be important in helping to reduce floods and maintain the quality of the water. The annually flooded hardwood swamp wetlands provide very productive forest sites. Many of the most valuable timber species were cut decades ago, but potential for modern productive forest management remains on many sites.

NORTH AMERICAN WATERFOWL MANAGEMENT PLAN

In response to a steep decline in continental waterfowl numbers (ducks, geese and swans), Canada and the United States agreed in 1986 on an international approach to waterfowl restoration that involves federal, state, provincial and non-governmental organizations. Called the North American Waterfowl Management Plan, its major objective is the protection and management of about 2.4 million hectares (5.9 million acres) of high-priority waterfowl wetland habitats in both countries. The United States Fish and Wildlife Service and the Canadian Wildlife Service administer the plan and nearly 200 other public and private organizations (such as Ducks Unlimited), representing over 30 million individual members, participate.

The two nations have agreed to share the costs of the programme, the United States and Canada both contributing US$30 million per year for five years, with matching funds to come from provincial and private organizations. Over 30 areas of major concern have been identified and certain of these have been designated high priority. Among the high-priority sites are three that cross the national border, the Prairie Potholes/Aspen Parklands, the Lower

The North American Waterfowl Management Plan is aimed at conserving migratory species such as these greater snow geese.

Great Lakes and St Lawrence River Basin, and the Middle-Upper Atlantic Coast.

In addition to acquiring and managing wetland habitat, public education materials have been produced; population monitoring is funded; and research on species of special concern, such as Arctic goose

species and the black duck (*Anas rubripes*), is supported. It is intended to expand the plan to include Mexico. The experience of the North American nations under this kind of cooperative effort could be useful among other nations whose wetlands support a common migratory bird resource.

The West Coast Wetlands

The wetlands of the Rocky Mountains and western river basins are scattered, but highly important as waterbird breeding and migratory areas - since they occur in a region where water is scarce and annual precipitation is highly variable. Both alkaline and fresh lakes provide waterbird habitats and many of these same areas are important to agriculture. Artificial water control is necessary in many areas to meet the needs of farms as well as of waterbirds. In some cases the waterbird habitat is an unplanned by-product of irrigation or some other modification of the water supply.

In many cases waterbirds breed considerably more successfully on the managed marshes of state and federal refuges at some of these western sites than they do in even the best natural prairie habitats on the continent. Malheur and Summer Lake in Oregon, the Klamath Basin on the Oregon-California border, Stillwater Refuge in Nevada and the Great Salt Lake borders in Utah are among the most important breeding places in this region.

Along the northern Pacific coast the picture is slightly different. Here it is the role of the wetlands as reservoirs that absorb and store water and thus help to reduce flood hazards that is most important. Another key role, both locally and regionally, is in filtering water for nutrients, sediments and pollution.

The wetlands along this stretch of the coast are internationally important, especially as sites in the migration patterns of birds and anadromous fish, such as salmon, that leave the sea to spawn in freshwater. Over 50 per cent of the ducks that winter in Canada do so in the wetlands of the Fraser Delta. The streams associated with wetlands support commercially important salmonoid and other fish populations. Some peatlands serve as highly productive market and small fruit gardens, and as sources of horticultural peat.

The marine wetlands on the shoreline of Washington and the other states to its south provide an important food source for sea otters (*Enhydra lutris*) and various fish, including commercially important species such as salmon, halibut (*Paralichthys californicus*) and turbot (*Hypsopsetta guttulata*). Estuarine wetlands support vascular plants that are an important food source for brant and snow geese.

The Dungeness crab (*Cancer magister*) and the Pacific oyster (*Crassostrea gigas*) are important commercial species that depend on the wetland estuary complex for food or to complete their life cycle. Oyster culture has been started in these same waters. Clams are commercially important in Washington and derive their food from the wetland estuary complex as well.

As for fin-fish harvests: 6-7 per cent of the

The Suwannee Canal, started in 1891 and used to float out cypress logs, was a failed attempt to drain the Okefenokee Swamp, Georgia.

Mechanized agriculture is an inappropriate practice in the wet-meadow wetlands.

commercial catch from California coastal waters, 37 per cent of the Oregon catch and 54 per cent of the Washington catch is estuarine dependent. The fate not only of coastal wetlands, but also of freshwater wetlands along streams used by anadromous fish, could be highly important. Over 40 per cent of commercial salmon landings in Washington and virtually all commercial salmon landings in Oregon and California are estuarine wetland dependent.

Inland, the Central Valley and San Francisco Bay wetlands are the major wintering grounds for waterbirds that migrate along the western side of the continent. The Central Valley is also important to agriculture, which occupies large areas of former wetlands.

THREATS, MANAGEMENT AND CONSERVATION
Most wetlands in the northern half of North America are still in their natural state. From southern Canada to Mexico huge areas of wetlands have been drained and considerable pressure is being placed on those that remain.

In Canada, over one-seventh of the wetland area that existed before European settlement has been converted to other uses. In the United States (excluding Alaska) between 30 and 50 per cent of the original wetland area has been lost. Agriculture has been the leading cause of loss, with urban development, construction of port facilities, roads, industrial parks and hydroelectric projects also responsible for significant losses. In Canada,

agricultural conversions have been most significant in the prairie potholes, in the Atlantic salt marshes and in the lakeshore and rivershore areas in southern Ontario and the St Lawrence Valley. In the United States, agricultural losses have been significant in the prairie states of North Dakota, Nebraska and Minnesota, with further extensive losses in the Gulf coastal states of Louisiana, Mississippi, Arkansas, Texas and Florida as well as in North Carolina on the Atlantic coast.

The conversion of wetlands for urban expansion has been significant along the shorelines of the St Lawrence River and the lower Great Lakes, in Atlantic salt marshes and Pacific estuarine marshes and around every large coastal city.

Industrial and pollution degradation is another factor, and this is not limited to regions near major cities. It also includes damage caused to the environment by potash and salt extraction plants in the Canadian prairies and by agricultural run-off from irrigation systems in the western United States and from sugar-cane farming near the Florida Everglades. Alaskan wetlands are, in their turn, threatened by development of oil and gasfields, pipeline construction and the building of ports.

Hydroelectric development on both the Peace-Athabasca River system and the Saskatchewan River Delta has had a major adverse impact on wetlands. Similar damage seems likely at the James Bay in Quebec, Churchill Falls in Labrador, the Nelson River

The pools occupying the centre of cypress domes may be used as sites for natural treatment of waste water from small rural communities in the southeastern United States.

URBAN WETLAND LOSSES

The regions around Boston, Massachusetts and San Francisco, California provide examples of how major wetland areas have been lost, for different reasons, near major coastal cities in North America.

Prior to 1814, the city of Boston was located on a peninsula in Boston Harbour, attached to the mainland by a narrow neck of land. Between the city and the mainland lay large tidal flats and marshes. By 1821 the wetland area was dyked off by an earth and stone dam to capture tidal energy to run mills. In 1836 more fill was placed to support

railroad tracks across the flats into the city. The dam and rail bed reduced tidal flushing, causing stagnation and odours at low tide that offended the Bostonians. The remaining wetland basin was filled and a major part of the city now stands on former wetland.

The earliest conversions of the San Francisco area marshes were for agriculture and small salt evaporation ponds. In the 1850s hydraulic mining for gold sent huge amounts of sediment down the rivers to the bays, providing material that made it easier for shoreline dyking and filling to proceed.

Major dredging for navigation started in 1868 and by the 1870s ownership of the shoreline had largely passed out of public domain into the hands of individuals who dyked and filled the marshes, laying the foundation for urban development of the shoreline. But little regard has been given to the nature of the soft bay mud under the fill foundations and highways. It constitutes a hazard to surface structures because they liquify during earthquakes. The public costs and consequences of converting these wetlands to other uses will continue to mount in the future.

---

in Manitoba, the Liard River in British Columbia, the Slave River in Alberta and several estuaries on the Pacific coast.

Canada has mined peat for over 50 years. Despite an annual increase in demand for peat for horticultural, agricultural and fuel use, the nation has no national peatland policy. In the United States peat is being considered for power generation and other uses in the Great Lakes region, Maine and on the mid-Atlantic coast.

Forest harvesting on sensitive, easily damaged black spruce stands is a problem in certain regions of Canada, largely due to a lack of good forest management practices. In parts of the southeastern United States, forests in bottomland hardwood wetlands have been cut, dyked and converted for soybean production. Altering the flooding regime of these wetlands by dyking has eliminated fish stocks and wildlife habitat, increased flood crests down-

stream and threatens commercial fishing in the estuarine reaches of the river mouths.

The continuing loss of estuarine wetland is greatest in the United States, especially along the Gulf coast of Louisiana where the wetlands are unique, complex and extensive. Large areas of coastal marsh are being inundated by the sea because the accumulation of sediments is not keeping pace with natural coastal submergence. Sediments from the Mississippi River, that once nourished the coast, have been diverted out to deeper sea waters by man-made flood-control and navigation devices and by dredging. Loss has been accelerated by construction of canals for oil exploration.

The huge and biologically rich Chesapeake Bay system has been severely damaged by industrial pollution and changes in salinity. The Everglades are also threatened - by diversion of water for human uses and by pollution from intensive agricultural practices, especially sugar-cane farming.

Water hyacinth, an exotic floating plant that may clog waterways in the southern United States, can also remove pollutants from the water.

Canada geese take advantage of well-fertilized lawns, and degrade water quality, where development has encroached on a former wetland.

The management and conservation of wetlands in North America takes several forms. Canada's federal government manages 29 per cent of all the country's wetlands: those located on federal (Crown) lands and waters, particularly in northern territories. The United States Fish and Wildlife Service manages nearly 9.3 million hectares (23 million acres) of inland wetlands and about 809,000 hectares (2 million acres) of estuarine wetlands. A further 2 million hectares (5 million acres) of wetlands are under state management in the United States.

Many of the wetlands acquired by the governments of Canada and the United States have been purchased in order to set up a large-scale system of wildlife refuges. This is necessary to meet national obligations under the several migratory bird conventions signed by Canada, the United States, Mexico, the Soviet Union and Japan.

Private non-governmental organizations are also active in wetland protection in North America. Several million hectares are protected by private conservation agencies in the United States. A private Canadian conservation organization, Ducks Unlimited - Canada, has placed high priority on the prairie pothole region in its wetland lease, purchase and management programme. Private sector initiatives have protected at least 1 million hectares (2.5 million acres) of wetlands in Canada. The 600,000 members of

Ducks Unlimited Inc. raise about US$60 million annually, most of which goes to wetland aquisition, management and creation. Other private agencies in the United States, such as the National Audubon Society (71,000 hectares - 175,000 acres) and Nature Conservancy (728,000 hectares - 1.8 million acres), acquire land that includes important wetlands.

Thirty-eight wetland sites in North America (30 in Canada, 8 in the United States) have been designated for the list of Wetlands of International Importance under the Ramsar Convention. But the United States has only named sites that are already in protected ownership and thus is not using this international treaty as a means of encouraging protection of sites that are in need of additional protection.

Both Canada and the United States have, however, designated high-priority wetlands for protection. Canada's national policy has put high priority on protection of Arctic, sub-Arctic and Boreal wetlands. Under the North American Waterfowl Management Plan, Canada and the United States are jointly committed to additional wetland aquisition, restoration and management. The Plan has identified over 20 million hectares (49 million acres) of wetlands in the United States and Canada for acquisition, restoration and management, at a cost of more than US$1.5 billion dollars over 15 years.

Thirty-four habitat areas of major concern have

been identified. Of these top priority has been given to the Central Valley of California, the prairie parklands and potholes, the lower Mississippi River, its delta and associated Gulf coast, the lower Great Lakes-St Lawrence Basin, and the middle and upper Atlantic coast from South Carolina in the United States to New Brunswick and Nova Scotia in Canada. Additionally in Canada, goose, black duck, and eastern duck habitats have been given high priority.

Buying wetlands is not the only means of protecting wetlands in North America. In the United States, state and federal governments have enacted laws that regulate wetland alterations on all lands, public and private. Regulatory programmes started on the state level and are now in effect for freshwater wetlands in 14 states, primarily in the northeast and north-central part of the United States. Every coastal state has some level of regulation on marine wetlands. These regulations usually require any person who wishes to alter a wetland first to obtain a permit. If a permit is issued, it contains conditions that the applicant must follow to ensure that the proposed project does not impair the public health, welfare and safety functions of wetlands.

United States law does not permit governments to control the use that a private individual makes of his or her land unless that use puts the public interest at risk. Thus, the regulatory process is likely to give higher consideration to the importance of wetlands in relation to flood control and water quality than to wildlife and fish habitats.

The United States federal government, through the Army Corps of Engineers and the Environmental Protection Agency, regulates dredge and fill activities in wetlands of all states under the federal Clean Water Act. The corps issues the permits and the EPA sets the standards for the programme. The main weakness of this programme is that it does not regulate activities, like agriculture, that are most destructive of wetlands; it has also taken the two agencies many years to agree on techniques and standards.

The Canadian province of Ontario has adopted a policy that ensures that the functions and values of wetlands are taken into consideration during the process of land-use planning. The province of Quebec has implemented policies to enhance protection of wetlands as wildlife habitats and to control river and shoreline development.

CONTRIBUTOR: D.A. SCOTT

Latin America and the Caribbean

THE NEOTROPICAL REALM - broadly, Mexico, Central America, the Caribbean and South America, but excluding the highlands of Mexico, Guatemala and Honduras in the north and the extreme southern tip of South America - is biologically much the richest and most diverse of the world's eight major bio-geographical regions. It is also one of the least known, and offers great opportunities for the taxonomist seeking species new for science. Recent studies in the Amazon, for example, have indicated that in some families of invertebrates, up to 80 per cent of the species to be found there remain undescribed.

With a total human population of about 310 million, the South American continent has an overall population density of less than 18 inhabitants per km² (47 inhabitants per sq mile). The bulk of this population is concentrated on the northern and central coasts and along the major navigable rivers. Much of the interior and south are very sparsely populated and retain vast tracts of almost pristine habitats, including wetlands. By contrast, most of the small Caribbean states are very densely populated, the average density for the region being 160 inhabitants per km² (415 inhabitants per sq mile). Many of the islands have been subjected to centuries of intensive exploitation, and little natural habitat survives intact, except in the rugged interior of some of the larger islands, such as Jamaica. Middle America (Mexico to Panama) lies between these two extremes. Environmental degradation is proceeding rapidly in densely populated regions, especially in Mexico and Panama, but large areas of natural habitat remain, including many wetlands.

GEOGRAPHY AND CLIMATE

Latin America and the Caribbean cover a land area of approximately 20.5 million km² (7.9 million sq miles) and extend for over 12,000 km (7,500 miles) from north to south between latitudes 32°30 North and 56°00 South. This vast region contains almost the full spectrum of the world's major ecosystems, from the coral reefs and mangrove swamps of the Caribbean to the permanent snowfields and glaciers of the Chilean Fjordland, and from the towering peaks and barren plateaus of the high Andes to the vast rainforests of Amazonia. The Atacama Desert of northern Chile and southern Peru is one of the world's most lifeless deserts, while just across the Andes there are humid forests supporting the greatest diversity of plant and animal life on Earth.

The mountain ranges of Mexico and Central America and the mighty Andes of South America form an almost uninterrupted barrier between the Pacific and Atlantic lowlands, the only real gap being the low-lying Isthmus of Panama, only 65 km (40 miles) wide at its narrowest point, which bridges the North and South American land masses. In general, the foothills and lowlands on the Pacific side of the mountain chains receive considerably less rainfall than those on the Caribbean and Atlantic side. Thus the former tend to support desert vegetation, dry thorn forest or a Mediterranean type of scrub, while the latter support rainforest and wet savannas. There are, however, some notable exceptions on both slopes - for example, the humid forests of southeastern Costa Rica, western Colombia and southern Chile in the Pacific watershed, and the arid regions of northern Colombia, northwestern Venezuela, northeastern Brazil and Patagonia in the Atlantic watershed. Within the mountain ranges themselves, there is a great complexity of climatic conditions: desert vegetation in rain shadow areas often occurs within a few dozen kilometres of luxuriant forests in valleys exposed to humid winds from the oceans. The same is true for the Caribbean islands, many of which have strikingly different wet and dry sides.

WETLANDS OF SOUTH AMERICA

The wetlands of South America may be subdivided into three major systems: those of the Pacific lowlands (west of the Andean chain), those of the Andean chain itself, and those of the Atlantic-Caribbean lowlands (north and east of the Andes).

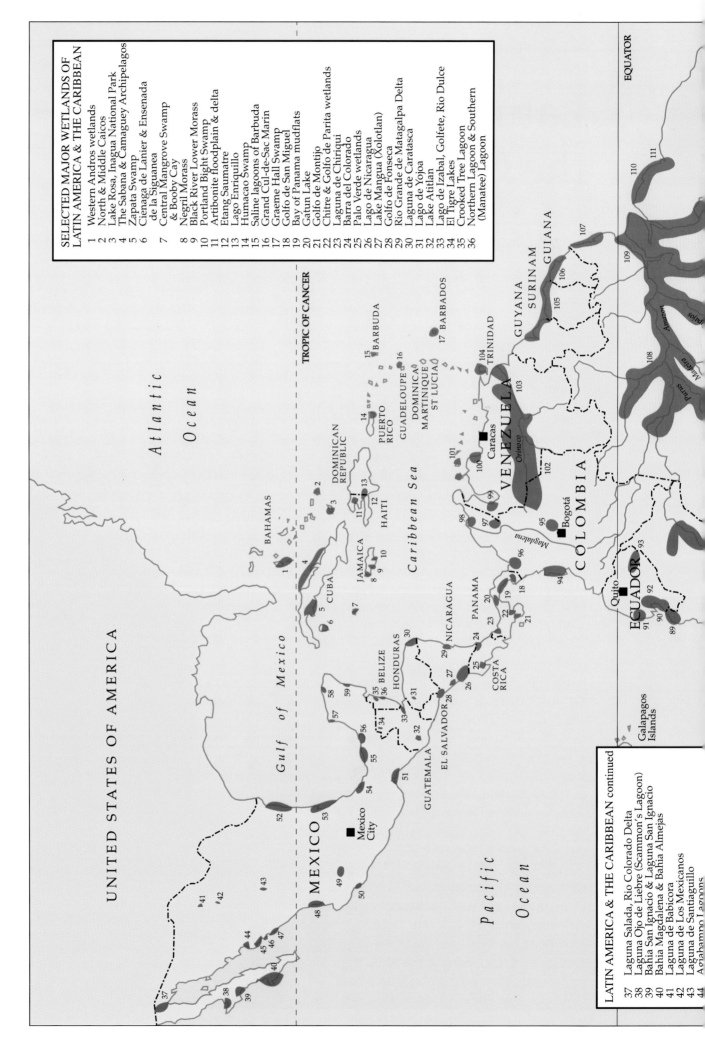

SELECTED MAJOR WETLANDS OF
LATIN AMERICA & THE CARIBBEAN

1 Western Andros wetlands
2 North & Middle Caicos
3 Lake Rosa, Inagua National Park
4 The Sabana & Camaguey Archipelagos
5 Zapata Swamp
6 Cienaga de Lanier & Ensenada
   de la Siguanea
7 Central Mangrove Swamp
   & Booby Cay
8 Negril Morass
9 Black River Lower Morass
10 Portland Bight Swamp
11 Artibonite floodplain & delta
12 Etang Saumatre
13 Lago Enriquillo
14 Humacao Swamp
15 Saline lagoons of Barbuda
16 Grand Cul-de-Sac Marin
17 Graeme Hall Swamp
18 Golfo de San Miguel
19 Bay of Panama mudflats
20 Gatun Lake
21 Golfo de Montijo
22 Chitre & Golfo de Parita wetlands
23 Laguna de Chiriqui
24 Barra del Colorado
25 Palo Verde wetlands
26 Lago de Nicaragua
27 Lake Mangua (Xolotlan)
28 Golfo de Fonseca
29 Rio Grande de Matagalpa Delta
30 Laguna de Caratasca
31 Lago de Yojoa
32 Lake Atitlan
33 Lago de Izabal, Golfete, Rio Dulce
34 El Tigre Lakes
35 Crooked Tree Lagoon
36 Northern Lagoon & Southern
   (Manatee) Lagoon

LATIN AMERICA & THE CARIBBEAN continued

37 Laguna Salada, Rio Colorado Delta
38 Laguna Ojo de Liebre (Scammon's Lagoon)
39 Bahia San Ignacio & Laguna San Ignacio
40 Bahia Magdalena & Bahia Almejas
41 Laguna de Babicora
42 Laguna de Los Mexicanos
43 Laguna de Santiaguillo
44 Agiabampo Lagoons

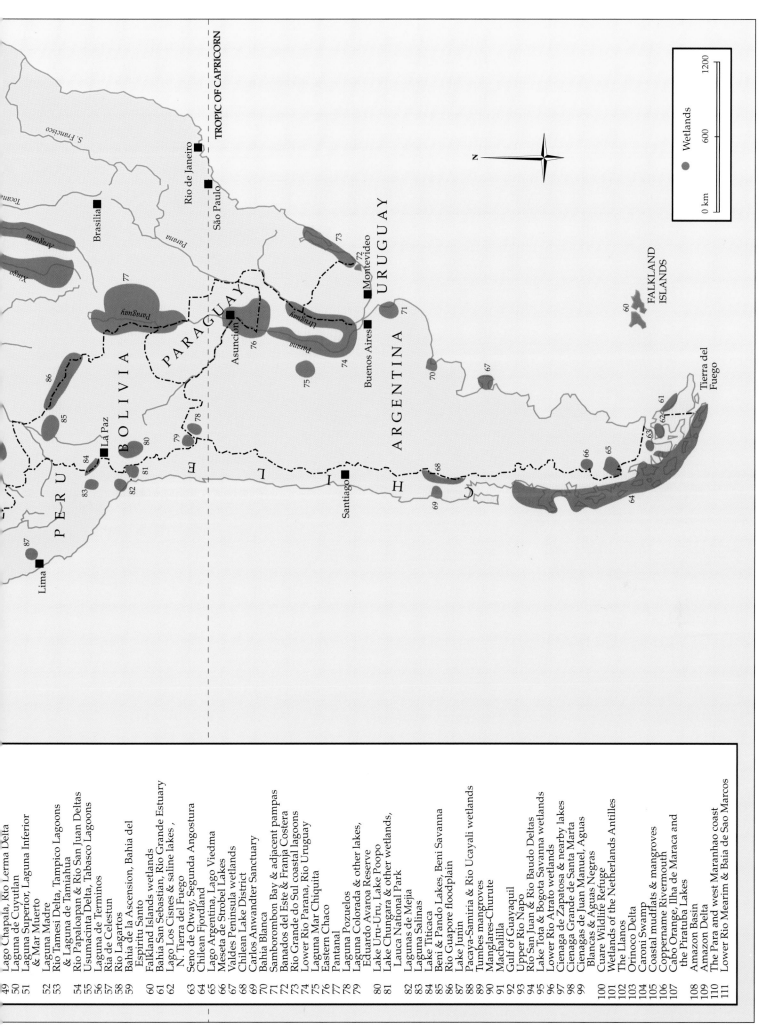

Lake Tota in the Colombian Andes, home to a number of threatened species including the Colombian grebe, last reported in 1977.

The Pacific Lowlands

The entire Pacific coast of South America is dominated by the Andean chain which rises steeply from a narrow coastal plain to altitudes in excess of 6,900 m (22,640 ft). High rainfall in the Pacific watershed of Colombia and Ecuador gives rise to many short, fast-flowing rivers which generally enter the sea through estuarine systems with mangrove swamps. Some of the most important wetlands include extensive mangroves in the deltas of the Rio San Juan and Rio Baudo in Colombia, and a vast complex of riverine and estuarine marshes, freshwater lakes, seasonally flooded grassland, swamp forests and mangrove forests at the head of the Gulf of Guayaquil in Ecuador.

Farther south, semi-desert and desert conditions prevail for over 3,500 km (2,170 miles) from southern Ecuador to central Chile. Mangroves reach their southernmost limit in the extreme north of Peru. The coastal plain then becomes extremely arid; indeed, there are regions of the Atacama Desert in southern Peru and northern Chile where it virtually never rains. The principal wetlands are small brackish coastal lagoons and marshes at the mouths of large rivers rising in the high Andes. One of the best examples is the Lagunas de Mejia in southern Peru, a complex of brackish lagoons and marshes behind a sea-beach, with small freshwater ponds and marshes fed by springs. Plans to drain the wetland for agricultural purposes raised a public outcry which led to the establishment of a nature reserve in 1982.

Increasing rainfall south of the Atacama Desert gives rise to a Mediterranean type of climate in central Chile and a humid temperate climate farther south. Coastal lagoons and estuaries remain the principal wetlands, although there are some small freshwater lakes inland, such as Lago Penuelas near Santiago, and extensive riverine wetlands, particularly in the south. A good example of these is Chile's sole Ramsar site, the Carlos Anwandter Nature and Scientific Investigation Sanctuary. This wetland comprises the braided section of the Cruce River north of Valdivia, with associated swamps and marshy ground. The major part of the wetland was created as a result of earthquake-induced subsidence in 1960.

From Chiloé Island southwards, the coastline is highly indented with countless offshore islands. This region, known as the Chilean Fjordland, includes approximately 6.5 million hectares (16.1 million acres) of wetland habitat. It stretches in a belt up to 220 km (135 miles) wide for over 1,000 km (620 miles) from the Golfo de Guafo in the north to Tierra del Fuego in the south. The coastline is mainly rocky with a few sandy beaches and many small estuaries. Inland, there are numerous freshwater lakes, marshes, wet meadows and areas of seasonally flooded grassland and swamp forest. On the higher ground and in the south, tundra vegetation alternates with boggy areas fed by melting glaciers and snow. Almost the entire region is included within a chain of national parks and forest reserves.

The Andes

Wetlands occur throughout the Andes, from the glacial lakes and paramo wetlands of Venezuela and Colombia in the extreme north to the tundra wetlands, permanent snowfields and glaciers of Tierra del Fuego in the far south.

Many of the wetlands in the northern Andes occur in the paramo zone. Paramo is a humid grass-shrub vegetation that borders the upper limits of temperate forests. Small lakes are scattered throughout the paramo, and bogs occur in poorly drained areas. The largest wetland in this region is Lake Tota, a freshwater lake with extensive fringing marshes at 3,015 m (9,892 ft) above sea level in the highlands of Colombia. Once famous for its endemic fish and large populations of waterbirds, Lake Tota has come under serious pressure from reclamation and development. Although most of the waterbirds are still there, the Colombian grebe (*Podiceps andinus*) is believed to have become extinct in the late 1970s, and the endemic fish have virtually disappeared.

The high Andes of Ecuador also possess a number of freshwater lakes, marshes and bogs in the paramo zone. Some of the more remote wetlands, such as Laguna Cuicocha, a deep crater lake in the Cotacachi-Cayapas Ecological Reserve, and Limpiapungo Paramo in Cotopaxi National Park, remain in almost pristine condition, but most of those at lower elevations are now much degraded and polluted. Lago San Pablo, the second largest lake in Ecuador, has been the victim of shoreline developments and use for recreation activities, while Lago Yaguarcocha is now encircled by an automobile race track.

Farther south, in the Andes of northern and central Peru, there are numerous small lakes and bogs at high altitudes, but very few large lakes, one notable exception being Lake Junín, a freshwater lake of almost 300 km^2 (115 sq miles) in the Andes northeast of Lima. The lake is surrounded by extensive freshwater marshes and up to 10,000 hectares (24,710 acres) of seasonally flooded grassland. Emergent rushes extend up to 6 km (3.7 miles) out into the lake, and provide breeding sites for the endangered Junín grebe (*Podiceps taczanowskii*), a species known only on this lake.

The Andes split into two main branches in southern Peru and northern Bolivia; the plateau (altiplano) between these two branches has an average height of 3,800 m (12,467 ft), and constitutes an enormous inland drainage system with large lakes and salt basins, notably Lake Titicaca, Lake Uru-Uru, Lake Poopo, Salar de Uyuni and Salar de Coipasa. The region is characterized by its rigorous climate with extremely low temperatures and low rainfall;

LAKE TITICACA, BOLIVIA AND PERU

Lake Titicaca is a deep freshwater lake at 3,812 m (12,506 ft) above sea level in the Andes, on the border between Peru and Bolivia. With an area of 828,900 hectares (2.05 million acres), it is the largest lake in South America and the highest large lake in the world. A broad fringe of emergent rushes extends up to 12 km (7 miles) out into the lake. The water supply comes from a number of rivers and streams rising in snow-melt on the surrounding high peaks. The lake has a maximum depth of 272 m (892 ft), the water level fluctuating by about 1 m (just over 3 ft) and reaching its maximum at the end of the rainy season (November to March).

Lake Titicaca near Puno, Peru, with reed boats.

Lake Titicaca supports a thriving Indian community of hunters, fishermen and pastoralists. Fishing is very important in the local economy, the fishermen still using their traditional reed boats. Reeds are also harvested for mat-weaving and other local handicrafts. The seasonally inundated grasslands around the lake support large herds of llamas, alpacas and other domestic livestock.

Lake Titicaca is an extremely important area for most of the waterbird species typical of the high Andes, and is also a major wintering area for some migrant shorebirds from North America. It has a rich and diverse endemic fish fauna, including 14 species of *Orestias*, as well as a large population of introduced trout.

Lake Titicaca is threatened by pollution from domestic sewage, which is causing eutrophication in some bays. Mining in surrounding areas is also polluting the lake with zinc, lead and magnesium, and there is some oil pollution from the heavy boat traffic. Excessive fishing and the introduction of exotic fish species have caused a drastic decline in populations of native fish species, and indiscriminate hunting and the collection of birds' eggs are a problem in some areas. Only two small portions of the lake are protected, both within the Titicaca National Reserve (36,180 hectares - 89,400 acres) in Peru.

Lake Parinacota in Lauca National Park, at 4,520 m (14,829 ft) in the Andes of northern Chile.

the typical puna vegetation consists of dry grassland with low shrubs and cushion plants.

Many of the saline lakes of the altiplano are important for flamingos. One of the most famous is Laguna Salinas in southern Peru, a semi-permanent and very shallow hypersaline lake lying 4,295 m (14,091 ft) above sea level in a basin in the western Andes. This lake regularly supports a high proportion of the world population of James' flamingo (*Phoenicoparrus jamesi*) along with large numbers of Chilean flamingos (*Phoenicopterus chilensis*) and Andean flamingos (*Phoenicoparrus andinus*).

Farther south, there is an important group of saline lakes and bogs at 4,250-5,780 m (13,943-18,963 ft)

above sea level in the Eduardo Avaroa National Faunal Reserve in the southeastern corner of Bolivia. One of the principal lakes is Laguna Colorada, a hypersaline lake of glacial origin with about 100 hectares (247 acres) of ice islands of great antiquity. This lake, the main breeding area for James' flamingo, has a bright orange colour due to the presence of a dense population of the flagellate *Dunaliella salina*.

The altiplano extends still farther south into northern Chile and northwestern Argentina. Some of the finest high Andean wetlands occur at altitudes of 4,500-4,600 m (14,760-15,090 ft) above sea level in Lauca National Park in northern Chile. The 500 km² (192 sq miles) of wetlands in the park include a variety of freshwater, brackish and saline lakes, numerous fast-flowing rivers and streams and large areas of wet meadows (known as bofedales). The most important of the altiplano lakes in northwestern Argentina is Laguna de Pozuelos in Jujuy Province. This saline lake of 10,000 hectares (24,710 acres) supports very large populations of waterbirds and is one of the most important breeding areas for the endangered horned coot (*Fulica cornuta*).

In the southern Andes of Argentina and Chile, a humid temperate climate supports dense deciduous and evergreen forest with extensive wet meadows and peat bogs. The abundant rainfall and snow-melt from permanent snowfields in the high Andes feed a chain of large freshwater lakes along the base of both slopes of the Andes. On the Argentinian side in western Patagonia, the larger lakes include Lago Huechulafquén, Lago Nahuel Huapí, Lago Argentina and Lago Viedma. These lakes, set against a backdrop of forested mountainsides, glaciers and snow-capped peaks, are the centre of a major tourist industry. Most are included within an extensive system of national parks and reserves.

Laguna Salinas, a saline lake famous for its flamingos, on the altiplano of southern Peru, with James' flamingos.

A typical creek on the lower Rio Negro in central Amazonian Brazil. These habitats support a huge diversity of plants and animals.

The so-called Chilean Lake District is no less famous for its scenic grandeur. It consists of a chain of large, deep, freshwater lakes in the foothills of the southern Andes. There are about 300,000 hectares (741,300 acres) of lakes and associated marshes, the principal lakes being Villarrica, Ranco, Puyehue, Rupanco, Todos los Santos and Llanquihue. The region abounds in fast-flowing rivers and streams, and there are numerous small freshwater lakes, marshes and bogs at higher elevations in the Andes. Farther south still, another chain of large freshwater lakes extends through the southern Andes of Chile from Lago Patena in the north to the vast Lago Buenos Aires in the south. Most of these wetlands, the total area of which exceeds 300,000 hectares (741,300 acres), are included within an extensive network of forest reserves and national parks.

The Atlantic and Caribbean Lowlands
The most extensive wetlands in Latin America occur in the lowlands of eastern South America, and are fed by a number of great rivers rising in the Andes and tablelands of central Brazil. In the north, the Caribbean watersheds of Colombia and Venezuela include a number of large rivers with extensive wetlands along their lower courses. Some of the finest examples are the Ciénaga Grande de Santa Marta, a complex of brackish to saline lagoons, mangrove swamps and freshwater lakes near the mouth of the

Río Magdalena in Colombia, and the Ciénagas de Juan Manuel, Aguas Blancas and Aguas Negras, a complex of fresh to brackish lagoons, seasonally flooded alluvial plains and swamp forests on the plains to the west of Lago de Maracaibo in Venezuela. Other wetlands along Venezuela's rather arid Caribbean coast include a number of saline lagoons and estuarine systems with mangrove swamps, such as the wetlands in Cuare Wildlife Refuge, Venezuela's sole Ramsar site.

There are also some small saline lagoons and mangrove swamps on the offshore islands of Aruba, Bonaire and Curaçao in the Netherlands Antilles. Five of these have been listed under the Ramsar Convention, along with the breeding site of Caribbean flamingos (*Phoenicopterus ruber*) situated in the midst of a large complex of saltpans on Bonaire.

Trinidad lies only 12 km (7 1/2 miles) off the Venezuelan coast and its flora and fauna have much more in common with those of the South American mainland than with those of the other Caribbean islands. The island is well watered, with many of the rivers ending in coastal lagoons and mangrove swamps. The largest wetland is Caroni Swamp, a complex of brackish to saline lagoons, mangrove swamps and seasonally inundated marshes near Port of Spain. Large portions of the swamp have been reclaimed for agriculture, and the once famous flocks of scarlet ibis (*Eudocimus ruber*) are now sadly depleted in numbers.

THE LLANOS, VENEZUELA

The Llanos of Venezuela comprise about 180,000 km² (69,480 sq miles) of savanna and 60,000 km² (23,160 sq miles) of semi-deciduous forest, gallery forest and cultivated land in the basin of the Orinoco River. Large areas flood during the rainy season (June to October), creating as much as 10 million hectares (24.7 million acres) of wetlands. These consist of an intricate network of meandering rivers and streams with associated oxbow lakes, riverine marshes and swamp forest, numerous freshwater lakes and ponds, and large areas of inundated grassland and palm savanna dominated by the Llanos palm (*Copernicia tectorum*). By the end of the dry season in April or May, most of the plains are dry, and many of the smaller rivers are reduced to a series of pools.

Much of the region is privately owned in huge cattle ranches. There is also a considerable amount of subsistence agriculture, as well as some fishing and sport hunting. A few landowners are successfully 'farming' capybaras; on one large ranch in Apure state, a population of about 44,000 capybara supports an annual harvest of some 8,000 animals.

The Llanos are famous for their huge concentrations of waterbirds, particularly herons, egrets, storks, ibises and ducks.

The Llanos, Venezuela - part of the Orinoco floodplain, one of the largest wetlands in South America.

Scarlet ibises are common and conspicuous, the breeding population of about 65,000 pairs representing a large proportion of the world population of this species. Two species of tree duck, the white-faced tree duck and the black-bellied tree duck, are particularly abundant, and occur in massive and spectacular concentrations during the moulting season.

The mammalian fauna is also very rich, and there are unusually high densities of capybara and white-tailed deer (*Odocoileus virginianus*). The spectacled caiman is abundant, and the endangered Orinoco crocodile is still present in small numbers.

The principal threat to the wetlands is a general increase in human population and gradual transformation of the natural ecosystems into pasture land and agricultural land. Uncontrolled hunting also poses a major threat to some wildlife species. However, several large protected areas have been established, notably the Aguaro-Guariquito National Park (569,000 hectares - 1.41 million acres) and Estero de Chiriguare Wildlife Refuge (44,500 hectares - 109,960 acres), and some private landowners have taken a considerable interest in conservation, managing their properties on a sound ecological basis.

The Atlantic coast of Venezuela is dominated by the delta of the Orinoco River. This comprises a vast mosaic of some 3 million hectares (7.4 million acres) of mangrove swamps, permanent freshwater swamps with groves of palms, seasonally flooded palm savanna, swamp forest and higher ground with tropical evergreen forest, all interwoven with an intricate network of river channels.

The floodplain of the Orinoco River and its major tributaries comprises one of the largest wetlands in South America - the Llanos of eastern Colombia and Venezuela. Much the greater part of the Llanos lies in Venezuela, stretching in a broad belt from the Colombian border in the west to the Orinoco Delta in the east, but there are very extensive wetlands along several major tributaries of the Orinoco, notably the Arauca, Meta and Vichada, in eastern Colombia.

To the east of the Orinoco Delta as far as the Essequibo River in Guyana, the shoreline is mainly a narrow coral-sand beach. There then begins a series of coastal wetlands which extends through eastern Guyana, Suriname, French Guiana and northern Brazil to the mouth of the Amazon. The extensive tidal mudflats and mangrove swamps along this coast are some of the most productive on the continent, supporting huge numbers of waterbirds, including several million migratory shorebirds (waders) from North America. The mudflats and mangrove swamps are frequently bordered inland by brackish and saline lagoons and swamps, which in turn are bordered by a belt of freshwater marshes with patches of swamp forest and large areas of peat swamp. Some 310,000 hectares (766,000 acres) of coastal wetland survive in Suriname, and one of the most important sites, at the mouth of the Coppename River, has been designated as a Ramsar site. However, in Guyana and French Guiana, large tracts of coastal swamp have been destroyed for agriculture and shrimp farming, and much of this region is now intensively cultivated for sugar cane and rice.

The Amazon River and its tributaries comprise the greatest riverine system on earth, discharging over one-sixth of the freshwater entering the world's oceans. The delta itself comprises some 3.5 million hectares (8.65 million acres) of broad river channels, low-lying islands, mangrove swamps, inter-tidal mudflats, brackish lagoons and marshes, palm swamps and seasonally flooded grassland and swamp forest.

The Amazon and its 1,100 tributaries drain a catchment of about 7 million km² (2.7 million sq miles).

Before the recent massive clearance of forest for agricultural land, the greater part of the basin was under humid tropical forest. Natural non-forested areas include scattered patches of wet and dry savanna, patches of low vegetation on white sand (known as campinas) and extensive floodplain and lake systems along the major rivers. No reliable estimate of the total area of wetland habitat is available. However, it has been estimated that in Brazil alone there are between 70,000 and 100,000 km² (27,000 and 38,600 sq miles) of floodplain habitat, and over 100,000 km² of lakes and swamps.

Two major divisions of aquatic system are widely recognized: black water and white water. Black-water systems arise on sandy soils; the water is a clear dark brown, highly acidic and very poor in nutrients. White-water systems arise mainly in the Andes and foothills; the turbid waters carry large quantities of sediments in suspension and have a fairly high nutrient content. Black waters have a very low productivity, while white waters are highly productive.

All of the major rivers of the Amazon Basin fluctuate widely in water level. Rivers flowing south from the northern parts of the basin reach flood peaks between June and August; those flowing north into the Amazon, peak between February and June.

The Amazon itself usually reaches its maximum level at the end of June. Most of the lakes in the basin are floodplain lakes along the lower courses of these rivers. They are shallow lakes connected with rivers for at least a part of the year, allowing an exchange of nutrients, energy and biological material on an annual basis. Many are oxbow lakes formed in abandoned river channels, and most are subject to wide fluctuations in water level.

Extensive flooding occurs along white-water rivers during the rainy season. Many of the floodplain lakes unite to form vast shallow lakes, and large areas of low-lying forest are inundated. This seasonally flooded forest along the banks of white-water rivers is commonly referred to as varzea. At the height of the flood season, there may be as much as 6.4 million hectares (15.8 million acres) of floodplain lakes and flooded varzea forest along the Solimoes-Amazon alone, in a strip 20-100 km (12-62 miles) wide. Flooding occurs to a lesser extent along black-water rivers, and here the flooded regions are covered by igapo, a characteristic type of forest which can survive flooding for several months of the year.

The coastline east of the Amazon Delta is extremely indented with over 35 major inlets and estuaries fringed with mangrove swamps and separated by headlands with white-sand beaches and coastal sand dunes. The largest wetlands in this region are around São Marcos Bay and in the lower basin of the Río

A water-storage reservoir in Brasilia National Park on the outskirts of Brasilia; one of many in the arid interior of eastern Brazil.

A clear mountain stream in Serra da Canastra National Park, central Brazil: a vanishing habitat and last refuge for the endangered Brazilian merganser.

Mearim. Here there are over a million hectares (2.47 million acres) of wetlands including extensive mangrove swamps, about 80 permanent freshwater lakes and a vast area of seasonally inundated marshes along the lower courses of the Mearim, Pindare and Grajau Rivers. There are many smaller coastal wetlands in eastern Brazil, scattered all along the coast as far south as Rio de Janeiro and São Paulo states. Most are estuarine or lagoon systems with mudflats and mangrove swamps, but many have been reclaimed for agriculture, and almost all of the remainder are under threat, especially from urban development and pollution.

Central Brazil is dominated by the Brazilian Tableland which includes the headwaters of several great rivers, including the Paraguay, Guapore, Tapajós, Xingu, Tocantins and Araguaia. In a few well-protected national parks, the mountain rivers and streams remain clear and unpolluted, and provide a last refuge for the endangered Brazilian merganser (*Mergus octosetaceus*); elsewhere, however, most rivers are heavily silted as a result of severe soil erosion on the vast cattle ranches which dominate the region.

In the upper basin of the Río Paraguay lies one of the world's greatest floodplains - the Pantanal. At its

THE PANTANAL, BRAZIL, PARAGUAY AND BOLIVIA

The great marshy plain of the Pantanal, covering some 200,000 km² (77,200 sq miles), is one of the largest floodplains in the world. It lies in the upper drainage of the Río Paraguay, and comprises a vast region of seasonally flooded palm savannas with an elaborate network of meandering rivers and streams, and numerous small freshwater lakes and marshes. Heavy rainfall during the summer months (December to March) and impeded drainage cause extensive flooding which may persist until the middle of June.

The principal activity throughout the Pantanal is cattle ranching, but fishing is very important in some areas, and hunting is widespread. The wetlands are extremely rich in wildlife, supporting huge breeding populations of waterbirds, a wide variety of mammals, such as the giant river otter,

capybara, marsh deer, common tapir and jaguar (*Leo onca*), as well as two species of caiman, the spectacled caiman and the broad-nosed caiman (*Caiman latirostris*).

In recent decades, there has been a great expansion in agriculture, industrial development and mining activities throughout the region. Massive deforestation in the catchment area of the major rivers has led to severe soil erosion and increased siltation in the wetlands. The construction of huge dams for hydroelectricity and irrigation is altering the hydrology of the entire region, while the pollution of rivers from new industrial developments and pesticide run-off is becoming a serious problem. Gold mining has been particularly harmful, flushing large quantities of sand and clay into the rivers and poisoning plants and animals

with the mercury used in gold extraction.

Illegal hunting of caimans for their skins and the trapping of birds, mammals and reptiles for the international zoo and pet trades now pose a serious threat to many species. Every year, Brazilian poachers kill hundreds of thousands of caimans and smuggle their skins over the border to Bolivia and Paraguay from where they are exported to Europe and North America.

Only two relatively small protected areas have been established in the Pantanal, both in the Brazilian portion. In 1987, the Mato Grosso state government halted all gold mining in the Pantanal lowlands in Brazil, and placed a ban on fish exports in an attempt to prevent further depletion of the threatened fish stocks.

LAGUNA MERIM AND THE BAÑADOS DEL ESTE, BRAZIL AND URUGUAY

Laguna Merim lies at the centre of a huge complex of wetlands (1.2 million hectares - 2.97 million acres) spanning the border between Brazil and Uruguay and separated from the Atlantic Ocean by a broad belt of coastal dunes. The lagoon (in Portuguese Lagoa Mirim) is brackish and supports little emergent vegetation, but there are extensive freshwater marshes, shallow lakes, peat swamps and areas of seasonally flooded grassland and palm savanna to the west and south, especially in the Bañados del Este in Uruguay. The water supply comes from local run-off (mainly winter rainfall) and a number of rivers and streams rising in hilly areas to the west.

The lakes are used for irrigation purposes in summer; there is some commercial fishing, and the region is popular for outdoor recreation. Much of the area is privately owned in large ranches.

These wetlands are amongst the richest for waterbirds in South America, supporting a wide variety of breeding

The Bañados del Este, the first and only Ramsar site in Uruguay.

species, migrants from the southern part of the continent during the austral winter, and migrants from North America during the austral summer. Coscoroba swans and black-necked swans breed here at the northern limit of their ranges, along with many species of duck and three species of coot. The marshes also support large populations of coypu and capybara, along with

much smaller numbers of La Plata otter, marsh deer and broad-nosed caiman.

The principal threats are drainage for pastureland and cultivation, and widespread use of pesticides. There has been an increasing tendency in recent years to move away from ranching to rice-growing, and large areas of wetland have now been converted to rice paddies, particularly in the Bañados del Este. Excessive commercial hunting of fur-bearing mammals has resulted in a drastic decline in numbers of the important species, and this industry is now dying out.

Some 200,000 hectares (494,200 acres) of wetlands in the Bañados del Este were designated as a Biosphere Reserve in 1976 and listed as a Wetland of International Importance under the Ramsar Convention in 1984. On the Brazilian side of the border, over 32,000 hectares (79,000 acres) of lakes, marshes and wet grassland are protected in the Taim Ecological Reserve.

---

southern edge, this borders on the Grand Chaco, a vast low-lying plain extending from eastern Bolivia and Paraguay to northern Argentina.

The western parts of the Chaco lie in the rain shadow of the Andes; rainfall is light, and there are few major wetlands, most notably the Bañados de Figueroa in Argentina. Heavier rainfall in the east, however, gives rise to several very important wetlands, especially along the Río Paraguay and its tributaries. In eastern Paraguay alone there are some 4.5 million hectares (11.1 million acres) of wetlands, comprising a vast complex of seasonally flooded grasslands and palm savannas, with numerous small permanent freshwater lakes and marshes. Most of the area dries out completely from April to August, but with the onset of the rains and flooding from the Río Paraguay, huge areas are inundated.

Similar wetlands occur farther south in the humid Chaco plains of northern Argentina. By far the most extensive of these are the Bajos Submeridionales in Chaco and Santa Fé provinces, a million hectares (2.47 million acres) of permanent and seasonal lakes and marshes, swamp forests and seasonally inundated palm savannas on the west bank of the Río Paraná.

In the semi-desert areas to the south of the Chaco, there are several isolated wetlands, the largest of which is Laguna Mar Chiquita (200,000 hectares - 490,000 acres) in Córdoba province. This is a highly saline lake with some brackish marshes and tamarisk thickets at the mouths of rivers, and vast

areas of mudflat during the dry season.

The wetlands of the humid eastern Chaco are contiguous in the east and south with extensive wetlands that run along the lower reaches of the Paraguay, Paraná and Uruguay Rivers in the basin of the Río de la Plata. The Pantanal de Neembucú of southern Paraguay is one such wetland covering 800,000 hectares (1.98 million acres) between the confluence of the Paraguay and Paraná Rivers. In neighbouring Argentina, there is a similar but even larger wetland, the Esteros del Ibera, comprising 1.1 million hectares (2.7 million acres) of freshwater lakes and swamps with extensive floating vegetation, slow-flowing rivers and streams shaded by gallery forest, and seasonally inundated grassland.

The extreme south of Brazil has a temperate climate and a landscape similar to that of neighbouring Uruguay and Argentina. Mangroves extend south along the coast to 28° 30 South; from there almost as far as Montevideo in Uruguay the shoreline is a sandy beach backed by dunes and a succession of freshwater lakes and brackish lagoons. The largest of these is Lagoa dos Patos (985,000 hectares - 2.43 million acres), the largest lake in Brazil. It is a deep freshwater lake 250 km (155 miles) in length with a broad connection with the sea at Rio Grande. Farther south still, Lagoa Mirim, Lagoa Mangueira and a number of smaller lakes and marshes comprise a vast coastal wetland system spanning the border between Brazil and Uruguay.

The vast humid grasslands or pampas of Argentina

The low human population density has meant that numerous unspoilt wetlands remain in the Pampas region of Argentina.

are dotted with numerous shallow lakes, permanent swamps and seasonal marshes noted for their large concentrations of waterbirds. One of the most extensive wetland areas occurs around Samborombón Bay on the south shore of the Río de la Plata estuary. Here the extensive inter-tidal mudflats and tidal salt marshes are backed by a broad belt of seasonally flooded marshes and low-lying grassland dissected by numerous canals and streams.

To the south, the pampas give way to the much colder and drier steppe-like plains of Patagonia. There are many important lake systems on these plains, especially on the Meseta de Strobel, a basaltic plateau in Santa Cruz province. The 540 lakes in this region are extremely important for breeding ducks, geese, swans and shorebirds, and support almost the entire world population of the recently discovered hooded grebe (*Podiceps gallardoi*). Along the Patagonian coast, there are several huge bays and estuarine systems with extensive tidal mudflats important for migratory shorebirds. Chief amongst these are Bahía Blanca in the north, the complex of bays around the Valdés Peninsula in Chubut province, and Bahía Bustamente and Golfo San Jorge in the south.

In the extreme south, the rolling plains of eastern Tierra del Fuego comprise a region of bleak, windswept grasslands and tundra with numerous freshwater lakes, marshes and peat bogs supporting large breeding populations of ducks and sheldgeese. Along the east coast of the island, there are extensive inter-tidal mudflats which, in the austral summer, provide 'wintering areas' for large numbers of Hudsonian godwits (*Limosa haemastica*), red knots (*Calidris canutus*) and white-rumped sandpipers (*Calidris fuscicollis*) from breeding grounds in the Arctic.

Out in the South Atlantic, less than 400 km (250 miles) northeast of Cape Horn, lie the Falkland Islands, a group of rather low islands with gently sloping hills rising to no more than 700 m (230 ft). Over most of the islands, the soil is blanket peat of variable thickness dotted with countless shallow freshwater ponds and marshes. There are, however, no large lakes or extensive marshes, and estuaries are very small with limited areas of mud in some bays.

WETLANDS OF MIDDLE AMERICA
The wetlands of Middle America can be subdivided into three major groups: those of the temperate zone which includes Baja California, the northern coast of the Gulf of Mexico and the interior highlands of

Mexico and Guatemala; those of the tropical Pacific lowlands; and those of the tropical Gulf coast and Caribbean lowlands. The wetlands of the temperate zone show close affinities in their flora and fauna to those of the United States, and are generally regarded as lying within the same bio-geographical region (the Nearctic Realm). Some of the most important coastal wetlands in this zone are Laguna Madre and the extensive delta marshes of the Río Grande on the Gulf coast. Others are a chain of shallow sea bays, estuarine systems and coastal lagoons in Baja California such as Bahía San Quintin, Laguna Ojo de Liebre and Bahía Almejas.

The interior highlands of northern and central Mexico consist of an immense plateau bordered by two great mountain systems with peaks rising to over 3,000 m (9,800 ft). Almost the entire plateau is dry; in the past, there were numerous natural freshwater and brackish lakes with extensive marshes on this plateau, but many have dried out as a result of natural causes; others have been either seriously reduced in size or completely drained for agriculture and urban development. Of those that remain, several are noted for their large populations of waterbirds, while others are renowned for their endemic turtles, salamanders, fishes and snails.

In the highlands of Guatemala, much the largest lake is Lago de Atitlán, a large freshwater lake to the west of Guatemala City. The water level fluctuates by up to 22 m (72 ft) on a 40 year cycle; the lake is currently in the low phase of this long-term cycle. The level dropped by 7 m (23 ft) during an earthquake in 1976, and as a result, much of the fringing marsh vegetation disappeared.

The tropical lowlands on the Gulf coast of Mexico are well watered and rich in wetlands. The broad coastal plain is crossed by numerous rivers many of which form large deltas with extensive lagoon systems and marshy areas subject to seasonal flooding. One of the most extensive of these wetlands is the Usumacinta Delta and associated lagoons on the plains of Tabasco. Other wetlands of comparable significance include the Tampico lagoons and extensive delta marshes of the Río Tamesi and Río Panuco in the north, the deltas of the Río Papaloapán and Río San Juan in Veracruz and Laguna de Terminos in Campeche.

Much of the Yucatán Peninsula is a calcareous plain with subterranean water courses which come to the surface near the coast and give rise to a series of coastal lagoons and marshes. A chain of saline lagoons and small estuaries along the north shore of the peninsula supports a large breeding population of Caribbean flamingos. One of the most important sites, Río Lagartos, has been designated a Ramsar site. The largest wetland complex on the east coast of the peninsula is at Bahía de la Ascensión and Bahía del Espíritu Santo (Sian Ka'an) in Quintana Roo. These two large shallow sea bays are studded with numerous mangrove-covered islands and are fringed by extensive mangrove swamps. The mangroves back on to a vast area of shallow lagoons, swamps and seasonally flooded savannas. The entire region, which spreads over 528,147 hectares (1,304,523 acres), was established as a Biosphere Reserve and World Heritage site in 1986, and is now the third largest protected area in Mexico.

Farther south, there are extensive mangrove

USUMACINTA DELTA, MEXICO

Covering about 1 million hectares (2.47 million acres), the Usumacinta Delta is the most extensive wetland on the Gulf coast of Mexico. The delta marshes comprise a vast complex of freshwater lagoons, swamps and seasonally inundated plains, within a maze of distributary channels belonging to the Río Usumacinta and several other large rivers rising in the Chiapas Highlands to the south. Gallery forest extends in fingers along the main river channels. There are tidal lagoons and forested beach ridges along the coast, backed by brackish lagoons and mangrove swamps. Extensive flooding occurs throughout the region during the summer rainy season.

The nutrient-laden waters of the rivers support a major commercial

fishery. Shrimp production plays an important role in the local economy, and is dependent on the delta lagoons which provide the nursery grounds for the juvenile shrimps. There is also a considerable amount of subsistence hunting in the delta, as well as some forestry, agriculture and livestock grazing.

The delta marshes are noted for their rich and diverse fauna, and are especially important as a breeding and wintering area for waterbirds. The huge breeding colonies of herons, egrets, storks, ibises and spoonbills were estimated to contain about 250,000 birds in the late 1970s. Large numbers of shorebirds come here on passage, and in winter the marshes teem with migratory ducks and coots from breeding grounds

in North America. The West Indian manatee still occurs in small numbers, along with the endangered Morelet's crocodile (*Crocodylus moreletii*).

Huge oilfields have been discovered beneath the region, and their development is likely to cause tremendous ecological damage. There have already been serious incidences of oil pollution, and most rivers and lagoons have now been affected. Drainage for agriculture poses an ever-increasing threat, and mangroves are being heavily exploited for timber in some areas. Nevertheless, large parts of the delta are difficult to get to and remain relatively undisturbed. Several studies have been made on the natural resources of the delta, but no special protection measures have yet been taken.

swamps, freshwater lakes and saline lagoons in the lowlands of Belize. The coastal waters are generally shallow, and there is an almost continuous line of reefs and small coral islands (cays) 20-90 kms (12 1/2-56 miles) offshore, stretching the full length of the country. This comprises the longest barrier reef in the Northern Hemisphere.

The Caribbean lowlands of Guatemala are also rich in wetlands. Most of the country's lakes are located in this region, including the largest, Lago de Izabal, a slightly brackish lake with extensive fringing marshes and some swamp forest. The lake drains into the Caribbean through the Río Dulce, a very slow-flowing river with a lake-like section (Golfete) up to 7 km (4 1/2 miles) wide. Winter flooding creates one vast freshwater lake, but in summer, as water levels fall, seawater flows back up the Río Dulce into Lago de Izabal which then becomes brackish.

The Caribbean lowlands of Honduras, Nicaragua, Costa Rica and Panama are traversed by numerous rivers which enter the sea through extensive coastal lagoons and deltas. Mangrove swamps occur widely along the coast and are particularly extensive around some of the larger lagoons. The most important wetlands along this coast include Laguna de Caratasca in Honduras, the delta systems of the Río Grande de Matagalpa and Río Kurinwas in Nicaragua, a complex of lakes, lagoons and palm

swamps at Barra del Colorado in Costa Rica, and the Sansan, Changuinola and Chiriqui lagoons in Panama.

The Pacific coast of Middle America is generally much drier than the Caribbean coast. Nevertheless, important wetlands do occur along the entire length of the coast from the Gulf of California to eastern Panama. Most are brackish to saline lagoons, river deltas and estuarine systems with extensive mangrove swamps. One of the last large wetland areas which remains relatively intact on the Pacific coast of Mexico is the Marismas Nacionales in Sinaloa and Nayarit, a vast network of brackish lagoons, mangrove swamps, mudflats and marshes. One of the largest wetlands on the Pacific coast of Central America is the Golfo de Fonseca, an extensive system of estuaries with inter-tidal mudflats, mangrove swamps and sand beaches around a large sea bay shared by El Salvador, Honduras and Nicaragua. The section in Nicaragua, known as Estero Real, includes some of the largest stands of mangroves on the entire coast.

The coastal zone of southern Nicaragua includes two vast freshwater lakes, Lake Managua and Lake Nicaragua, both of which have large areas of permanent and seasonally flooded marshes. Lake Nicaragua (870,000 hectares - 2.15 million acres) is much the larger of the two, with extensive marshes along the north shore and at the mouth of the Río

Lake Atitlán in Guatemala, home of the Atitlán grebe which is believed to have become extinct within the last few years.

Humacao Swamp, the largest wetland in Puerto Rico, is threatened by pollution and urban and agricultural development.

Pacora. Farther east, there are extensive freshwater lakes and marshes in Palo Verde National Park and Wildlife Refuge in Costa Rica and many fresh to brackish lagoons, marshes and mangrove swamps on the Golfo de Parita in Panama. A broad strip of inter-tidal mudflats, mangrove swamps and brackish marshes stretches eastwards along the shores of the Bay of Panama for 130 km (80 miles) from the southern entrance of the Panama Canal to Punta Brujas. During the dry season (January to mid-April), the upwelling of nutrient-rich waters in the bay supports huge populations of crustaceans, fish and waterbirds.

WETLANDS OF THE CARIBBEAN

Many of the Caribbean islands have important wetlands, mostly coastal lagoons, mangrove swamps and inter-tidal mudflats, although some of the higher volcanic islands possess interesting freshwater lakes in old volcanic craters. Despite their relatively small size, many of these wetlands are of considerable interest because so many of their flora and fauna are endemic.

The principal wetlands in Bermuda, the Bahamas, the Turks and Caicos Islands and the Cayman Islands are mangrove swamps, shallow brackish lagoons and inter-tidal mudflats. Almost every island contains some wetland habitat, and several of the Bahama islands, notably Grand Bahama, Abaco, Andros and Great Inagua, have enormous wetlands. The largest is a complex of mudflats, brackish lagoons and mangrove swamps covering some 270,000 hectares (667,000 acres) on the western side of Andros island. 'Blue holes' occur throughout this area; these are inland pools connected to the sea through subterranean cave systems.

Cuba has the most extensive wetlands in the Caribbean, principally shallow sea bays with fringing mudflats and mangroves swamps, brackish coastal lagoons and small offshore islands or cays. Much the most important wetlands, for their unique flora and fauna, are the vast swamps of the Zapata Peninsula on the main island and Ciénaga de Lanier on La Juventud (Isle of Pines). Both are complexes of fresh to brackish lakes, saline lagoons and seasonally flooded sawgrass swamps adjacent to shallow sea bays. With an area of 340,000 hectares (840,000 acres), Zapata Swamp is the largest wetland of its type in the Caribbean.

Most of Jamaica's wetlands are shallow sea bays,

ZAPATA SWAMP, CUBA

Zapata Swamp (340,000 hectares - 840,140 acres) is much the largest wetland in the Caribbean. It comprises a vast complex of brackish to saline lagoons and marshes, mangrove swamps and inter-tidal mudflats along the Zapata Peninsula. Much of the wetland consists of sawgrass swamps with wooded hummocks, and there is only one significant freshwater lake, Laguna del Tesoro. Extensive flooding occurs during the rainy season (May to October). Most of the marshes dry out during the dry season, but there are numerous small hollows (casimbas) that remain flooded and provide dry season refuges for crocodiles and turtles.

The swamp supports a wide variety of wildlife, but is of special importance for the high number of endemic and endangered species which occur there. It is the only known locality for the Zapata rail (*Cyanolimnas cerverai*), the Zapata wren (*Ferminia cerverai*) and nominate race of the Zapata sparrow (*Torreornis inexpectata*), and is the most important breeding area for the endangered Cuban race of the sandhill crane (*Grus canadensis nesiotes*). The West Indian manatee still occurs in small numbers, but the very rare dwarf hutia (*Capromys nanus*), a small rodent known only from the swamp, has not been reported since 1937 and may now be extinct. Reptiles include an endemic sub-species of the lizard *Anolis luteogularis* and a small population of the endangered Cuban crocodile. Unfortunately, most of the crocodiles have been moved to enclosures at Laguna del Tesoro where there has been hybridization with captive American crocodiles (*Crocodylus acutus*).

An introduced mongoose (*Herpestes auropunctatus*) has recently invaded the swamp and could pose a serious threat to the Zapata wren. The only other serious problem has been accidental fires, which have destroyed large areas of marsh vegetation in the past, and could pose a threat to the Zapata rail. Some 300,000 hectares (741,300 acres) of the swamp are protected in the Zapata National Park, an important regional centre for outdoor recreation and nature tourism.

---

tidal creeks or brackish to saline lagoons with mangrove swamps. There are, however, two large peat swamp systems, the Black River Lower Morass along the Black River and the Negril Morass near the western tip of the island. Both are under threat from peat mining, and the Negril Morass has been greatly modified by drainage, which has led to a spread of sawgrass and invasion by shrubs and trees.

The most extensive wetlands in Haiti are the floodplain and delta of the Artibonite River. These comprise some 47,500 hectares (117,325 acres) of brackish coastal lagoons, mangrove swamps, seasonally flooded marshes and saline flats along the lower reaches of the Artibonite River. Here, as else-where in Haiti, extensive tracts of freshwater marsh have been converted into rice paddies, but the country's largest inland lake, Étang Saumâtre, and most of the 22,000 hectares (54,340 acres) of coastal mangrove swamps have remained more or less undisturbed.

In the neighbouring Dominican Republic, much of the land is mountainous and rather arid. Nevertheless, there are several important lakes and lagoons, much the largest of which is Lago Enriquillo (26,500 hectares - 65,455 acres), a land-locked hypersaline lake near the Haitian border. It lies at 46 m (151 ft) below sea level in an old sea channel, and is of considerable scientific interest as a fossil marine ecosystem. The water is sulphuric, and the salinity can rise to as high as 90 parts per thousand.

Puerto Rico is the easternmost and smallest of the Greater Antilles. Although there are few permanent rivers, subterranean water courses are abundant and there are some important thermal springs with sulphurous waters - at the Baños de Coamo, for example. The largest wetland is Humacao Swamp, a complex of fresh to brackish lagoons, mangrove swamps, herbaceous swamps and seasonally flooded marshes along the Anton Ruiz River, with a small patch of *Pterocarpus* swamp forest.

The Lesser Antilles comprise a chain of hundreds of small islands stretching in an arc from the Virgin Islands near the eastern end of Puerto Rico to the island of Grenada, only 150 km (93 miles) off the Venezuelan coast. The islands are divided into no fewer than 14 political entities, all of which possess some wetlands. The great majority of the wetlands are saline lagoons and mangrove swamps, although there are interesting freshwater marshes and patches of *Pterocarpus officinalis* swamp forest on some of the larger islands, and deep crater lakes on several of the volcanic islands, such as Soufrière Lake on St Vincent. The largest saline lagoon is Grand Étang de Simsonbaai (1,250 hectares - 3,088 acres) on St-Martin, and the most extensive mangrove swamp is in the Grand Cul-de-Sac Marin (7,000 hectares - 17,290 acres) on Guadeloupe. Although all of the wetlands are small by continental standards, collectively they support a rich and diverse flora and fauna, and are of considerable importance for migratory birds.

FLORA

Throughout tropical Latin America and the Caribbean, shallow freshwater lakes and permanent swamps support a luxuriant growth of aquatic vegetation often dominated by tall stands of cattail or reedmace (*Typha* species) and extensive floating mats of water hyacinth (*Eichhornia crassipes*). Below the surface, hornwort (*Ceratophyllum*), bladderworts (*Utricularia* species) and wild celery (*Vallisneria*) are often abundant. Widespread floating species include

Regalia lilies near Manaus in central Amazonian Brazil.

water lilies (*Nymphaea* and *Nymphoides* species), water lettuce (*Pistia stratiotes*), and several species of water ferns (*Salvinia*), mosquito ferns (*Azolla*) and duckweeds (*Lemna*). Common species in the emergent marsh vegetation include *Montrichardia arborescens*, spike-rushes (*Eleocharis*), club-rushes or bulrushes (*Scirpus*), nut grasses (*Cyperus*), marsh grasses (*Paspalum* and *Paspalidium*) and ferns of the genus *Acrostichum* which also occur in mangrove swamps.

Along the rivers of the Amazon Basin, newly formed sandbanks are first colonized by thickets of willows (*Salix* and *Tessaria* species). These are succeeded by a transitional forest dominated by species of fig (*Ficus*), *Cecropia* and *Erythrina*. Dense stands of the tall cane (a *Gynerium* species) are also typical of this habitat, which is often known as zabolo. In some of the quieter backwaters, the spectacular regalia lily (*Victoria amazonica*) grows in profusion and forms a firm platform for courting frogs and jacanas. Swampy areas around oxbow lakes are dominated by species of rushes and sedges, with scattered stands of the palm *Mauritia flexuosa*.

Large tracts of permanently swampy forest and

seasonally flooded forest occur in low-lying areas along many of the major rivers, varzea on white-water rivers and igapo on black-water rivers.

The vast seasonally flooded savannas to the north and south of the Amazon Basin, such as the Llanos and the Pantanal, are characterized by open grasslands with species of *Paspalum, Stipa* and *Andropogon*, interspersed with groves of palms. Tall gallery forest and dense scrub often occur as belts of varying width along river courses. North of the Amazon, *Mauritia flexuosa* is the most abundant palm; in the Pantanal and humid eastern Chaco of Paraguay and northern Argentina, *Copernicia australis* predominates.

On the cold and windswept plains of Patagonia, Tierra del Fuego and the Falkland Islands, most lakes have little emergent vegetation, although some are almost entirely covered with extensive beds of water milfoil (*Myriophyllum* species) and some have dense submergent beds of horned pondweed (*Zanichellia*) and pondweeds (*Potamogeton* species).

Most wetlands in the highlands of Mexico and Central America lie below 2,000 m (6,560 ft) above sea level and support a mixture of tropical and temperate species. Characteristic aquatic plants include stoneworts (*Chara* species), ditch grass (*Ruppia*), naiad (*Najas*), wild celery, pondweed, water lily, lotus (*Nelumbo nucifera*), water hyacinth, mosquito fern and duckweeds. The marshes are typically dominated by reedmace, club-rush, nut grass and witch grass (*Panicum*).

By contrast, most of the large wetlands in the Andes lie over 3,500 m (11,480 ft) above sea level in the temperate and alpine zones. Deep glacial lakes and salt lakes generally have little aquatic vegetation other than phytoplankton and algae, but many of the shallower freshwater lakes support a rich growth of pondweed, bladderwort, stonewort, water milfoil, mosquito fern and duckweed, and are surrounded by extensive marshes and areas of seasonally inundated grassland. Some of the larger lakes, such as Lake Titicaca and Lake Junín, support vast emergent stands of reedmace and the rushes *Scirpus californicus* and *Schoenoplectus tatora*. The marsh vegetation typically includes species of pennyworts (*Hydrocotyle*), persicarias (*Polygonum*), docks (*Rumex*), sedges (*Carex*) and rushes (*Juncus*), while the seasonally flooded grasslands are dominated by species of spike-rush, small-reed (*Calamagrostis*) and *Distichia*.

Many of the large freshwater lakes in the southern Andes are steep-sided and deep, supporting little emergent aquatic vegetation except at the deltas of rivers. Here there are often extensive *Phragmites* reed beds and marshy meadows with species of plantain (*Plantago*), pennywort, dock and rush, and the grass *Holcus lanatus*.

Throughout tropical Latin America and the Caribbean, the dominant vegetation in most coastal wetlands is mangrove forest. Mangroves occur widely along the Pacific coast from the lower Gulf of California in Mexico to the Tumbes region in the extreme north of Peru, and along the Atlantic coast from the Gulf coast of Mexico to Santa Catarina in southern Brazil. They also occur throughout the Caribbean islands, and as far north as Bermuda. In 1983, there were estimated to be some 67,000 km^2 (25,860 sq miles) of mangroves in the New World, with 37 per cent of these in Brazil.

In contrast to the mangrove ecosystems of the Old World, however, those in the New World are remarkably poor in species. Only four species of true mangrove, black mangrove (*Avicennia germinans*), buttonwood (*Conocarpus erectus*), white mangrove (*Laguncularia racemosa*) and red mangrove (*Rhizophora mangle*) are at all common and widespread. There are, though, a few other species which commonly grow in association with mangroves, notably mangrove ferns, the palm *Mauritia flexuosa* and the swamp forest tree *Pterocarpus officinalis*. The last of these normally grows in freshwater, and is the dominant tree species

Paramo vegetation at Paramo Chisacal near Bogotá in the high Andes of Colombia.

Dense mats of the floating and purple-flowered water hyacinth at a lowland swamp in Brazil.

Igapo forest on the lower Rio Negro, a black-water river near Manaus in central Amazonian Brazil.

in many of the freshwater swamp forests of Central America and the Caribbean.

Saline coastal lagoons typically have little if any aquatic vegetation, although salt-tolerant species such as glasswort (*Salicornia*), cord grass (*Spartina*) and saltwort (*Batis maritima*) may grow around their margins. Brackish systems often support extensive marshes dominated by reedmace, sawgrass (*Cladium*), club-rush, nut grass, spike-rush and witch grass, while some coastal lagoons have extensive beds of wigeon grass (*Ruppia maritima*) or turtle grass (*Thalassia testudinum*) and algae of the genera *Chara, Enteromorpha, Spyrog ra* and *Chlorella*.

FAUNA

The wetlands of Latin America support an extremely diverse fish fauna, but our knowledge of many regions remains fragmentary; it is certain that numerous species remain unknown to science. Thus, for example, studies in the Amazon Basin during the past 15 years have recorded some 3,000 species of fish of which 300 to 400 were new to science. Well-known fishes of the great riverine and floodplain systems of northern and central South America include several huge catfish of the Siluriformes, the notorious piranha (*Serrasalmus*) species and the electric eel (*Electrophorus electricus*). In Central America and the Caribbean, many wetlands such as Crooked Tree Lagoon in Belize and Caroni Swamp in Trinidad are famous for their large

tarpon (*Megalops atlantica*), a popular sport fish.

The region also possesses a wide variety of amphibians, although again our knowledge remains rather fragmentary. One of the most widespread and conspicuous species is the giant toad (*Bufo marinus*). Unfortunately, no fewer than eight amphibian species are thought to be endangered, including the giant frog (*Batrachophrynus macrostomus*), known only from Lake Junín in Peru, and three species of *Ambystoma* salamander, each of which is known only from a single locality in the highlands of Mexico. One of these is the axolotl (*Ambystoma mexicanum*) of Lago Xochimilco near Mexico City.

Of the numerous aquatic reptiles in the tropical regions of the New World, much the most conspicuous are the freshwater turtles, terrapins, crocodiles and caimans. Freshwater turtles are particularly common along river banks and around oxbow lakes in the Amazon Basin. Many of the larger species, such as the South American river turtle (*Podocnemis expansa*), yellow-spotted sideneck turtle (*Podocnemis unifilis*) and red-headed Amazon turtle (*Podocnemis erythrocephala*), have been subjected to heavy hunting pressure and are now rare and

The giant coot is found in high Andean lakes from south Peru to northern Chile and Argentina.

declining, although some other species that are commonly hunted for food, such as the mud turtle (*Kinosternon scorpioides*), seem to be holding their own.

Of the nine crocodilians occurring in the region, seven are threatened by massive exploitation for the skin trade. Two species, the Cuban crocodile (*Crocodylus rhombifer*) and the Orinoco crocodile (*Crocodylus intermedius*), are now on the verge of extinction. The spectacled caiman (*Caiman crocodilus*) remains widespread over much of South and Central America despite heavy hunting pressure, but the other four crocodilian species are all declining rapidly throughout their ranges and are now extinct in many areas.

Despite their vast extent, the wetlands of Latin America are home to few species of mammal.

Two large rodents, the capybara (*Hydrochoerus hydrochaeris*) and the coypu (*Myocastor coypus*), remain common and widespread through most of the region, despite being hunted on a large scale for their fur. The capybara is particularly abundant in the Llanos, and is reported to be increasing in Amazonia as the clearance of forest for agriculture and ranching provides increased feeding areas. The seven small cetaceans of South American rivers include the scarce Amazon river dolphin (*Inia geoffrensis*) in the Amazon Basin and La Plata dolphin (*Pontoporia blainvillei*) in the basin of the Río de la Plata, as well as five more common river dolphins of the genus *Sotalia*.

Otters occur throughout the region, but all eight species are hunted for their fur. Intensive hunting has brought the giant river otter (*Pteronura brasiliensis*), the world's largest otter, to the verge of extinction throughout much of its range in Amazonia and central South America; and the marine otter (*Lutra felina*) of coastal Peru and Chile, La Plata otter (*Lutra platensis*) of the basin of the Río de la Plata and southern river otter (*Lutra provocax*) of the southern Andes are all under serious threat.

Hunting also poses a serious threat to the region's two species of manatee, the Amazonian manatee (*Trichechus inunguis*) and the West Indian manatee (*Trocjecjis manatus*). The former is almost exclusively a freshwater species, occurring widely in the Amazon Basin, while the latter inhabits estuaries and coastal waters from southern Mexico and the Caribbean to northeastern Brazil. Manatees are exclusively herbivorous, consuming vast quantities of aquatic vegetation every day. This habit has recently been put to good use in Brazil, where the Amazonian manatee has been introduced into reservoirs to control the spread of aquatic vegetation.

The marsh deer (*Blastocercus dichotomus*) is an inhabitant of the vast floodplain wetlands of central South America from central Brazil and the Pantanal south to the basin of the Río de la Plata in Argentina. This too has been widely hunted, and is now considered to be a threatened species through most of its range. The two lowland species of tapir, the common tapir (*Tapirus terrestris*) of South America

and Baird's tapir (*Tapirus bairdi*) of Central America, are commonly found in and around wetlands, although they spend much of their time foraging in the rain forest.

As might be expected, the wetlands of Latin America and the Caribbean are home to a great diversity of waterbirds. No fewer than 255 species occur either as resident breeding species or regular winter visitors from North America. Of the resident species, 145 are endemic to the region, occurring nowhere else in the world. Some familiar groups of the Northern Hemisphere, such as divers, true geese and cranes, extend no farther south than Mexico, but these deficiencies are more than compensated for by a great diversity within some groups such as grebes (12 species), ibises (12 species), flamingos (4 species) and coots (8 species), and endemic groups such as the screamers, sheldgeese and sunbittern (*Eurypyga helias*).

Most resident species remain common, only 23 are threatened with extinction. Unfortunately, the prospects for several of these are exceptionally bleak. The Atitlán grebe (*Podilymbus gigas*) and Colombian grebe both appear to have become extinct within the last 15 years, and the extinction of the Junín grebe, which numbered only about 100 individuals in 1987, now seems imminent. The attractive little ruddy-headed goose (*Chloephaga rubidiceps*), once so

Brown pelicans nesting in mangroves in the Galapagos Islands National Park, established in 1936.

Crabs and other invertebrates inhabit the damp coastal forest wetlands such as those in Costa Rica.

Heavily grazed pastures around Laguna Salinas, a saline lake on the altiplano of southern Peru.

numerous in Patagonia that it was persecuted as an agricultural pest, is now all but extinct on the South American mainland, although it remains common in the Falkland Islands. The Brazilian merganser, once widespread along rivers and streams in central Brazil, Paraguay and northern Argentina, now survives only in remote upland areas with clear waters unaffected by forestry and ranching activities. In the Caribbean, the West Indian tree duck (*Dendrocygna arborea*) is suffering a similar fate, as more and more of its wetland habitats are being destroyed to make room for tourist developments, marinas and golf courses.

Some of the characteristic breeding species of

The scarlet ibis, at a breeding colony in the Llanos in Venezuela, is vulnerable to habitat loss and disturbance.

lowland lakes, swamps and floodplains in tropical Latin America include the olivaceous cormorant (*Phalacrocorax olivaceus*), anhinga (*Anhinga anhinga*), a wide variety of herons and egrets, three species of stork, several species of ibis, roseate spoonbill (*Ajaia ajaja*), three species of tree duck (*Dendrocygna*), Muscovy duck (*Cairina moschata*), Brazilian duck (*Amazonetta brasiliensis*), limpkin (*Aramus guarauna*), purple gallinule (*Porphyrula martinica*), sun grebe (*Heliornis fulica*), wattled jacana (*Jacana jacana*), southern lapwing (*Vanellus chilensis*) and black skimmer (*Rynchops niger*).

In the temperate regions of southern Chile and Argentina, ducks, geese, swans and shorebirds predominate, common breeding species including black-necked swan (*Cygnus melancoryphus*), Coscoroba swan (*Coscoroba coscoroba*), upland goose (*Chloephaga picta*), ashy-headed goose (*Chloephaga poliocephala*), steamer ducks (*Tachyeres*), many dabbling ducks (*Anas*), three species of coot (*Fulica*) and various oystercatchers, plovers and dotterels. Another group of species occurs only on wetlands in the high Andes; these include short-winged grebe (*Rollandia micropterum*), puna ibis (*Plegadis ridgwayi*), Andean flamingo, James' flamingo, Andean goose (*Chloephaga melanoptera*), giant coot (*Fulica gigantea*), Andean avocet (*Recurvirostra andina*), Andean lapwing (*Vanellus resplendens*) and puna plover (*Charadrius alticola*).

The majority of breeding species in South America are either sedentary or only short distance migrants. Many species concentrate around permanent lakes and swamps during the dry season, and spread out onto the floodplains during the rains, while others, breeding high in the Andes, undertake altitudinal migrations with the changing seasons, but there is nothing to compare with the mass migrations of waterbirds in the Northern Hemisphere. Even in mid-winter, weather conditions in southern Chile and Argentina are not very severe, and large numbers of waterbirds can overwinter there without difficulty. A few species of ducks, sheldgeese and shorebirds do, however, undertake true migrations, deserting their breeding grounds in the extreme south to winter in central Chile and northern Argentina, but few individuals travel as far north as Paraguay and southern Brazil, and none crosses the Tropic of Capricorn.

In contrast, about 90 species of waterbirds which breed in temperate and arctic regions of North America undertake lengthy migrations to spend the non-breeding season in Latin America and the Caribbean. Several species, particularly some of the diving ducks, geese and sandhill crane (*Grus canadensis*), go no farther than the north coasts and highlands of Mexico, while many others, including a variety of herons, ducks, shorebirds, gulls and terns, winter south through the Caribbean and Central America to northern South America. Some 28 species of shorebirds and several terns continue on deep into the continent, and a handful of species travel as far as Tierra del Fuego and the Falkland Islands.

VALUES AND USES
Wetlands in Latin America and the Caribbean, as elsewhere in the world, are highly productive ecosystems capable of providing a wide range of goods and services on a sustainable basis. However, in contrast to other parts of the world, these potential uses of wetlands have to a large extent been overlooked or ignored in this region. Subsistence hunting and fishing make a major contribution to the livelihood of many of the indigenous tribes, but on the whole the more recent colonists have tended to see wetlands merely as areas potentially suitable for conversion to other uses, and have either destroyed them or simply left them alone. The fact that so much excellent wetland habitat still survives in South America is more a reflection of the low human population density than of any special conservation efforts.

Only about 6 million people inhabit the Amazon Basin, and they are mostly concentrated along the main watercourses because of their dependence on the rivers for transportation. Floodplains close to the main rivers are extensively cultivated, particularly around the main centres of habitation where maize, rice and jute are the principal crops. Rice production is, however, increasing rapidly and is likely to take over large areas of floodplain in the future.

In more densely populated areas, such as the lowlands of Mexico, Central America, southern Brazil and northern Argentina, large areas of wetland have

Fishing in the Río Magdalena, northern Colombia.

been converted to rice paddies and other kinds of agricultural land. Similarly, in areas with low rainfall, such as the coastal plain of Peru and Chile and the altiplano of the central Andes, many wetland areas have been lost to arable land.

Wetlands are also widely grazed by domestic livestock. Huge areas of the Llanos, Pantanal, humid eastern Chaco and pampas have been given over to cattle ranching, and virtually all of the marshy grasslands around high Andean lakes are now heavily grazed by sheep, cattle, llamas and alpacas. At Lake Junín in Peru, as elsewhere, large areas of marsh vegetation are regularly burned to improve the grazing, while aquatic vegetation is harvested as a source of fodder.

Communities living around lakes with extensive reed beds often harvest the reeds for thatch, and produce a variety of handicrafts such as baskets, carpets and furniture. Such is the case at Laguna Zapotlán in Mexico, Lake Atitlán in Guatemala, Lake Tota in Colombia, Lake Junín in Peru and especially Lake Titicaca in southern Peru and Bolivia, where the indigenous Indians have developed a remarkable skill in boat-building using nothing but reeds.

Lakes and rivers provide water for domestic

A tourist lodge set amidst the spectacular scenery of Torres del Paine National Park in the southern Andes of Chile.

consumption and irrigation, and rivers are also widely used for hydroelectric power. Virtually all of Brazil's major rivers have now been dammed to produce hydroelectricity. Some lakes have even been artificially raised in level to permit the generation of electricity, for example Lake Junín in Peru.

In parts of Mexico, Central America, the Caribbean and northern South America, saline coastal lagoons have been converted to saltpans. Salt production is also the principal activity on some of the saline lakes in the high Andes of Peru and Bolivia, although the extent of many of the Andean lakes is such that,

Educational material about the scarlet ibis, Trinidad's national bird, is provided for visitors to Caroni Swamp in Trinidad.

in general, the salt workings have had negligible impact on local wildlife.

Mangrove forests, although very extensive in Latin America, lack the diversity of tree species found in similar forests in the Asian and African tropics, and have less commercial value as a source of timber. There is some commercial exploitation of mangrove forests in parts of Central America, on the Caribbean coast of Colombia and Venezuela and on some Caribbean islands, but in most areas the forests are used only as a source of fuelwood for local people or to produce tannin for curing hides.

The value of mangrove forests in preventing coastal erosion and providing protection against storms is well appreciated in the Caribbean, where mangrove-fringed lagoons provide safe shelters for boats during hurricanes. The primary value of mangrove swamps is, however, as spawning and nursery grounds for fishes and crustaceans, including many commercially important species. Recent studies in Surinam have indicated that 60-80 per cent of fish sold in coastal markets originate from mangrove areas. Throughout Central America and northern South America, major shrimp fisheries such as those in the Usumacinta Delta, Gulf of Fonseca, Gulf of Panama and Orinoco Delta are dependent on the high productivity of coastal mangrove swamps, as are the significant harvests of crabs, clams and oysters.

The great riverine and floodplain systems of South and Central America also support a number of very important subsistence and commercial fisheries. Although overfishing has become a problem in some densely populated regions, fish stocks remain high in much of South America. It has been estimated that the fisheries potential of the Amazon could exceed 600,000 tonnes (590,520 tons) of fish per year, but only a small fraction of this is currently being harvested. An investigation of the importance of the Amazon floodplains for fish populations concluded that about 75 per cent of the commercial fish catch in the Amazon depended on food chains originating in the seasonally flooded forests.

Hunting for food and skins has long been an important activity in wetlands throughout the region. In the Amazon Basin, there was a massive trade in skins of crocodiles, capybara and otters in the 1950s and 1960s, but with the virtual extermination of some species and subsequent prohibition of commercial hunting, the level of harvest dropped off considerably. Capybara, coypu and otters are still widely hunted elsewhere in South America, and indeed, in the Llanos of Venezuela populations of capybara are actively managed for their meat. Crocodiles and caimans continue to be heavily hunted for their skins, despite the fact that in most countries this is now illegal.

Waterbirds provide a valuable source of meat for subsistence hunters throughout the region, and sport hunting is popular in some areas, particularly in Mexico, parts of the Caribbean, Colombia, Venezuela, southern Brazil, Argentina and Chile. Illegal hunting is widespread, and there is even some illegal commercial hunting, for example in the Maranhão wetlands of northeastern Brazil, but over much of South America the overall hunting pressure on waterbirds is light.

Many of the region's wetlands have little to attract the general tourist and are far too remote and inaccessible to provide outdoor recreation for city dwellers. However, there are several lakes of great beauty in Central America and the northern Andes which have already become popular holiday resorts, while the spectacular lakeland scenery of the southern Andes has become a tourist destination of world renown. Locally, wildlife spectacles are also providing a tourist attraction; at Caroni Swamp in Trinidad, the large roosting flocks of scarlet ibises attract thousands of tourists each year. Specialist nature tours are increasingly visiting some of the more spectacular wetlands, such as the Llanos, the Pantanal and the lakes of the Peruvian Andes, and this sector of the tourist industry is likely to expand rapidly in the coming years.

THREATS, MANAGEMENT AND CONSERVATION

Until the early part of the present century, vast tracts of wetland habitat in Latin America remained in almost pristine condition, subject only to low levels of subsistence hunting and fishing, grazing by domestic livestock and some primitive agriculture. However, within the last few decades, a rapid increase in human population, the associated expansion and extension of human settlements and a resulting massive increase in agricultural and industrial development have put enormous pressure on wetlands almost throughout the region. As might be expected, pressures are greatest in the densely populated areas of the Caribbean, Mexico and Central America, and lowest

Destruction of mangroves for saltpans on the shore of Baia de São Marcos in Maranhão, northeastern Brazil.

109

in the thinly populated areas of southern South America.

Almost throughout Mexico, Central America, the Caribbean and northern and central South America, the drainage and reclamation of wetlands for human settlement, agriculture and industrial development has been the principal cause of wetland loss. In arid regions, such as parts of Mexico, coastal Peru and northwestern Argentina, the conversion of wetlands to farmland and the diversion of water supplies for irrigation purposes have left few natural wetlands intact. In the Amazon Basin, the floodplain wetlands of white-water rivers have come under considerable pressure because of the fertility of the soils, and this habitat has now largely disappeared from the major navigable rivers of central and lower Amazonia. In the Guianas, Chile, Uruguay and parts of central and southern Brazil, the conversion of wetlands into rice fields has occurred on a large scale, and this continues at an accelerating pace.

A rapid development of the mining and petroleum industries in the Amazon Basin in recent years has greatly improved transportation networks, thereby facilitating further colonization by settlers. This increasing human activity has been accompanied by widespread deforestation and transformation of wetlands into agricultural land. Wetlands on the Gulf coast of Mexico have also been affected by the development of the oil industry, which has entailed the construction of oil and gas pipelines across large tracts of wetland. Mining activities are causing serious problems at some of the lakes in the high Andes, such as Lake Junín in Peru, while the mining of peat for fuel poses a serious threat to wetlands in Jamaica.

The deforestation of watersheds is adversely affecting many wetlands. Throughout the highlands of Mexico, Central America, the northern Andes and central Brazil, deforestation is causing changes in the amount of discharge, sediments and dissolved substances in rivers and streams. These are becoming increasingly turbid; at the same time, lakes and marshes are silting up, and in some areas flash-flooding is becoming a problem. Overgrazing by domestic livestock can also create serious problems in wetlands. In Patagonia, for example, heavy grazing by sheep causes erosion of terrestrial habitats and prevents the formation of emergent vegetation along lake margins.

One of the most serious threats to riverine wetlands in Amazonia is the construction of dams for hydroelectric power. As many as 40 dam projects have been put forward, affecting every major river in the basin. Several enormous dams have already been completed, such as the Tucurui Dam on the Tocantins River, while many others are under construction or planned. Such dams have a profound effect on the ecology of wetlands downstream, by reducing or eliminating flood cycles and changing the water chemistry and sediment loads of the rivers. They have an adverse effect on fish populations by reducing the extent of floodplain habitat available for spawning and by disrupting the long migrations made by many species.

Pollution is fast becoming one of the most serious threats to wetlands, particularly in Mexico and Central America where almost 40 per cent of the important wetlands are badly affected. Wetlands around urban centres are almost invariably polluted with domestic sewage and industrial waste, while in rural areas, large quantities of pesticides and fertilizers used on agricultural land are finding their way into rivers and lakes. This problem is particularly serious in rice-growing areas, but even in Amazonia pollution from pesticides is becoming a serious problem. Defoliant sprays have been used to clear forest at dam construction sites, and the effects of

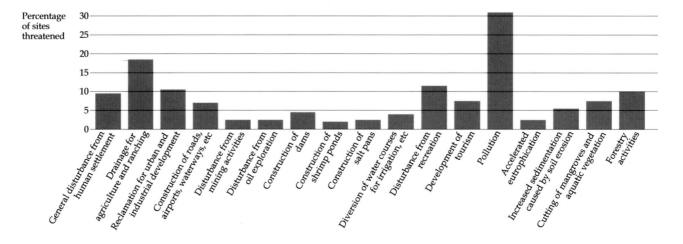

Major threats to wetlands in Latin America and the Caribbean. Based on information from 620 wetlands in South and Central America and the

Mining activities and forest clearance in the Amazon rain forest have led to the widespread soil erosion and pollution now affecting wetlands throughout Amazonia. The wetlands have also become more accessible as transport systems develop.

these have been felt far downstream. In many wetlands, contamination with domestic sewage and fertilizers is causing rapid eutrophication with consequent dramatic changes to the aquatic vegetation. This is a major threat at several lakes in the Andes of Colombia and Ecuador.

Of the major types of wetland in Latin America and the Caribbean, the mangrove ecosystem is undoubtedly the most widely threatened. The principal problems are filling in for urban, industrial and tourist development, the cutting of

trees for timber, firewood and fodder, conversion to shrimp ponds and rice paddies, and the dumping of rubbish. The situation is particularly serious in the Caribbean, but mangrove swamps are also under extreme pressure in parts of Central America, Ecuador and eastern Brazil. In Ecuador, there has been an explosive expansion of the shrimp industry in recent years. Over 20 per cent of the mangroves have disappeared as a result of this expansion, and the remainder are seriously threatened.

Commercial and subsistence hunting are wide-spread throughout the region, and threaten many species with local extinction, especially crocodiles and caimans, freshwater turtles, manatees, otters and some waterbirds such as the Orinoco goose (*Neochen jubata*). In French Guiana, birds are hunted for their feathers, which poses a serious threat to colourful species such as the scarlet ibis, while in the Bolivian Andes, the collection of eggs for human consumption is becoming a serious problem at some of the flamingo colonies.

The introduction of exotic species has caused some problems for native fish faunas. *Tilapia* from Africa have already escaped into the wild in parts of Amazonia, and it is feared that a great expansion in fish culture in the region will result in the spread of new diseases and parasites amongst native fish stocks.

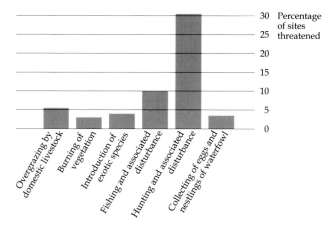

Caribbean described in A Directory of Neotropical Wetlands.

111

Biologists from the Venezuelan Wildlife Service in the Llanos, rounding up moulting black-bellied tree ducks for banding as part of a long-term study of the movements of this popular game species.

At Lake Tota in Colombia, trout were introduced in the 1940s, and since then the endemic fish have virtually disappeared.

Nowhere are the pressures on wetlands more acute than in the small Caribbean islands, where availability of land is very limited and human population pressure very high. The main threats to wetlands are land reclamation for urban and industrial development, construction of roads, airports, tourist hotels and marinas, conversion of wetlands to agricultural land and cutting of mangroves for timber, fuel and animal fodder. Some of the salt ponds have been opened to the sea and dredged or partly filled to create marinas, while mangroves have been cleared for boat anchorages and harbours. Many wetlands are being used as rubbish dumps, and in a number of areas sand mining is having a detrimental effect on nearby mangrove and marine ecosystems.

Almost throughout Latin America and the Caribbean, an overriding desire for rapid economic development, coupled with exploding human populations and crippling international debts, has meant that very little attention has been given to the conservation of wetland resources. Indeed, wetlands and their margins have more often been viewed as areas suitable for human settlement, agriculture and industry rather than as rich and productive ecosystems which should be managed wisely for their own intrinsic values. Despite a great increase in environmental awareness in recent years, particularly amongst the younger generations, the situation continues to deteriorate.

In most countries, the only significant steps taken to conserve wetland ecosystems have been the inclusion of some important wetland sites within national networks of protected areas. In several countries, notably Argentina, Chile, Brazil, Mexico and Venezuela, the establishment of national parks and other protected areas began as early as the 1930s and 40s, and by the early 80s, most countries had set up elaborate networks of parks and reserves many of which included huge tracts of wetlands. In 1985, the total area of wetlands under protection was estimated at 16 million hectares (39.5 million acres). Even when bearing in mind their small size, most Caribbean states lag far behind the Central and South American countries in the establishment of wetland reserves. By early 1985, six Caribbean states had still not created any wetland reserves, and seven others had protected no more than 100 hectares (247 acres) of wetlands.

As natural resources have been depleted in unprotected areas, it has become harder to maintain the integrity of the existing reserves. The enforcement of regulations within protected areas leaves much to be desired through most of the region. Indeed, some of the wetlands that are currently most seriously under threat are, in fact, among those that are supposed to be under complete protection.

Most countries have passed some legislation relevant to the conservation of wetland resources. For example, in Brazil, a law regulating the use of rivers, lakes and lagoons was introduced as early as 1934, while in Colombia, the government passed a law in 1974 regulating the use, supply and management of all water resources. This law also established the rule that a major obligation in any development is to conduct environmental impact studies in order to determine to what extent a land-use project is harmful or beneficial.

In Puerto Rico, a variety of US federal laws and

regulations favour the protection of wetlands. These include: the Clear Water Act, one of the most effective mechanisms for preventing the harmful modification of wetlands; the Endangered Species Act, which provides protection to certain species and habitats, and the National Environmental Policy Act, which requires an evaluation of the environmental impact of important development projects. Elsewhere in the Caribbean, legislation covers such matters as the exploitation of fishes, crustaceans and sea turtles, control of oil pollution, prevention of pollution of fresh waters, and regulation of irrigation and reclamation schemes. Unfortunately, the level of enforcement of this type of legislation is generally very poor throughout the region.

Most countries have also passed legislation relating to hunting, but again the level of enforcement is poor. Commercial hunting has been banned throughout Brazil since 1967, and sport hunting is permitted only in those states that are able to demonstrate on a scientific basis that an open season can be justified.

Since 1980, the only state able to do this, and therefore the only state in which hunting has been permitted, is Rio Grande do Sul. Unfortunately, the enforcement of this admirable piece of legislation is reported to be almost non-existent outside the reserve network. In most other countries the situation is no better, and illegal hunting is prevalent throughout the region.

Although the future for wetlands in the Neotropical Realm still looks rather bleak, some progress is now being made. Already in 1986, an inventory of the most important wetlands in the region had been compiled. In several countries, the aesthetic, scientific and economic values of wetlands are now widely recognized, and some efforts are being made to save and restore them, not only by the voluntary conservation bodies, but also at government level through environmental legislation. Considerable attention is being given to obtaining local support for wetland conservation through environmental awareness campaigns which focus on the values of wetlands and ways in which they can be

The catch of black-bellied tree ducks, ready for banding in the Llanos, Venezuela.

used on a sustainable basis. The World Wide Fund for Nature (WWF) has given its support to several such campaigns, for example at Monterico Protected Biotope in Guatemala, at Laguna Jocotal in El Salvador and at Tortuguero National Park in Costa Rica.

At an international seminar on wetland conservation and sustainable development in Brazil in 1986, representatives from 13 Latin American countries met with international experts and drew up a Wetlands Action Strategy which identifies a number of national and international priorities for conservation action in the region. In 1988, the World Conservation Union (IUCN) initiated a regional wetlands programme in Central America with three major objectives: to disseminate widely information on the benefits wetlands offer to people; to provide technical assistance to national institutions in the development and implementation of wetland conservation and management activities; and to identify priorities for research in the functioning and management of wetland ecosystems.

Another major international effort focusing on wetlands in the region is the Western Hemisphere Shorebird Reserve Network (WHSRN), initiated in 1987 as a collaborative effort for the protection of shorebirds and the management of their habitat. WHSRN functions by bringing together organizations and individuals throughout North and South America with an interest in the conservation of shorebirds. The programme promotes the establishment of reserves at sites of special importance for migratory shorebirds, and designates reserves of outstanding importance as Hemispheric Reserves. By 1990, local networks had been established in Argentina, Chile and Brazil, and four sites (three in Surinam and one in Argentina) had been designated as Hemispheric Reserves.

In 1991, a joint venture was launched by the International Waterfowl and Wetlands Research Bureau, the WHSRN and Ducks Unlimited. Under the title Neotropical Wetlands Program, this venture will draw together networks of experts and data-gathering programmes to provide better technical support for wetland conservation initiatives.

The Ramsar Convention has been slow to gain momentum in the Neotropical Realm. Indeed, by the end of 1985, ten years after the convention came into force, only three countries, Chile, Surinam and Uruguay, had joined and each had designated only one wetland as a Ramsar site (although the government of the Netherlands had listed six sites in its small territories in the Caribbean). However, another six countries have joined the Convention since then, and it seems that the region's governments are at last beginning to appreciate the value of the Convention as a tool to promote the conservation of wetlands.

CONTRIBUTOR: P. DENNY

Africa

A FIRST-TIME VISITOR TO Africa, especially one travelling by air, will almost certainly be impressed by the immense size and diversity of the continent.

Flying from the north African coast over the Nile Delta and then, for many hours, southwards following its course, there can be little doubt that this great river is a lifeline to survival. Thin green strips, the result of management and irrigation schemes, expand and contract on each side of the river, whilst barrages, such as the Aswan High Dam, create massive man-made lakes in an otherwise dry and inhospitable environment. Towards the Equator, the landscape changes: the desert gives way to lush green vegetation; and the Nile expands into an enormous wetland, the Sudd, created from the waters of the White Nile as they flow from the great lakes of equatorial Africa.

Leaving the Nile, the flight might then pass over Lake Victoria which lies across the Equator between the Western and Eastern Rift Valleys and is surrounded by rivers and lakes. If the Cape is its destination, it is now halfway.

Continuing south, the land no longer looks so green. Intensive agriculture can be distinguished. As with the Nile, the water courses of rivers are highlighted by the emerald sheath of vegetation expanding into more extensive wetlands.

Towards the end of the journey, the harsh peaks of the Drakensburg Mountain range glisten with rivulets and streams that carry the snow-melt of the southern spring. Beyond Table Mountain comes the Cape of Good Hope where onshore breezes or winds from the South Atlantic Ocean determine the distinctive wetland types of the region. The journey has covered some 8,000 km (5,000 miles), passing through 60 degrees of latitude and several major climatic zones, crossing land masses that range in height from sea level to more than 6,000 m (19,700 ft).

Clearly, over such a vast and diverse continent the wetland types vary greatly with the major geographical features and climatic conditions. These same features add to the distinctive nature of African wetlands.

GEOGRAPHIC SETTING

Africa comprises some 50 countries ranging in size from 21,000 km² (8,100 sq miles) - such as the Gambia - to more than 2.5 million km² (965,000 sq miles) - such as Sudan.

The continent is some 100 million years old, having previously been part of the supercontinent of Gondwanaland. Present-day Africa divides into Low Africa to the north and west (most of which lies below about 600 m - 1,970 ft) and High Africa to the south and east. The largest rivers, the Nile, Niger and Zaïre and lake basins such as that of Lake Chad are in sedimentary basins of Low Africa.

High Africa is largely the result of intense pushing up of the earth's surface over the last 25 million years. A broad belt of land running approximately northeast-southwest, mainly over 1,000 m (3,280 ft) high and up to 800 km (500 miles) wide, now stretches from Eritrea in the north, down the east of the Rwenzori Mountains, to the Zambezi in the south.

The central equatorial area subsequently sagged and created the precursor to Lake Victoria (altitude: 1,130 m - 3,710 ft). The radial pattern of streams and rivers that flowed into the lake accounts for the numerous valley swamps now surrounding Lake Victoria. It is in this region that the Great Lakes of the Western and Eastern (Gregory) Rift Valleys evolved; this series of deep lakes includes Lake Tanganyika, the second deepest lake in the world - 1,470 m (4,820 ft).

Farther south lie the Cubango and Kalahari internal drainage basins. Water collects in the centre of these and supports the beautiful wetlands of Botswana's Okavango Delta. If there are exceptionally heavy rains in the Angolan Highlands water will overflow from Okavango into the Zambezi via the Selinda Spillway. The extensive Makgadikgadi saltpans in the south are connected to the Okavango Delta by the Boteti River; they are the result of the accumulation of salt through evaporation.

Farther south again is the Karoo Basin, a generally dry area draining via the Vaal and Orange Rivers into the Atlantic Ocean. During the Jurassic period,

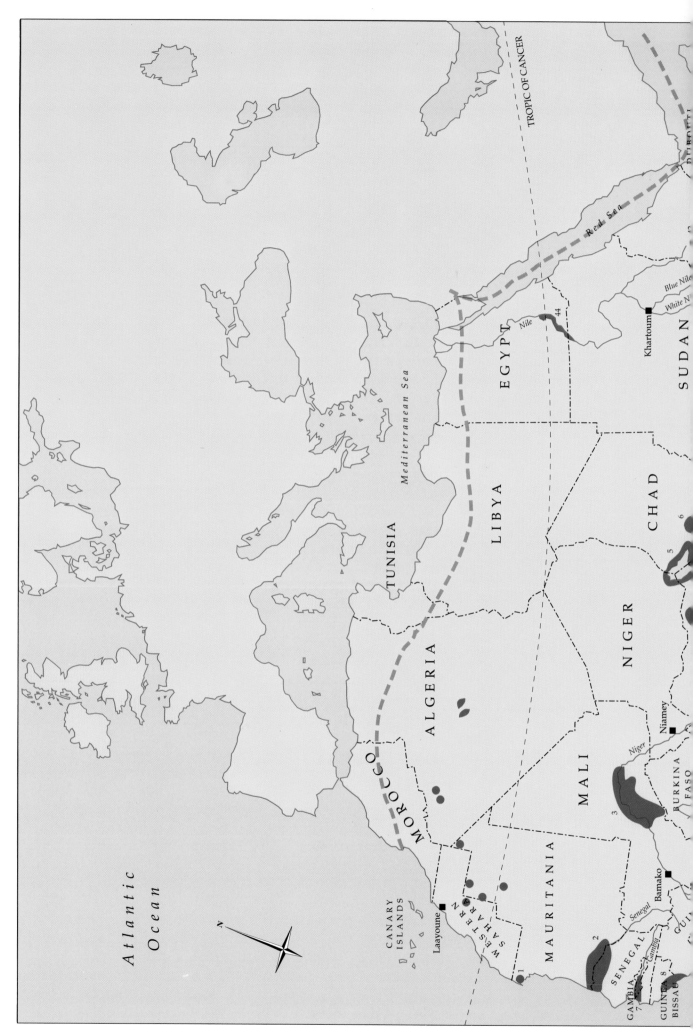

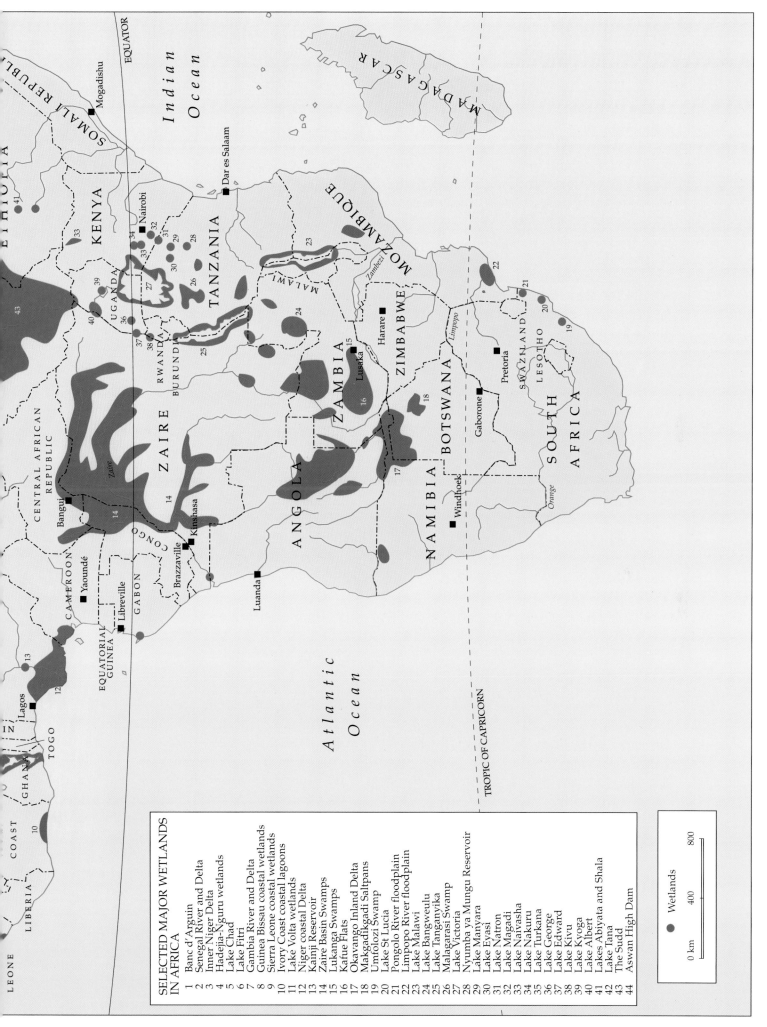

SELECTED MAJOR WETLANDS
IN AFRICA

1 Banc d'Arguin
2 Senegal River and Delta
3 Inner Niger Delta
4 Hadejia-Nguru wetlands
5 Lake Chad
6 Lake Fitri
7 Gambia River and Delta
8 Guinea Bissau coastal wetlands
9 Sierra Leone coastal wetlands
10 Ivory Coast coastal lagoons
11 Lake Volta wetlands
12 Niger coastal Delta
13 Kainji Reservoir
14 Zaire Basin Swamps
15 Lukanga Swamps
16 Kafue Flats
17 Okavango Inland Delta
18 Makgadikgadi Saltpans
19 Umfolozi Swamp
20 Lake St Lucia
21 Pongolo River floodplain
22 Limpopo River floodplain
23 Lake Malawi
24 Lake Bangweulu
25 Lake Tanganyika
26 Malagarasi Swamp
27 Lake Victoria
28 Nyumba ya Mungu Reservoir
29 Lake Manyara
30 Lake Eyasi
31 Lake Natron
32 Lake Magadi
33 Lake Naivasha
34 Lake Nakuru
35 Lake Turkana
36 Lake George
37 Lake Edward
38 Lake Kivu
39 Lake Kyoga
40 Lake Albert
41 Lakes Abiyata and Shala
42 Lake Tana
43 The Sudd
44 Aswan High Dam

● Wetlands

0 km   400   800

there were dramatic earthquakes and long fissures opened up in the east of this region; basaltic lava poured out and overlay the sandstones and shales of the Mesozoic era to a thickness of 1,500 m (4,920 ft).

Alongside the Drakensberg Range, the Maloti mountains in Lesotho have the highest peaks south of Kilimanjaro.

CLIMATE AND SOILS

Broad high-pressure belts overlie the subtropical regions of Africa, while a low-pressure belt - known as the Equatorial Trough - overlies the central, equatorial zone. The Trough migrates north and south through the year according to the season and thus brings about the climatic regimes that are characteristic of the various regions. The tragic drought conditions in the Sahel, for example, are thought to result from the reduced northward movement of this rain-bearing trough.

Northeast and Southeast Trade Winds blow onshore from the Indian Ocean, respectively north and south of the migrating Trough. In the Southern Hemisphere, in July, the Southeast Trades can swing around to the southwest and west. These westerlies pick up moisture from the Atlantic Ocean and are responsible for the monsoon rains of western Africa. In general, sinking air currents in the subtropics bring hot, dry conditions and clear skies; rising air in the Equatorial Trough brings clouds and precipitation. Thus, a belt of high rainfall occurs in the equatorial zone, monsoons in the inner tropics and dry, clear skies in the outer tropics and subtropics.

The movement and position of the sun is responsible for the pattern of the seasons. Towards the northern and southern extremities of Africa, spring and summer follow winter as in other temperate parts of the world. Closer to the Equator this seasonal rhythm becomes less and less well defined.

In the subtropics there is one hot season each year (May to July in the Northern Hemisphere and November to January in the Southern Hemisphere). Nearer the Equator, there are two hot seasons (April and August in the north and October and February in the south).

In the inner tropics and equatorial zones, the noon sun is practically overhead for the whole year. As a result, the mean annual temperature range (the difference in temperature between the coldest and warmest months) is minimal at the Equator, but increases towards the north or south. Near the coast, temperatures are moderated by ocean temperatures and wind directions. Inland, great extremes can occur, though where there is ample water they are reduced by the heat-storage capacity of the water and the cooling effect of evaporation. Large swamps and lakes are important in reducing extremes of temperature.

Rainfall migrates with the Equatorial Trough. At the limits of the Trough's migration, in the outer tropical zone, there is a single rainfall peak: August in the north and February in the south. In latitudes over which the Trough passes twice - that is, the inner tropical zone - there are two rainfall peaks. In view of these variations, seasons in the tropics tend to be distinguished as dry and rainy.

Heavy annual rainfall is confined to the equatorial zone while the subtropical margins contain dry deserts. Precipitation of up to 2,000 mm (79 in) a year occur around 5 degrees latitude, whereas in the Trade Wind belt (roughly, 15° North) precipitation is much lower at about 600 mm (24 in) per year. Cloud cover reduces evaporation in the Equatorial Trough zone; maximum evaporation is found in the Trade Wind belt where it is facilitated by steady strong winds. Thus, there is a trend towards high evaporation in regions of low rainfall - potentially disastrous for those living in the Sahel region.

A few examples highlight the differences in patterns of rainfall in the tropical and equatorial zone.

First, the coastal regions of western Africa. Dakar in Senegal lies near the northernmost limit of the zone over which the Equatorial Trough migrates. It has an intensely dry period lasting seven months and a light summer rain season corresponding to the summer movements of the Trough. Slightly farther south, Freetown in Sierra Leone has longer, heavier monsoonal rains (3,500 mm - 138 in - a year) with a single peak in July. Towards the Equator there are two rainfall peaks of equal intensity separated by a severe dry season. In the Zaïre Basin, which lies on the Equator, few areas receive more than 2,000 mm (79 in) a year; severe rainstorms are rare and short dry periods can occur throughout the year. South of the Equator, towards the southern limit of the Trough's migration, the rainfall pattern is the mirror image of that of Dakar.

The rainfall pattern in central and eastern Africa is more complex. In Khartoum (Sudan), on approximately the same latitude as Dakar, the total precipitation is much lower than in Dakar (150 mm - 6 in - a year) and very variable. Entebbe (Uganda) is on the Equator and has two rainfall peaks, but, for the latitude, annual rainfall is relatively low: 1,500 mm (59 in) a year. The Equatorial Trough extends south and just reaches Bulawayo (Zimbabwe), to produce a single rainy season.

Even as far south as Lesotho adequate summer rains prevail, with generally dry winters of low night temperatures and clear sunny days. The highlands of Lesotho have a relatively high mean annual rainfall of around 770 mm (30 in), which makes them an

Lake Victoria is a shallow lake with numerous broad inflow valleys. This encourages the development of extensive swamps, especially papyrus, in the bays and inlets.

attractive proposition for water-storage dams.

Outside the tropical zone, the summer rain pattern gives way to a predominantly Mediterranean-type climate with winter rain and a long summer drought season. During the winter southernmost Africa comes under the influence of westerly winds and cyclones occur.

In the tropics, rain generally falls in intense storms which cause erosion and compaction of the soil surface. If vegetation in the catchment areas is sparse, streams and rivers with heavy burdens of silt and clay will prevail. The lake and estuarine deltas which form when these sediments are deposited comprise some of the most extensive and finest wetlands in Africa: for example, the Inner Niger and Nile Deltas.

High rainfall, in the equatorial zone especially, encourages heavy leaching producing thick, nutrient-poor soils. In areas of basic rock, 'black cotton' soils or 'cracking' clays occur. As the name of the latter implies, deep fissures develop in the surface layers of the soil during the dry season, but when the rains come the expanding lattices of the clays produce an impervious lining which, in depressions, results in valuable seasonal wetlands and dambos. Where there is a marked dry season, red laterite soils are common. Bases are leached out and oxides of iron and aluminium are precipitated so that hard, impervious, metallic crusts or pans are formed. In the rains the pans become flooded, producing, once again, seasonal wetlands.

WETLANDS

Africa is known for its hot deserts - yet about 1 per cent of its surface (totalling at least 345,000 km² - 133,170 sq miles) is occupied by wetlands. This figure excludes the multiplicity of smaller or seasonal

wetlands, many of which have yet to be mapped, but which are of major importance to people and wildlife. Wetlands are predominant in the zone influenced by the Equatorial Trough, that is, approximately between latitudes 15° North and 20° South.

In equatorial Africa alone are three of the largest wetland systems: the Zaïre swamps (covering 80,000 km² - 50,000 sq miles), the Sudd in the Upper Nile (over 50,000 km² - 31,000 sq miles) and the multitude of wetlands in the Lake Victoria Basin (about 50,000 km²). Other major wetlands include those of the floodplains of the Niger and Zambezi Rivers, the Chad Basin (approaching 20,000 km² - 12,000 sq miles) and the Okavango Delta (16,000 km² - 9,900 sq miles). In southern Africa below the Limpopo River are perhaps another 12,000 km² (7,400 sq miles). Around the coast and in estuaries, mangrove swamps are common.

A simple categorization which highlights the prominent and important types of wetlands found in Africa has been chosen for the present purposes. These are: freshwater forests; mangrove forests, coastal lagoons and mudflats; floodplains; saline lakes and saltpans; herbaceous swamps; and high altitude swamps, bogs and mires.

In nature there is no such demarcation between, say, a permanent swamp, floodplain, and savanna. This is because wetlands are the dynamic interface between dry land and water in which the water table or depth of water is a regulator. Seldom is the water regime identical each year and the tolerance of plants to these hydraulic cycles determines the migrations and somewhat diffuse edges of vegetation zones.

Freshwater Forests

Few tree species can tolerate long periods of deep flooding and so the diversity of species increases as flooding decreases. The diversity in Africa is disappointingly low when compared with the rich swamp forests of Southeast Asia. The largest expanses of wetland forests are in the equatorial zone and around the tropical coastline.

Freshwater swamp forests are best developed in the Zaïre Basin and to a lesser extent, in regions of the coastal Niger Delta; most rivers also have various types of swamp forest associated with them. Remnants of substantial lacustrine forest - that is, forests associated with lakes - occur around the edge of Lake Victoria but a rise in the lake's water level in the early 1960s has reduced them significantly; so too has tree felling for firewood.

Equatorial swamp forests grade from permanent to seasonal swamps and then to rain forest (where the soil is free draining). At greater latitudes, forests more usually grade into woodland or savanna.

The swamp palms in the upland valleys of Uganda provide material for building, thatching and matting. Many of these valleys are now being drained for agriculture.

Swamp forests contain dense stands of trees 10-45 m (33-148 ft) tall.

In permanent swamps the trees are specifically adapted to long periods of flooding and waterlogged soils. The canopy is somewhat open: the species diversity poor with *Raphia* species and *Phoenix reclinata* palms in the wettest areas. The primordial-looking *Pandanas candelabrum* is widespread.

The forests of the Zaïre Basin have the richest diversity of plants in Africa. The trees around the shores of the Great Lakes in East Africa suffered when the water levels rose, but are showing some recovery. At the mouth of the Kagera River on the southwestern side of Lake Victoria is a unique forest which contains not only species typical of Zaïre (particularly *Baikiaea insignis*) but also species, such as *Podocarpus falcatus* and *Podocarpus latifolius*, that are characteristic of more mountainous regions.

Seasonal swamp forests are, not surprisingly, best developed in regions with distinct seasons where there is regular flooding by rivers. The levee of the rivers (that is, their raised banks) is occupied by gallery forest while the floodplains support seasonal swamp forests. Characteristic species vary from region to region. In southern Africa, in the Pongolo floodplain system, for example, the species are different from those of, say, Senegal: they include *Ficus sycomorus* (a wild fig that can reach a height of 18 m - 59 ft), *Rauvolfia caffra* which dominates the levee and *Acacia xanthophloea*, common at the edge of the floodplain.

The higher diversity of species in the seasonal swamp forests is due to the more variable water regime. Which species grow in particular swamps depends upon seasonality and flooding. *Acacia nilotica*, for example, is a tropical floodplain species which can tolerate two to three months of flooding, but must have flowing water for good aeration in the root zone.

Acacia xanthophloea occurs at the very edge of seasonally flooded areas where malaria-bearing mosquitoes abound, and is often used as an indicator of the upper limits of flooding. It cannot tolerate prolonged waterlogging. Because of its particular niche at the edge of swamps, it became known as the fever tree.

Borassus and *Hyphaene* palms are found towards the fringes of floodplains and are common on levees. They also form pockets of 'Palm Savanna' in rain-fed pans and dambos where they can tolerate shallow flooding for several months.

Mangrove Forests, Coastal Lagoons and Mudflats

Coastal and inter-tidal areas of tropical Africa are dominated by mangrove forests. On the western side they extend north to Mauritania and south to Benguela in Angola. In the east, they extend north to the Gulf of Aqaba and south to East London in the Republic of South Africa.

Interestingly, the species occurring in west Africa are the same as those on the eastern shores of tropical America, yet entirely different from the flora on the east coast of Africa. The west African mangrove communities have five species only. The normal succession is from the pioneer species *Rhizophora racemosa* (which likes a soft muddy substrate and can grow 45 m - 148 ft - tall in the Niger Delta), through *Rhizophora harrisonii* to the shrubby *Rhizophora mangle* in the shallowest zones. *Avicennia*, which prefers a sandy substrate and grows between the high tide and spring tide zone, occurs behind the *Rhizophora* zone.

One of the finest and most extensive developments of mangroves with this type of succession occurs in the Niger Delta where, on the landward side, it grades into substantial freshwater swamp forests.

The mangrove flora in eastern Africa is richer with nine species, none of which occur on the Atlantic coast. *Heritiera littoralis* is confined to the equatorial area. Others thin out north and south, *Avicennia marina*, *Bruguiera gymnorrhiza* and *Rhizophora mucronata* having the widest range. As a rule, *Sonneratia* occurs in the deepest water which is uncontaminated by freshwater, and then comes *Rhizophora*. Behind the *Rhizophora* is *Ceriops tagal* and finally, *Avicennia*.

The west coast of Africa and eastern South Africa have a number of indentations forming lagoons. These can contain freshwater, but others are periodically inundated by seawater and can become

THE GAMBIA RIVER

In the course of its 1,090 km (677 mile) journey from the Fouta Djalon Highlands of Guinea (at the divide of the headwaters of the Upper Niger) to the Atlantic, the Gambia River produces some of the most splendid mangrove swamps, mudflats and floodplains in Africa. They act as host to a large and spectacular bird population which has become a focus of the tourist trade. The riverine flats (known locally as 'banto faro') support vital agriculture including the growing of groundnuts, rice and horticultural crops. (Some 100,000 tonnes - 98,420 tons - of groundnuts are harvested annually.)

The meandering river has created large areas of muddy, ramifying swamp, penetrated by tidal waters a substantial distance up its water course. *Rhizophora* borders the waterways whilst *Avicennia* forms bush to the limit of high water spring tide. Beyond the *Avicennia* are extensive mudflats 150-300 mm (6-12 in) higher than the mangrove belt. These are devoid of vegetation and become very salty, hot and parched in the dry season.

hypersaline. The lagoons, Lake Sibaya and Lake St Lucia, bordering the Indian Ocean in South Africa, are examples. The former is a freshwater lake completely isolated from the sea whilst its neighbour to the south has a salinity which can rise to 120 per cent of seawater in times of drought. Salinity within one particular system may vary spacially and seasonally. The coastal lagoons of the Ivory Coast have salinities ranging from almost freshwater in the upper reaches to full seawater, but during the two rainy seasons substantial flushing and dilution occurs.

The vegetation of coastal lagoons and their associated fauna is governed largely by tidal influences and freshwater flushing regimes. Within the mangrove climatic belt the shores of the lagoons may be colonized by mangroves which give way to gallery forest in freshwater locations. Along the coast of Ghana, for example, mangroves grow principally in

Shallow, freshwater lagoons, colonized by submerged and floating-leaved plants such as water lilies, are a refuge for wildlife.

lagoons which either have permanent outlets to the sea or are closed except for a couple of months during the monsoonal rains.

The open water of lagoons may be colonized by seagrasses and marine macro-algae in the saline areas, by salt-tolerant freshwater plants such as *Potamogeton pectinatus* in the variable salinities and by obligate freshwater plants such as the water lilies (*Nymphaea* species) in freshwater zones.

Production in coastal lagoons is variable. Those in Sierra Leone are generally nutrient-poor and, although they retain a surprisingly high population of fish, they cannot sustain commercial fisheries. On the other hand, those of the Ivory Coast are highly productive and support large communities of freshwater and marine fish. Annual fish production from three lagoons with a total area of 1,180 km^2 (455 1/2 sq miles) can reach 20,000 tonnes (19,680 tons).

Lagoons are a focus for wildlife. During the winter they become valuable stopover sites for tens of thousands of migratory birds as well as supporting a diversity of resident species. In west Africa they also offer an important refuge to the rare aquatic mammal, the African manatee (*Trichechus senegalensis*). But, like so many other places, coastal lagoons in west Africa are being developed for commerce, the waters are being regulated and pollution is increasing. In South Africa for example, Lake St Lucia, a wetland of international significance for its wildlife, is under imminent threat from mining development.

In warm, deltaic regions where rivers burdened with suspended sediment enter the sea, stability of the coastline is aided by the mangrove development. However, mudflats may occur in the more open areas, and inland from the mangroves. If the climate is very hot and the land is only covered occasionally by water, the mudflat soils can become very saline and inhospitable. Such areas are found in the Gambia Delta. In latitudes where mangroves are sparce or absent - the coast of Mauritania is a good example - regularly inundated mudflats may be extremely valuable sites for wildlife, especially birds.

THE BANC D'ARGUIN, MAURITANIA

The Banc d'Arguin archipelago forms the major wintering grounds of shorebirds in the east Atlantic. Lying on the Mauritanian coast, it is surrounded on one side by the Sahara and consists of 500 km² (193 sq miles) of muddy tidal flats partly covered with seagrass. The mudflats manage to attract over 2 million shorebirds each winter, an extraordinarily high density. These include over 800,000 dunlin (*Calidris alpina*), 360,000 knots (*Calidris canutus*), 500,000 bar-tailed godwits (*Limosa lapponica*) among numerous other species; for many species, these are the largest known concentrations in the east Atlantic and possibly in the world.

During migrations, another 1.5 million shorebirds use the Banc d'Arguin as a vital stopover on their way to and from wintering areas farther south, especially in coastal Guinea-Bissau.

The islands of the Banc d'Arguin are also home to large breeding colonies of spoonbills (*Platalea leucorodia*), greater flamingos, great white pelicans,

The islands of the Banc d'Arguin are breeding sites for the great white pelican which feeds on the fish in the coastal waters.

cormorants and terns. Altogether, there are up to 40,000 pairs of 15 species, including an endemic subspecies of the grey heron (*Ardea cinerea monicae*). The unreliability of the food supply sometimes results in mass deaths of pelican chicks.

In addition, the rich seagrass bed provides a habitat for the threatened green turtle (*Chelonia mydas*) as well as the best fish nurseries in the region.

It thus supports traditional fisheries. The Imragen tribe have been living in this rich environment for centuries, and still use the same fishing methods as in the fifteenth century. Despite designation as a national park and as a Ramsar site, it is uncertain if this wetland which is on the verge of an expanding desert will be able to resist a threatened invasion by modern, commercial fishing boats.

Floodplains

Floodplains are complex wetlands. In this section they are taken to include seasonally flooded areas alongside rivers and lakes and rain-fed impervious depressions, such as dambos and pans.

Most lakes have floodplains associated with them; good examples are the floodplains of Lakes Chad, Victoria and Chilwa. The vegetation is restricted to the fringe of lakes between seasonal low and high water and is in intense competition with the more aquatic vegetation. Man-made lakes (including small ones, such as farm ponds, and very large ones, such as Lakes Volta, Cabora Bassa and Kariba) have created their own habitats, but do not necessarily provide good floodplain environments. Regulation of the water level can produce very rapid changes, preventing the vegetation from covering the bare expanses exposed during draw-down. If draw-down takes place in the hot, dry séason then re-colonization by opportunist species is especially difficult.

Riverine floodplains are those associated with rivers which have a seasonal rainfall catchment area. They are formed from the regular spilling of the river into the surrounding plains. All the great rivers - the Nile, Niger, Zaïre and Zambezi - have colossal floodplains which are vital to the African economy and wildlife. The Sudd in the Upper Nile has some

30,000 km² (11,600 sq miles) of floodplain or 'toiche' associated with it; the Inner Niger Delta occupies 20,000-30,000 km² (7,700-11,600 sq miles) at peak flood; the Zambezi system includes the Barotse Plains (9,000 km² - 3,470 sq miles) and the Kafue Flats (6,000 km² -2,320 sq miles) whilst the Okavango system has some 13,000 km² (5,020 sq miles) of floodplain.

Floodplains of smaller rivers are just as important and are critical to the well-being of people and wildlife. The Hadejia-Nguru wetlands of the Hadejia and Jama'are Rivers in the Chad Basin, which cover some 3,500 km² (1,350 sq miles), are good examples. They are estimated to support some 25,000 farmers and are particularly valuable to many species of birds.

Rain-fed seasonal wetlands, where the vegetation is regulated by the soil's water content, come in many forms. Some are extensions of the riverine floodplains; others are associated with pans and dambos.

One area that has been studied carefully is the swamps and floodplains of the Sudd. Beyond the reach of the Nile floodwaters the black (cracking) clay soils are inundated by rainwater for varying periods of the year and support some 15,800 km² (6,100 sq miles) of grasslands. These areas are very important for the Dinka and Nuer tribesmen in their transhumant cattle movements. The cattle can graze the rain-fed grasslands when the riverine floodplain is

The riverine and rain-fed floodplains of the Sudd are the lands of the Dinka, Nuer and Shilluk tribes. These tribes are predominantly pastoralists with half a million cattle and over 100,000 goats and sheep. They live in harmony with tens of thousands of wild herbivores including buffalo, elephant, gazelle, tiang, Nile lechwe and white-eared kob. All depend upon the seasonal flooding of this great expanse.

still under water and the higher grounds (where the homesteads are sited) are overgrazed.

African floodplains are predominantly grasslands that are waterlogged for periods of the year. Their species composition and vegetation dynamics are rather complicated. Furthermore, heavy grazing and anthropogenic activities, especially burning, may establish sub-climax vegetation. They contain a wide diversity of species with a plant succession from wetter to drier conditions. The position of a particular species depends upon a number of inter-related variables.

In the Sudd floodplains, for example, large expanses of wild rice (*Oryza longistaminata*), which

The Hadejia-Nguru floodplains in Nigeria are home to more than a million people and their cattle.

dominates 13,100 km² (5,060 sq miles) of the grassland, occur only in deep-water areas flooded for 135 to 287 days a year to depths of 0.65 to 1.21 m (2-4 ft). Farther up the floodplain where flooding is never deep, wild rice is replaced by *Echinochloa pyramidalis* grasslands. Beyond are the vast areas (15,800 km² - 6,100 sq miles) of rain-fed wetlands dominated by *Hyparrhenia rufa* grasslands. The woodlands of the Sudd floodplain ecosystem are dominated by two tree species: *Acacia seyal* woodlands occur in the lower areas and cover 5,400 km² (2,100 sq miles) while *Balanites aegyptiaca* woodlands cover some 5,300 km² (2,040 sq miles) of the upper floodplain.

One of the most important floodplain systems in southern Africa is the Kafue Flats in Zambia. The flats lie in a shallow alluvial depression covering some 6,000 km² (2,320 sq miles) of floodplain. The Kafue River enters the flats through a narrow constriction at Itezi-tezi (now dammed) and then meanders 450 km (280 miles) before passing over the Kafue Gorge (also dammed) to become a major tributary of the Zambezi River. From 3,000 to 5,000 km² (1,160 to 1,930 sq miles) of floodplain were normally inundated each year to a maximum depth of 2 m (6.6 ft), for up to seven months in the deepest areas. The Itezi-tezi Dam now regulates the floods. Like the Sudd floodplains, the soil is a cracking clay.

A distinct vegetation zonation is apparent over the flats. The levees have two main tree species, the Borassus palm (*Borassus aethiopum*), and the swamp acacia (*Acacia albida*). Where it has not succumbed to grazing, the swamp grass, *Vossia cuspidata*, colonizes much of the levee. Open lagoons have a diversity of floating-leaved, rooted and totally submerged waterplants, including water lilies (*Nymphaea* and

As the waters of the floodplain recede a bountiful harvest of fish is anticipated.

Nymphoides species) and various submerged plants. Emergent swamp vegetation is somewhat limited, confined mainly to the permanently wet areas near the river, and dominated by papyrus (*Cyperus papyrus*) and bulrush (also called cattail, *Typha domingensis*) communities. Palm savanna with *Borassus aethiopum* and *Hyphaene ventricosa* palms marks the limit of flooding.

Nearly 40 per cent of the *Vossia/Echinochloa* vegetation is consumed through grazing. Wild rice is a favourite food of lechwe antelope (*Kobus leche kafuensis*) but the *Paspalidium* water meadow, which normally floods to about 1 m (just over 3 ft), is the most impressive community. It is heavily grazed by lechwe during the early rain season and then grows rapidly during the floods to keep its shoots above

water. Up to 82 per cent is grazed as either fresh shoots or dry biomass.

The overall impression of the Kafue Flats is of a highly productive grassland; perhaps one of the most productive in the world which sustains intense dry season grazing by cattle owned by the Ila and Tonga tribesmen. In the drier areas some crops such as maize are cultivated and a few large-scale agricultural projects, particularly sugar-cane production, exist. High productivity ensures a rich aquatic environment and floodplain fisheries are a vital part of the country's protein production and economy - but the over-riding importance of the wetlands is for the great diversity of wildlife it supports.

The productivity of floodplains is determined by the continued input of nutrients into the system,

THE NIGER RIVER

The Niger is roughly 4,200 km (2,610 miles) long and has an overall catchment of some 1.25 million km² (0.48 million sq miles). Monsoonal rains fall at the head-waters of the Upper Niger between May and September, and create a surge in September which arrives at the river's inner delta a month or so later.

The inner delta region can extend over as much as 25,000 km² (9,650 sq miles) in the floods, but shrinks to only 4,000 km²

(1,540 sq miles) in the dry period. It receives practically no rainfall and the surge is a lifeline to survival for the local people. The surge gets dissipated in the swamps of the delta and silt is deposited.

Clear water leaves the inner delta to travel another 1,500 km (932 miles) or so, arriving some four or five months later (peak floods, January to March) in Kainji, where there is a man-made lake. As the water from the delta is clear but

darkened by iron salts, it is known as the 'black flood'. This distinguishes it from the 'white floods' of the Sokoto which are heavily laden with silt and peak in Lake Kainji in September following heavy rains to the northeast between April and October. Thus, at Lake Kainji there are two independent flooding regimes. Down river these are moderated by the barrage at the outflow to the lake.

PRODUCTION IN THE INNER NIGER DELTA

The floodplains of the Inner Niger Delta are dominated by highly productive grasslands which support many hundreds of thousands of people in fishing and pastoralism. Land is also cleared for rice cultivation. Productivity fluctuates with rainfall and flood levels, so when conditions are good, recorded fish landings may exceed 100,000 tonnes (98,000 tons), but in drought years this may be halved. Similarly, rice production in the southern half of the delta peaked at 85,000 tonnes (84,000 tons) in 1978, dropping to 4,600 tonnes (4,500 tons) in the droughts of 1984-85.

Livestock are numerous and a key component of the ecosystem, attracted by the rich flood recession pastures. Some 2 million cattle and 3 million sheep and goats were present before the numbers halved in the droughts. The delta is extremely important economically, exporting fish, livestock and rice to other parts of Mali and neighbouring countries.

Fish caught from the floodplain are smoked or dried in the sun to preserve them.

The cycle of seasonal flooding provides ideal wintering and passage condition for migratory birds, mostly from the Palearctic region. The gradual decline in water level from November to March concentrates the fish in drying pools and exposes mud rich in seeds and invertebrates. Over a million waterbirds winter on a regular basis. A few hippopotami and manatees still survive in the river, but their populations are threatened.

Human activities are generally compatible with bird populations and serious conflicts are rare. The single greatest determinant of the delta's ecology (and economy) is the fluctuating rainfall and the resultant flow of the River Niger. This has caused some land degradation and pasture loss due to drought and excessive grazing.

Three Ramsar sites covering 1,620 km² (625 sq miles) were declared by the Malian Government in 1987 in recognition of their importance for migratory birds.

and the cycling of nutrients within the system. The floodwaters carry fine, nutrient-rich sediments. On deposition these produce a thin veneer which enriches the floodplain and guarantees its continued productivity. The rising water drowns vegetation which cannot adapt to the new depths. In the Pongolo floodplains of South Africa, for example, *Cynodon dactylon* grass shoots are inundated and rot. The detritus and decomposition of the tissues provide enrichment to the rising water. The nutrients released enter the aquatic food cycle through plankton and periphyton.

A prolific invertebrate fauna, including crustaceans, insects and snails, develops rapidly. With the microorganisms and with the new growth of submerged plants, a rich food base for the floodplain fisheries is ensured.

As the water recedes the newly exposed land enriched by the floods sprouts to life. The dormant underground runners of *Cynodon* push up new shoots available for another season's grazing. During the season cowpats will enrich the land; hippopotami (*Hippopotamus amphibius*) wander off to the water to defecate using their little tails to propel their endproducts far and wide, and the cycle continues. This pattern, in one form or another, is repeated throughout Africa.

Floodplains are of major importance for both fish life and fishing activities. Nearly all river fishes make use of them and some remain on the floodplains, or its margins, throughout their lives. Initial flooding may

be accompanied by a short-lived reduction in oxygen levels and, in dense swamps, persistent oxygen depletion may preclude lateral migration by all except oxygen-thrifty or air-breathing fish.

For the majority of fish, however, the start of flooding triggers breeding activity. Spawning takes place at the edges of small rivers, or far out on the floodplain itself. Natural migrants intent on spawning are usually found at the leading edge of the flood as it channels out or spills on a broad front. With increasing depth, larger species emerge often to construct nests in flooded vegetation. Eventually the young disperse onto and over the floodplain. High water affords the main feeding, growing and fattening for the fish as the littoral area is then richest in food supply.

At draw-down a reverse migration back to the river ensues. It is led by fishes most sensitive to a changing aquatic environment on the foodplain. Large numbers of fish are invariably stranded during draw-down. Some are especially adapted to survive in floodplain swamps and shallows but others will perish unless they find persistent lakes or river backwaters.

Floodplains typically provide the most productive fisheries in river systems. Emerging species can become trapped, especially in flood channels, but at high water, when fish may be dispersed over wide areas, fishing becomes more difficult. The most intensive fishing activity typically takes place at

LAKE NAKURU AND LAKE NAIVASHA, KENYA

Over the course of millions of centuries, the tectonic forces which are tearing Africa apart have created the Rift Valley and contributed to the formation of many saline and soda lakes. Among them, Lake Nakuru has become known as the 'lake of a million flamingos'. The rich *Spirulina* algae and plankton which thrive in its alkaline waters attract vast numbers of lesser flamingos. Declared a bird sanctuary as early as 1961, this 40 km² (15 sq mile) lake is now a national park and a recently declared Ramsar site.

Nakuru is more than just the home of flamingos, which in fact do not breed here but come from Tanzanian lakes such as Lake Natron. Over 18,000 great white pelicans have been counted, as well as thousands of cormorants, herons, storks, ibises and shorebirds. Among the most prominent of these are the yellow-billed stork (*Mycteria ibis*), the marabou (*Leptoptilos crumeniferus*), the African spoonbill (*Platalea alba*), as well as 20 species of shorebirds and abundant grey-headed gull (*Larus cirrocephalus*).

In contrast, Lake Naivasha is one of the few freshwater lakes in Kenya. Its richer aquatic vegetation supports an extraordinarily diverse community of waterbirds. In January 1991, a count came up with 65 species, of which the red-knobbed coot (*Fulica cristata*), with 15,000, was the most abundant. Naivasha harbours almost the entire range of ducks and herons to be found in eastern Africa. The spectacular African fish eagle is particularly abundant.

There is good reason to hope that these wonderful wetlands will be preserved intact for future generations, since both lakes are major tourist attractions in a country where conservation and the national economy are closely linked through tourism.

---

draw-down. Trapping, netting, long-lining and spearing are all used to obtain a glut of fish from isolated lakes, pools and backwaters, and along swamp margins. The fishing is often shared with flocks of fish-eating birds and massive reduction of fish stocks takes place.

Saline Lakes and Saltpans

Africa is blessed with a number of saline wetlands of non-marine origin. This is not surprising when one considers the amount of volcanic activity that has taken place to form base-rich volcanic soils. When this is coupled with hot, dry conditions, evaporation from the soils - and lakes formed within them - will tend to concentrate the salts. If there is no flushing of the system, saline lakes and saltpans will result. Some volcanic crater lakes, such as Lake Katwe in

Spits in lakes and rivers often act as basking and preening places for waterbirds after they have fished. Hippopotami wallow in the shallows to evade the scorching tropical sun.

Uganda, are so saline that the salt deposits around the shores are collected for commercial purposes.

The eastern Rift Valley is peppered with hills and mountains of volcanic origin (the most famous being Mount Kilimanjaro and Mount Kenya) which deposited deep volcanic ash in the valley bottom. Thus, many of the shallow lakes in the eastern Rift, from Ethiopia to the east and south of Lake Victoria, are saline. Some of the better-known ones are: Lakes Nakuru, Magadi, Natron, Eyas and Manyara (which is part of a National Park and Game Reserve in Tanzania).

In the hot, more arid regions of southern Africa, such as the Zambezi Valley, dambos are prone to salination and saltpans are common. Indeed, in Botswana, the Makgadikgadi saltpan (an extended arm of the Okavango floodplain), at 37,000 km² (14,282 sq miles), has the distinction of being the largest in the world.

The vegetation of saltpans and saline lakes is very dependent upon salinity and hydrology. Some saltpans are only intermittently flooded: others are flooded seasonally. The centres of pans, with thick encrustations of salt, are devoid of vegetation.

In saline lakes, few 'freshwater' submerged macrophytes can tolerate salinities greater than one-tenth of seawater. *Potamogeton pectinatus* and *Najas marina* are more tolerant and can survive salination of up to one-third of seawater with temporary inundations of higher concentrations. Above this value algae tend to dominate, especially blue-green algae (Cyanophyta) such as *Spirulina* species.

In standing saline waters, emergent fringe vegetation may be dominated by *Cyperus laevigatus*, *Juncus maritimus* or *Dactyloctenium* species with *Diplachne fusca* on the grasslands and saltpans. The grass *Sporobolus spicatus* is also tolerant of relatively high salt concentrations but other species, such as *Sporobolus robustus,* will only survive moderate salinities. Around the edge of the Makagikgadi saltpan, where salinity is reduced, *Hyphaene* palms form a welcome respite from the monotonous landscape.

The salt-deposit areas of saltpans are inhospitable to wildlife but the fringes of pans and lakes provide grazing and feeding sites for game and bird life.

The centre of the Makgadikgadi saltpan, for example - a very hot and dry area - has no wildlife. It is crossed occasionally by ostriches (*Struthio camelus*) which need little water and can withstand heat and salt by excreting excess salt from their bodies through special nasal glands. At the edges of the pan an unusual lizard, the Makagikgadi spiny agama (*Agama hispida*), lives under the salt bushes and feeds on beetles and termites.

When the rains come the pan is transformed. The freshening water encourages lush growth of the grasslands and game in their thousands migrate to the newly created pastures, taking advantage of the salty vegetation.

The development of blue-green algae and the emergence of millions of brine shrimps in the water provides the basis of a rich food chain which attracts enormous flocks of birds, including greater and lesser flamingos (*Phoenicopterus ruber* and *Phoenicopterus minor*), from far and wide. It is suggested that they may migrate from the saline lakes of east Africa to form the largest breeding colonies of flamingos in Africa.

Permanent Herbaceous Swamps

African herbaceous swamps conjure up images of leech-ridden, crocodile-infested, mosquito-plagued environments. In reality, they are wetlands of great beauty which support a variety of dynamic ecosystems, and are classed amongst the most productive in the world. Papyrus, for example,

Papyrus can grow 6 m (18 ft) tall and is very difficult to pass through. Often, the base is floating on the surface of the water.

a dominant emergent waterplant in many swamps, can be twice as productive as maize or sugar cane. Even the production of submerged plants can nearly match that of maize and is five times higher than that of wild rice on the floodplains.

Permanent herbaceous swamps are found where the soil is permanently waterlogged or flooded. They are most extensive in the shallow Lake Victoria Basin where drowned valley swamps radiate from Lakes Victoria and Kyoga (approaching 30,000 km² - 11,580

PRODUCTIVITY OF AFRICAN WETLANDS

African wetlands include, arguably, the most productive ecosystems in the world.

The annual primary production of herbaceous swamps is the most impressive. Papyrus is estimated by some to have a production of up to 143 tonnes per hectare (57 tons per acre) under optimal conditions, though a more likely figure would be nearer 100 tonnes per hectare (40 tons per acre). Values for *Typha* and reed range from 30 to 70 tonnes per hectare (12 to 28 per acre). Surface-floating plants have

values in excess of 40 tonnes per hectare (16 tons per acre) or more.

Most surprising, perhaps, is the annual production of some submerged plants, often considered as dwarfs among giants. Potamogetons are reliably reported to produce up to 40 tonnes per hectare (16 tons per acre) per year. Sudd floodplain grasses can produce 8-10 tonnes per hectare (3-4 tons per acre) of biomass each year.

The Kafue Flats, Zambia, are, perhaps, the most productive floodplains: the *Paspalidium* water meadows produce 17

tonnes per hectare (7 tons per acre) and the *Vossia/Echinochloa scabra* grasslands produce 40 tonnes per hectare (16 tons per acre) of which 80 per cent and 40 per cent respectively, are removed annually by grazing.

As a yardstick, it is interesting to compare these values with those, say, of a highly productive crop plant such as sugar cane (63 tonnes per hectare - 25 tons per acre) and maize (60 tonnes per hectare - 24 tons per acre); and they need nurturing, irrigating and feeding regularly.

Floating vegetation can break away from the fringe swamp and form floating islands. Islands of Typha domingensis, *for example, blow across Lake Jipe, Tanzania. They congregate on the windward shore and make it impossible for the fishermen to get to the open water.*

sq miles) and the vast Sudd (20,000 km^2 - 7,720 sq miles). Other extensive swamps include those of the Okavango Delta (15,000 km^2 - 5,790 sq miles) and the Chad Basin (estimated at 7,000 km^2 - 2,700 sq miles - in 1976 but very susceptible to change). The swamps consist of a variety of competing plant communities, in zones regulated by the depth of water.

For convenience herbaceous swamps can be grouped into three main life-form categories: emergent plants; floating-leaved and submerged plants, plus those with both floating and submerged leaves; and (free) surface-floating plants.

The herbaceous swamp is the grande finale at the aquatic end of the floodplain succession. With increasing depth of water the floodplain grasses give way to emergent swamp, then to floating-leaved, rooted water plants (often called the lily zone) and finally to submerged plants which grow down to a maximum depth beyond which light intensity is inadequate. The free-floating vegetation, of course, is not regulated by depth of water.

The emergent plant communities of tropical Africa are tall and impenetrable. In the swamps of the Upper Nile, stands of papyrus and *Phragmites karka* reach over 6 m (roughly, 20 ft) tall. They rarely grow comfortably together but tend to form single-species stands, each with their associated flora. Papyrus overhangs the open waterways and gives the impression of massive expanses, similar to those of the drowned valley swamps of Uganda. In fact, the papyrus fringe is relatively narrow, obscuring vast areas of *Typha* behind. *Phragmites* is not so prevalent and tends to occur nearer the main river channels. *Vossia* fringes the swamp in competition with surface-floating macrophytes.

The wildlife habitats of emergent swamps can be divided into inner and fringe regions. Curiously, although the inner swamp supports high plant biomass, this is not balanced by an equivalent profusion of animals. The reasons for this are not known for certain. There is no doubt that the inner region is not easily accessible and is inhospitable to terrestrially adapted animals. Indeed, our own knowledge is severely limited by this very problem.

Few studies have been carried out on the invertebrate fauna of emergent vegetation, but indications are that, although diversity may be high, total numbers are variable and the actual amount of plant biomass removed by grazing is insignificant. Maybe this is a credit to the defensive mechanisms of the plants.

Aquatic invertebrates and fish, unless specially adapted, are restricted by low oxygen concentrations in the inner swamp. Swamp fish survive in shallow water and pools of irregular oxygenation. Lungfish (*Protopterus* species) and catfish (*Clarias* species) are examples. But again, limited information suggests they are more common near the edges than in the centre of a swamp.

The outer fringe, on the other hand, is very productive. The extraordinarily rich fish populations and fisheries potential have been mentioned in sections on floodplain ecology. The ecology and dynamics of the interface between the swamp edge and open water will be discussed later.

Floating rafts of emergent vegetation occur in many African swamps. The integrity of the raft is dependent upon buoyant rhizomes forming a strong, intertwining mat which acts as a base for the vegetation. A number of species has this ability, foremost amongst them papyrus. The mat can be up to 4 m (13 ft) thick and, with time, it consolidates to provide a sufficiently stable environment for the establishment of trees.

Floating swamps grow out from rooted swamps, and can stretch across bodies of water, no matter how deep. Wave and wind action can detach the raft from its rooted anchor and islands of vegetation, sometimes colossal in area, are conveyed by wind and current across bodies of water. The larger ones have enormous momentum and are notorious for blocking navigation ways and harbours. The Sudd derived its name from the Arabic, meaning, 'blockage'; the boats of early explorers seeking the source of the Nile River were frequently blocked by islands of floating vegetation. Surface-floating plants (not to be confused with rafts of emergent swamps) also form thick mats of floating vegetation which cause similar problems.

Floating swamps (of surface floating plants or emergent vegetation) have special features which affect the ecology and dynamics of the ecosystem. First, the raft acts as a blanket suppressing the exchange of gases between the air and water surface. The underside of the mat becomes deoxygenated and it is not unusual for the entire water column to be anoxic. The deoxygenated water can be toxic to macro-invertebrates and lake fish.

Plants in the zone of deeper water beyond the emergent vegetation grade from floating-leaved to submerged species. It is a species-rich zone which can extend down to depths of 10 m (33 ft), although

On the Nile, large floating islands of papyrus are used by people to convey themselves, their livestock and their ware, downstream.

Potamogeton thunbergii, *a floating-leaved water plant, is commonly found at the interface between emergent swamp and open water.*

turbidity and phytoplankton blooms often restrict the depth of colonisation to a few metres. Water lilies, floating-leaved Potamogetons and water chestnut (*Trapa natans*) are all widely distributed. Amongst the submerged species, Potamogetons, strapweeds (*Vallisneria spiralis*), bladderworts (*Utricularia* species), *Lagarosiphon* species and *Ceratophyllum demersum*, are perhaps the most common. The last two can become particularly troublesome weeds.

The submerged plants are vitally important in oxygenating the water, whilst shoots provide a vast surface area for colonization by attached algae, bacteria and protozoa; these provide ideal conditions for grazers, particulary invertebrates and young fish.

Some fish, especially the commercially important *Tilapia*, nibble away at vegetation, and hippopotami from Lake Turkana, Kenya, have been reported to consume substantial volumes of *Potamogeton pectinatus*. The food storage organs and fruits of those plants are favourite foods of waterbirds and many come to feast on the rich harvest. Many juvenile fish hiding and feeding in the vegetation are preyed upon by cormorants (*Phalacrocorax africanus*) and darters (*Anhinga rufa*).

Forming a distinctive zone, commonly called the interface zone, many of these plants act as a nutrient filter between the swamp fringe and open water. The biological and chemical interactions at this zone create some of the most fertile habitats in the aquatic environment in terms of biodiversity and productivity.

The high fish production potential there has not escaped the attention of local fishermen. It has been estimated that 36 per cent of the freshwater fish catch in Africa comes from swamp fringes and floodplains.

In the Bangweulu Swamp, Zambia, for example, gill-net catches around the vegetation are three times greater than in open water.

The breadth of the zone may be only a few metres or it may spread out over a wide area. Like, for example, the Okavango Delta, where shallow, meandering waterways form an intricate network of ever-changing channels through the vegetation mass.

How does the interface zone function and why is it so important? Basically, it is a buffer zone. When there are water level changes water will move between the floodplain, the emergent swamp and the lake or river through the submerged and floating-leaved vegetation. Run-off water will flush through the swamp taking with it, perhaps, ions and partially oxygenated water from below a floating raft, or organic detritus from a rooted swamp.

The vegetation will oxygenate the incoming water and trap nutrients. The efficiency of trapping is variable and depends upon local conditions. Where submerged plants are growing rapidly under low nutrient conditions, the retention of nutrients can be almost complete. In lakes, these nutrients can be carried down with the colder, denser water from the swamp into deep water where they may be irretrievable.

The outer fringe of the swamp, together with all the plants and attached organisms, provide refuge, breeding sites and a rich food base in a highly productive food web.

Surface-floating plants such as the Nile lettuce (*Pistia stratiotes*), water fern (*Azolla nilotica*) and members of the duckweed family (Lemnaceae) are indigenous, but others, especially the water hyacinth (*Eichhornia crassipes*) and Kariba weed (*Salvinia molesta*) have been introduced to African swamps.

In Africa, most surface-floating plants have exceptionally high rates of growth causing some to become serious weeds. Water hyacinth, for example, grows rapidly in the backwaters and inlets of the Sudd, and the upper reaches of the Zaïre River. Some are dislodged by wind, wave action and fluctuating water levels, and detached plants are carried down river. They join up with those from other inlets and tributaries to form islands of floating vegetation which only too readily form weed barrages. Bridges, landing stages and other man-made structures may be swept down river by the force of the jammed vegetation and navigation becomes virtually impossible.

Most rivers and channels in Africa are susceptible to this potential problem and where weeds impair drainage an ideal habitat for carriers of some of the most unpleasant water-associated diseases, such as bilharzia snails and malaria mosquitoes, is provided.

Surface-floating plants can exhibit prodigious growth under sheltered conditions with a good nutrient supply: for example, the Kariba weed infestations on Lake Kariba and the water hyacinth plague on Hartebeespoort Dam, South Africa. One of the most dramatic water plant invasions ever was on Lake Kariba in 1963; vast mats of Kariba weed covered over 1,000 km² (386 sq miles) of the water surface. Generally, however, as new man-made lakes settle down, the normal course of events is for nutrients to become limiting, populations of waterweeds to decline, and for a more diverse and naturally-balanced foodweb to develop.

Although surface-floating water weed problems are most dramatic in man-made lakes they are not confined to such environments. Lake Chad and the Sudd have long been troubled with occasional profusions of Nile lettuce growth.

The positive side of surface-floating water plant existence sometimes get overlooked. Some species, such as duckweeds, are highly nutritious and are grazed by a range of fauna including aquatic invertebrates and waterbirds. Usually, leaves of surface-floating plants are relatively unpalatable - yet, even they provide refuge and support for a bustling community of leaf-trotters, frogs and toads, emerging pupae and nesting waterbirds. The rich faunal communities associated with the roots bear witness to the valuable habitat they provide, particularly for fish fry. The Nile lettuce, for example, has leathery leaves not easily chewed, except occasionally by hippopotami, but the stems, leaf bases and roots are host to a range of invertebrate nibblers, grazers and burrowers. The high biomass, of course, can always be harvested for man's use.

High Altitude Swamps, Bogs and Mires

Compared with the total area of Africa, upland regions are very restricted. Wetlands represent only a small proportion of the uplands and are largely uncharted. The high-altitude African wetlands have a quite different structure from lowland swamps. Temperatures are lower and, consequently, decomposition in the wetlands is slower. Largely as a result of these factors, organic detritus accumulates, and peats are formed.

Three vegetation zones can be recognized in the uplands: the Afro-montane zone, the sub-(afro)alpine zone (or Ericaceous Belt) and at the highest altitudes, the Afro-alpine zone. Where these zones begin and end depends upon the size of the plant community, their climate, their aspect, and their latitude. Generally speaking, the higher the latitude the lower the altitudes at which the zones begin. For example, in east Africa the Afro-montane region starts at about 1,800 m (6,000 ft), whereas in the Drakensberg Mountains in southern Africa, it lies between about 1,200 and 1,800 m (4,000 and 6,000 ft).

The Ethiopian Highlands constitute some of the larger wetland areas. In other mountainous regions - such as the Rwenzori Mountains, Mounts Kenya, Elgon, Kilimanjaro and the Usambara Range in eastern Africa; the Cameroon and Fouta Djallon Highlands in western Africa; the Mlanje and the Drakensberg Ranges in southern Africa - upland wetlands remain largely uncharted and unclassified. High population pressures have ensured that those that are accessible either have been destroyed or are under imminent threat.

In east Africa, high altitude mires are dominated by tussocks of sedges, usually *Carex runssoroensis* at the

A saddlebill stork in the Sudd swamps of the Upper Nile. In the background, expanses of water hyacinth, the invasive water plant which has largely replaced Pistia *in the Sudd.*

131

The upland bogs of Lesotho regenerate very slowly. They are threatened by a proposed massive Highland Water Project.

higher altitudes (above about 3,300 m - 10,800 ft) and *Pycreus nigricans* at the lower altitudes (about 2,000 to 3,300 m - 6,560 to 10,800 ft). *Sphagnum* moss is frequent in the *Carex* mires of the Rwenzori and Aberdare mountains but is rare on Mount Elgon.

The Afro-alpine vegetation is easily destabilized. Few people live in the region although lumbering continues its upward expansion. Clearance, inevitably, will destroy the accompanying wetlands. In the higher regions, soil erosion from excessive tourism, climbing and mountain walking can quickly break up the terrain. At these high altitudes and low temperatures, growth rates are minimal and recovery of the communities is very slow.

At the lowest altitude of the montane region papyrus can dominate the mire, but it dies out at 2,100 m (6,890 ft). Mires can become overgrown by ericaceous plants and bushes such as *Erica kingaensis* and the refreshingly scented African bog myrtle, (*Myrica kandtiana*). The mires can even support closed-canopy swamp forest (especially, *Syzygium cordatum*) or thicket.

The eastern foothills of the Rwenzori Mountains in southwestern Uganda, Rwanda and Burundi are regions of great geomorphological upheaval and volcanic history (some are still active). The back-tilting or volcanic damming of many valleys has allowed lakes (such as Bunyonyi and Mutanda), swamps and mires to evolve. The overall effect is one

of breathtaking beauty: steeply terraced or wooded hills capped with montane forests forming a perfect backdrop to the glistening lakes and emerald green valley swamps. All produce soils of high organic content or are peat-forming. Pools, bogs and flushes abound wherever depressions occur or springs emerge.

The wetlands in the Drakensberg Mountains make an interesting comparison to those of the Rwenzori. The mountain kingdom of Lesotho in the southern half of the range has one of the highest mean altitudes in the world and is known as Africa's Switzerland. The climate is one of summer rains and dry winters with hard frosts and occasional heavy snowfalls in the highlands.

Lesotho's Afro-montane belt occupies a narrow strip of land roughly encircling the country. (In the centre of the Kingdom massive basaltic extrusions overlie the sandstone.) Streams and rivers which come rushing from the highlands meander their way through the softer lowland formations cutting deep gullies in the land.

Soil erosion is acute, aggravated by poor land management, heavy grazing and trampling, and poorly designed roads. Lakes and pools tend to be clouded by suspended sediments and their water levels fluctuate drastically with season. The fringes of lakes (usually farm dams and reservoirs), the banks of rivers and their floodplains and seepage areas are colonized by common emergents such as *Miscanthidium*, *Typha* and *Phragmites*. The latter was widespread in damp areas but cultivation, burning and overgrazing has reduced its distribution substantially.

Lesotho's sub-alpine and alpine belts occur within the basaltic zone. The streams and rivers from the mountains are numerous, fast-flowing and with little sediment burdens. The tree line is at about 2,300 m (7,550 ft) and 100 m (328 ft); above this no further cultivation is possible.

The nutrient-poor soils and vegetation are determined by the hard rock; bogs and mires nestle in waterlogged depressions. The wetland vegetation is very different from the lowland reed beds.

Two main forms of alpine and sub-alpine wetlands can be identified in Lesotho, although sometimes they are intermixed: first, those characterized by tallish vegetation (up to 1 m - 3 $1/3$ ft high) and, second, those characterized by flat, carpet-like vegetation not more than a few millimetres above the water. Both are composed primarily of flowering plants.

Tall tussock grasses, especially *Danthonia* species, line the banks of the rivers and streams and colonize wet areas. Spikey tussocks of moseha grass (*Merxmuellera macowanii*) also form a distinctive community along stream banks. Above flushes, the beautiful bog red hot poker (*Kniphofia caulescens*) with *Geum capensis* add colour to the scene, whilst pipeworts (*Eriocaulon* species) form mats between the tussocks.

The carpet bogs are dominated by various cushion angiosperms. Mosses and liverworts are rarely dominant and, surprisingly, the bog moss (*Sphagnum*) has not been recorded from Lesotho. The overall height of the bog vegetation decreases with increased altitude. *Kniphofia caulescens* and *Danthonia drakensbergensis* are often the only species which give any semblance of height. Above about 3,000 m (9,840 ft), the vegetation is usually less than 200 mm (8 in) tall and decreases to 10 to 20 mm ($2/5$ to $4/5$ in) in the highest bogs.

Bogs at the heads of the valleys and others on the hills and mountain tops moderate the release of water to the streams and so reduce erosion to a minimum. The peat layer in the shallow depressions is thin, but in other areas it reaches a depth of 2 m (6 $1/2$ ft). These bogs are said to be of late- or post-glacial age, and lay down peat at the impressively slow rate of about 0.25 mm ($1/100$ in) a year.

A feature of the Lesotho bogs are the raised hummocks often capped with the white composite, *Athrixia fontana*. Their origin has aroused much speculation: some reckon they are earthworks made

by mole-rats (*Cryptomys natalensis natalensis*) or real moles (*Chlorotalpa guillarmodii*); others suggest that they are ice-induced. Sedge meadows dominated by *Carex* species occur around the edges of the bogs. Not all the wetlands are peat-based and the edges of streams and pools can support vleis (marshes).

The global importance of the African upland vegetation is its uniqueness and limited distribution. It has been considered an 'archipelago' of widely distributed islands of vegetation on the African mainland. It is a very sobering thought to realize that the wetlands represent only a small fraction of that limited area. Often they occur in relatively inaccessible regions or inhospitable environments and our knowledge of the them is sadly lacking.

FLORA AND FAUNA
The plants which make up the African wetland vegetation are an integral part of, and a driving force in, the dynamics of the wetlands. Therefore, they have not been treated as a separate entity: rather, the plant associations which determine the types of wetlands, and their functioning, have been included in the wetland descriptions. Likewise, the secondary producers, which are a composite part of the wetland ecosystem - particularly the invertebrates and fish - have been considered with the sections on wetland dynamics.

African wetlands offer crucial refuges, watering places and feeding grounds for a profusion of game and birds. Indeed, they support and provide sanctuary for the greatest wildlife spectacles in the world. The survival of African 'Big Game' and migratory and resident waterbirds, which are the basis of a thriving tourist industry, are heavily dependent upon the wetlands. Thus, the role of wetlands in African game and waterbird survival has been selected for special attention.

African Game
The floodplains and temporary pools are of special significance. As well as supporting nomadic tribesmen and their cattle, Africa's floodplains are crucial to a wide range of wildlife. Two examples are sufficient to highlight the balance of nature in the floodplains, but variations can be found throughout Africa.

The white-eared kob (*Kobus kob leucotis*) is an extremely rare antelope only found in the floodplains of the Upper Nile in southern Sudan and along the borders of Ethiopia. Each year the population, a million strong, undertakes a massive migration of over 1,500 km (930 miles). This represents one of the largest masses of migrating animals in the world,

African wetlands are vital to wild animals, especially in the dry season. An elephant in Queen Elizabeth National Park, Uganda, cools itself in the Kasinga Channel.

far exceeding the migrations of wilderbeest (*Connochaetes taurinus*) in the Serengeti Plains.

The kob start their journey from the Kidepo River and floodplains on the border of Uganda and southern Sudan at the end of the rains in September. When the grass has dried up they head north towards the *Echinochloa* floodplains of the Upper Nile. Here, the black cotton soils, with their pastures lush from the receding floodwaters, become the kob's temporary home.

While in the region the kob play a vital part in the life of the local people. Each year some 5000 individuals (less than 0.5 per cent of the population) are hunted by the Murle tribe for protein. None of the meat is wasted, the excess being sun-dried for later use.

By December, these floodplains have become parched and the migration proceeds to its northern limit - the permanent swamps of Gwom. Wildlife in these swamps at this time of year is rich and varied: fish are concentrated in the pools, and yellow-billed (*Ibis Ibis*) and open-billed storks (*Anastomus lameltigerus*) abound. After December bush fires cause the kob to move east to their breeding grounds in Ethiopia. In late February and March, at the height of the dry season, the Neubari River, and its pans and floodplains, provide vital sustenance to the herd (and to crocodiles and other predators). After mating in April the kob move towards woodlands and then start their long trek back to Kidepo.

The dynamics of the floodplains in the southern Sudan have, thus, over thousands of years, created a

behaviour pattern in the kob which supports an entire way of life in terms of predators (including man) and prey. If this is to be disturbed, say by changing the flooding regime, then the ecosystem may be destroyed.

The Okavango Delta and Kafue Flats offer refuge to some of Africa's most glorious wildlife. The Okavango Delta will be discussed in the next section. First to the Kafue Flats where two national parks, Blue Lagoon and the Lochinvar, have been established as wildlife sanctuaries. The meandering Kafue River attracts enormous and diverse bird populations. Indeed, the national parks are listed amongst the 10 best bird sanctuaries in the world.

During the dry season large herds of wild game come to graze: zebra (*Equus burchelli*); buffalo (*Syncerus caffer*); oribi (*Ourebi ourebi*), a small, very graceful antelope; and kudu (*Tragelaphus strepsiceros*) - to mention just a few. Inevitably these are accompanied by their predators, such as lion (*Panthera leo*), wild dog (*Lycaon pictus*) and spotted hyena (*Crocuta crocuta*).

Of prime importance is the Kafue lechwe, an endemic race of antelope with particularly fine horns. Lechwe graze the floodplain grasses following the rising and falling waters; they wade out to depths of 600 mm (2 ft). These are the most common antelope on the floodplain and are largely responsible for the intensive grazing. The Kafue Flats offer one of its last strongholds.

Permanent swamps provide very different functions and habitats for wildlife and attract game from far and wide, especially in the dry season. The outer (landward) zones particularly, provide watering holes and wallows for game and their predators. Amongst the big game, crocodiles, elephant (*Loxodonta africana*), buffalo and hippopotamus favour the semi-aquatic environment.

In contrast, few large herbivores are at home in the inner regions of dense emergent swamps. The lechwe and sitatunga (*Tragelaphus spekei*) have enlarged, supple, elongate hooves adapted for swamp conditions, but they are not normally found in great numbers. The Okavango Delta is a refuge for the sitatunga. A shy animal, it is ideally adapted to the floating vegetation. When danger lurks it submerges itself in the water, its nose poking out.

Perhaps one of the few widespread resident game animals found around emergent swamps is the hippopotamus. But it rarely ventures into the heart of the swamp, confining itself to the periphery and well-trodden tracks leading to wallows and pools. For feeding, it prefers the lush grasses at the swamp edge and floodplains.

The little egret (Egretta garzetta), *fishing in a pool in gallery forest in the Gambia.*

Similarly, few birds specifically inhabit and solely depend upon the inner swamp, although the fringes may be a hive of activity.

Waterbirds
The wetlands of Africa provide vital wintering grounds for Palearctic waterbirds. They use two main migration routes: the east Atlantic route which leads into west Africa, and the so-called 'eastern African flyway', used by millions of ducks and shorebirds which follow the Nile and Rift Valleys south to winter in the vast Sudd marshes, or South Africa after flights of up to 14,000 km (8,700 miles).

With over 230 species, the waterbird community of the Afro-tropical realm is a rich one, further enhanced by a variety of warblers and raptors. (It does, however, lack some striking waterbird groups of the Northern Hemisphere, such as swans and true geese.)

Some of these species are threatened. Madagascar alone, for example, has 12 endemic species, but the alaotra grebe (*Tachybaptus rufolavatus*) is gradually hybridizing with a continental invader, the little grebe (*Tachybaptus ruficollis*). The Madagascar pochard (*Aythya innotata*), not seen since 1970, may be extinct. On the mainland, some species have a dangerously restricted range or a low population: the shoebill (*Balaeniceps rex*) is down to 11,000 birds. Others in

danger include the slaty egret (*Egretta vinaceigula*), the damara tern (*Sterna balaenarum*) and the yellow swamp warbler (*Calamonastides gracilirostris*) found only around Lake George in western Uganda.

Fortunately, many species have a wider distribution. These include: the crowned crane (*Balearica pavonina*), one of Africa's most famous birds; the African fish eagle (*Haliaeetus vocifer*), conspicuous in trees that dot wetlands; and various egrets, ibises and storks which are found even in the middle of villages and towns, where they sometimes breed. The hammerkop (*Scopus umbretta*), although hardly distinctive in its drab brown plumage, is famous for its disproportionately huge nests. Southern and eastern Africa host several endemic but widespread ducks, such as the red-billed teal (*Anas erythrorhyncha*), the yellow-billed duck (*Anas undulata*) and the maccoa duck (*Oxyura maccoa*); the vast Okavango in Botswana is one of their most famous haunts.

The interface zone between the emergent swamp and open water is a favourite hunting ground and roosting area for a plethora of bird life. They are attracted, of course, by the rich harvest of fish and amphibians. Fish eagles, cormorants, egrets (*Egretta* species), hammerkops, pelicans (*Pelecanus* species), a plethora of ducks and geese, and a confusion of lily-trotters, waders, storks and so on all congregate above the interface zone. The rousing chorus of toads and frogs to be heard in the evenings reminds one of the amphibian life. This profusion of wildlife in its turn attracts scavengers and predators, including humans.

Surprisingly, the drought-stricken Sahel holds the largest concentrations of migrant ducks in Africa. Nearly a million garganey (*Anas querquedula*) and up to 300,000 pintail (*Anas acuta*) winter in the Niger floodplains in Mali, which also has most western Palearctic glossy ibises (*Plegadis falcinellus*) and ferruginous ducks (*Aythya nyroca*). Lake Chad may hold up to a million wintering ducks, and the Bijagos in Guinea Bissau similar numbers of shorebirds.

Strikingly, Afro-tropical species form a minor proportion of most concentrations of wetland birds in west Africa. The numbers of the Afro-tropical species are thought to be limited by the dry season, when their migrant cousins return to their Arctic and temperate breeding grounds. However, some ducks like the white-faced whistling duck (*Dendrocygna viduata*), the spur-winged goose (*Plectropterus gambensis*), or the knob-billed duck (*Sarkidiornis malanotos*) can gather in non-breeding time in flocks of tens of thousands.

Some tropical species breed in huge colonies. The Inner Niger Delta may have over 80,000 pairs of

15 species of cormorant, heron and ibis. The great white pelican (*Pelecanus onocrotalus*) has some 25 colonies in the whole continent, some numbering as many as 40,000 pairs - the colonies at Lake Abijatta-Shalla in Ethiopia and Lake Rukwa in Tanzania, for instance.

Some ducks and shorebirds, such as the ruff (*Philomachus pugnax*), have been able to adapt to conditions in the many natural wetlands that have been converted to agriculture uses, particularly rice fields, but they are now accused of damaging crops. Furthermore, the increasing use of pesticides in crops may, in fact, soon pose serious problems to the survival of these species.

VALUES AND USES

A discussion of the values and uses of African wetlands can be be divided into four sections: first, their contribution to global issues; second, their functional values; third, their habitat and biological values; and, last, their anthropogenic values - that is, their values in relation to human activity. This division is one of convenience, to focus the mind.

Global Values

Put together, the wetlands of Africa constitute one of the largest expanses of wetland in the world. As the continent spans the tropics, warm average temperatures ensure a high rate of biological activity. Decomposition is fast and the rapid cycling of carbon and nutrients is normal. It is not difficult, therefore, to make a case for the conservation of wetlands on the grounds of their importance for carbon cycling and to avert the threat of global warming.

On another front, the biodiversity and gene pools of Africa are very rich. The concept of island evolution is particularly relevant. Jonathan Kingdon in *Island Africa, The Evolution of Africa's Rare Animals and Plants* has argued that thanks to the development of geological and geographical barriers and climatic zones, the flora and fauna of Africa became isolated into centres or biogeographical 'islands' and in these the evolution of many endemic species occurred. White in *Vegetation of Africa* recognizes nine centres of endemism for vegetation, each having 'more than 50 per cent of its species confined to it and a total of more than 1,000 endemic species'.

The high number of centres ensures a great degree of biodiversity as well as valuable gene pools. Each centre can itself be considered as an archipelago of wetlands which enhance genetic diversity even further. Among plants alone are all the plants with nutritional or medicinal value for which the wetlands provide the habitat and gene pool: the genetic stocks of wild rice plants and oil palms come to mind.

The many small uncharted permanent and seasonal wetlands in dambos, pans and pools provide a refuge for aquatic plants and animals and act as stepping stones for gene flow.

Functional Values

African wetlands have important functional values and, in the light of the extraordinary pressures upon the wetlands, it is important to stress these. For instance, the influence of wetlands on microclimate. Even though concrete data are few, it is important to be aware of potential links. The Sudd and the Okavango Delta can be taken as models: viridescent jewels set in seas of sand.

The Sudd floodplains and accompanying rain-fed, seasonal wetlands of the Upper Nile comprise one of the largest wetland areas in the world. The Sahara Desert lies immediately to the north and is encroaching southwards. The Sudd spans a very hot, dry climatic zone and evapotranspiration is enormous (estimated to be 2,150 mm - 85 in - annually).

If the wetland shrinks, evapotranspiration, which effectively reduces extremes of temperature, will be reduced accordingly. At the same time, a rise in mean daytime temperatures over the Sudd may be expected. If temperatures rise, potential evaporation will be greater, but over a more limited area. The path of rising warm moist air masses is still uncharted, but it is safe to say that many territories in already marginal rainfall areas would be likely to suffer further deprivation. Within the Sahel, the consequences would be incalculable.

There are similar concerns for the Okavango Delta. Permanent swamp occupies about half the wetland, the rest being seasonal floodplain. It is a massive oasis in the middle of a desert. A staggering statistic is that some 95 per cent of the water is lost to evapotranspiration. If the flow of water to the delta is impeded, then total evaporative loss will be reduced

An aerial view of the Okavango River.

The wetlands provide essential habitats and refuges to a wide diversity of game. The Nile crocodile is under threat from hunting and loss of habitat. If the flow of rivers and natural flood cycle is impeded many habitats will disappear.

and, once again, there is the question of effects on microclimate. In Namibia, there is a proposal to divert 3 per cent of the Okavango River flow, and upstream in Angola, water demand is likely to increase with development programmes.

A frequently expressed asset of a wetland is its ability to act as a sponge, thus reducing the damaging effects of floods. The wetland absorbs run-off from the catchment, filters out accompanying sediments and nutrients and releases the excess. During dry periods, slow release sustains and replenishes streams below. In a continent where dry seasons can last all too long, this is particularly valuable.

Habitat Values

One of the most familiar and eye-catching values of African wetlands is their provision of wildlife habitats. The habitats, scattered over 60 degrees of latitude and spanning the Equator, range from non-marine and marine saline wetlands (mangrove swamps, mudflats, saltpans, salt lakes and so on) to rain-fed peat bogs, swamp forests, lake littorals, permanent swamps and seasonal floodplains.

Just as important as habitat diversity is the range in size of the wetlands. Inevitably those wetlands, such as the Okavango Delta, Lake Nakuru or Senegal Delta, which provide wildlife spectacles are the best known by the general public in many countries. However, it is important to bear in mind that the innumerable pans, dambos, seasonal wetlands, tiny lakes and transient ponds, as well as man-made habitats, all contribute to the mosaic of African habitats.

Wetland wildlife can be divided into two main categories: indigenous residents and transient or migratory species. African wildlife relies heavily on wetlands. The big game animals are, perhaps, the most emotive. Already under pressure from human activities, the continued existence of a number of species is at risk if wetland habitats are mismanaged further. Of immediate concern are those species under imminent threat, such as the African manatee and shoebill stork. But other, more common animals such as crocodiles and elephant are also in danger.

Transient and migratory populations of animals and birds are also reliant on wetlands. The annual migration of vast numbers of Palearctic birds along the Nile and across the wetlands of eastern coastal Africa to the west African floodplains as far south as the Cape Province is legendary.

On a less grand scale is the seasonal migration of game. The long treks of the white-eared kob from floodplain to floodplain across southern Sudan to Ethiopia and back has already been mentioned. In the Sudd, the kob share the territory with up to 16 other large herbivorous species. The most numerous are the tiang antelope (*Damaliscus korrigum*) which in the dry season, while the white-eared kob migrate towards the northeast floodplains and Ethiopia, move to the northwest floodplains of the Nile. For all these species the wetlands are their refuge and sustenance. Therefore, not only is the presence of a wetland important to wildlife survival, but the animals are also often geared to the dynamics of particular wetlands. If these change, or are changed, the animals may not be able to adapt.

Anthropogenic Values

Is it possible to evaluate the use of wetlands for human beings and their quality of life? To whom should the valuation be directed? The criteria for nations and for local inhabitants can be very different. Athropogenic activities can be separated into two categories: extrinsic and intrinsic values.

Nursery beds of rain-fed upland rice in Sierra Leone. As long as there is not excessive use of agrochemicals these do little damage to the environment.

Extrinsic values concern mainly governments, national and international organizations, large landowners and those who exploit wetlands for commercial purposes. In developing countries, governments with desperate needs to feed their peoples and to raise hard currency for foreign exchange participate in, and sanction, a number of activities under the umbrella of 'development'. These activities are not always in harmony with the environment and can result in fundamental change to the ecosystem. Forestry, paddy rice schemes, intensive agriculture, cattle ranching and large-scale water extraction for industrial and domestic purposes come into this category.

The value of wetlands for tourism must not be overlooked. In 1988 Botswana welcomed over 300,000 tourists who contributed some US$47 million to the country's balance of payments. Many of the tourists will have visited the Okavango Delta, advertized as one of the last wildernesses in the world. The tourist trade in Kenya, Zimbabwe, the Gambia and many other countries is focused on wildlife. The wetlands are an integral and spectacular part of the wildlife habitats. Although tourists are looked upon with mixed feelings, they may provide a lifeline for some of the larger wetlands.

As for intrinsic values, the lives of people in many rural economies are geared to, and revolve around, the functioning of wetlands. At the individual, family, village and community level, the wetland is there to serve their needs. In an African village abutting a wetland, the elegantly reed-thatched houses and huts might well, for example, be constructed from wetland materials - be they timbers from mangroves, trunks from palm trees or bundles of papyrus. The walls might be of bricks or of clay and muds from the wetland sediments; the floors might be strewn with dried cattail and myrtle (*Myrica* species) for sweet aromas or with mats woven from reeds, raphia palm leaflets or papyrus.

The range of wetland food plants that such communities rely on is impressive: starch from, for example, water lilies, water chestnuts and wild rice; oil from the oil palm; wine and beer from the oozing sap of palm trees; and fruits in season. Wetland trees and shrubs provide fuelwood; their leaves provide fodder. Goats, sheep, poultry and cattle graze the water meadow, browse the swamp edge and drink the water.

Countless items, which in themselves hardly warrant a mention and are practically worthless in monetary terms, are interwoven in an intricate sociological structure which is the basis of survival. When a wetland is modified or destroyed these 'little things' get forgotten. Yet they represent individual life styles and ways of sustainable existence which are rarely replaced.

Wetlands are also important for cottage industries and home markets. In Uganda, for example, during 20 years of civil war when commodities were limited, a plethora of entrepreneurial activities sprang up around swamps. Foremost amongst these in the lowland clay-based swamps is brick-making, which has in fact created its own problems. Swamp edges are now pitted with clay excavations and dotted with brick kilns fired by fuelwood. Unfortunately, wetlands have been damaged as a result. The pits also form a hazard to small children; the cutting of fuelwood has destroyed many trees, and malaria mosquitoes are now prevalent.

The natural produce of wetlands is always a source

Fisherman in Nyumba ya Mungu Reservoir, Tanzania, take advantage of the rich harvest of fish to be caught at the interface zone of a swamp.

In the Hadejia-Nguru floodplains of Nigeria, the fruits of water lilies are collected and dried in the sun for food. Water plants offer a wide range of nutritious foods to local communities. When wetlands are destroyed these 'hidden' values are rarely considered.

of income. Reeds cut for thatch provide an obvious example, whilst in village markets all over Africa brightly coloured mats, baskets and bowls made from the fibres of wetland plants enliven the ware. There is a profusion of fish in the swamps. In many communities it is the trapping, spearing, rod-and-line fishing and netting of fish in the areas where swamps meet open water that offers the most sustainable livelihood.

In the floodplains whole cultures and rural economies are based upon the regular ebb and flow of the waters across the land. It is most apparent in the larger floodplain ecosystems such as the Inner Niger Delta, the Lake Chad Basin, the floodplains of the Sudd, the Okavango Delta and the Kafue Flats, where so many people depend upon the natural cycle.

In some regions traditional husbandry still underpins the existence and survival of a community. The Nilotes in the Sudd region are an example. Numbering 300,000-400,000 people, and dominated by three main tribal groups, the Dinka, Nuer and Shilluk, the society depends upon the Nile floods and the associated rain-fed grasslands. Traditional grazing practices have developed over centuries to utilize most effectively the productivity of the grasslands.

Differences in custom between tribes ensure full utilization of the ecosystem. The Dinka and Nuer are pastoralists who prize their cattle: they may travel hundreds of kilometres a year. (Hard times have forced some of the Dinka to live right in the middle of the swamps and survive largely on fish, but it is said they would dearly love to return to a pastoral way of life.) The Shilluk are a sedentary people who have fewer cattle and maintain wet-season gardens on tenured land for cultivation. They particularly enjoy

fishing. Through necessity, all tribal groups support a mixed economy of livestock, crops (sorghum, maize, beans, groundnuts and so on) and fishing.

Other river and floodplain ecosystems have been greatly altered to take advantage of the alluvial soils, enriched annually by the life-giving veneer of silt. The Inner Niger Delta, supporting hundreds of thousands of people through fishing, pastoralism and cultivation, is a good example. The delta can now be considered as one enormous agricultural area based on traditional systems greatly modified by land clearance, drainage and irrigation schemes.

THREATS TO AFRICAN WETLANDS
Africa still has a good proportion of its natural wetlands but they are under threat. The question is how best to achieve a high standard of living for the disparate people of the continent without annihilating the environment. Examples of the threats to African wetlands will provide a basis of understanding for recommended management policies.

In the earlier part of the century, the growing need for energy and for water supply encouraged the building of massive dams across major rivers - the Aswan High Dam on the Nile; the Kainji Dam on the Niger; the Volta Dam on the Volta River; the Kariba and Cabora Bassa Dams on the Zambezi, to mention just a few - as well as numerous smaller dams and other water-regulation systems (to support irrigation systems, for example) across other waterways.

The benefits are for all to see: hydroelectric power supplies energy for heavy industry and domestic use; water storage supplies water to towns and villages, and for agriculture; and man-made lakes created behind the dams provide additional benefits

Highly toxic copper mine waste has been found to enter Lake George, a Ramsar site, in Uganda. This could be prevented if international organizations were prepared to help.

from fisheries. But at what cost?

Most dams have been placed in valleys where people tended to congregate and the richest soils (from seasonal flooding) occurred. Good agricultural land, valley swamps and floodplains were flooded and destroyed. Towns and villages, and whole communities of people, were forced to move and much wildlife perished (although there were valiant efforts to save the most emotive species, such as in 'Operation Noah' on the rising Lake Kariba). River fish could no longer migrate upstream to spawn. The reservoirs trapped the fine suspended sediments which previously nourished the floodplains and deltas downstream.

But, perhaps, the most insidious effects were to reduce or stop the natural flooding of the rivers and thus to damage critically the floodplain ecosystems and all that they supported, in terms of people and wildlife. Thus, the river systems of this magnificent continent, which provide the lifeblood for survival, have become clogged. The arterial and fine network of water transport in Africa is in a critical state, and requires rehabilitation through sympathetic treatment.

Taking into consideration all aspects of river and catchment management, including the people, the wildlife and the ecosystem dynamics, the needs of industrial and commercial development can be integrated with the desire for an improved quality of life. Controlled release of water from dams to emulate natural flooding cycles, less grandiose barrages across rivers, smaller and more diverse irrigation schemes incorporating more extensive wildlife refuges are a few possible ways in which this can be accomplished.

Among Africa's currently threatened wetlands is the Sudd, the largest wetland in the world. Plans are in hand to change the hydrology of the Sudd. The Jonglei Canal between Bor and Malakal is a projected bypass designed to carry a proportion of the waters of the White Nile more quickly northwards. Specifically, its construction aims to reduce evaporative water loss from the Sudd and provide more water downstream for irrigation schemes in Egypt and the Sudan. It will act as a navigation channel as well. Although started, civil war has impeded its completion.

Another area of threatened wetlands is in Lesotho. At high altitudes, the recovery of wetlands from damage is, at best, slow; at worst, it is irredeemable. The interwoven, delicate carpets of vegetation on the high peaks in Lesotho, once broken up by mouth, foot or hoof, are more likely to erode and shred than to mend. The actual area of wetlands in the uplands is only a small fraction of the total vegetation cover, yet their sponge or buffering effects play a vital role in regulating flow into headwater streams, which ultimately feed and sustain river systems.

The newly commenced Lesotho Highland Water Project, a massive water-storage complex designed to alleviate acute water shortages in the fertile agricultural lowlands of the Republic of South Africa, has to be sensitive to these dangers. Already, there is evidence of damage to bogs and mires, the loss of their buffering capacity, and of increased erosion.

The mass removal of hardwoods from swamp forests - such as those of the Niger Delta and Zaïre - raises the same emotions as the wanton destruction of tropical rain forests. Whilst much of the biomass, including the stems and branches, is wasted, the main trunks are shipped for export in exchange for hard currency.

Also under threat are the remnants of the high altitude (montane) *Syzygium cordatum* peat swamp forests in the Kabale district of southwestern Uganda. Although always limited, these forests were widespread in the valley swamps of the Rwenzori Mountains. Because of cutting and drainage for agriculture most of them have been destroyed. Probably the most complete one remaining is at a small inflow in a valley swamp entering Lake Mutanda. Trees on the (poorly maintained) terraced hillsides have been cleared and soil erosion is profound. But people desperately need land for subsistance agriculture, and fuelwood: as long as the pressure remains, no amount of legislation will protect the trees.

The cutting of swamp peat for energy in Rwanda is necessarily a destructive process. There are now plans to increase the amount of cutting; but this has to be measured against potential losses. Run-off from the catchment travels down the Kagera River to enter Lake Victoria through a magnificent swamp forest, soon to be declared a Ramsar site. If the hydraulics or sediment burdens of the river change, the forest may be damaged.

In Africa, colonial governments and subsequent aid programmes have instigated the drainage and clearance of wetlands for food production. There is no doubt that wetland clearance for agriculture has been highly successful. But the trade-off is in habitat loss and degradation of the environment. Pollution, eutrophication, agrochemical toxicity and hydrological imbalances are commonly associated with such schemes. One of the sadder trends is the conversion of seasonal wetlands for the growth of luxury crops for export markets; again, the need for hard currency is the driving force. The export of roses and carnations by Kenya is an example.

Since the explosive increase in human population which started in the mid-1950s, African wetlands have succumbed to agricultural exploitation as never before. Many of the valley swamps in Rwanda and

Local brick-making is an entrepreneurial activity that has sprung up in the lowland swamps of Uganda. They are a danger and an eyesore, and do irreversible damage to the swamp.

the upland areas of Uganda, for example, have been drained and are used intensively for horticultural crops. Unfortunately, the nutrient pool that was locked in the swamp vegetation has largely been lost during cutting and burning. The organic soil is nutrient-poor and residue nutrients are soon used up (as with the now disastrous 'slash and burn' practices in tropical rain forest clearance). Oxidation of the peat soil, and in volcanic areas, of the sulphides to sulphuric acid, culminate in serious acidification. The quality of the soil, therefore, deteriorates and crop production decreases. The water-buffering capacity of the valleys is reduced and flash floods downstream are perpetual threats.

With the ever-increasing demand for grain, tropical wetlands are attractive for rice-growing. In east Africa the expertise of the Chinese has enabled large stretches of wetland to be converted to grow swamp rice. For wildlife, this has good and bad points. The flat, shallow-flooded paddies attract a diversity of birdlife (including the pestiferous quelea, *Quelea quelea*) but it disturbs the breeding of others such as the crowned crane, *Balearica regulorum.* As the integrity of the wetland is partially maintained, aquatic organisms, including fish, can exist in the channels but original swamp inhabitants may not survive and the food web will be disturbed. The channels may also become purveyors of waterborne diseases, especially bilharzia (schistosomiasis) and malaria. To ensure high yields from the rice, agrochemicals, especially fertilizers and pesticides, are essential - and their detrimental side effects are inevitable.

In west Africa, the oil palm (*Elaeis guineensis*) is planted in profusion in boggy areas. Plantations are increasing year by year and problems similar to those with paddy rice are encountered. Any dense, monoculture crop, terrestrial or wetland, has serious environmental repercussions.

Recent trends in the Okavango Delta demonstrate some of the conflicting interests between commercial development of floodplains and the natural environment. The high (and reliable) primary productivity of the floodplain has meant that a rich wildlife based on large herbivores - antelopes, gazelles, buffalo - has evolved. These share the land with the Tswana tribes who use it for cattle grazing; cattle are an integral part of the tribes' heritage, culture and tradition. The people, their cattle and the wildlife have coexisted for centuries and the natural balance of the ecosystem has been in harmony with the carrying capacity of the floodplains.

However, beef cattle are now the biggest hard-currency earner, after minerals, for Botswana.

The introduction of beef cattle has been achieved at considerable environmental cost. Before the 1960s the Okavango Delta was a no-go area for domestic, exotic cattle because foot-and-mouth disease and sleeping sickness were prevalent amongst indigenous species. Since the 1960s the government has carried out intensive spraying programmes to eradicate the tse-tse fly, *Glossina* species (the carrier of the sleeping sickness parasite). This has been a resounding success and total eradication is imminent. On top of that, hundreds of kilometres of fencing have been erected to separate the beef cattle from the wild animals (carriers of foot-and-mouth). The net result is that for the first time, cattle will be able to graze the Okavango with impunity.

All this means, on the one hand, a certain amount of protection for the wetland; the fence protects major areas of the wetland from cattle grazing. On the other hand, the fence runs across wildlife migration routes and game are inhibited from travelling to their natural watering and grazing sites. In 1983 some 50,000 wildebeest died because they were unable to reach their traditional water supply. At the same time, the increased grazing pressures from goats and cattle put additional stresses on an already fragile floodplain ecosystem.

Worldwide, erosion is a major problem; the retention of vegetation is an essential first step in its alleviation. The value of wetlands in the uplands of Africa has been already been shown. No less significant are those in deltas and around coastal waters. Freshwater swamp forests, and more particularly mangrove swamps, are critical to sedimentation processes and in preventing coastal erosion.

MANAGEMENT AND CONSERVATION

The driving force for sound environmental policies must be a strong political will. In most countries of the world this is not yet the case. In Africa it is harder because of exploitation of the continent's natural resources by the industrialized world at minimum recompense, and because of the basic needs of local people.

A fundamental political strategy must be to ensure that the carrying capacity of the land is not exceeded. Africa is undergoing an enormous population explosion. In many African countries the best hope for long-term escape from poverty and for an increased quality of life is by population stability. If this is not achieved, wetland utilization may offer short-term relief, but a general decline will ensue as increasing numbers of people encroach upon, exhaust and destroy the ecosystem.

Local communities are often intricately linked to wetlands. They live near them and utilize many plants and animals.

If overseas governments, industrialists and developers paid African countries the true value of their produce - to allow the highest environmental protection policies to be implemented - pressures on wetlands would be reduced. One example will suffice to demonstrate a transcontinental problem. In Uganda, aid programmes are helping to re-establish the country's industrial base. To this end, the Kilembe copper mines near Lake George are being renovated. When they were last operational, effluent contaminated the surrounding countryside, which includes a national park. Recent evidence has confirmed that toxic metals also entered Lake George, Uganda's first wetland designated a Ramsar site.

Financially, Uganda is in no position to impose the most stringent environmental standards: it badly needs the foreign exchange from copper export. Why is the fullest financial support not given by international organizations to ensure sound waste management? That would protect a Ramsar site, provide Uganda with an environmentally acceptable, efficient industry, and demonstrate the industrial nations' true concern for environmental issues in the developing world.

In wetland management two basic factors need to be borne in mind: first, man's responsibility to future generations; second, the need for sustainable development. While it must be wise to conserve African wetlands, they cannot be preserved unconditionally: the pressures on nations are such that they are obliged to consider wetlands as legitimate resources for development. Therefore, a policy of conservation and sustainable development is required.

In a successful management scheme, the attributes and current uses of a wetland are assessed, and the opinions of all interested parties including the rural community, are canvassed before a final plan is concluded. The World Conservation Union (IUCN) review on wetland conservation and management has some very practical guidelines. Preferably, any decision should be taken within the framework of a national policy on wetland management. The government of Uganda, for example, within its Ministry of Environment Protection, has a National Wetlands Conservation and Management Programme to do just this.

African wetlands have a staggering diversity of natural and anthropogenic use. Looking at the pressures many are under, there is no doubt they have a remarkable resilience; but excessive pressures result in irreparable damage. To protect their long-term survival it is essential to assure that present demands made upon them are tempered with environmental considerations for the future.

Conservation Areas

Some wetlands may have overriding biological and environmental values which demand the highest protection. Establishing conservation areas such as national parks and wildlife sanctuaries may be the appropriate mechanism to provide this. Profits from regulated wildlife tourism can be sufficient to maintain the conservation areas and give much needed hard currency to the nation. For them to

succeed, local communities must gain from their own efforts. Thus, if tourism is a source of wealth generation, those who underpin it (such as wardens, guides, hotel workers and drivers as well as scientific, technical and managerial staff) must all receive tangible benefits. This requires a policy of decentralization wherever feasible.

The Ramsar Convention provides international assistance for the protection of wetlands of international importance. Uganda was one of the first countries in Africa to take advantage of this when it declared the Lake George wetlands a Ramsar site. A second site, the freshwater swamp forest at the mouth of the Kagera river in Lake Victoria is soon to follow. The Ramsar Bureau can support monitoring of sites as well as training and education programmes. The people of the country then become more appreciative of their wetlands, and internationally important wetlands have a better chance of surviving.

Establishing conservation areas does not imply that people should be evicted from the areas or visitors forbidden from entering them. The rural community is an integral part of the wetland ecosystem; often it has maintained the wetland's current state for generations. The balance of the local community's activities and wetland utilization is an essential part of

A well-managed papyrus swamp in Uganda harvested for matting and building material. This swamp is cut in rotation every eight months.

Public awareness of the values of wetlands is critical to their survival. This notice is by the side of a large swamp in Uganda.

the dynamics. Conservation areas are designed to maintain that balance and ensure that changes in circumstances (in, for instance, housing, transport, community activities and population structure) do not destabilize the balance irreversibly.

Multi-Purpose Utilization

Many wetlands do not warrant the legislative protection given to conservation areas, even though their overall maintenance is desired. How can this be achieved?

The three major demands on wetlands are: ecosystem and wildlife survival; tourism; and anthropogenic exploitation. Whilst wildlife and tourism are natural bedfellows (in moderation), the exploitation of wetlands is often destructive. The most damaging kinds of wetland 'development' are those which utilize the entire wetland for a single purpose -

drainage for agriculture, clearing for paddy rice, flooding for reservoirs, infilling for industrial expansion and so on. This sort of approach needs to be replaced with a more enlightened one, the basic aim of which is to integrate the most prized environmental and anthropogenic values of each wetland - that is, multi-purpose utilization of the wetland.

Floodplain ecosystems demonstrate this well. Most are vital to people and wildlife alike. As long as the arrival of the floods at any particular place can be predicted, exploitation of the natural flooding cycle can benefit people without destruction of the wildlife. For centuries, Africans have utilized flooding regimes for seasonal agriculture, for cattle, sheep and goat grazing and for fisheries.

Wildlife, river and floodplain fish and vegetation have all evolved according to particular flood regimes. The tragedy over the last half-century has been the apparent lack of regard for these natural processes which has led to flows being impeded, regulated or otherwise exploited by man's activities. The 'controlled release' option whereby the water released through barrages mimics the natural pattern, has been mentioned as a better management strategy.

Sound hydrological management is important. So is the need to manage floodplains on a sustainable basis. This is easier said than done. Human pressures make ever-increasing demands. In Nigeria's Hadejia-Nguru wetlands, a sanctuary for resident and migratory birds, the government has created the Hadejia-Nguru Wetlands Conservation Project. The aim was to protect the wildlife whilst allowing traditional utilization of the wetlands.

The Kenya Marine and Fisheries Research Institute, Mombasa, has a development programme for the cultivation of oysters. Mangroves provide the necessary enrichment and protection for culture beds.

However, agricultural developments, supported by large subsidies (particularly for wheat cultivation) from international organizations, have encouraged land clearance. In 1988-89 alone, some 10 km² (nearly 4 sq miles) of floodplain was cleared even though wheat is not an appropriate crop for the area - and wholesale clearance generates a potential dust bowl. Much of the blame can be levelled at absentee landlords who reap the rewards of subsidies. Inappropriate subsidies tend to work against sustainable development: they cause heavy use of agrochemicals and overproduction of crops which then flood the market and destabilize the rural economy. It is also apparent that sustainable development requires radical land reforms so that local communities own their land. This gives them a vested interest in good land husbandry: absent landlords all too often increase personal wealth at the expense of sound land management.

Similar concerns apply to the Okavango Delta and Kafue Flats where heavy grazing pressures and irrigation projects threaten the stability of the fragile ecosystems. It is imperative that a balance is struck between wildlife conservation, tourism, rangeland management and agricultural development.

APPROPRIATE INTERMEDIATE TECHNOLOGY
A move away from prestigious and expensive 'high tech' developments towards more appropriate intermediate technologies based on local resources and self-help schemes goes hand in hand with sustainable development. In fact, the multi-purpose

The Kariba weed is one of the most troublesome water weeds in Africa. Yet its rapid growth and high biomass could be put to man's advantage.

utilization of wetlands employing appropriate technologies is a great hope for the future of African wetlands. Upkeep and maintenance of the managed wetland are often easier and cheaper, do not require continued highly skilled manpower and are usually more acceptable environmentally. Most importantly, they are sustainable if well designed.

Proclaiming the need to use appropriate technological developments is now part of the rhetoric of international organizations; the benefits of such schemes are well documented, but their implementation seems to present untold problems. In the first place, it is difficult for organizations and government departments to support multi-purpose wetland developments. Bureaucratically, it is easier to administer, say, a rice scheme development, than a multi-purpose development for wildlife, fisheries, seasonal grazing, horticulture and rural handcrafts based on appropriate technologies. Politically too, it is often more prudent to support schemes with projected (impressively) high maximum yields than those with lower sustainable yields, even though the investment and hidden costs in the former may be far greater.

Although still in the early stages, the development and use of appropriate technologies in African wetlands deserve every encouragement - and financial support. Three fields in which this is particularly evident is in biomass production, waste water treatment and integrated farming/fish polyculture.

Biomass Production
One of the most impressive features of African wetlands is the high biomass production of the vegetation, often under limited nutrient supply. This is why the floodplains support rich fisheries and heavy domestic and wildlife grazing. But what of those hectares of wetlands in which the standing crop appears to be untouched? Surely that biomass can be put to man's advantage without destruction of the wetland? Following a United Nations Environmental Programme (UNEP) report, the Ministry of Environment Protection in Uganda has initiated investigations into all aspects of wetland biomass production and utilization.

Initially, it is vital to get an idea of yield on a sustainable basis. The wetland can then be cropped at suitable intervals without damage to its overall integrity. If the cropping is by rotation then a high proportion of the wetland will be undisturbed and the wildlife will suffer little. The development and use of appropriate technology for harvesting the biomass (rather than importing massive machinery with high

Swamp fish that can tolerate variable oxygen concentrations congregate in the outer swamp where there are channels. Convoluted barriers, made from emergent vegetation, are put across the channels to trap the fish. These fish provide vital protein for the local people.

maintenance costs) is essential. A cottage industry with manpower and management at the village level will encourage the long-term conservation of the swamp.

The same principles apply for the use of other wetland vegetation, including water weeds such as the water hyacinth, and Kariba weed. Why, for example, the knee-jerk reaction to eliminate noxious water weeds with very expensive, dangerous chemicals, when it may be feasible to turn the high biomass production to man's advantage?

Thanks to the new emphasis on intermediate technology for sustainable development and technological advances particularly in biotechnology, the time is now ripe for re-examining the use of wetland vegetation for fibre and construction products, fodder, mulches and bio-gas energy. Special attention should be directed towards the use of the plant biomass for fuel. If this can be achieved, then, maybe, the trees of the savanna and tropical rain forests will get a well-deserved reprieve. Biological fermentation processes for alcohol and bio-gas production are other avenues under investigation. In addition, Rwanda and Uganda have pilot experiments for the production of briquettes from papyrus. The Ugandan process is particularly attractive as it is on a village scale designed for rural communities.

Waste Water Treatment

The treatment of waste water is another area in which appropriate intermediate technology can play an important role. Water plants have long been used in various parts of the world for waste water treatment. However, over the last 15 years or so there has been a concerted effort to develop wetlands for the treatment of industrial and domestic wastes. There are two main approaches: either to discharge suitable effluents into natural wetlands, or to construct artificial wetlands designed specifically for the purpose.

Natural wetlands have to be used with caution, and the implications assessed, before they are allowed to receive effluent. Problems associated with the use of natural wetlands include: disease transfer; eutrophication of the wetland; bad aromas; and accumulation of toxic wastes, such as heavy metals, in the wetland. However, under strict management, the treatment of suitable wastes (usually tertiary waste from domestic treatment plants) is highly satisfactory. For non-toxic domestic effluents, the accompanying nutrient enrichment can be used to increase fish production.

The use of constructed wetlands is a very promising approach to waste water treatment. There are many different designs, but apart from a pilot plant in Egypt based on temperate climate technology, there are few, if any, constructed wetlands for waste water treatment in Africa. However, they could become a major means of treatment of domestic waste at the home and small community scale. The warm climate of most parts of the continent should encourage aquatic plants and their accompanying microbiological flora (which are responsible for the functioning of the system) to perform very efficiently. Properly designed they will be odour and disease-free. In addition, the high water plant biomass production could, perhaps, be cropped for fuel generation.

The beauty of this system is the low technology and low maintenance required. Every household could

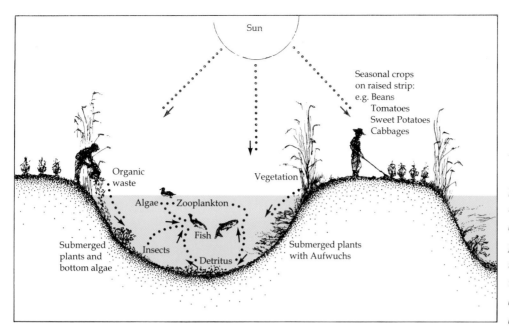

A schematic cross-section through finger ponds - a proposed development for swamp edges in which ponds are dug into the swamp for fish polyculture, and the sediment removed is used for raised bed cultivation. The arrows indicate major inputs and an aquatic food web.

have one. With financial support from international agencies, experimental plots and pilot plants could be established in different parts of Africa to develop the most appropriate technologies for local conditions.

Integrated Farming and Fisheries

The interface zone between swamp and open water is particularly valuable for swamp fisheries production. Production can be increased by extension of the interface area, naturally or artificially. Thus cutting inlets into a swamp, to create open spaces where light can penetrate to the water surface, will encourage the growth of food for many fish. In the multi-purpose utilization of permanent wetlands, inlets, bays and ponds within the swamp can provide suitable environments for sustainable fisheries. Pools must be of an appropriate size and shape for good oxygenation of the water and photosynthesis of the algal biomass (phytoplankton and periphyton). This can be taken a step further to create finger ponds and fish ponds.

Finger ponds are constructed at the edge of swamps by digging out a series of parallel 'fingers' towards the centre of the swamp. The soil removed is used to provide raised beds between the ponds. The edges of the ponds are fringed with emergent vegetation to provide feeding and refuge areas for the fish. The vegetation also protects the raised beds from soil erosion. The raised beds can be used for horticultural cash crops such as potatoes, tomatoes, beans, cassava, cucurbits and so on.

The ponds themselves are stocked by natural migration during flooding or from culture ponds, with a variety of fish to take advantage of a broad food web. Lake fish such as tilapia are much sought after, but others should be stocked as well. Swamp

waters are often nutrient-poor and so enrichment of the ponds is necessary. This is achieved by controlled input of organic wastes such as kitchen refuse, manures and decomposing vegetation. Manure from chicken, ducks and turkeys is particularly good. Care has to be taken to release the waste in regulated doses so that deoxygenation of the water does not occur. The nutrients released are quickly taken up by

The fish catch from the Sudd is hung out to dry in the sun.

the algae which form the base of the food web.

Thus, the ponds are sustained by sunlight and nutrients from organic wastes. No agrochemicals are used and, although production may not be as high as in intensive fish farming, it will provide a continuous supply of protein on a sustainable basis for local consumption. Crops from the raised beds supplement the diet.

This integrated livestock and fish farming is common in Asia but is rarely practiced in Africa. In Rwanda, sustainable-yield fish ponds have been constructed in some of the high-altitude valley swamps with a degree of success. Uganda had just embarked upon the construction of some experimental ponds in wetlands near Lake Kyoga. The attraction of such ponds is the low technology required for their construction and maintenance.

For these proposals to have a chance of success, local people must be involved from the early planning stages. There must also be a long-sustained programme of training and education. Ignorance is likely to be the bugbear; education the saviour.

GENERAL CONCLUSION

African wetlands support the largest numbers and greatest variety of wildlife in the world. For this reason alone, they deserve the highest conservation attention.

They also support, and are the livelihood of, many hundreds of thousands of indigenous peoples - permanently resident, transhumant and nomadic populations. These people are an integral part of the wetland ecosystems and for generations have lived alongside the wildlife, and have utilized the wetlands in a balanced and sustainable manner.

However, over the last half-century the population of Africa has increased dramatically and the wetlands are now under serious threat. If steps are not taken, they will be destroyed at an ever-increasing rate. International organizations and governments must be prepared to take firm action on behalf of future generations. Population control is the over-riding issue. Within the framework of sustainable development, multi-purpose utilization of the wetlands, incorporating appropriate technologies wherever possible, offers greatest hope. African countries are generally poor and concerted efforts must be made to assist them in their environmental tasks. Education and training programmes in environmental studies and wetland management at all levels of society are required for the long-term success of wetland conservation and management.

Acknowledgements

Jamie Skinner kindly supplied information on the Inner Niger Delta and the relevant feature box; Roland Bailey provided valuable information on floodplain fisheries and Christian Perennou provided information on waterbirds and for the Banc d'Arguin and Lake Nakuru and Naivasha boxes.

CONTRIBUTOR: D.A. SCOTT

Asia and the Middle East

STRETCHING from the Bosporus and the Urals in the west to the Pacific Ocean in the east, and from the High Arctic in the north to the Arabian Peninsula and island systems of Indonesia in the south, Asia comprises almost 30 per cent of the world's land surface. It covers approximately 44 million km^2 (17 million sq miles) and is by far the largest continent.

It contains significant elements of four of the world's eight major biogeographical regions. Much of the Middle East and the whole of northern and central Asia north of the Himalayas lie within the Palearctic region, while the Indian subcontinent, Southeast Asia and the island groups of the Philippines, Borneo, Sumatra and Java make up the Indo-Malayan region.

In the southwest, the southern tip of the Arabian Peninsula has many similarities in its fauna and flora with Africa, and is generally included within the Afro-tropical region, while in the extreme southeast, the island groups of Sulawesi, the Moluccas and the Lesser Sundas (collectively known as Wallacea) straddle the transition zone between the Indo-Malayan and Australasian regions. Not surprisingly, therefore, Asia possesses a bewildering diversity of animal and plant life much of which is now under threat as a result of direct competition for space with the continent's huge human population.

Asia is home to almost 60 per cent of the world's population, with China alone containing over 20 per cent and India a further 14-15 per cent. The great fertile plains of the Indus and Ganges in the Indian sub-continent, the Mekong and Red River in Southeast Asia, and the Yangtze and Yellow River in China are the birthplaces of some of the world's oldest civilizations, and are now among the most densely populated places on Earth, with densities in rich rice-growing areas approaching 2,000 people per km^2 (5,180 per sq mile).

GEOGRAPHY AND CLIMATE

Situated between latitudes 10° South and 80° North, and extending for over 9,600 km (5,960 miles) from east to west, Asia embraces almost the full complement of the world's climatic and biotic zones,

from the Arctic tundra and boreal forests of Siberia to the tropical rain forests and mangrove swamps of Borneo and Sumatra, and from the deserts of the Middle East to the tropical islands and coral seas of the Philippines.

An almost unbroken chain of high mountain ranges traverses the continent, from the Taurus Mountains of Turkey and the Alborz Mountains of Iran through the mighty Hindu Kush and Himalayas to the contorted ranges of northern Burma and southwestern China. In southern China, the Qinghai-Tibetan Plateau, often referred to as the 'roof of the world', rises to an average height of 4,000-5,000 m (13,000-16,500 ft) above sea level, while in the Himalayas, 14 peaks rise to over 8,000 m (26,000 ft), including Mount Everest, at 8,840 m (29,028 ft) the highest mountain in the world. By contrast, vast areas of the Caspian Basin lie below sea level, as do the salt lakes of the Turpan Depression in Xinjiang (Sinkiang). The Great Rift Valley descends to 394 m (1,292 ft) below sea level on the shores of the Dead Sea, the lowest point on the Earth's surface.

Many of the world's great rivers have their headwaters in Asia's backbone of mountain ranges. To the north flow the Ob, Irtysh, Yenisey and Lena; to the east, the Amur, Yellow and Yangtze Rivers; and to the south, the Tigris, Euphrates, Indus, Ganges, Brahmaputra, Irrawaddy and Mekong Rivers. Asia includes the world's largest inland body of water, the Caspian Sea; its largest delta, that of the combined Ganges, Brahmaputra and Meghna Rivers; and some of its most extensive mangrove swamps, in the coastal lowlands of Sumatra and Borneo. It also includes some of the world's most inhospitable deserts, stretching in a broad belt from the Arabian Peninsula across Iraq, Iran and Afghanistan to western China and Mongolia.

The climatic extremes over this vast region are enormous. In parts of the Arabian Peninsula, it never rains for years on end and temperatures can soar to 50°C (122°F) or more, while in the extreme continental climate of northeastern Siberia, average January

149

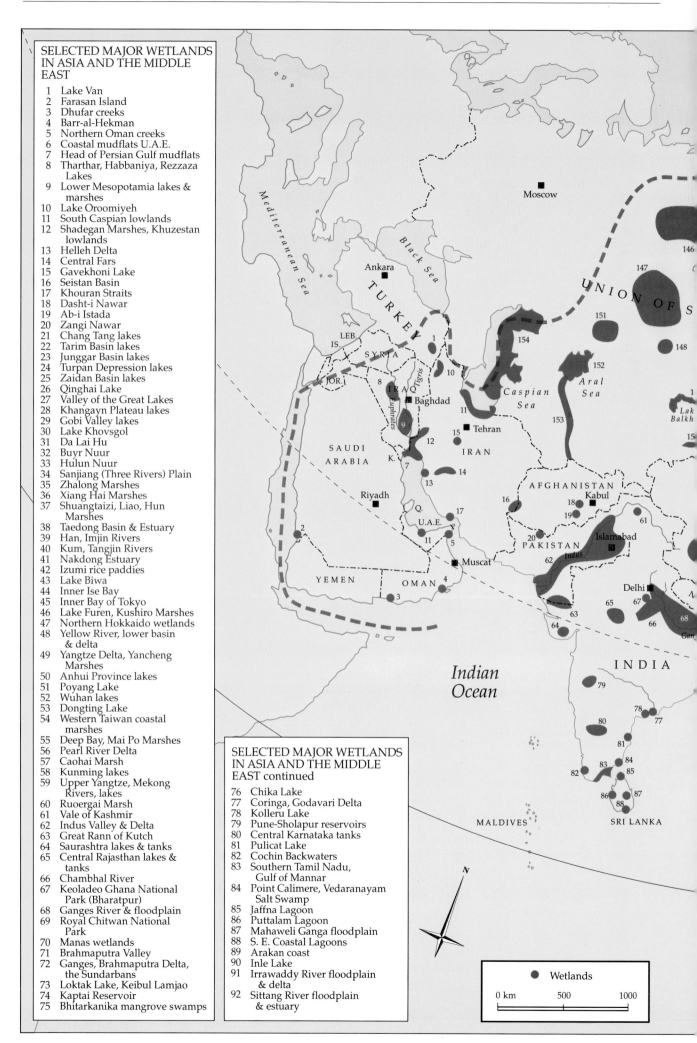

SELECTED MAJOR WETLANDS IN ASIA AND THE MIDDLE EAST

1. Lake Van
2. Farasan Island
3. Dhufar creeks
4. Barr-al-Hekman
5. Northern Oman creeks
6. Coastal mudflats U.A.E.
7. Head of Persian Gulf mudflats
8. Tharthar, Habbaniya, Rezzaza Lakes
9. Lower Mesopotamia lakes & marshes
10. Lake Oroomiyeh
11. South Caspian lowlands
12. Shadegan Marshes, Khuzestan lowlands
13. Helleh Delta
14. Central Fars
15. Gavekhoni Lake
16. Seistan Basin
17. Khouran Straits
18. Dasht-i Nawar
19. Ab-i Istada
20. Zangi Nawar
21. Chang Tang lakes
22. Tarim Basin lakes
23. Junggar Basin lakes
24. Turpan Depression lakes
25. Zaidan Basin lakes
26. Qinghai Lake
27. Valley of the Great Lakes
28. Khangayn Plateau lakes
29. Gobi Valley lakes
30. Lake Khovsgol
31. Da Lai Hu
32. Buyr Nuur
33. Hulun Nuur
34. Sanjiang (Three Rivers) Plain
35. Zhalong Marshes
36. Xiang Hai Marshes
37. Shuangtaizi, Liao, Hun Marshes
38. Taedong Basin & Estuary
39. Han, Imjin Rivers
40. Kum, Tangjin Rivers
41. Nakdong Estuary
42. Izumi rice paddies
43. Lake Biwa
44. Inner Ise Bay
45. Inner Bay of Tokyo
46. Lake Furen, Kushiro Marshes
47. Northern Hokkaido wetlands
48. Yellow River, lower basin & delta
49. Yangtze Delta, Yancheng Marshes
50. Anhui Province lakes
51. Poyang Lake
52. Wuhan lakes
53. Dongting Lake
54. Western Taiwan coastal marshes
55. Deep Bay, Mai Po Marshes
56. Pearl River Delta
57. Caohai Marsh
58. Kunming lakes
59. Upper Yangtze, Mekong Rivers, lakes
60. Ruoergai Marsh
61. Vale of Kashmir
62. Indus Valley & Delta
63. Great Rann of Kutch
64. Saurashtra lakes & tanks
65. Central Rajasthan lakes & tanks
66. Chambhal River
67. Keoladeo Ghana National Park (Bharatpur)
68. Ganges River & floodplain
69. Royal Chitwan National Park
70. Manas wetlands
71. Brahmaputra Valley
72. Ganges, Brahmaputra Delta, the Sundarbans
73. Loktak Lake, Keibul Lamjao
74. Kaptai Reservoir
75. Bhitarkanika mangrove swamps

SELECTED MAJOR WETLANDS IN ASIA AND THE MIDDLE EAST continued

76. Chika Lake
77. Coringa, Godavari Delta
78. Kolleru Lake
79. Pune-Sholapur reservoirs
80. Central Karnataka tanks
81. Pulicat Lake
82. Cochin Backwaters
83. Southern Tamil Nadu, Gulf of Mannar
84. Point Calimere, Vedaranayam Salt Swamp
85. Jaffna Lagoon
86. Puttalam Lagoon
87. Mahaweli Ganga floodplain
88. S. E. Coastal Lagoons
89. Arakan coast
90. Inle Lake
91. Irrawaddy River floodplain & delta
92. Sittang River floodplain & estuary

Wetlands

0 km   500   1000

temperatures can be as low as -51°C (-60°F). The climate of much of southern and southeastern Asia is dominated by the monsoons. During summer a vast low pressure zone over central Asia draws moisture-laden winds in from the ocean, and these deposit heavy rains over most of the Indian subcontinent, Southeast Asia and southern China between May and October. Ranges of mountains and hills exposed to the full force of the southwest monsoon can receive in excess of 5,000 mm (200 in) of rainfall within the space of four months.

WETLANDS

For convenience in treating the wetlands, Asia has been subdivided into five regions: northern Asia (the USSR), southwestern Asia (Asia Minor and the Middle East), eastern Asia (China, Mongolia, Korea and Japan), southern Asia (the Indian subcontinent) and southeastern Asia (mainland Southeast Asia and the island systems of the Philippines, Greater Sundas and Wallacea).

Northern Asia

The Soviet Union is the world's largest country, covering approximately one-sixth of the Earth's land surface. About one-quarter lies west of the Urals and Caspian Sea, in Europe; the remainder stretches across the Asian continent from the deserts of the Middle East and mountain ranges of central Asia north and east to the Arctic Ocean and Bering Sea. This huge territory possesses vast areas of wetlands, including three of the world's ten largest lakes, the Caspian Sea, the Aral Sea and Lake Baykal, and three of its ten longest rivers, the Irtysh, Amur and Lena.

The tundra zone extends from the High Arctic wildernesses of Severnaya Zemlya, Novosibirskye Ostrova and Wrangel Island in the Arctic Ocean south through the tundra proper of the Mid Arctic to the shrub-tundras and forest-tundras of the Low Arctic. Wetlands abound, with spring snow-melt flooding vast expanses of low-lying land in river valleys and along the coast, and creating myriads of shallow lakes and ponds. Extensive bogs, dominated by mosses and sedges, occur in depressions and on gentle slopes with a permanent supply of water from melting snow. Permafrost underlies these wetlands at shallow depths and tends to concentrate the available moisture at the surface. The intense cold in winter causes cracking of the surface, producing characteristic polygon fens and bogs.

The most extensive tundras in the Russian Arctic occur on the Taymyr Peninsula. This peninsula, most of which is included in a nature reserve of over 1.3 million hectares (3.2 million acres), contains the full range of tundra ecosystems from barren Arctic wilderness in the north to forest-tundras in the south. The dwarf larch (*Larix*) forests in the southern part of the reserve are remarkable in being the most northerly forests on Earth, while Lake Taymyr - 4,600 km² (1,775 sq miles) - is much the largest lake in the Russian Arctic. Other regions of the Arctic tundra with important wetland areas include the Yamal Peninsula and Gydan Peninsula in the west; the delta of the Lena River and lower basins of the Indigirka and Kolyma Rivers in Yakutia; and the Chaun Basin, Wrangel Island and coastal zone of the Chukchi (Chukotka) Peninsula in the east.

The forests of the taiga extend from the Urals to

LAKE BAYKAL, USSR

Lake Baykal (3.2 million hectares - 7.9 million acres) is the largest freshwater lake in Eurasia, and the deepest (max. 1,620 m - 5,315 ft) lake in the world. It lies in the heart of Siberia, surrounded by the coniferous forests of the taiga. The lake is reputed to contain about 20 per cent of the world's freshwater, and its water was until recently claimed to be some of the purest water on Earth. It owed its purity primarily to the enormous numbers of a tiny crustacean (*Epischura baicalensis*) which lives in the surface waters and feeds on algae. The lake freezes over in early January, when air temperatures drop to -30°C (-22°F), and remains frozen until April or May.

Lake Baykal is famous for its breathtaking scenery and unique flora and fauna which contain a high proportion of endemic species. The extremely rich plankton supports about 50 species of fish, which in turn support a major fishery. The lake also has its own endemic seal, the Baykal seal.

Lake Baykal is in great peril. Extensive logging in the Baykal region has resulted in soil erosion, landslides and loss of many streams. Atmospheric pollution from nearby industrial centres is causing acid rain, and there is serious pollution from over 100 factories on Baykal's shores. The most notorious sources of pollution are two pulp and cellulose mills. The larger of the two, at Baykalsk, began operating in 1966, and since then has poured more than 1.5 billion m³ (53 billion cu ft) of industrial waste into the lake.

The effects of the high levels of pollution are now strikingly evident. The small crustaceans which purify the water are dying out; some fish species no longer spawn naturally and have to be maintained artificially, and thousands of Baykal seals have died within the last few years.

Some measures have been taken to clean up the lake, such as the introduction of a ban on logging along the lake's shore in 1988, a government resolution to phase out the Baykalsk pulp mill's harmful operations by 1993, and a resolution calling for measures to curb air pollution. However, these measures have turned out to be largely inadequate, and the progressive pollution of Lake Baykal continues.

Lake Baykal is reputed to contain about 20 per cent of the world's freshwater.

Kamchatka, bordering the forest-tundra in the north and the steppe zones of western Siberia and the mountain ranges of central Asia in the south. Throughout this vast region of dark, coniferous forests, there are countless lakes, marshes and bogs which drain north via a series of great rivers, notably the Ob, Irtysh, Yenisey, Lena and Kolyma, into the Arctic Ocean. It has been estimated that there are some 83 million hectares (205 million acres) of peat bogs and swamps in the USSR, as well as about 90 million hectares (220 million acres) of marshy ground subject to seasonal flooding. Most of these wetlands are in the taiga zone.

The two main types of wetland are nutrient-rich peat swamps and nutrient-poor peat bogs. The former occur in dead arms of rivers, in old oxbow lakes, around the margins of lakes and in any depression where there is a good supply of water. Some are forested with dense willow thickets or more open forest of birch, alder and larch. The peats are rich in minerals and support an abundant growth of aquatic vegetation such as sedges, cattails and reeds.

Nutrient-poor peat bogs form in depressions where the principal source of water is local rainfall. They are dominated by *Sphagnum* mosses, and often become dome-shaped as the accumulation of *Sphagnum* peat in the centre of the bog outpaces that around the periphery. The bogs have a very low mineral content, and generally support little vegetation other than the mosses themselves and a few stunted pines and birches.

The most extensive region of lakes, swamps and bogs is in the middle and lower basin of the Ob and Irtysh Rivers in western Siberia, and covers about 1.8 million km^2 (695,000 sq miles). This is the great 'duck factory' of western Siberia, producing many of the ducks which winter in the Mediterranean Basin, the Middle East and the western half of the Indian subcontinent; it is thus comparable with the prairie pothole country of North America. Other important wetlands for breeding waterbirds occur along the middle and lower reaches of the Yenisey River, in the middle basin of the Lena River, along the middle and lower courses of the Amur River, on the north end of Sakhalin Island and in the coastal lowlands of the Kamchatka Peninsula.

Of the many thousands of lakes in the taiga zone, much the most famous is Lake Baykal, the largest freshwater lake in Eurasia and the deepest in the world.

In the extreme southeastern corner of the USSR, the coniferous forests give way to mixed forests of coniferous and deciduous broadleaf species. Here, on the Chinese border, lies Lake Khanka (Xinghai Hu), the largest lake in northeastern Asia. This shallow, freshwater lake of 4,830 km^2 (1,864 sq miles) is fringed by extensive reed beds, willow thickets and peat bogs.

The rolling steppes of the west Siberian lowlands extend from the southern end of the Urals east through the upper basins of the Ob and Irtysh to the upper basin of the Yenisey. Large tracts of these grasslands have been converted to agricultural land, while other areas are heavily grazed by domestic livestock. The whole region is dotted with countless small lakes, ponds and marshes - some permanent and some seasonal, some freshwater, some brackish and others saline. The greatest concentrations of freshwater lakes and marshes occur in the north, in the basins of the Ob and Irtysh, and farther south, along the Tobol and Ishim Rivers. The largest wetlands of this region are Lake Tengiz, a shallow saline lake noted for its large breeding population of greater flamingos (*Phoenicopterus ruber*), and Lake Kourgaldzhin, a complex of lakes and channels with varying salinities, some supporting abundant aquatic vegetation and extensive reed beds.

The desert zone of the southwestern USSR extends from the Caspian Sea east to the base of the Tien Shan and Altai Shan on the borders of China and Mongolia. Although extremely arid, ample rainfall in the high mountain ranges to the south feeds several large rivers which flow into the desert and end in large salt lakes. The Caspian Sea itself is one such lake, and is the world's largest inland body of water, covering some 371,000 km² (143,200 sq miles). The salinity is approximately half that of sea water, and the northern end freezes over in winter.

About 500 km (310 miles) east of the Caspian Sea lies the Aral Sea (67,340 km² - 25,990 sq miles), the world's fourth largest lake. The lake once formed part of the Caspian Sea, and was separated from it in recent geological times. Until recent historical times, the salinity was fairly low, and the lake supported a rich fauna and significant commercial fishery. However, the large-scale diversion of water from the main inflow rivers for irrigation schemes has reduced the lake to about half its former size and caused an ecological catastrophe. Ironically, the huge water-storage reservoirs and irrigation dams on the inflow rivers now provide a chain of extensive wetland habitats in a region which only 50 years ago was hostile desert. Hundreds of thousands of waterbirds

have been recorded on these new wetlands in Turkmenistan.

The Turgai Depression, to the northeast of the Aral Sea, contains a large group of mostly brackish to saline lakes fed by the Turgay and Irgiz Rivers. Freshwater habitats with extensive reed beds and sedge meadows occur along the floodplain of the Turgay River. Farther to the east lies Lake Balkash (18,300 km² - 7,060 sq miles), a huge, shallow, brackish lake surrounded by desert and fed by rivers rising in the Tien Shan Ranges to the southeast.

South of Lake Balkash lies one of the world's greatest mountain lakes, Issyk Kul. This brackish lake lies in a basin at 1,608 m (5,275 ft) in the Tien Shan. Its great depth (max. 700 m - 2,300 ft) and a series of hot springs along the north shore help to keep the lake ice-free in winter. The lake supports a rich planktonic and fish fauna, and is of great limnological interest.

Southwestern Asia

Although much of Asia Minor and the Middle East is semi-arid or arid, the high mountain ranges and plateaus in the north attract sufficient rainfall to feed several major river systems which in turn supply water to a number of impressive wetland systems. These include the wetlands of Mesopotamia in Iraq, the wetlands of the Orumiyeh Basin, south Caspian

A Marsh Arab village in the Mesopotamian Marshes, Iraq. How far these communities have been disrupted by recent conflicts is unknown.

THE MESOPOTAMIAN MARSHES, IRAQ

The wetlands of Mesopotamia comprise a vast complex of shallow freshwater lakes, marshes and seasonally inundated plains between the Tigris and Euphrates rivers in lower Iraq. The numerous reed-fringed lakes are inter-connected by an intricate network of river channels and canals. Winter rainfall in the head-waters of the Tigris and Euphrates causes extensive flooding throughout Mesopotamia and fills up the lake systems in the south.

After passing through the marshes, the two rivers unite near Basra to form the Shatt al Arab which enters the Persian Gulf some 90 km (56 miles) farther downstream.

The lakes and marshes are among the most important wintering areas for migratory waterbirds in western Eurasia, supporting several million cormorants, pelicans, herons, flamingos, ducks, geese, coots and shorebirds throughout the winter months.

For at least 5,000 years, the Ma'dan or Marsh Arabs have lived in the marshes, building their reed houses on artificial islands made from layers of mats, reeds and mud, and obtaining virtually all of their needs from the surrounding lakes and marshes. The Ma'dan are

White pelicans on the Mesopotamian Marshes near Fuhud, Haur Al Hammar in Iraq.

primarily buffalo herders and fishermen, although they also cultivate a little rice. Traditionally spear-fishermen, the Ma'dan now use nets to catch fish for export to Basra and Baghdad. Mat-weaving is an important source of income, and demand continues to grow for the pliable mat coverings used in housing, fencing and packaging. In a region where travel is possible only by boat, the vast stretches of water and reeds have served to isolate the Ma'dan from the outside world; for this reason, their fascinating culture has changed

very little over the centuries.

The diversion of water from the Tigris and Euphrates for irrigation has resulted in some loss of wetland habitat. Parts of the marshes have been reclaimed for agriculture and oil exploration, and recent wars have undoubtedly had some adverse affects. As no special measures have been taken by the Iraqi government to conserve these marshes, their continued survival as one of the finest and most extensive natural wetland ecosystems in western Eurasia must now be in some doubt.

---

lowlands, Khuzestan and central Fars in Iran, and the wetlands of the Seistan Basin on the Iran-Afghanistan border.

Much of Turkey may be considered as falling in the Mediterranean and Black Sea regions, but the eastern part of the country, containing the upper valleys of the Tigris and Euphrates Rivers, is truly part of Asia.

Wetland vegetation at Pahlavi Mordab in the South Caspian Lowlands is dominated by reeds and lotus lilies.

There are many wetlands in the region of Van Golu, a vast soda lake near the Turkish/Iranian border. These include areas of wet meadow, freshwater lakes and marshes, and brackish to saline lakes.

The interior of the Arabian Peninsula contains some of the world's harshest desert areas, and lacks major natural wetlands. In contrast, there are some very extensive wetlands on the coast. Inter-tidal mudflats occur widely, and are particularly extensive in Kuwait, along the shores of the United Arab Emirates, at Barr-al-Hekman on the Oman coast and around Farazan Island in the Red Sea. Sheltered bays and coastal lagoons in the United Arab Emirates and northern Oman support simple mangrove communities, while in Yemen and southern Oman, the slight influence of the southwest monsoon provides sufficient rainfall to maintain a chain of brackish creeks and lagoons on the narrow coastal plain.

The most extensive wetlands in the Middle East occur in Iraq. Two great rivers, the Tigris and the Euphrates, traverse Iraq from northwest to southeast, uniting as the Shatt al Arab shortly before entering the Persian Gulf. Dam-building in central Iraq has converted several large saline depressions into huge water-storage basins, the most important being Lakes

Islets in Lake Rezaiyeh, Iran, provide a traditional breeding site for greater flamingos.

Tharthar, Habbaniya and Rezzaza. In their lower courses, the Tigris and Euphrates create a vast complex of shallow lakes and marshes covering about 15,000 km² (5,800 sq miles), the Mesopotamian Marshes, home of the famous Marsh Arabs.

Iran possesses a great diversity of wetlands. In the north, there is an almost unbroken chain of freshwater lakes and marshes, brackish lagoons, irrigation ponds (locally known as 'ab-bandans') and rice paddies stretching for some 700 km (430 miles) along the southern edge of the Caspian Sea. Two of the most important wetlands in these lowlands are Anzali Mordab in the west, a complex of shallow lakes and tall reed beds with surrounding flood meadows, and Gorgan Bay in the east, a large, shallow, brackish lagoon with extensive seasonally flooded sedge marshes and tamarisk thickets.

The Orumiyeh Basin in the highlands of Azarbaijan in northwestern Iran includes a number of important wetlands. Lake Orumiyeh (483,000 hectares - 1.2 million acres) is a vast hypersaline lake with spectacular breeding colonies of pelicans and flamingos. Although the lake is too saline to support any plants or animals other than the alga

Enteromorpha and the brine shrimp *Artemia*, the numerous small fresh and brackish water lakes and marshes along the rivers which enter the lake support abundant aquatic vegetation and are very rich in wildlife.

Near the eastern end of the Zagros Mountains, in south-central Iran, there is a group of large wetlands set in broad valleys between rugged mountain ranges. These wetlands include freshwater lakes and marshes, such as Dasht-e Arjan, and salt lakes with extensive brackish marshes, such as Parishan, Bakhtegan and Tashk. Three large rivers, the Karun, Dez and Kharkeh, which rise amidst the snow-capped peaks of the Zagros Mountains, debouche on to the plains of Khuzestan and create a vast complex of seasonal floodplain wetlands which extend west to the Iraqi border and south to the head of the Persian Gulf. The most important of these wetlands is Shadegan Marshes, some 290,000 hectares (717,000 acres) of seasonally flooded sedge marsh and brackish lagoons adjacent to the extensive inter-tidal mudflats at the head of the Gulf.

In the very heart of the great deserts of eastern Iran and western Afghanistan lies a vast complex of freshwater lakes and reed beds, which at times of peak flooding can cover over 200,000 hectares (490,000 acres). These wetlands, in the Seistan Basin, are unusual in that although the three main lakes, the Hamoun-e Puzak, the Hamoun-e Sabari and the Hamoun-e Helmand, lie within an internal drainage basin, they are predominantly freshwater. The system is fed by the Helmand River, which during long periods of drought supplies sufficient water to flood only the uppermost of the lakes, the Hamoun-e Puzak. However, during years of unusually heavy rainfall, floodwaters sweep through all three lakes and overflow into a vast saline waste area, flushing the salts out of the system. The only other wetlands of note in Afghanistan are two salt lakes in the eastern highlands, Dasht-i Nawar and Ab-i Istada, renowned for their flamingos.

Eastern Asia

Eastern Asia possesses at least 280,000 km² (108,000 sq miles) of wetlands. The People's Republic of China, which comprises over 80 per cent of this region (and indeed over 20 per cent of the whole of Asia), has more than 25 million hectares (62 million acres) of wetlands including about 11 million hectares (27 million acres) of marshes and bogs, 12 million hectares (30 million acres) of lakes - both natural and artificial - and 2 million hectares (5 million acres) of coastal salt marshes and mudflats. To this can be added about 1.5 million hectares (4 million acres) of lakes and marshes in Mongolia, over 1 million hectares (2.5 million acres) of wetlands, mainly estuarine systems and coastal mudflats, in the Korean

Peninsula, and perhaps 0.5 million hectares (1.2 million acres) of lakes, bogs and estuarine systems in Japan.

The Qinghai-Tibetan Plateau of western China is the largest high-altitude plateau in the world. It is dotted with innumerable lakes, ponds and bogs, and includes the sources of several of the world's greatest rivers: the Yellow, Yangtze, Mekong and Salween in the east, and the Indus, Ganges and Brahmaputra in the south. Much of the plateau consists of inland drainage systems, and most of the larger lakes are saline. Qinghai Lake (458,000 hectares - 1.13 million acres) in the east is the largest saline lake in China. The total area of lakes and marshes is unknown, but probably exceeds 5 million hectares (12.5 million acres). To the north, the great inland drainage systems of the Xinjiang deserts include several large saline lakes, such as those of the Tarim Basin, Turpan Depression and Junggar Basin. This whole region of China is undergoing dessication as the uplift of the Himalayas increasingly blocks the inflow of moist trade winds from the south; most of the lakes of the Qinghai-Tibetan Plateau are shrinking in size, and the largest lake in Xinjiang, Lop Nur, has dried out completely in recent years.

Most of Mongolia's principal lakes occur in the Central Asian Internal Drainage Basin. There are three main systems: a group of large freshwater and saline lakes in the Valley of the Great Lakes; a chain of saline lakes at the foot of the Gobi-Altai in the Gobi Valley; and a group of mostly saline lakes on the Khangayn Plateau. All have numerous characteristics in common since they were once part of a vast body of water

Qinghai Lake on the Qinghai-Tibetan Plateau, China, lies in a large inland drainage system.

POYANG LAKE, CHINA

Poyang Lake is a large freshwater lake with associated marshes and wet grassland, south of the Yangtze River in central China. The lake is fed by five rivers which enter at the south end, and also by back-flow from the Yangtze River. At the height of the wet season, from April to July, the lake can cover as much as 4,600 km² (1,780 sq miles); during the dry season, it fragments into many smaller lakes and ponds, the emerging mudflats supporting a rich growth of grasses.

Poyang Lake stores up floodwaters from the Yangtze River and other rivers during the rainy season and thereby plays a vital role in flood protection. It supports a significant commercial fishery and a small freshwater pearl industry, as well as providing valuable grazing land for domestic water buffalo. Local villagers cut grasses and aquatic vegetation for fodder, fuel and thatching; during the dry season, many parts of the wetland are cultivated for vegetable crops and rice.

The lake is world-famous for its wintering population of the endangered Siberian crane (*Grus leucogeranus*). These cranes were first discovered in the winter of 1980/81, and it is now known that as many as 1,500 may be present in mid-winter, along with large numbers of two other endangered species of crane, the white-naped crane and hooded crane The lake also holds some 5,000 swans, 100,000 geese and 600,000 ducks during the winter months.

The construction of dykes to prevent seasonal flooding, as well as the reclamation of land for agriculture and the removal of water for irrigation, has resulted in the loss of some wetland habitat. In the long term, however, damming projects on the Yangtze River and other source rivers could have a much more drastic impact upon the lake.

Poyang Hu Nature Reserve (22,400 hectares - 55,400 acres) was established in 1982 to provide a refuge for the cranes and other waterbirds. A laboratory, museum and bird observatory have been constructed, and wildlife tourism is now being encouraged with the building of tourist accommodation near the lake.

which covered the entire region in more humid times. The whole region still abounds in relict features such as ancient lake banks and dry river courses.

Some of the largest freshwater marshes in Asia occur in northeastern China. There are over 1 million hectares (2.5 million acres) of marshes on the Sanjiang (Three Rivers) Plain alone. This region, sometimes known as the Plain of Reeds, consists of a vast complex of shallow freshwater lakes, reed beds and peat bogs near the confluence of the Heilong (Amur), Sungari and Wusuli (Ussuri) Rivers. Other extensive systems of freshwater lakes and marshes include the Zhalong Marshes and Xiang Hai Marshes. All three of these wetlands are of great significance as breeding and staging areas for huge numbers of waterbirds, including four endangered species of cranes.

The alluvial plains of the Yellow and Yangtze River Basins in eastern China contain the greatest concentration of large freshwater lakes in the country, totalling over 2.2 million hectares (5.4 million acres). The Yangtze Basin in particular is famous for its lakes, such as the Dongting Lakes, the Wuhan Lakes, Poyang Lake and Shengjin Lake. All are freshwater, and many are fringed with extensive reed beds.

Most of China's 2.1 million hectares (5.2 million acres) of coastal marshes and mudflats occur in three main areas in the north: at the mouth of the Yangzte River and along the adjacent coast; around the estuary of the Yellow River; and in the estuarine system of the Shuangtaizi, Liao and Hun Rivers. Most of the rivers flowing into the Yellow Sea carry large amounts of sediment, resulting in rapid build-up of deltas and continuous creation of new wetlands.

Much of China's south coast is rocky, with extensive wetlands occurring only at the mouths of the larger rivers, for example in the delta of the Pearl River. Virtually all of these coastal wetlands have, however, now been converted to rice paddies and aquaculture ponds. Mangroves still occur patchily along the coast as far north as central Fujian province and the west coast of Taiwan, and are particularly well preserved in Deep Bay in Hong Kong. The famous Mai Po Marshes Nature Reserve incorporates a portion of this mangrove ecosystem along with a large area of adjacent shrimp ponds.

Most of the Korean Peninsula is mountainous. The only large wetlands are located along the west and south coasts, where there are numerous estuaries and shallow sea bays with extensive inter-tidal mudflats and many small offshore islands. The northeast shore of Korea Bay has one of the highest tidal ranges in the world, with neap tides of 5.5 m (18 ft) and spring tides of 9.3 m (30 1/2 ft). South Korea alone possesses about 630,000 hectares (1.56 million acres) of mudflats on its west and south coasts. In some areas, there is a broad coastal plain with many small lakes, extensive reed beds and large areas of rice paddy. Other notable wetlands include several lakes of volcanic origin in the mountains along the Chinese border, as well as some small bogs of great botanical interest in the northern highlands.

Japan possesses a great diversity of natural wetlands, although most have been adversely affected by development in recent decades. Most lakes are very small, Lake Biwa (67,380 hectares - 166,500 acres) in central Honshu being a notable exception. This large freshwater lake is one of the few lakes in Japan of pre-glacial origin. There are several other large lakes, mostly of volcanic origin, in Hokkaido.

A kei wai shrimp-culture pond dug in what was originally a mangrove wetland at Mai Po in the New Territories, part of Hong Kong.

Extensive freshwater marshes still persist in some of the more remote areas, particularly in eastern Hokkaido. This region also contains the majority of the country's coastal lagoon and salt marsh systems of which Lake Furen is the largest. Elsewhere, most of the lowland marshy habitats and coastal lagoons have been drained for agricultural land. Some of this now provides important feeding habitat for wintering waterbirds, for example the large area of rice paddies at Izumi in Kyushu, which harbours up to 8,000 hooded and white-naped cranes (*Grus monacha* and *Grus vipio*). Japan's largest areas of inter-tidal mudflats are in estuaries and bays along the Pacific coast, such as the Bay of Tokyo and Inner Ise Bay, where there are particularly large tidal ranges, but much of this habitat has now been lost to development. Mangrove swamps are confined to the Amami Islands and Ryukyu Islands in the south.

Southern Asia

There are estimated to be about 33 million hectares (82 million acres) of wetlands in the Indian subcontinent, excluding areas under paddy cultivation. The riverine, floodplain and deltaic wetlands of the Indus, Ganges and Brahmaputra account for a large proportion of this area. However, throughout the rest of the subcontinent there are innumerable small water-storage reservoirs and irrigation ponds, known as tanks, which in total exceed 1.5 million hectares (3.7 million acres), and constitute the only significant bodies of standing water over much of the subcontinent's arid interior. Other major wetland types include the coastal lagoon systems of peninsular India and of Sri Lanka and the salt lake systems of Pakistan and western India. Mangroves once occurred widely along the coasts of the subcontinent, but these have been drastically

KUSHIRO MARSH, JAPAN

Kushiro Marsh, in the lowlands of eastern Hokkaido, is a marshy floodplain along the Kushiro and Akan Rivers, with several small freshwater lakes, extensive reed beds, sedge marshes and peat bogs. There are many springs, some of which are warm and maintain small areas of open water throughout the long, cold winters.

The marsh is one of the largest and most important natural wetlands remaining in Japan, supporting a very rich and diverse fauna. The shallow marshes are particularly important as a breeding and wintering area for the endangered red-crowned crane (*Grus*

japonensis). The entire Japanese population of these birds breeds in eastern Hokkaido and the great majority of the birds winter in the Kushiro area - as many as 380 birds in recent years. About 21 pairs remain throughout the summer to breed. Large numbers of swans, geese, ducks and shorebirds occur during the migration seasons, and as many as 1,000 whooper swans (*Cygnus cygnus*) overwinter.

The clearing of forests for agriculture and the straightening and deepening of rivers in the catchment area have led to increased siltation in the marshes, excessive flooding in spring and drought

in summer. Road-building and the urban sprawl around Kushiro City have also resulted in a loss of wetland habitat.

Some 5,000 hectares (12,400 acres) of the marsh have been listed under the Ramsar Convention. The Ramsar site is located in the centre of the marsh where all the rivers converge. This area was first designated as a Special Protection Area in 1935; it is now a National Wildlife Protection Area, and has also been designated as a Special Natural Monument. Several feeding stations have been established for the wintering cranes, and large quantities of food have been provided every year since 1952.

The famous Bharatpur wetland in India is artificial. It was specifically created for duck hunting.

reduced in extent by man's activities, and are now largely confined to the remoter areas of the Indus and Ganges-Brahmaputra Deltas.

There are relatively few wetlands in the Himalayas, other than the river systems and a scattering of small, freshwater lakes and bogs at medium to high altitudes. However, where the rivers leave the foothills and spread out on to the plains, there are often extensive wetlands - the so-called 'terai' - such as those along the Rapti and Narayani Rivers in Royal Chitwan National Park in Nepal and along the Manas River on the border between Bhutan and India. Severe flooding during the summer monsoon and constant shifting of the river channels have created wide floodplains with a mosaic of sand and shingle banks, oxbow lakes, patches of riverine forest, marshes and seasonally flooded grasslands.

In northwestern India, a broad valley parallel to the folds of the Himalayas contains the Jhelum River, a tributary of the Indus. Here, in the Vale of Kashmir, the broad valley floor is covered with a dense network of rivers and canals linking a group of large freshwater lakes, each with an abundant growth of aquatic vegetation. One such wetland is Dal Lake, on the outskirts of Srinagar, famous for its great scenic beauty and once a major tourist attraction, but now under serious threat from siltation and eutrophication.

The Indus is one of the great rivers of Asia, rising in Tibet and flowing for over 3,000 km (1,900 miles) to its delta on the Arabian Sea. Virtually all of Pakistan's wetlands depend to some extent on this river and its tributaries. The rivers themselves comprise over 3 million hectares (7 million acres) of wetland - the broad-braided river channels with their extensive mudflats, sand banks, reed beds and tamarisk thickets creating an ever-changing mosaic of wetland habitats, all of which are of great importance for wildlife.

Since the earliest days of civilization on the Indus, the waters of the river have been tapped for irrigation through an elaborate system of canals. This system now extends almost throughout the plains of Pakistan and carries water year-round, not only to cultivated

The Indus River Dolphin Reserve, Sindh Province, Pakistan is severely threatened by the construction of numerous dams.

land, but also to many natural wetlands which would otherwise have dried out during the dry season. Some natural wetlands are now linked to the canal system and managed for specific purposes; for example, Haleji Lake is maintained as a stop-gap water supply for Karachi. In addition, the unintentional seepage of water from the canals and excess water from irrigated land have created large areas of new wetland habitat on the once arid plains. Many of these are freshwater or brackish wetlands with extensive reed beds and tamarisk thickets. The recent construction of huge reservoirs on the larger rivers

has added to the extent of wetland habitat. Some of these dams and barrages, such as Chashma and Taunsa, have developed a rich growth of aquatic vegetation and now support important commercial fisheries and large concentrations of waterbirds.

The delta of the Indus River is a vast complex of tidal river channels and creeks, low-lying sandy islands, mangrove swamps, inter-tidal mudflats and bare salt flats covering about 600,000 hectares (1.48 million acres). In the east, it merges into the vast saline lagoons and salt flats of the Great Rann of Kutch, which are famous for their large breeding colonies of flamingos.

Most of the wetlands of northern India lie within the basin of the River Ganges, which also rises in Tibet and flows for over 2,500 km (1,550 miles) to its mouth in the Bay of Bengal. The alluvial plain of the Ganges stretches for over 2,000 km (1,200 miles) from Calcutta to Amritsar, comprising a vast lowland, some 250-300 km (155-190 miles) wide, studded with innumerable small freshwater lakes with luxuriant vegetation. Most of these are oxbow lakes, marking the historical courses of the Ganges and its tributaries. Heavy monsoon rains in the months of July to October and the accompanying floods inundate these lakes and the surrounding plains, but by the end of the dry season (March-June), most of them are completely dry.

One of the most famous waterbird sanctuaries in Asia, the Keoladeo Ghana National Park (Bharatpur),

The fish-eating painted stork is common throughout the Indian subcontinent and may raise up to four chicks per year.

The Sundarbans (literally 'beautiful forests') are a vast complex of tall mangrove forests, mudflats, river channels and tidal creeks in the combined deltas of the Ganges, Brahmaputra and Meghna Rivers. This region contains one of the largest continuous stands of mangroves in the world (between 600,000 and 700,000 hectares - 1.48 million and 1.73 million acres). The whole area is subject to inundation during spring tides and extensive flooding with freshwater during the monsoon season (May to November).

The mangrove forests have been exploited since time immemorial, the principal activities being fishing, the collection of wild honey and beeswax, and the cutting of mangroves for timber, pulp-wood and firewood. The Sundarbans provide vital breeding and nursery grounds for a large proportion of the fish and crustaceans that make up the extremely important marine fishery in the Bay of Bengal. The mangrove forest also protects the densely settled agricultural areas to the north from the full force of cyclonic storms and tidal waves.

The Sundarbans support a very rich and diverse fauna, including a substantial population of estuarine crocodiles and the world's largest single population of royal Bengal tigers (500-

Fishermen in the Sundarbans mangrove forests in Bangladesh.

600 individuals), notorious for their man-eating tendencies.

A long-term ecological change is taking place in the Sundarbans as a result of the eastward migration of the Ganges and the diversion of water for irrigation. Decreased flushing with freshwater has resulted in increased saline intrusion, and this has affected the natural regeneration of mangroves. Approximately half of the mangrove forest has been cleared for agriculture and human settlement, and the remainder is being heavily over-exploited for timber. Wildlife

populations are threatened by illegal hunting, and several large mammals have become extinct in recent times.

The whole of the Bangladesh Sundarbans has been declared a Forest Reserve which includes three wildlife sanctuaries totalling over 32,000 hectares (79,000 acres). Across the border, over 258,000 hectares (637,500 acres) of the Indian Sundarbans were declared a Tiger Reserve in 1973. Various management plans have been prepared, the aim of these being to ensure that future exploitation of the forest does not conflict with wildlife conservation.

lies on the rim of the Gangetic Plain in Rajasthan. This artificial complex of shallow freshwater lakes and marshes was created in the 1850s when the Maharajah of Bharatpur constructed a system of extensive lagoons in order to attract ducks and geese for hunting.

Near its mouth, the Ganges unites with another of Asia's great rivers, the Brahmaputra. The floodplain of the Brahmaputra in Assam extends for over 600 km (370 miles) from Upper Assam to the frontier with Bangladesh, and contains some of the country's finest wetlands. The river itself changes course frequently, leaving permanent or seasonal lakes and marshes in the abandoned channels, and maintaining a mosaic of riverine habitats. In wet years, the floodplain becomes a single vast wetland, some 500,000 hectares (1.24 million acres) in extent. The wetlands of Assam have fared better than those elsewhere in India, and the Brahmaputra Valley retains relicts of natural ecosystems which have all but disappeared from the rest of India.

The combined floodplains of the Ganges and Brahmaputra Rivers in Bangladesh and West Bengal

comprise the largest deltaic system in the world. The entire region is criss-crossed with an intricate network of rivers, streams and canals. During the rainy season, vast areas of the low-lying alluvial plains between the rivers are flooded; indeed, at this time of year, about half of Bangladesh could be classified as wetland. The floodwaters remain for two to five months; then, as the floods recede, the exposed land can once again be cultivated for rice, jute and other crops. Numerous shallow lakes and marshes remain after the flooding, and many of these retain water throughout the dry season. Along the southern edge of the delta, at the head of the Bay of Bengal, lies a vast complex of mangrove swamps, river channels, tidal creeks, mudflats and low-lying sandy islands known as the Sundarbans.

In the western part of peninsular India, the narrow coastal plain is abundantly watered by rivers rising in the Western Ghats, and there are several important lagoon systems, such as the Cochin Backwaters in Kerala, but most of the original mangrove swamps have now disappeared.

In marked contrast, the east coast is relatively low-lying with extensive alluvial floodplains and deltas. There are several very large brackish lagoons on the coast, notably Chilka Lake and Pulicat Lake, and freshwater lakes in the interior of the deltas, notably Kolleru Lake. The great Vedaranayam Salt Swamp near Point Calimere is a complex of open mudflats and lagoons behind a 50 km (31 mile) long sand bar. Some well-preserved areas of mangrove forest remain, as at Bhitarkanika in the delta of the Brahmani and Baiterani Rivers and at Coringa in the Godavari Delta.

The principal coastal wetlands of Sri Lanka are estuaries and lagoons, many of which contain small patches of mangrove forest. Many of the 45 or so estuaries belong to the basin type, where rivers discharge into a relatively shallow basin, which in turn opens into the sea (for example, the Puttalam, Negombo and Jaffna Lagoons). Of the 40 or so true lagoons, most are found along the south and east coasts. Many of these are seasonal, drying out completely during the dry season, while others become hypersaline as sources of freshwater dry up.

Freshwater habitats include numerous rivers and streams, extensive riverine and floodplain marshes, and many small permanent and seasonal ponds. Although there are no large natural lakes in Sri Lanka, there are some 12,500 hectares (30,900 acres) of small floodplain lakes, known as 'villus', particularly in the Mahaweli river system in the east. Villus range in size from 10 to 550 hectares (25 to 1,360 acres); most contain freshwater, but there is a unique group of saline villus far inland in Wilpattu National Park, in the west. In addition to these natural wetlands,

there are over 10,000 small irrigation ponds or tanks, locally known as 'wewa', which form part of an intricate water-supply system used for rice cultivation and dating back at least 1,500 years.

Southeastern Asia

Most of the major wetlands of mainland Southeast Asia are situated in the lower basins and deltas of the Irrawaddy, the Chao Phraya, the Mekong and the Red River. A long history of rice cultivation, coupled with the very dense human population, has meant that most wetland areas amenable for rice-growing have already been converted to paddies, and little natural wetland habitat survives today. The most extensive wetlands of Malaysia, Indonesia and the Philippines are typically coastal mangrove swamps with their associated mudflats, and freshwater and peat swamp forests which often occur inland from the mangrove forest. In remote regions of Sumatra and Borneo, vast areas of mangrove forest and swamp forest have survived until recent times, although they are now under great pressure from logging.

Burma possesses several very large estuarine and delta systems with extensive mangrove swamps. Mangroves, covering in all more than 500,000 hectares (1.2 million acres), are mostly located in the Irrawaddy Delta and on the Tenasserim and Arakan coasts. However, only a small proportion of this forest remains in an undisturbed condition, and the once extensive forests of the Irrawaddy Delta are now badly degraded. Inland, much the most extensive wetlands are the seasonally inundated floodplains of the Irrawaddy-Chindwin, Sittang and Salween Rivers.

One of the many trout streams in the Horton Plains National Park, Sri Lanka.

163

Intha fishermen wrap their legs around a single oar to propel their boats across Inle Lake, Burma.

Large areas of floodplain have been bunded (dyked) and reclaimed for permanent agriculture, and most land still subject to seasonal inundation is used for rice cultivation during the dry season.

Similarly, in south-central Thailand, the once extensive wetlands on the floodplain of the Chao Phraya and several other large rivers have been almost entirely converted to agricultural land. Extensive flooding still occurs during periods of heavy rainfall, but under normal circumstances the monsoon flooding is highly restricted, and by January standing water is restricted to small lakes, ponds and

Paddy fields are used to take advantage of the high productivity of lowland wetland ecosystems in many parts of Asia.

water courses. Some significant freshwater lakes and swamps remain in central and northern Thailand, but most have been modified for irrigation purposes and rice-growing. The largest lake in central Thailand, Beung Boraphet, was formed in 1930 by the damming of a large swamp, and now constitutes the single most important wintering site for ducks in the country. Much the largest wetland in the south is Lake Songkhla, a huge shallow coastal lagoon of fresh to brackish water. There are also many estuarine systems with mangrove swamps and mudflats along the coast, the most extensive and species-rich ecosystems occurring along the west coast.

The Mekong is one of the great rivers of Asia, the twelfth longest river in the world and sixth in terms of discharge. It rises on the Qinghai-Tibetan Plateau in China, and flows for 4,160 km (2,585 miles) to its delta in Vietnam. In northern Cambodia, the river enters a fluviatile lowland landscape with broad floodplains and extensive backwater swamps, many of which remain flooded throughout the dry season. Just below Phnom Penh, it divides into two main channels at the apex of its vast delta which comprises much of southern Cambodia and southern Vietnam. The Great Lake and Tonle Sap River, in central Cambodia, form an integral part of the Mekong floodplain system. The Great Lake is the largest lake in Southeast Asia. It lies in a vast shallow basin to the west of the Mekong, and is surrounded by a broad belt of freshwater swamp forest. During the dry season, the lake drains into the Mekong via the Tonle Sap River. However, as the water level in the Mekong rises during the rainy season, the flow in the Tonle

Sap is reversed and the Mekong floodwaters enter the Great Lake. At the height of the flood season in September and October, the lake and its inundation zone cover 1.3 million hectares (3.2 million acres).

The Red River (Song Hong) is the largest river in northern Vietnam. It rises in the mountains of Yunnan Province in China, and flows generally southeast into the Gulf of Tonkin. The river carries a very large silt load (115 million tonnes - 113 million tons - per year), giving the water its reddish colour. Almost the entire delta (12,600 km² - 4,860 sq miles) has been converted to agricultural land and aquaculture ponds, or drained for forestry and urban development, and very little natural wetland habitat now remains, except for a few remnants of the mangrove/mudflat ecosystem along the outer coast. The most important of these is at Xuan Thuy, at the mouth of the main branch of the Red River.

The principal wetland systems throughout peninsular Malaysia and the Greater Sundas (Borneo, Sumatra, Java and Bali) are mangrove swamps and inter-tidal mudflats, freshwater swamp forests and peat swamp forests, although locally there are some important freshwater lake systems.

The most extensive mangrove forests occur along the eastern coast of Sumatra and around the island of Borneo, but there are still some significant stands in the states of Perak, Selangor and Johor in peninsular Malaysia. In many places, the adjacent inter-tidal mudflats extend for several kilometres out to sea. The nipa palm (*Nypa fruticans*) often occurs in association with mangroves, lining the tidal reaches of rivers and sometimes forming huge swamps in delta areas, such as on the Klias Peninsula in Sabah.

Freshwater swamp forests are to be found on permanently or seasonally flooded mineral soils on coastal plains and in river basins in the lowlands. They often form fringes, up to 5 km (3 miles) wide, along the lower reaches of large rivers, or in a broad belt around some freshwater lake systems. There, they are commonly succeeded by peat swamp forests. The largest areas of freshwater swamp forest occur in the lowlands of Sumatra and Kalimantan, along Sabah's eastern coast, along the lower reaches of certain rivers in Sarawak, and in parts of peninsular Malaysia. The richest and most extensive peat swamp forests are in Sumatra and Borneo. There are about

MEKONG DELTA, VIETNAM AND CAMBODIA

The Mekong Delta forms a vast fertile plain of approximately 55,000 km² (21,000 sq miles) with extensive floodplain wetlands, where freshwater swamp forests are dominated by paperbark, mangrove forests and inter-tidal mudflats. By the end of the monsoon season in September or October, the combination of floodwaters from the rivers, local rainfall and tidal inundation can result in the flooding of 3.4 million hectares (8.4 million acres) of the delta.

The delta includes some of the most productive agricultural land in Southeast Asia. Approximately 3.7 million hectares (9.1 million acres) are under cultivation, principally for rice, and yield about 6.5 million tonnes (6.4 million tons) of rice per year. The delta also supports a major fishery involving over 200 species of fish as well as many shellfish, mussels, clams, prawns and shrimps. The mangrove and paperbark forests constitute an important forestry resource, and also play a very important role in coastal protection in a region prone to several typhoons a year. The marshes support a large population of the rare eastern sarus crane (*Grus antigone sharpii*), and the mangrove and paperbark forests provide nesting sites for huge numbers of cormorants,

Dong Thap Muoi comprises a large seasonal floodplain on the Mekong River.

herons, egrets, storks and ibises.

Rapid growth in human population and intensive development of the delta for agriculture pose a major threat to the wetlands. Various developments upstream on the Mekong River, including hydroelectric, irrigation and flood-control projects, are changing the hydrology of the delta; water quality, and therefore the fishery, is being affected by industrial and domestic

wastes, pesticides and fertilizers. Six reserves have been established in Vietnam to protect representative examples of the wetland ecosystems, and large areas of former mangrove and paperbark forest have been replanted. In some areas, following the failure of attempts to drain wetlands for agricultural purposes, considerable efforts have been made to restore the wetlands to their natural condition.

2 million hectares (5 million acres) in Malaysia, of which about 75 per cent are in Sarawak. Estimates of the total area of peat swamp forests in Sumatra and Kalimantan vary between 16.5 and 27 million hectares (41 and 66.5 million acres).

Most of the region's lakes are associated with riverine systems, such as the Lake Sentarum complex in West Kalimantan, Tasek Cini in peninsular Malaysia, Loagan Bunut in Sarawak, and the numerous oxbow lakes along the meandering lower reaches of several major rivers in Sarawak and Sabah. Some, however, are of volcanic origin, such as Lake Toba in western Sumatra, a very large crater which, with a maximum depth of 450 m (1,475 ft), is the deepest lake in Southeast Asia.

The Philippines formerly supported extensive mangrove forests, tidal mudflats and coastal swamps, but these have been severely degraded as a result of conversion to shrimp ponds and reclamation for agriculture. Large stands of mangrove still persist in Ragay Gulf in southeastern Luzon, in Davao Gulf in Mindanao, and on many of the smaller islands. The country is rich in freshwater lakes, many of which are of volcanic origin, such as Taal Lake on Luzon, Lakes Balinsasayao and Danao on Negros, and Lake Lanao, a very large lake formed by the collapse of a volcano on Mindanao. The largest lake in the Philippines is Laguna de Bay near Manila. This shallow freshwater lake, formerly an extension of Manila Bay, has been extensively developed for its fisheries, and about 70 per cent of the lake's surface has now been enclosed in fish pens. Most swamps and marshes have been drained for agriculture, but there remain three extensive lowland marshy habitats of considerable importance for their wildlife: Candaba Swamp in central Luzon, and Agusan and Liguasan Marshes in Mindanao.

Mangroves occur in sheltered bays throughout the region, and are particularly extensive in southern Sulawesi, on Buru in the Moluccas, at Maumere Bay on Flores, in western Timor and in the Tanimbar Islands. There are large areas of alluvial plain with freshwater swamp forest and peat swamp forest in central Sulawesi, along the west coast of northern Sulawesi, and also to a lesser extent on the island of Seram. The region has a number of interesting lakes, many of which are of volcanic origin, such as Gunung Gamkonora crater lake on a steep-sided volcano on Halmahera, and the Kelimutu crater lakes on Flores, each of which has its own distinctive colour caused by the high content of minerals and gases. The Malili lake system in central Sulawesi is remarkable in having no fewer than 16 endemic fish species. Other freshwater lakes in Sulawesi with endemic fishes include Lake Poso and Lake Lindu in the central highlands, and a group of three lakes, Tempe, Buaya and Sidenreng, in the southern lowlands.

FLORA

In the High Arctic wilderness, the thin soils support only the simplest plants. Species of algae, lichens and mosses dominate, although a few species of flowering plants such as poppies (*Papaver*), cinquefoils (*Potentilla*), chickweeds (*Stellaria*), saxifrages (*Saxifraga*) and sedges (*Carex*) maintain a tenuous foothold during the brief Arctic summer. Farther south, in the tundra zone, the soil cover becomes more extensive, and the number of species increases rapidly. Mosses and lichens are gradually replaced by flowering plants, and stunted shrubs begin to appear, mainly birches (*Betula glandulosa*) and willows (*Salix*). Boggy areas are dominated by *Sphagnum* mosses and tussocky grassland with various sedges and cotton grasses (*Eriophorum*). Farther south still, the open tundra gives way to the forest-tundra zone, with patches of tundra alternating with forest dominated by larches and birches.

Throughout the great taiga forest zone, the nutrient-poor bogs are dominated by *Sphagnum* mosses. Here, the nutrient-rich lakes and marshes have much in common with similar wetlands in the deciduous forest, steppe and desert zones to the south. Indeed, there is a remarkable similarity in the vegetation of freshwater lakes and marshes across the whole of temperate Asia.

Although severely degraded in some areas, paperbark forests are being replanted in the Mekong Delta.

The Tutong Marshes, Brunei are included within the Tasek Merimbun National Park.

Throughout this vast region, the submerged vegetation is typically dominated by species of pondweeds (*Potamogeton*), water milfoils (*Myriophyllum*), bladderworts (*Utricularia*), hornworts (*Ceratophyllum*), naiads (*Najas*) and stoneworts (*Chara*). Floating vegetation generally consists of the leaves of water lilies (*Nymphaea* and *Nuphar* species) and free-floating species such as duckweeds (*Lemna*), water chestnut (*Trapa natans*) and water lettuce (*Salvinia natans*). The common reed (*Phragmites australis*) and species of reed mace, cattail or bulrush (*Typha*) are often the most conspicuous of the emergent species, forming huge reed beds on many of the large shallow lakes. Other common emergent species include spike-rushes (*Eleocharis*), club-rushes (*Scirpus*), bur-reeds (*Sparganium*) and rushes (*Juncus*). Forested wetlands are generally dominated by species of alder (*Alnus rugosa*), birch and willow. Overall, the wetland vegetation is very diverse and variable.

Most of the plant genera characteristic of freshwater lakes and marshes in the temperate regions of Asia are also common and widespread in similar wetland ecosystems in subtropical and tropical regions. However, the number of species in tropical wetlands is generally much higher. Some of the most widespread and conspicuous plants include the submerged *Hydrilla verticillata* and rooted-floating species such as the East Indian lotus (*Nelumbo nucifera*), water lilies of the genus *Nymphoides* and the giant water lily (*Euryale ferox*). Conspicuous free-floating species are water fern (*Azolla pinnata*), water

soldier (*Pistia stratiotes*), water hyacinth (*Eichhornia crassipes*) and water lettuce (*Salvinia molesta*). The last two are introduced plants from South America and are major pests in many parts of Asia, forming vast floating mats over the surface of lakes and reservoirs, and clogging up rivers and canals.

Emergent plants characteristic of tropical freshwater wetlands include wild rice (*Oryza sativa*), rushes, sedges of the genus *Cyperus* and marsh grasses of the genera *Echinochloa, Panicum, Paspalum* and *Paspalidium*. Floodplain grasslands, where not heavily grazed by domestic livestock, are often dominated by elephant grass (*Saccharum spontaneum*, for example) and *Arundo donax*.

Man-made lakes generally have a much simpler aquatic flora than natural lakes because of the large seasonal fluctuations in water level. At low water levels, grasses and annuals invade the zone normally covered by water but now exposed, and are often subjected to heavy grazing by domestic livestock.

The marshes and bogs of the great Qinghai-Tibetan Plateau in central Asia possess a highly distinctive flora dominated by a mixture of species of rushes (*Kobresia*), sedges (*Carex*), mare's-tails (*Hippuris*), arrow-grasses (*Triglochin*) and club-rushes (*Blysmus*).

The saline wetlands of internal drainage basins, such as those in many parts of the Middle East, Pakistan, northwestern India and central Mongolia, support extremely simple plant communities. In highly saline conditions, only certain algae may survive. Where some inflow of freshwater creates brackish conditions, salt marsh vegetation may develop, with characteristic species being glasswort (*Salicornia*), sea-blite (*Suaeda*), saltwort (*Salsola*) and various salt-tolerant species of rush (*Juncus*) and sedge (*Carex*). Tamarisk (*Tamarix*) thrive in saline soils subject to seasonal inundation, and form an extensive shrub zone around some salt lakes.

Through most of southern Asia, mangroves dominate the inter-tidal zone. Indeed, mangrove vegetation is believed to have reached its optimal development in Southeast Asia, and in that region comprises an extremely diverse ecosystem. In Indonesia, 92 plant species have been reported in the mangrove swamps, including 38 genuine mangrove tree species. The dominant tree genera in Southeast Asia are *Acanthus, Aegiceras, Avicennia, Bruguiera, Ceriops, Excoecaria, Heritiera, Kandelia, Lumnitzera, Rhizophora, Sonneratia* and *Xylocarpus*. Other plant species commonly associated with mangroves include the mangrove fern *Acrostichum aureum*, creepers of the genus *Derris*, the shrub *Hibiscus tiliaceus*, the palms *Nypa fruticans* and *Phoenix paludosa*, and the grass *Imperata cylindrica*.

Local villagers collecting shellfish on mudflats at Ao Ban Don in peninsular Thailand.

Towards the northern and western limits of mangrove distribution in Asia, species diversity declines. At the northern limit, on the coast of Fujian Province in China, only a single mangrove species, *Kandelia candel*, is common, while at the western limit, in the southern Persian Gulf, again only a single species is present, this time *Avicennia marina*.

Two other main types of forested wetlands occur in Southeast Asia: freshwater swamp forest and peat swamp forest. Freshwater swamp forest is very rich in tree species compared to mangrove forest, with over 120 canopy tree species recorded, for example, at one site in peninsular Malaysia. These forests are rich in epiphytes, rattans and palms, and are usually dominated by species of *Campnosperma*, *Terminalia*, *Shorea*, *Barringtonia* and paperbarks (*Melaleuca*). The most disturbed sites, particularly those which have been subjected to repeated burning, are rather poor in species and are usually dominated by the paperbark *Melaleuca leucodendron*, as is the case in the Mekong Delta.

Peat swamp forests are characterized by a species-rich forest community growing on waterlogged peat. They are botanically very rich, with an average of 30-55 tree species per hectare (12-22 species per acre) in parts of Indonesia. The vegetation in these peat swamps is typically zoned around a central dome; the vegetation varies from mixed forest with up to 100 species in the outer zone to virtually monospecific stands of species such as *Shorea* in the inner zones.

FAUNA

The wetlands of Asia support an extremely rich and diverse fish fauna. In the cold lakes and rivers of temperate and Arctic regions, salmonids predominate. Many of these spend most of their lives at sea and migrate up the rivers of northern Asia to spawn. This is true, for example, for almost all of the fishes in the lakes and rivers of the Kamchatka Peninsula in the USSR. The most unusual fish in Lake Baykal is the viviparous Baykal oil fish (*Comephorus baicalensis*), a small fish lacking scales and almost translucent in colour. It lives at depths in excess of 300 m (980 ft) during the day, rising to 50-100 m (160-330 ft) below the surface at night to feed. In early summer, the females rise to the surface where the reduced water pressure causes their abdomens to burst open, releasing their live fry.

In the freshwater lakes on the high plateaus of central Asia, many cyprinid fishes hibernate in burrows not only during the long cold winters but also partly in summer, to avoid the intense daytime solar radiation and low temperatures at night.

Throughout the inland freshwaters of southern and eastern Asia, species of carp and catfish dominate. Other widespread groups include the murrels, featherbacks, climbing perch and gouramis. Species of tilapia (especially *Tilapia mossambica*) have been introduced from Africa and comprise an important component of the commercial catches. In the larger rivers of the Himalayas, two species of carp known as mahseer (*Tor tor* and *Tor putitora*) are very popular sport fish.

No fewer than 850 species of fish have been recorded from the lower Mekong Basin, but many are poorly known. One of the most remarkable is the giant catfish (*Pangasianodon gigas*), which can measure over 3 m (nearly 10 ft) in length and weigh 250-300 kg (550-660 lb). It reportedly migrates several thousand kilometres from Cambodia to spawning grounds in the province of Yunnan in China. Probably the best-known fish of Southeast Asia, however, is the now highly endangered Asian bonytongue or arowana (*Scleropages formosus*), an inhabitant of freshwater lakes and peat swamp forests in Malaysia and Indonesia. Unfortunately, it is much sought after by collectors for their aquaria and fish ponds, especially the red variety which may sell for as much as US$2,700 per fish.

The wetlands of Asia boast seven species of crocodile. The marsh crocodile or mugger (*Crocodylus palustris*) and estuarine or salt water crocodile (*Crocodylus porosus*) are still widely distributed, but the others are all rare, and three are on the brink of extinction. The total population of Chinese crocodiles (in fact, alligators: *Alligator sinensis*) is probably less than 2,000 individuals; the Philippine crocodile (*Crocodylus mindorensis*) may now survive in viable numbers only at Liguasan Marsh in Mindanao, and the Siamese crocodile (*Crocodylus siamensis*) is confined to a few isolated wetlands in Vietnam and possibly also Cambodia.

Turtles and terrapins remain, on the whole, common and widespread in central and southern Asia, although, even so, no fewer than 18 species are considered threatened. One of the largest species,

the river terrapin (*Batagur baska*), has declined catastrophically throughout its range in Bangladesh, Burma and Southeast Asia as a result of direct persecution of adults and massive collection of eggs for human consumption. The dark soft-shell turtle (*Trionyx nigricans*) is known to science only from a single semi-domesticated population at a small artificial pond at the shrine of Hazrat Sultan Bayazid Bostami in southeastern Bangladesh. The 150-200 turtles survive almost entirely on scraps thrown to them by visitors.

Very few mammals are closely associated with wetlands in the Arctic and temperate regions of Asia, and those that are tend to be extremely widespread and still at least locally common if not abundant. Such species include the water shrew (*Neomys fodiens*), beaver (*Castor fiber*), water vole (*Arvicola terrestris*), root vole (*Microtus ratticeps*), muskrat (*Ondatra zibethicus*) and common otter (*Lutra lutra*). The coypu (*Myocastor coypus*), a native of South America, has become widely established in Europe and has recently extended its range into western Asia. The moose or elk (*Alces alces*) of the northern forests habitually forages in marshes during the summer months, and the very widespread wild boar (*Sus scrofa*)

The Kaziranga National Park in Assam, India, has the largest population of the Indian one-horned rhinoceros in the world, although it is threatened by poaching.

The waterbird breeding colony of Vedanthangal, India was protected by local villagers for 200 years before becoming a bird sanctuary.

frequents damp thickets and reed beds.

Two especially noteworthy aquatic mammals of temperate Asia are the land-locked seals of the Caspian Sea and Lake Baykal. The Caspian seal (*Phoca caspica*) spends the summer primarily in the south Caspian and migrates north in autumn to give birth to its pups along the edge of the pack ice. It spends much of the winter out of the water and on ice floes. At Lake Baykal, however, air temperatures drop so low that the Baykal seal (*Phoca sibirica*) must spend most of the winter under the pack ice to keep warm.

In contrast to northern Asia, southern Asia possesses a wide variety of mammals that depend on wetlands for their survival. Many of these are now threatened with extinction, as their habitats are modified by man. Three small cetaceans are confined to Asia's great river systems: the Ganges river dolphin (*Platanista gangetica*) in the Ganges-Brahmaputra systems, the Indus river dolphin (*Platanista minor*) in the Indus River and the Chinese river dolphin or baiji (*Lipotes vexillifer*) in the Yangtze River. The Ganges river dolphin remains common, but the other two species are on the verge of extinction.

Other mammals associated with the wetlands are the fishing cat (*Felis viverrina*) and four species of otter - the common otter, smooth-coated otter (*Lutra perspicillata*), hairy-nosed otter (*Lutra sumatrana*) and oriental small-clawed otter (*Aonyx cinerea*). The Chinese water deer (*Hydropotes inermis*) remains fairly common around lakes in the Yangtze Valley and in the extensive coastal marshes north of Shanghai. Domestic and feral water buffaloes are common throughout southern Asia, but the truly wild ancestral stock of the Asian water buffalo (*Bubalus bubalis*) is on the verge of extinction as a result of hybridization with domestic animals.

The marshes, seasonally flooded grasslands and swamp forests of the Himalayan terai support a variety of threatened species, such as the Asian one-horned rhinoceros (*Rhinoceros unicornis*), swamp deer (*Cervus duvauceli*) and pygmy hog (*Sus salvanius*), which have all but disappeared elsewhere. Similarly, the freshwater swamp forests and peat swamp forests of Southeast Asia provide relatively safe refuges for several rare and endangered species such as the Sumatran or Asian two-horned rhinoceros (*Dicerorhinus sumatrensis*), Javan or lesser one-horned rhinoceros (*Rhinoceros sondaicus*), Sumatran tiger (*Panthera tigris sumatrana*) and otter civet (*Cynogale bennettii*).

The extensive mangrove forests of the Sundarbans support a rich and diverse mammalian fauna, including some 300-350 royal Bengal tigers (*Panthera tigris*) and large numbers of rhesus macaques (*Macaca mulatta*), spotted deer (*Axis axis*) and wild boar. Mangrove forests in Southeast Asia are home to other species such as the widespread crab-eating macaque (*Macaca fascicularis*) and the rare proboscis monkey (*Nasalis larvatus*), known only in Borneo.

Waterbirds are the most conspicuous form of animal life on most Asian wetlands. Of the 310 species which occur regularly, the great majority are to some extent migratory, even in tropical regions where many species undertake lengthy movements to take advantage of seasonal wetlands flooded by the monsoon rains. Other species undertake relatively short altitudinal migrations between breeding areas on the high plateaus of central Asia and wintering areas in the foothills or plains of eastern China and northern India. A good example is the rare black-necked crane (*Grus nigricollis*), which breeds on the Qinghai-Tibetan Plateau and winters in sheltered valleys at lower elevations in the eastern Himalayas and southwestern China.

However, about 160 species of Asian waterbirds are true long-distance migrants, travelling annually between breeding grounds in Arctic and temperate Asia and wintering grounds in Europe, southern Asia, Africa and Australasia. Huge numbers breed on the tundra and forest-tundra of the Arctic and on the countless wetlands in the taiga and steppe zones. The great majority of these are species of ducks (31), geese (10) and shorebirds (waders) (60). Each autumn, many millions of waterbirds begin their long migrations south, some taking a southwesterly route to winter in Europe and the Mediterranean Basin, others a more southerly route to the Middle East, East Africa and in some cases even South Africa, while still others head south or southeast into the Indian subcontinent, Southeast Asia, Australia and New Zealand. There are even a few birds breeding in northeastern Asia, such as the snow geese (*Anser caerulescens*) of Wrangel

Island, which winter in North America.

Many species, notably the swans, most of the ducks and geese, several of the cranes and most of the gulls, go no farther than they have to, spending the winter in suitable habitats not far beyond the southern limit of ice and snow cover. Huge concentrations of birds occur in the wetlands of the Middle East, Pakistan, northern India, eastern China, Korea and Japan. Swans reach their southern limit in the south Caspian region and central China, while geese and most ducks reach theirs in Mesopotamia, central India, Burma and Vietnam. Many other species, notably species of shorebirds, undertake much longer migrations to wintering areas along the southern shores of Asia and in Africa and Australasia. For the very long distance migrants, which winter in southern Africa, Australia and New Zealand, many of the coastal wetlands of south and east Asia provide vital refuelling areas during the spring and autumn.

Characteristic resident waterbirds of freshwater wetlands in southern Asia include three pelicans, four cormorants, oriental darter (*Anhinga melanogaster*), about 20 herons, egrets and bitterns, various storks, ibises and spoonbills, several ducks, many rails, crakes and waterhens and two jacanas. In the coastal zone, extensive mangrove forests provide the security required for breeding, and often support large nesting colonies of cormorants, herons and egrets. In parts of Southeast Asia, mangrove forests are critical for the survival of rare species such as the spot-billed pelican (*Pelecanus philippensis*), milky stork (*Mycteria cinerea*), black-necked stork (*Ephippiorhynchus asiaticus*) and

lesser adjutant (*Leptoptilos javanicus*). Freshwater swamp forests and peat swamp forests are also important for colonies of large waterbirds, particularly in the Mekong Delta, Sumatra and Borneo.

Despite the massive destruction and degradation of Asia's wetlands, large numbers of waterbirds survive in many areas. Migratory species seem to have fared slightly better than sedentary species, presumably because most of their main breeding areas in the USSR and many of their terminal wintering areas in the Middle East and Australasia have remained relatively intact. Nevertheless, of the 310 or so species of waterbirds of regular occurrence in Asia, no fewer than 54 (17.4 per cent) are considered to be threatened.

VALUES AND USES
Asian wetlands play an important role in sustaining the living standards of hundreds of millions of people, particularly in southern Asia where economies have been intimately linked with wetlands since about 4500 BC, when according to the latest archaeological research lowland rice cultivation began.

Almost throughout the region, the level of exploitation of wetlands is very high. Most of the region's rice, fish, shrimp and other food production is derived from wetlands, as well as substantial quantities of fuel and materials for weaving and thatching. Wetlands provide water for domestic and industrial consumption, and in arid regions provide water for irrigation. Large rivers provide important

Many rural communities in India depend on wetlands and their fish for their subsistence.

communication networks and the means for generating hydroelectricity. Saline wetlands provide an abundant source of various salts. Swamps and marshes offer luxuriant grazing for livestock and fodder for the winter months, while mangrove and swamp forests offer timber, fuel, fodder and many other forest products. In addition, the great numbers of waterbirds and other wildlife which frequent wetlands provide a valuable source of protein for the subsistence hunter, game for the sportsman and endless fascinating spectacles for the naturalist and photographer.

The high productivity of lowland wetland ecosystems is reflected in the extremely high human population densities which they can support. Approximately one billion people, or almost 20 per cent of the world's population, inhabit the floodplain systems and deltas of southern Asia's 10 greatest river systems, where population densities can exceed 1,500 people per km² (3,880 per sq mile). In Vietnam, 42 per cent of the country's 60 million people live in the deltas of the Mekong and Red River which comprise only 15.7 per cent of the land area, while in China, some 95 per cent of the massive population is concentrated in the eastern half of the country, principally on the vast alluvial plains of the major rivers.

In many of Asia's rivers and floodplain wetlands, fisheries production is extremely high. The lower Mekong Basin supports one of the largest inland fisheries in the world, producing an annual yield of over 500,000 tonnes (490,000 tons) in Cambodia and Vietnam alone, and providing some 40-60 per cent of the animal protein intake of the people. In Bangladesh, more than 5 million people depend on fishing for their livelihood. The annual harvest of fish, crustaceans and frogs in this country is currently estimated to be in the region of 675,000-725,000 tonnes (664,000-714,000 tons), of which 64 per cent comes from the rivers, 16 per cent from the floodplain lakes and the remainder from marine systems.

Inter-tidal mudflats and mangroves are of enormous importance to fisheries. Not only are these habitats extremely rich in edible invertebrates such as crabs, shrimps, oysters and clams, but they also constitute vital breeding and nursery grounds for a wide variety of inshore and marine species of fish. For example, in Indonesia over half of the commercial fish catch consists of species dependent on the estuarine systems at some stage during their life cycles.

In many parts of Southeast Asia, inter-tidal flats are used for the culture of the oyster *Crassostrea gigas* and other molluscs. In Hong Kong, for example, the harvest of oysters from Deep Bay in 1983 was estimated at about 235 tonnes (231 tons), worth approximately US$1 million. This type of aquaculture is growing in importance in South Korea where, with government support, the farming of molluscs, particularly oysters, as well as seaweeds has increased dramatically in recent years.

The construction of fish and shrimp ponds in the coastal zone exploits the extremely high productivity of the mangrove-mudflat ecosystems. Such aquaculture ponds are now widespread throughout

Shrimp production in the Red River Delta, Vietnam, has risen sharply with the development of numerous aquaculture schemes.

The mudflats and mangrove swamps of Brunei Bay, Brunei, support a rich aquaculture and fishing industry.

southern China and most of Southeast Asia. All too frequently, however, the ponds have been developed at the expense of the mangrove swamps and mudflats upon which they depend for their supply of nutrients.

Mangroves have many other values. In the Sundarbans, they are exploited for a wide range of forest products, especially timber, pulp-wood and firewood. The leaves of the nipa palm are used for thatching, and those of the palm *Phoenix paludosa* for making house walls. In addition, large quantities of honey and beeswax are gathered from wild bees' nests. Nipa palms are also widely used in Malaysia to provide traditional attap roofing, while in Sarawak, sugar is extracted from the nipa and then refined and distilled into alcohol.

Mangrove forests also play a vital role in coastal

Excessive commercial logging still threatens the remaining peat swamp forests of Malaysia and other countries in Southeast Asia.

protection, stabilizing the shoreline and creating a buffer against coastal erosion caused by ocean currents and storms. Furthermore, by accumulating sediments around their roots, mangroves accelerate the accretion of new land.

Freshwater swamp forests and peat swamp forests play a valuable role in the mitigation of flooding, acting as natural reservoirs which absorb and store excess water during the rainy season and thereby reduce flooding in adjacent areas. They also constitute important forestry resources, with many valuable timber species and other locally important products, such as rattans, gums, resins, tannins, scented woods, oils, medicines and edible fruits.

Throughout southern Asia, floodplains, river banks and lake shores are used for the cultivation of vegetables or rice as water levels recede during the dry season. Cattle and water buffalo graze the marsh vegetation, and aquatic plants are harvested to provide fodder during the monsoon. In some countries, such as China and Bangladesh, huge numbers of domestic ducks are raised in the wetlands, both for eggs and for meat. Reeds are widely used for thatching and weaving purposes or as fuel, while in northeastern China, they are harvested on a commercial basis for the production of high-quality paper.

Hunting of waterbirds is widespread almost throughout Asia. Sport hunting is popular in the USSR, Japan, the Koreas and parts of the Middle East and Indian subcontinent, and accounts for the deaths of huge numbers of migratory ducks and geese each year; elsewhere, waterbirds are shot, netted or trapped primarily for their meat. In some regions, such as the south Caspian lowlands in Iran, eastern Ganges

The floating market on Dal Lake, Srinagar, Kashmir. Early each morning, vegetables are brought to the market from all sides of the lake.

Valley in India, Yangtze Valley in China and coastal wetlands of Java, enormous numbers of waterbirds are harvested on a commercial basis and provide a livelihood for many thousands of people.

Many wetlands, particularly mountain lakes, are scenically very attractive, while others support a great abundance of wildlife, thus giving them considerable potential for recreation and tourism. Many of Asia's best-known national parks and wildlife sanctuaries are wetlands, such as Keoladeo Ghana (Bharatpur) and Kaziranga in India, Poyang Lake in China and Mai Po Marshes in Hong Kong. Dal Lake in Kashmir, one of the most beautiful lakes in the world, now receives an estimated 500,000 visitors each year.

THREATS, MANAGEMENT AND CONSERVATION
There are still some remote regions of the northern USSR, Mongolia and western China where wetlands remain in an almost pristine condition, disturbed only by the occasional hunter, fisherman or shepherd with his flocks. But such sites are now becoming a great rarity throughout the more densely populated parts of Asia. Almost everywhere, wetlands have come under extreme pressure from human activities. Vast areas have been drained for agriculture and urban development, or converted into rice paddies, aquaculture ponds, water-storage reservoirs or saltpans. Rivers have been dammed and diverted;

mangrove and swamp forests have been clear-felled for their timber; and wetlands of all types have been polluted with domestic sewage, herbicides, pesticides, fertilizers, industrial effluents and other waste products. Fish stocks are being over-exploited and wildlife populations decimated by excessive hunting. Catchment areas are being denuded of their forest cover, leading to soil erosion and flash-flooding; rivers and lakes are silting up, and the entire hydrology of river basins is being altered. The situation is particularly serious in southern and eastern Asia, where most natural wetland ecosystems are now under threat.

The most serious threat has been drainage or 'reclamation' for agriculture, aquaculture, industry and urban development. Since much of Asia's human population is concentrated in the coastal lowlands, coastal wetlands in particular have come under pressure from drainage. In the Republic of Korea, a shortage of land suitable for agriculture has prompted the government to pursue a major programme of land reclamation in estuaries and shallow bays on the south and west coasts. It is anticipated that 155 sites will eventually be reclaimed, resulting in the loss of some 65 per cent of the country's coastal wetlands. In nearby Japan, about 35 per cent of the total area of mudflats has been lost to reclamation since 1945.

In much of the western USSR and eastern China,

reclamation of wetlands for agricultural land, often linked to public health campaigns, has greatly reduced the area of lakes and marshes. It has been estimated that in the 30 years from the 1950s to the 1980s, the number of natural lakes in China decreased from 2,800 to 2,350, and the total area of lakes shrank by 11 per cent.

Siltation is a serious problem in many parts of southern Asia, where deforestation, overgrazing and potentially wasteful agricultural practices such as slash-and-burn farming have led to severe soil erosion. Many of Asia's major rivers are becoming choked with silt, a notable example being the Yellow River in China, probably now the world's greatest earth-mover. With the bed of the river currently rising at the rate of 75-150 mm (3-6 in) per year, the chance of disastrous flooding is constantly increasing. The simultaneous shrinkage of floodplain lakes due to siltation and reclamation has lowered their capacity to store floodwaters, further increasing the likelihood of flooding downstream. Such problems are particularly serious along the lower reaches of the Yangtze River in China and in the delta of the Ganges-Brahmaputra in Bangladesh, where flash-flooding is becoming a common phenomenon.

Most of Asia's major rivers have been dammed for irrigation, the generation of electricity and flood control. Many of the dams and barrages have had serious downstream effects; floodplains, essential for the reproduction of many riverine fishes, have been destroyed, and the seasonal migrations of fish have been disrupted. As a result, there have been major declines in many riverine fisheries.

In arid regions, many wetlands have disappeared through the construction of large water-storage reservoirs on the major rivers and diversion of water supplies for irrigation. A reduction in the flow of fresh water at river mouths during the dry season has resulted in greater saltwater incursion into delta areas with consequent loss in agricultural potential and damage to mangroves. Such problems are particularly serious in the Indus and Ganges-Brahmaputra Deltas.

Nowhere have the adverse effects of dam construction and diversion of water supplies been more apparent than in the Aral Sea in the USSR. This vast, shallow inland sea once supported a major fishing industry, and was surrounded by fertile agricultural land. However, the massive diversion of water supplies for irrigation projects along the Syr Darya and Amu Darya Rivers has greatly reduced the amount of freshwater reaching the lake. As a result, the lake has shrunk to about half its original size,

A close-up of infestation of a canal by water hyacinth in the Cau Mau Marshes, Mekong Delta, Vietnam.

exposing almost 30,000 km² (11,600 sq miles) of bare salt flats and leaving fishing villages 60 km (37 miles) from the water's edge. The local climate has become more extreme, with colder winters and hotter summers; dust storms are now frequent, and wind-blown salt has destroyed large areas of agricultural land around the lake. The salinity of the lake has almost tripled, killing off 20 of the 24 species of fish and destroying the commercial fishery. A highly productive wetland ecosystem supporting a thriving human population and abundant wildlife has been converted into a harsh and unproductive desert.

Pollution from domestic sewage, industrial waste and agricultural chemicals is a serious problem in many parts of Asia. Many coastal wetlands and inshore waters are now heavily polluted with sewage, heavy metals, pesticides, PCBs, oil and other contaminants, and with increasing industrialization taking place, the situation is likely to deteriorate still further. Water pollution from logging and mining in catchment areas threatens many lakes in Malaysia, Indonesia and the Philippines, while in Sri Lanka, sand mining is adversely affecting water quality in many of the coastal lagoons and estuaries.

Forested wetlands have suffered widely from over-exploitation. In the more densely populated rural areas, local demand for timber, fuel and fodder has exceeded regenerative ability, resulting in a gradual degradation of the forest ecosystems. In India, Thailand, China, Vietnam and the Philippines, large areas of mangrove have been destroyed to make room for aquaculture ponds, while in eastern Malaysia and many parts of Indonesia, vast areas of mangrove and swamp forest have been clear-felled for timber and the production of chipboard.

Although peat swamp forest is of only marginal use for agriculture, clearance for aquaculture ponds remains a major threat, together with non-sustainable logging. Under current practice, it is predicted that all of Sarawak's peat swamp forest will have been logged before the year 2000.

War has also taken its toll of the mangrove and swamp forests of Southeast Asia. In Vietnam, some 40-50 per cent of the mangrove forests in the Mekong Delta were destroyed by herbicides during the Vietnam War. Furthermore, the use of the powerful herbicide Agent Orange has had a lasting effect on the soils, limiting the success of subsequent reafforestation programmes.

Overfishing is common in southern Asia, and is often aggravated by the use of harmful fishing practices such as dynamiting and poisoning. This, coupled with the loss of floodplains and mangrove forests vital as spawning and nursery grounds, has resulted in a decline in natural fisheries production in many parts of Asia.

The economic welfare of the peoples of Asia depends to a large extent upon the sustainable utilization of wetlands; indeed, large sectors of the human population depend on wetlands for their everyday survival. Grave mistakes have been made in the past, and these are reflected in the increasing frequency of so-called 'natural' disasters, which have inflicted enormous suffering on millions of people.

In Asia, perhaps more than anywhere else on Earth, the importance of wetland conservation is becoming apparent. The need to protect watersheds to prevent soil erosion and flash-flooding, the vital role of many floodplain wetlands in water storage and flood control, and the value of mangrove swamps in

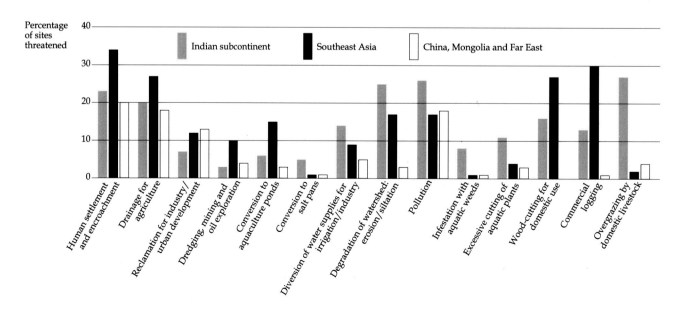

Major threats to wetlands in southern and eastern Asia.

Haleji Lake, only a short distance from Karachi in Pakistan, is a popular area for recreation and has a conservation visitor centre.

fisheries production and coastal protection are now becoming widely recognized. Major steps are being taken to protect and restore watersheds, to reduce siltation and pollution, and to conserve fisheries. Destructive policies are being reversed; mangroves are being replanted; wetlands are being restored, and ways of managing natural wetlands for food production are being chosen in preference to reclamation for farmland or fish ponds. Many

countries are at long last addressing the problem of population growth, although success to date has been poor, and it seems likely that for the next two or three decades at least, Asia's population will continue to grow at an alarming rate.

The conservation status of Asian wetlands varies widely from one region to another. In some remote parts of the USSR, the Middle East, western China and Mongolia, human population pressure remains low and many wetland ecosystems survive almost intact. On the other hand, in the western USSR, eastern China and countries such as India, Indonesia, Iran, Japan, Malaysia, Pakistan, Sri Lanka and Vietnam, wetlands have come under considerable pressure from population growth and development, and much has already been lost.

However, the governments of these countries have become aware of the need for wetland conservation and have launched programmes and policies which might yet save significant tracts of wetland habitat as functioning natural ecosystems. In several countries, notably the USSR, China, India, Indonesia, Iran and Pakistan, numerous wetland reserves have been created in recent years to ensure the survival of representative examples of the major wetland types. There are, however, several countries such as Bangladesh, Burma, South Korea, Iraq, Thailand, Turkey and the Philippines where the pressures on wetlands are extremely high

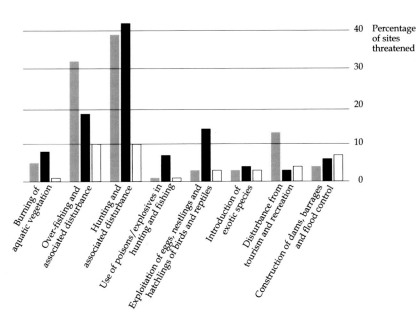

177

and the destruction of natural wetland ecosystems continues unabated. Until recently at least, wetland conservation has been accorded low priority by the governments of these nations.

In several countries, such as China, India and Pakistan, major campaigns have been launched to focus the attention of the general public on wetlands and the need for their conservation. These campaigns have included television and radio programmes, newspaper articles, roadside advertisements, lectures in schools and universities, wildlife posters, wildlife films and a variety of booklets and brochures. In China, special attention has been given to protecting the nation's eight species of crane, five of which are threatened with extinction. Cranes are very popular birds in China, and have long been revered in Chinese art and literature. They are characteristic birds of many of the country's most important wetland areas, and have thus provided an ideal focus for wetland conservation efforts through much of the country.

Wetlands impinge upon many aspects of the economic sphere, and as a consequence have often been subjected to a great many uncoordinated developments. In some cases, several projects with mutually incompatible goals have been carried out at a single site. Because the small-scale utilization of wetland resources by villagers living around wetlands is so widespread and the pattern of use so complex and varied, the benefits reaped by local communities have proved difficult to evaluate and have often been neglected when assessing the costs of large-scale development schemes. In addition, the assessment of environmental impact insofar as wildlife conservation is concerned has often been omitted.

Fortunately, the need for fully integrated management plans for the exploitation of wetland ecosystems is now widely recognized. Such plans have been completed for specific wetland sites in several Asian countries, for example at Songkla Lake in Thailand and at the Sundarbans in Bangladesh. The need for an integrated approach to the management of the coastal zone is also widely recognized, and frameworks for sustainable utilization of the many natural resources of estuaries, lagoons and mangroves

are now being developed in several countries.

Most nations have introduced legislation to conserve wildlife, especially migratory waterbirds. Indeed, in Mongolia official protection for waterbirds dates back to the thirteenth century. Furthermore, major efforts are now being made to save many of Asia's threatened species. In India, for example, the government is involved in the conservation and captive-breeding of marsh crocodiles, estuarine crocodiles and gharials (*Gavialis gangeticus*). Thirteen sanctuaries covering an area of approximately 800,000 hectares (1.98 million acres) have been established, and successful captive-rearing, and in some cases breeding, are taking place at 23 crocodile centres and 12 zoos scattered throughout the country.

In recent years, the international conservation community has supported a variety of initiatives focusing on Asian wetlands. These have included an inventory of wetlands of international importance in south and east Asia, and the Asian Waterfowl Census, an annual mid-winter waterfowl census throughout southern and eastern Asia. In 1987, the Asian Wetland Bureau was founded, with headquarters in Malaysia, to promote the protection and sustainable utilization of wetland resources in Asia. Although active primarily in Southeast Asia (with regional offices in the Philippines and Indonesia), the bureau is gradually expanding into other parts of the continent. It currently focuses on conservation education and training, wetland surveys, wetland and waterbird research, and production of guidelines for coastal development.

Although the Ramsar Convention has its roots in Asia (the final text being approved and opened for signature at an international conference held at Ramsar on the shores of the Caspian Sea in Iran in 1971), only nine Asian countries have so far joined the Convention: India, Iran, Japan, Jordan, Nepal, Pakistan, Sri Lanka, the USSR and Vietnam. Between them, these countries have designated a total of 45 wetlands as Wetlands of International Importance under the terms of the Convention - the areas thus designated cover just over 3 million hectares (7 million acres) of valuable habitat.

CONTRIBUTOR: C.M. FINLAYSON

Australasia and Oceania

WITH LANDSCAPES that range from the baking deserts of the Australian interior to the palm groves of Pacific atolls, from the snow-capped peaks of New Zealand's Southern Alps to the jungle-clad slopes of the central cordillera of New Guinea, the landmasses of Australasia and Oceania encompass a wide spectrum of contrasts. They vary tremendously in landform, in size, in the extent of human development; many are separated from each other by vast stretches of ocean. In land area the Australian continent dwarfs the others, and itself contains the extremes of an arid interior and snow-capped peaks. Only in a broad and very general geographic sense can these landmasses be treated as a single entity.

For the purposes of this chapter, Australasia is taken to include the large landmass of Australia and the smaller landmasses of New Guinea and New Zealand. Oceania takes in the multitude of small islands in the South Pacific. The Australasian and Oceanic political entities have special and individually characteristic features. These are reflected in, amongst other things, the range of wetland types and in the nature of their exploitation.

Australia has the largest population, but at 16 million people this is low on a world scale. Aboriginal people have been in Australia for some 40,000 to 60,000 years and currently make up 1.5 per cent of the population. The first European settlers arrived relatively recently, about 200 years ago. The population is now predominantly of European origin. More than 70 per cent are crowded into a few cities and towns along the southeastern and eastern rim of the continent; Brisbane and Adelaide have 1.5 million people each, Melbourne 2.7 million and Sydney 3 million. There are very few large inland cities. On the western coast is Perth, with 1.4 million people. Canberra, the national capital, has 250,000 people; Darwin, the northern outpost, has only 60,000.

New Zealand was first settled by Maori people from Polynesia some 700 years ago. European traders came in the early part of the nineteenth century and in 1840 the British formally annexed the islands. The population stands at 3.2 million with 460,000 people in both Wellington, the national capital, and Christchurch and 915,000 in Auckland.

The total population of the Oceanic islands is close to 2 million, with 646,000 in Fiji, 234,000 in the Solomons, 157,000 in Western Samoa and 151,000 in French Polynesia. Papua New Guinea has an estimated 3 million people with 100,000 in Port Moresby and 50,000 in Lae. The rest are found in a myriad of small villages often separated by steep jungle-covered slopes.

GEOGRAPHIC SETTING

Australia

As already stated, Australia is by far the largest landmass. It comprises the mainland and the island of Tasmania, and covers 7,682,300 km² (2,965,400 sq miles). The land is extremely old and appears overwhelmingly flat. The mountain ranges that exist are worn and reduced to blunt-topped peaks, none of which are permanently above the snow line. The Arnhem Land Plateau and the Hamersley Ranges are stark examples of the rugged, barren and inhospitable nature of these highland areas. The Eastern Highlands (Great Dividing Range) extend from Cape York in the north to Victoria in the south; Tasmania is an extension of this mountain chain.

Mount Kosciusko (2,228 m - 7,310 ft) in the Eastern Highlands is Australia's highest point, while the lowest point is Lake Eyre at 16 m (52 ft) below sea level. Arid regions cover one-third of the continent and devastating floods and droughts are regular events.

The usually dry interior contains expansive drainage systems that often take the form of chains of dry salt lakes. When the unpredictable rains arrive floodwater can spread out over hundreds of hectares of land adjacent to the rivers. Often too, the lakes are connected by the floodwater. The waters of some of these lakes flow enormous distances before they literally disappear into the desert. Much of the water never reaches the coast. Australia's seemingly non-directional or inland-flowing rivers gave rise to European settlers' dreams of a vast inland sea.

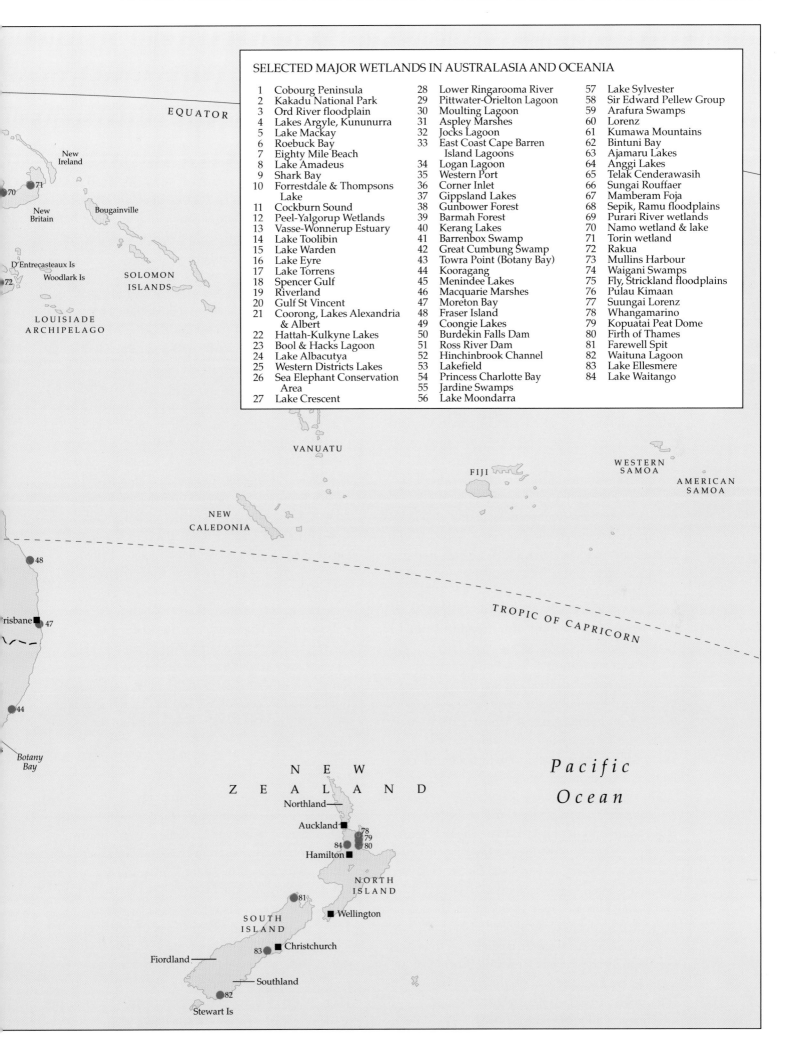

SELECTED MAJOR WETLANDS IN AUSTRALASIA AND OCEANIA

1	Cobourg Peninsula	28	Lower Ringarooma River	57	Lake Sylvester
2	Kakadu National Park	29	Pittwater-Orielton Lagoon	58	Sir Edward Pellew Group
3	Ord River floodplain	30	Moulting Lagoon	59	Arafura Swamps
4	Lakes Argyle, Kununurra	31	Aspley Marshes	60	Lorenz
5	Lake Mackay	32	Jocks Lagoon	61	Kumawa Mountains
6	Roebuck Bay	33	East Coast Cape Barren	62	Bintuni Bay
7	Eighty Mile Beach		Island Lagoons	63	Ajamaru Lakes
8	Lake Amadeus	34	Logan Lagoon	64	Anggi Lakes
9	Shark Bay	35	Western Port	65	Telak Cenderawasih
10	Forrestdale & Thompsons	36	Corner Inlet	66	Sungai Rouffaer
	Lake	37	Gippsland Lakes	67	Mamberam Foja
11	Cockburn Sound	38	Gunbower Forest	68	Sepik, Ramu floodplains
12	Peel-Yalgorup Wetlands	39	Barmah Forest	69	Purari River wetlands
13	Vasse-Wonnerup Estuary	40	Kerang Lakes	70	Namo wetland & lake
14	Lake Toolibin	41	Barrenbox Swamp	71	Torin wetland
15	Lake Warden	42	Great Cumbung Swamp	72	Rakua
16	Lake Eyre	43	Towra Point (Botany Bay)	73	Mullins Harbour
17	Lake Torrens	44	Kooragang	74	Waigani Swamps
18	Spencer Gulf	45	Menindee Lakes	75	Fly, Strickland floodplains
19	Riverland	46	Macquarie Marshes	76	Pulau Kimaan
20	Gulf St Vincent	47	Moreton Bay	77	Suungai Lorenz
21	Coorong, Lakes Alexandria	48	Fraser Island	78	Whangamarino
	& Albert	49	Coongie Lakes	79	Kopuatai Peat Dome
22	Hattah-Kulkyne Lakes	50	Burdekin Falls Dam	80	Firth of Thames
23	Bool & Hacks Lagoon	51	Ross River Dam	81	Farewell Spit
24	Lake Albacutya	52	Hinchinbrook Channel	82	Waituna Lagoon
25	Western Districts Lakes	53	Lakefield	83	Lake Ellesmere
26	Sea Elephant Conservation	54	Princess Charlotte Bay	84	Lake Waitango
	Area	55	Jardine Swamps		
27	Lake Crescent	56	Lake Moondarra		

Cymodocea serrulata *seagrass meadow at Green Island, Queensland. Some of the most extensive and species-diverse seagrass meadows in the world occur around the Australian coast.*

New Guinea

New Guinea lies between the Equator and a latitudinal line 10° South. It contains, in its western half, the political state of Irian Jaya, the most easterly province of Indonesia, and, in its eastern half, the independent nation of Papua New Guinea. The border between these countries follows the meridian 141° East for most of its length. Papua New Guinea also embraces the Trobriand, Louisade, D'Entrecasteaux, Bismarck and Woodlark Islands, as well as some of the Solomon Islands, most notably Bougainville. In all, it covers 462,500 km² (178,500 sq miles). Irian Jaya covers 421,981 km² (162,900 sq miles), making it the third largest landmass of the 13,000-island Indonesian archipelago.

A dominant feature of New Guinea is the spectacularly folded cordillera that runs the length of the island. Mountain peaks reach 4,400 m (14,400 ft) in the Central Highlands and 4,000 m (13,100 ft) in the Owen Stanley Range of Papua New Guinea. The cordillera extends into Irian Jaya where it is known as Pegunungan Maoke.

The ranges that compose the cordillera are flanked by extensive alluvial plains. North of the central ranges, the Sepik-Ramu-Markham trough is an area of swamps, floodplains, plains and lowlands that are some 150 km (93 miles) wide near the Sepik River. South of the ranges are swamps, alluvial plains and undulating hills. In Papua New Guinea, the southern plains and lowlands cover about 100,000 km² (38,600 sq miles) and are crossed by meandering rivers with very high discharges and large numbers of oxbow lakes. In the highland reaches the rivers are extremely fast flowing. Irian Jaya similarly has extensive swamps and alluvial plains flanking the cordillera.

New Zealand and the Pacific Islands

The combined land area of New Zealand's two main islands is 269,000 km² (103,800 sq miles). The islands are part of the Pacific Ring of Fire, an arc of volcanoes that stretches northwards around the western Pacific and across to Alaska. The North Island is frequently shaken by earthquakes. All major mountains are volcanoes, some of them still active.

The northernmost third of the North Island has a lower relief than the rest of the island; the Tutamoe Plateau has an average elevation of only about 700 m (2,300 ft). To the south lie fertile plains and lowland areas. Ranges rise along the east coast.

The Southern Alps run for 600 km (370 miles) down the centre of the South Island and contain 16 peaks over 3,000 m (9,840 ft). The highest is Mount Cook (3,764 m - 12,349 ft). To the north of the Alps lie alluvial plains, with a discontinuous alluvial plain to the west. The Canterbury Plains lie to the east of the Alps and comprise the largest lowland area in New Zealand.

Melanesia, Micronesia and Polynesia make up some 10,000 islands in the South Pacific. Some are independent states (for instance, Vanuatu, Solomon Islands and Fiji) whilst others are administered by France (New Caledonia and French Polynesia), New Zealand (Cook, Niue and Tokelau Islands), Great Britain (Pitcairn Island), the USA (Samoa and Guam) and the United Nations (Pacific Islands).

Islands such as the Marianas, the Solomons and Fiji were formed by faulting and folding of the Australian and Asian continental shelves. Most of Polynesia and Micronesia, on the other hand, are volcanic mountains that have protruded above sea level. Many have built up coral deposits and over thousands of years have formed extensive reefs. If the island is later submerged all that remains is a coral atoll, such as the Kwajalein Atoll in the Marshall Islands.

CLIMATE

Northern Australia has a monsoonal climate with two seasons: the wet and the dry. The wet season starts late in the year and lasts for three to four months. Annual rainfall varies from 1,500 to 3,500 mm (60 to 140 in), with very little falling during the dry season. Rainfall levels increase from south to north over northern Western Australia and the Northern Territory, and from southeast to northeast over Queensland. These areas are warm to hot all the year round; during the wet season, when cloud cover is high, relative humidity often reaches 80 per cent. There is less cloud over the dry interior; this gives rise to overnight convective cooling and frosts.

Central Australia is arid with high evaporation. Most of the rain comes from violent thunderstorms during the warmer months. Rain-bearing cyclonic depressions can move inland from the coast and drench vast areas of the interior.

Farther south, the climate varies from wet-tropical in coastal Queensland; alpine in Tasmania, northern Victoria and southern New South Wales; and Mediterranean in coastal South Australia and southwestern Western Australia. On the east coast rain falls mainly in the summer, though below a line running 34° South winter rain is also common. On the west coast, winter rain is common below a line running 30° South. To the north rainfall is erratic. The southern coast receives winter rain. In Tasmania continuous westerly winds bring rain at all times of year and large areas have snow for most of the winter.

Most of New Guinea has a high annual rainfall of 2,500-3,500 mm (100-140 in). Lowland areas can be drier; Port Moresby receives less than 1,000 mm (40 in). Most of the highland areas receive over 4,000 mm (160 in), some being deluged with more than 12,000 mm (470 in). Three basic rainfall patterns occur on New Guinea: rainy season in the middle of the year in some regions; relatively uniform distribution of rain over the year in other regions; and a rainy season from December to March in yet others. The high

rainfall goes hand in hand with high humidity and cloud cover. This in turn reduces evaporation from the lakes and streams. Air temperatures are consistently high. In coastal regions daily maximum temperatures average 32°C (90°F) and minimum ones 23°C (73°F). Above 2,200 m (7,200 ft) frosts can occur, and snow occasionally falls on the mountains.

New Zealand is by far the most temperate of the Australasian landmasses. Strong moisture-laden winds blow in from the Pacific and drop rain along the west coast: the western side of the Southern Alps gets 7600 mm (300 in) per year. To the lee, there is a rain shadow receiving about 300 mm (12 in) of rain. Rainfall distribution over the year is fairly even and over most areas it is generally between 630 and 1,530 mm (25 and 60 in).

The mean temperature at sea level varies from about 15°C (59°F) in the far north to 9°C (48°F) on Stewart Island in the south. The contrasts of temperature would be more extreme but for the moderating influence of the surrounding seas. Permanent snow occurs in Fjordland in the south, and all the mountains get snow. Summer temperatures are high, rising to the high 20s Centigrade (80s Fahrenheit).

Most of the Oceanic islands are small and close to the Equator. They have high rainfalls and temperatures, with little daily and annual variation.

Extensive hypersaline salt flats are found behind mangroves fringing the coast along the tidal reaches of rivers in northern Australia.

SHARK BAY, AUSTRALIA

Shark Bay is a large, shallow - mainly less than 15 m (50 ft) deep - semi-enclosed basin situated on the north-western Australian coast. It covers some 1.3 million hectares (3.2 million acres). The flow of water between the bay and the ocean is restricted and at low tide extensive hypersaline flats can be seen.

The largest seagrass meadows in the world are found in Shark Bay. With 12 species present, it is also one of the richest seagrass habitats. Some species have a southern temperate affinity (for example, *Amphibolus antarctica*) and others a tropical affinity (for example, *Syringodium isoetifolium*). *Cymodocea angustata* is endemic to this part of the coastline. *Amphibolus antarctica* grows in monospecific stands over 367,600 hectares (908,300 acres) and is the most widespread of the seagrasses. The small *Halodule uninervis* also occurs in mono-specific stands and is an important food source for the rare marine mammal, the dugong.

Turtles and a small number of dolphins frequent the bay and there is an abundant population of sea snakes. The stromatolites in Hamelin Pool are an (almost) unique feature. These are laminated, dome-shaped, rock-like structures that reach 1 m (just over 3 ft) in height and are formed from calcium carbonate accumulated in algal mats on the sand substrate. They resemble structures that were much more common 3,500 million years ago.

Development of tourism poses the greatest threat to Shark Bay. Important recreational fisheries depend on conservation of the shallow nursery areas, and the dugong population, although no longer hunted, is at risk from disturbance by power boats. Special marine reserves are proposed and should help protect the winter feeding grounds of these wondrous animals. Commercial fishing methods for prawns and scallops cause significant environmental impact, but these are limited to restricted areas in the bay.

Across most of the Pacific, air masses move towards the Equator from both the north and the south. This causes trade winds that drop rain on the windward, but not the leeward side of the islands. Typhoons (or hurricanes) are common in western Micronesia from July to November. The high winds, torrential rain and tidal waves can cause extensive damage.

THE WETLANDS

The major types of wetland in the Australasian and Oceanic region are: seagrass meadows, mangrove swamps, coastal salt marshes and flats, monsoonal freshwater floodplains, southern and inland swamps, lakes, river and creek channels and bogs.

Seagrass Meadows

The Australian coast boasts some of the largest seagrass meadows in the world. Over 30 seagrass species are found here; *Amphibolus* species are endemic. Seagrasses are flowering plants that grow completely submerged in the ocean. Under the right conditions they form dense meadows across enormous areas, swaying back and forth in stormy and turbulent seas. Hidden as they are from the sight of most people, these plants often lack common names.

The world's largest seagrass meadows are in Shark Bay (see box). In the Gulf of Carpentaria single-species meadows of the small *Halophila ovalis* and *Halodule uninervis* dominate the scene between high and low tide marks. The same species are common along the northeast coast of Queensland and the northwest coast of Western Australia. In deeper water there are dense stands of *Cymodocea serrulata*.

In southwestern Australia, *Posidonia* species are common and some, such as *Posidonia sinosa*, form very wide bands over hundreds of hectares of fringing reefs along the coast near Perth.

The southeastern coast also harbours extensive seagrass meadows. Spencer Gulf and Gulf St Vincent have a complexity of species. In Gulf St Vincent *Posidonia* species cover about 153,000 hectares (378,000 acres). *Amphibolis* and *Posidonia* species are common in Victorian and Tasmanian sub-tidal regions. *Zostera*, *Ruppia* and *Lepilaena* are considered as seagrass species in Australia (but not elsewhere) and are found in marine conditions on inter-tidal flats, with *Zostera mucronata* particularly abundant in South Australia.

Seagrass meadows are the habitat for a variety of fauna. In particular, they are major nursery grounds for commercial tiger prawn species (*Penaeus esculentus* and *Penaeus semisulcatus*) and endeavour prawn species (such as *Metapenaeus endeavouri*). They also provide food for two large vertebrates, the dugong (*Dugong dugon*) and the green turtle (*Chelonia mydas*). The dugong, or sea cow, is a large marine mammal that weighs up to 420 kg (926 lb). Some tens of thousands are found grazing in extensive seagrass meadows in shallow bays and channels that are protected against strong winds and heavy seas. The large green turtle, weighing up to 205 kg (452 lb), eats soft algae and seagrasses.

Different seagrasses do not necessarily support distinct fauna. Factors such as salinity, temperature and water movement determine which animals are present.

Many fishes occur in these communities. Herbivorous species seem more abundant in the seagrass meadows of southeastern Australia than in other temperate areas. Some fish break off seagrass leaf-blades to obtain encrusting invertebrates.

Large numbers of waterbirds feed on exposed tidal flats near or even amongst seagrass meadows. Roebuck Bay and Eighty Mile Beach in Western

Australia support some 850,000 birds, mainly migratory shorebirds (waders) flying in from their Arctic breeding grounds. Farther south the Vasse-Wonnerup wetlands support 150,000 waterbirds, from 75 different species. Many of these are migratory shorebirds. Similarly, the Peel-Harvey wetlands host many migratory birds.

The Gulf of Carpentaria contains vast areas of tidal flats that support some 250,000 waterbirds, again including many shorebirds. The entire world population of the eastern Siberian race of black-tailed godwit (*Limosa limosa*) may use the shores of the Gulf. In addition, tens of thousands of red knots (*Calidris canutus*) pass through en route to New Zealand.

Mangrove Swamps

Mangrove swamps develop on muddy sediments deposited in sheltered estuaries, inlets and bays throughout Australasia and Oceania. Around Australia they occupy an area of about 1.2 million hectares (2.9 million acres), mostly in the tropics - 460,000 hectares (1.1 million acres) in Queensland, 400,000 hectares (990,000 acres) in the Northern Territory, 250,000 hectares (620,000 acres) in Western Australia, dwindling to 9,900 hectares (24,000 acres) in New South Wales and 1,200 hectares (3,000 acres) in Victoria.

In Papua New Guinea extensive mangrove swamps occupy the estuarine reaches of large rivers and cover 925,000 hectares (2.3 million acres), that is, 2 per cent of the total land area. Some 160-200,000 hectares (395-494,000 acres) occur in the Gulf of Papua, where the

Fly River enters the sea. The Purari Delta contains 134,000 hectares (331,000 acres). In Irian Jaya, mangroves cover about 2.85 million hectares (7 million acres). Major areas of mangrove swamp occur along the coast from the deltas of the Pulau and Digul Rivers, the bay south of Cendrawasik, and along the coast to the east and west of the Mamberamo River. All major New Guinea estuaries support mangroves.

A small area of mangroves - with its main species a variety of *Avicennia marina* - occurs from North Cape to Tauranga on the North Island of New Zealand.

The Oceanic islands do not support large areas of mangroves - there are no more than about 64,000 hectares (158,000 acres) in the Solomon Islands, 20,000 hectares (49,000 acres) in Fiji and New Caledonia, and 1,000 hectares (2,500 acres) in Tonga - and mangroves are rare or absent on the Polynesian islands.

As for the varieties of mangrove growing in the region: up to 45 mangrove species occur in Australia. The number decreases from east to west and from north to south. Cape York Peninsula has over 40 species in forests where plants can reach as high as 30 m (98 ft). Fewer species occupying smaller areas are found in Australia's subtropical regions, while only *Avicennia marina* extends, in small pockets, into temperate Australia. Australia's mangrove forests are highly productive and a large amount of nutrient and organic material is carried by the tides out into the bays and estuaries.

In Australia, many mangroves grow in the kinds of

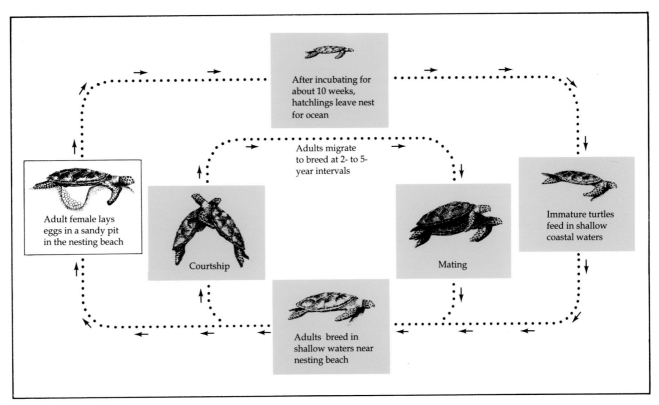

The life-cycle of the large green turtle, Chelonia mydas, *that frequents the warm tropical waters of Australia, New Guinea and Indonesia. Some Australian conservationists are worried by the extent of turtle-hunting in the Indonesian Archipelago.*

The estuarine or saltwater crocodile, Crocodylus porosus, *is common in northern Australia and New Guinea. Though now protected it is still considered as an endangered species.*

The little egret, Egretta garzetta, *is one of five white herons found in Australia and is also found in New Guinea. It nests in colonies in trees and feeds on fish and invertebrates.*

zone associated with them throughout the world - zones that are primarily determined by tide levels and flooding periods, and influenced by exposure, salinity and substrate type. Others, however, appear to grow throughout the tidal range and most species can be found in pure stands. Areas supporting mangroves in Australia are, therefore, extremely variable; it has been suggested that mangroves opportunistically colonize available habitats and are not simply confined to distinct zones.

The New Guinea mangrove flora is extremely diverse with over 60 species, richer on the north coast than on the south coast. Its complex pattern of distribution is influenced by tidal flooding, wave action, freshwater drainage, salinity and substrate type. Dense forests with tall trees abound. Rhizophoraceae species dominate, occupying more than half the total area of mangroves. *Bruguiera* and *Camptostemon* species are common.

Broad zones of mangrove species are recognizable along the New Guinea coast. Along the shoreline next to the coastal rainforest there is a narrow band of *Heritera littoralis* and then two much broader bands in the deeper water. The first band contains mainly *Bruguiera gymnorrhiza* and the second mainly *Rhizophora mucronata* trees.

Mangrove swamps in Fiji are extensive and also appear to grow in zones along the shoreline. Along the rivers, there is a fringe of *Rhizophora stylosa* and on higher ground a forest of *Bruguiera gymnorrhiza, Xylocarpus granatum* and *Lumnitzera littorea* trees mixed together. Along the Dumbea River in New Caledonia, *Rhizophora* and *Bruguiera* species grow in the lowest areas and *Avicennia officinalis* in higher areas. Other zonation patterns are found on other islands, particularly where the sea

level and sediment depth are different.

Mangrove swamps, dominated by *Rhizophora*, are well-developed in lagoons of Tongatapu on the island of 'Uta Vava'u and the totally enclosed lagoon of Nomuka on Tonga. They tend also to establish themselves where sandy or muddy substrates have built up over bare reef flats.

The first animals encountered by any visitor to mangrove swamps in Australasia are almost certainly invertebrates; they are most likely to be insects. Biting midges and mosquitoes, along with spiders, are common. Polychaetes, crustaceans and molluscs are also plentiful. Oysters and barnacles are conspicuous, while other molluscs, particularly gastropods, inhabitat the forest floor. The burrows of the mud lobster *Thalassina anomola* and the mud crab *Scylla serrata* are often seen in Australian mangroves.

The barnacle (*Elminius modestus*), oyster (*Saccostrea cucullata*), mussel (*Modiolus neozelandicus*) and crab (*Helice crassa*) are common amongst the New Zealand mangroves.

The invertebrate fauna of New Guinea has not been deeply researched. Clearly, however, crustaceans and molluscs and particularly insects are common. The island's vertebrate fauna is, by contrast, both well-known and plentiful. In the Purari and Kikori mangroves there are 143 species of fish from 58 families; 12 mammals; 59 birds; 20 reptiles and 4 amphibians. Three species of birds, the mangrove fantail (*Rhipidura phasiana*), the broad-billed flycatcher (*Myiagra ruficollis*) and the red-headed honeyeater (*Myzomela eythrocephala*), are confined to the mangroves. Another group of birds, including the mangrove robin (*Eopsaltria pulverulenta*) and mangrove golden whistler (*Pachycephala melanura*), are often found in mangroves, but are not restricted to this habitat.

Over 200 bird species have been recorded in Australian mangroves, but only 14 are restricted to mangrove swamps. The number of species increases from south to north, paralleling a similar increase in plant species. Near Sydney only the mangrove heron (*Butorides striatus*) is restricted to mangroves while other common species, such as the rufous whistler (*Pachycephala rufiventris*) and the white-faced heron (*Ardea novaehollandiae*), are also common in other habitats. On Cape York Peninsula, in contrast, 19 species depend largely on mangroves and seven are found only in mangrove forests. The pied cormorant (*Phalacrocorax varius*) and straw-necked ibis (*Threskiornis aethiopius*) nest in mangroves.

No mammals are endemic to Australian mangrove forests and only one, the rat *Xeromys myiodes*, uses these forests as its main habitat.

Reptiles are common in mangrove swamps, but many do not spend all their lives there. Undoubtedly the best-known reptile is *Crocodylus porosus*, the estuarine or saltwater crocodile. This 4-5 m (13-16 $^1/_2$ ft) creature is a relic from the age of dinosaurs. Since commercial crocodile hunting was banned in Australia in 1971 the population there has increased to about 30-40,000. However, some people are still worried about the survival outside nature reserves of this fearful creature from ancient times. The decline in crocodile numbers in Papua New Guinea, again brought about by hunting, has also been halted. Crocodile farming, but not hunting, is now allowed in both countries.

Fish are conspicuous in mangrove creeks and lagoons but, once again, few are confined to this habitat. Large numbers invade the swamps at high tide from adjacent estuaries and retreat to deeper water at low tide. In Australia the mud skipper species, *Periophthalmus* and *Periophthalmodon*, are often seen on exposed mudflats at low tide. The diverse fish community also includes the commercially important silver barramundi, *Lates calcarifer*.

Tidal Salt Marshes and Salt Flats

The salt marsh environment is hostile to most plants. The extremely high salt concentrations are toxic to all but a small number of species. This is in direct contrast to the species-rich tropical mangroves. Overall, in Australia, salt marshes cover about 920,000 hectares (2.3 million acres). In tropical Australia they are less widespread than in southern Australia and contain far fewer plants than the temperate southern marshes.

Australian salt marsh vegetation may be categorized as shrub, as sedge/rush, or as grass. Shrubs grow on well-drained soils that are

Sedgeland dominated by Eleocharis *species is widespread across the seasonally inundated floodplains of northern Australia.* Eleocharis *is a perennial species that forms bulbs to survive during the dry season. Magpie geese and brolgas eat the bulbs.*

187

Wandering whistling ducks, Dendrocygna arcuata, *fill the air with a shrill whistle made with their wings when they take to the air. They nest in tropical swamps.*

hypersaline between tidal flooding. Sedges and rushes are found in permanent and brackish water, the most widespread communities being dominated by *Juncus kraussii*. Grass-covered salt marshes are poorly developed in southern Australia.

Tropical salt marshes are usually located on the landward side of mangroves and adjacent to salt flats. The flats are encrusted with salt and often lack vegetation. Areas that are not frequently covered by tides have a very dry and hypersaline environment. Seasonal vegetation (for example, *Tecticornia australasica*) occasionally finds a foothold. Southern

coastal salt marshes rarely have an unvegetated zone. In southwestern Australia *Sarcocornia quinqueflora* grows in the more saline marshes, while grasses and sedges occupy the less saline areas.

In New Zealand the salt-tolerant samphire (*Salicornia australis*) grows in mixed stands behind the mangroves, and then by itself as the soil becomes more saline. In better-drained areas *Samolus repens* is dominant, while less salt-tolerant species occur in areas of freshwater influence. Under tidal flooding the rush *Juncus maritimus australiensis* can cover large areas. Where there is a freshwater inflow *Typha angustifolia* replaces the rushes.

In the North Island brackish water is marked by dense swards of the composite *Cotula coronopifolia*. In the South Island samphire gives way to a general mixed-species salt marsh. Brackish water supports species of *Scirpus*. In all these marshes, plant cover increases in a landward direction; above the level of the highest tides, a salt meadow of grasses and sedges is found.

A wide range of birds visit the marshes. The pied stilt (*Himantopus leucocephalus*) and oystercatchers (species of *Haematopus*) are particularly common in New Zealand.

Monsoonal Freshwater Floodplains

Extensive freshwater floodplains are found in Australia in the Northern Territory and Queensland. More is known about those in the Northern Territory than those in Queensland. The floodplains experience an annual wet-dry cycle that is caused by the monsoonal rainfall pattern. They are filled by floodwater from large streams after rainfall during the

The small water lily, Nymphoides planosperma, *grows in pools on top of sandstone outcrops in Kakadu National Park and Arnhem Land.*

wet season. At other times of the year they are generally dry, except for a few permanent billabongs (waterholes) and swamps.

Grasslands and woodlands are extensive across the Northern Territory floodplains. The annual wild rice (*Oryza meridionalis*) is very common and grows in seasonally inundated areas. There are five paperbark (*Melaleuca*) tree species in the floodplain woodland; some grow as high as 20 m (66 ft) and grow in areas subject to flooding 2-3 m (6 1/2-10 ft) deep. Sedge, water lily and grass species abound, displaying a picturesque mosaic of flowering plants at the end of the wet season.

The large reed *Phragmites karka* is common on floodplains that have not been intensively grazed and trampled by the feral Asian water buffalo (*Bubalus bubalis*). Buffaloes have destroyed an estimated 3,000-4,000 hectares (7,400-10,000 acres) of reed-swamp in Kakadu National Park. The introduced noxious weeds *Salvinia molesta* and *Mimosa pigra* are present and in places completely cover the water and crowd out many native plants.

Plant growth is influenced by changes in water depth. Many species start to grow after the first rains and reach their maximum height at the end of the rainy season. All plants have to cope with the extremes of annual flood and drought. Some, such as the perennial grass *Pseudoraphis spinescens*, adopt different growth forms for each season (short turf-like grass on the dry plains and long trailing stems that

grow up through the floodwaters of the wet season), whilst others rely on seeds and bulbs to survive the dry conditions.

Along the east coast of Queensland extensive herb, woodland and forested freshwater swamps are found. They are associated with streams and rivers that flood during the wet season. The herb swamps contain the same mosaic of plants common to the Northern Territory floodplains.

The wooded swamps are generally shallower than the herb swamps and are dominated by the large tree *Melaleuca quinquenervia*. Tall sedges, reeds and grass species grow beneath the tree canopy. Weed species are common. Water hyacinth (*Eichhornia crassipes*), often referred to as the 'noxious beauty', is widely distributed. Waterlogging, fire frequency and tree density influence the species composition.

The variety in these swamps is immense and the waterholes become a kaleidoscope of colour when the plants flower and the overhanging trees blossom. However, the diversity and colourful displays of the wet season vegetation give way to a parched monochrome by the end of the dry season. On occasion, fires sweep across the dry plains, blackening everything.

The animal-life of the floodplains is no less rich than their vegetation. The floodplains in the Northern Territory, in particular, support large numbers of vertebrates: freshwater and saltwater crocodiles, other reptiles such as turtles, fishes, and of course many

KAKADU NATIONAL PARK, AUSTRALIA

A wide variety of wetland types are contained within Kakadu National Park (Stages I and II) which is located in the Alligator Rivers Region, 220 km (135 miles) east of Darwin in the Northern Territory. Mangroves cover 660 km² (255 sq miles) on offshore islands, along the coast and fringing the rivers for about 100 km (60 miles) inland. Salt flats cover 16,000 hectares (40,000 acres) behind the mangroves. The creeks and rivers overflow onto extensive freshwater wetlands including 47,000 hectares (116,000 acres) of paperbark forests and woodlands, and 147,000 hectares (363,000 acres) of annually or seasonally flooded grasslands, sedgelands and swamp herbfields.

The marine coastal wetlands are subjected to twice-daily tides that can reach heights of 6 m (19 ft), and to seasonal freshwater discharges from the large rivers. The rivers flood after monsoonal rains and spill out onto the freshwater floodplains to a depth of several metres. During the dry season

the floodplains are parched with scattered vegetation. A number of permanent swamps and billabongs remain. Tidal influences extend 60-70 km (37-44 miles) upstream during the dry season.

The wetlands support up to 3 million waterbirds; magpie geese make up 85 per cent of these. Up to 400,000 wandering and 70,000 plumed whistling ducks, 20,000 radjah shelducks, 50,000 Pacific black ducks and 50,000 grey teal also use the area. Thirty-five species of shorebirds, many of them migrants from the Arctic, use these wetlands as well. The areas that retain freshwater during the dry season are important refuges for many species. The vegetation is speciesrich with, for example, 22 mangroves species and 225 freshwater plants on the Magela floodplain. The nearshore wetlands support turtles and the estuarine crocodile. The freshwater crocodile is also found. Aboriginal people gather plant and animal foods

from the wetlands.

Threats to the wetlands include introduced animals and plants. Buffalo were a major problem but have been virtually shot out. Very little is being done about pigs that also roam the floodplain fringes. The introduced prickly shrub *Mimosa pigra* is a major threat to the floodplain vegetation, but so far has been kept at bay by intensive monitoring and removal. The same success has not been achieved with biological control of the floating weed *Salvinia molesta*.

The more serious long-term problems centre on the disposal of wastes from a uranium mine situated next to Magela Creek. Almost every wet season there are proposals to release stored water from the mine site. Added to this annual argument is the debate over the fate of the large tailings (waste) dam. The longterm aspects of waste disposal in this area of incredible natural beauty and biological diversity will attract a lot more acrimonious debate.

Billabongs are common along the rivers that feed the floodplain wetlands of northern Australia.

waterbirds. All these animals are highly mobile and have mechanisms to withstand severe seasonal food shortages. For example, the freshwater crocodile (*Crocodylus johnstoni*) reduces its food intake during the dry season. These crocodiles, like the turtles, depend heavily on terrestrial foods. Some turtles are omnivorous; others eat leaves, flowers and fruit in the dry season; and yet others aestivate - that is, they

The pig-nosed or pit-shelled turtle, Carettochelys insculpta, *eats leaves, fruit and flowers. It is found in Australia and New Guinea.*

spend the dry season in a dormant state.

About 25 frog species are known from the Northern Territory floodplains and their inflowing creeks. In general, they are totally inactive during the dry season. Many species aestivate beneath the ground and require substantial rainfall to bring them to the surface.

The diversity of freshwater fishes is high. About 50 species occur in the Alligator Rivers Region, although only a few, such as the black anal-finned grunter (a species of *Pingalla*) and the Arnhem Land blue-eye (*Pseudomugil tennellus*) are restricted to the region.

Small juvenile fish are abundant in the muddy billabongs on the floodplains; larger juveniles and smaller adults are found in the areas that when flooded in the wet season connect the floodplains and billabongs; larger adults live in deeper floodplain billabongs. The silver barramundi breeds in sea water and either stays in the estuaries or migrates upstream to the freshwater. Juveniles spend their first weeks in brackish coastal swamps, though some migrate upstream.

Large flocks of magpie geese (*Anseranas semipalmata*), radjah shelduck (*Tadorna radjah*), wandering and plumed whistling ducks (*Dendrocygna arcuata* and *Dendrocygna eytoni*) move between the swamps and floodplains in search of food. Between 1983 and 1986, magpie geese on the floodplains in Kakadu National Park numbered 2-3 million.

In the wet season the birds disperse to nest. Catastrophic losses of nests from sudden flooding can occur about every seventh year, with less severe losses every third or fourth year. Low rainfall years also take their toll on breeding success. The geese concentrate on areas that still contain freshwater and food, such as *Eleocharis* bulbs, during the dry season. The floodplains of the Mary, Adelaide, Daly, South Alligator and East Alligator Rivers support the highest densities of birds in the Northern Territory.

These floodplains have been disturbed by feral animals - particularly the Asian water buffalo. Thus, in national parks and reserves they are being shot. Feral pigs (*Sus scrofa*) are also numerous and widespread. The cane toad (*Bufo marinus*) was introduced to Queensland more than 50 years ago and is now found in eastern parts of the Northern Territory.

The swamps and floodplains along rivers in eastern Queensland are also important habitats for waterbirds. They support thousands of birds during the dry season and during droughts. Some species, such as the Australian crane or brolga (*Grus rubicundus*), are resident on these floodplains. When the vegetation is lush and abundant many birds nest. The trigger for nesting is not known, but the young are hatched into an environment well-suited for their survival. Species that nest in these wetlands include magpie geese, Pacific black ducks (*Anas superciliosa*), wandering and plumed whistling ducks and occasionally black swans (*Cygnus atratus*). The entire eastern Australian population of brolga congregate on the floodplains near Townsville or on the northern shore of Princess Charlotte Bay.

Southern and Inland Swamps

Some of the inland-flowing rivers in Australia drain to the Murray-Darling system, but others, such as the Lachlan and the Macquarie, reach the larger rivers only during floods. Normally they terminate in extensive inland swamps: the Lachlan in the Great Cumbung Swamp, and the Macquarie in the Macquarie Marshes. Overflow swamps also occur along the rivers; floodwaters overflow the river banks, covering the swamps and forming large lakes. At times it is difficult to ascertain what is a swamp, what is a lake and what is a floodplain.

This section is confined to describing the general features of large swamps along the rivers. The plants in these swamps are also common along the inland rivers and fringe many freshwater lakes.

The Great Cumbung Swamp and Lowbidgee wetlands are located at the confluence of the Lachlan and Murrumbidgee Rivers. They cover 150,000 hectares (370,000 acres) with large stands of river red gums, reeds and lignum.

Many billabongs are found on the floodplains of the Murray-Darling Rivers. During high floods they can be connected to the rivers and serve as refuge areas for many species during the long dry spells when the streams and rivers are little more than a series of isolated waterholes.

When flooded, the swamps contain large expanses of turbid, shallow water. As the lakes dry out a ground cover of herbs and sedges develops. Cane grass (*Eragrostis australasica*) is prevalent in shallow marginal depressions. Stands of coolibah (*Eucalyptus microtheca*) or black box (*Eucalyptus largiflorens*) or lignum (*Muehlenbeckia cunninghamii*) trees grow along the deeper channels that crisscross the swamps.

At the confluence of the Lachlan and Murrumbidgee Rivers there are nearly 150,000 hectares (370,000 acres) of permanently wet to ephemeral wetland habitats. These wetlands are collectively known as the Great Cumbung Swamp and Lowbidgee wetlands. Here can be found large river red gum (*Eucalyptus camaldulensis*) forests, and extensive areas of reed and lignum. The latter has now fallen to an area of about 50,000 hectares (124,000 acres) following widespread clearing in the last 10 years.

Barrenbox Swamp is another large wetland, in New South Wales. It has suffered increased salinity and was changed from an ephemeral to a permanent wetland by the addition of water from an irrigation scheme. The vegetation is now dominated by reed and *Typha* (cumbungi species). In the floods of 1989 the swamp breached its banks and overflowed, causing extensive flooding of the surrounding land.

The Macquarie Marshes cover some 40,000 hectares (99,000 acres) along the highly regulated Macquarie River in New South Wales. The marshes were once characterized by periods of zero flow alternating with flash floods. This irregularity in flow has been totally eliminated. Large stands of *Acacia stenophylla*, river red gum and lignum line the channels in the northern part of the wetland. Wet channels contain cumbungi and reed. On sites that are only occasionally flooded coolibah and black box trees grow. Reeds grow in almost pure stands in the braided streams. Cumbungi species are now more common in channels and lagoons. The water couch *Paspalum paspaloides* is widespread and able to grow in open water and on exposed banks.

Swamps in Tasmania are much smaller than those on the mainland. However, they are locally important and are dominated by different plant species, namely *Baumea rubiginosa* or *Lepidosperma longitudinale*. Sedges, herbs and a variety of aquatic plants form a mixed plant community. *Triglochin procera* swamps are found at the shallow ends of lakes. In forests, the cutting grass *Gahnia grandis* dominates the swamp vegetation.

Floodplains and other areas of poor drainage in New Zealand contain swamps dominated by forest trees, shrubs or herbs. The forest swamps contain relatively few plant species other than the massive podocarp tree (*Dacrycarpus dacrylioides*). This can reach 35 m (115 ft) and is recognizable by a buttress trunk and pneumatophores - that is, specialized, upward-branching roots (similar to those of the mangrove) characteristic of certain swamp plants. Other plants that grow in the forest swamps are climbers, epiphytes, ferns, tufted grasses and sedges, and shrubs.

The dominant shrub is the high manuka (*Leptospermum scoparium*) which grows to 2-4 m (6 1/2 -13 ft). *Cordyline australis*, which grows as high as 6 m (20 ft), and the tufted grass *Cortaderia toetoe* also occur. Herb communities vary from one site to another. Raupo (*Typha orientalis*) grows in standing water. *Carex secta* can form a thick base of matted rhizomes and roots. In more permanent swamps flax (*Phormium tenax*) can form dense stands, excluding other species or associated with a mix of shrubs, rushes and aquatic herbs. In shallow water around lakes, *Juncus articulatus* often forms floating mats which extend outwards from a wet herb field on the shore.

Lakes

Many Australian lakes are non-permanent saline lakes that are only filled irregularly. This applies to Lake Eyre, the largest in Australia (860,000 hectares - 2.1 million acres). Extensive salt lake systems are found across southern Australia, while in the southwest widespread clearing of the native vegetation over the past 50-100 years, to make room for agricultural activities, has turned many irregularly filled freshwater wetlands into waterlogged, hypersaline lakes.

In Tasmania there are numerous permanent freshwater lakes as a result of glacial action and high rainfall. The only mainland glacial lakes are near Mount Kosciusko. Man-made lakes are now very common. Dune lakes occur along both the west and east coasts. The offshore islands of Queensland contain some of the largest. The dune lakes are locally important for waterbirds. For example, Forrestdale Lake near Perth supports 18,000 red-necked stints (*Calidris ruficollis*) and curlew sandpipers (*Calidris ferruginea*), as well as 10,000 ducks.

The vegetation of the lakes varies a good deal. Wave action and fluctuating water levels prevent plants growing in larger lakes. In tropical Australia several man-made lakes have been more intensively studied than many of the natural lakes. The Ross River Dam near the Queensland coastal city of Townsville is relatively shallow and contains a large number of aquatic plants, mainly submerged and floating-leaved species.

The vegetation in Lake Moondarra, also in Queensland but near the inland city of Mount Isa, was for many years dominated by the introduced floating weed *Salvinia molesta* and the native *Hydrilla verticillata*. The former covered 330 hectares (815 acres) and at times was able to double its area in four days. It was finally brought under control in 1981 when rapidly falling water levels stranded many plants and a weevil, *Cyrtobagous salviniae*, was released as part of a biological control programme against this weed.

COONGIE LAKES, AUSTRALIA

This complex of lakes, which covers an area of almost 1.98 million hectares (4.89 million acres), is strung along an unregulated river in a remote part of northeastern South Australia. The lakes receive most of the water that flows along the northwest branch of Cooper Creek. The major lakes flood in sequence as the water flow builds up. Only rarely does the water move beyond them to reach Lake Eyre. Lake Coongie is almost permanent whereas the other lakes hold water for limited periods only and some rarely fill.

The lakes are an important drought refuge for waterbirds. Some 20-35,000 birds generally use them all year, although a few may disperse after extensive rains elsewhere. Grey teal and pink-eared ducks are the most numerous, along with hardhead, Pacific black and wood ducks. Pelicans, coots, pied cormorants and black-tailed native hen (*Gallinula ventralis*) are also plentiful.

The Australian pelican can form large colonies; more than 200,000 congregated on Lake Eyre after it filled with floodwater in 1990. The pelican nests at any time of year if there is sufficient rain and water.

The rare freckled duck and Australasian shoveller (*Anas rhynchotis*) also find refuge on the lakes.

The biological diversity of the region is enhanced by wetlands that vary from ephemeral to permanent, open shores to capillary streams. The plant communities also vary, with flooded meadows, lignum swamps, coolibah woodlands, aquatic macrophytes and samphire flats.

Increasing numbers of tourists, as well as exploration for natural gas, threaten the integrity of these wetlands. Cattle grazing is widespread and potentially, if not already, a major problem. In December 1989 all of the Coongie Lakes complex and part of Cooper Creek were given reserve status and a draft management plan was released.

Lake Surprise and Lake Woods in the Tanami Desert are intermittent lakes in the interior arid zone. Lake Woods supports a plant community dominated by *Eleocharis pallens* and *Psoralea crinera* when dry and is fringed by coolibah and scattered lignum. Lake Surprise has not been extensively grazed and has an open coolibah woodland and a *Cyperus vaginatus* sedgeland. Lake Amadeus in the Amadeus Basin, Lake Bennett in the Burt Plain, and extensive playas (saltpans), such as that at Lake Mackay, also occur in the arid region.

The lakes of southern Australia have been the subject of a good deal of research, especially the salt lakes in the southeast. They are mostly ephemeral and many are endoreic - that is, they drain inland and not towards the coast.

Species of *Ruppia* and *Lepilaena* are widespread in salt lakes. The salt-tolerant *Suaeda australis* grows near many of the hypersaline lakes, but emergent or submerged plants are absent. The salty water in these lakes can be a red colour due to the presence of *Dunaliella*, a single-celled alga.

Lake Toolibin is one of the few remaining freshwater lakes in the southwest. It contains dense thickets of *Casuarina obesa* and a *Melaleuca* species. Emergent aquatic plants also develop. The thickets require periodic dry spells if they are to proliferate. Waterlogging can kill these shrubs, as has happened in nearby lakes.

The Kerang Lakes in northern Victoria contain many plant species. River red gum, black box and *Acacia stenophylla* trees are common, as are lignum shrubs in periodically flooded areas. These support reed, cumbungi, cane grass and numerous sedges. The vegetation composition and dominance is greatly influenced by the frequency and duration of floods. *Suaeda* species, *Juncus acutus*, and salt-tolerant grasses and shrubs grow in the more saline areas.

Spectacular floating islands can be seen in the Tasmanian lake known as the Lagoon of Islands. The island base is a mat formed of rhizomes and roots of sedges. *Carex appressa* binds the mat and develops a mound that is then colonized by woody shrubs and *Eucalyptus aggregata*. Eventually, the mats sink, the shrubs and trees die and the islands break up. This process seems to repeat itself.

Intermittent lakes in Australia fill only after substantial rainfall, but once full will hold water for two or three years. Fish populations can explode after the initial flooding and this in turn attracts thousands of waterbirds (such as cormorants, herons and pelicans). Large populations of brine shrimp (*Paratemia*) develop after the lakes are filled and form the basis of the food web. The thick brine attracts birds such as banded stilts (*Cladorhynchus leucocephalus*) and red-necked avocets (*Recurvirostra novaehollandiae*). A colony of 200,000 Australasian pelicans (*Pelecanus*

Lake Toolibin is one of the few remaining freshwater lakes in southwestern Australia. It is an important bird refuge and has been recognized as an internationally important wetland under the Ramsar Convention.

FAREWELL SPIT, NEW ZEALAND

Farewell Spit is located on the northwest extremity of the South Island, 38 km (23 miles) from Takaka in the Nelson district. It covers 11,388 hectares (28,140 acres) and contains a spit of quartz sand with sandflats and salt marsh exposed at low tide. Coastal dunes contain a series of damp hollows and small lakes, some of which have freshwater. The quartz sand derives from riverine drainage and is transported northwards to the spit by the Westland Current.

The spit extends 22 km (13 miles) into a bay. Some of the inter-dunal lakes are semi-permanent.

The spit is important for wintering shorebirds from the Arctic and sub-Arctic, including some 46,000 red knot, bar-tailed godwit and turnstone (*Arenaria interpres*). Up to 10,000 black swans use the area as a moulting reserve.

The native vegetation has been severely modified by burning, planting and grazing. Following removal of all cattle and sheep in 1975 it began to regenerate, and golden pingao (*Desmoschoenus spiralis*) started to grow, which in the absence of the introduced marram grass (*Ammophila arenaria*) would be one of the main sand-binding grasses. Other weeds still cause problems and, despite restricted access, off- road vehicles have caused some damage. It is planned to eradicate a number of introduced weeds.

The black swan is found mainly in southeast and southwest Australia. It has been introduced to New Zealand. When moulting the swans are flightless and gather in large numbers on open lakes.

conspicillatus) very quickly established itself in Lake Eyre after flooding in 1990. Similarly, banded stilts (*Cladorhynchus leucocephalus*) numbered around 100,000 in Lake Torrens after it flooded.

If lakes become hypersaline and dry out before the birds have left, many thousands will perish. In the late 1970s large numbers of pelicans and cormorants died as food supplies and freshwater became increasingly scarce after a series of large floods had filled many inland lakes, including Lake Eyre. Emaciated pelicans were literally dropping out of the sky as they vainly sought to reach food nearer the coast.

The freshwater Lake Toolibin in Western Australia, which is surrounded by a large number of unvegetated saline lakes, is a haven for waterbirds.

Over 40 species, with about half of them nesting, have been seen on the lake. It is particularly important for the rare freckled duck (*Stictonetta naevosa*), great egret (*Egretta alba*), yellow-billed spoonbill (*Platalea flavipes*), nankeen night heron (*Nycticorax caledonicus*) and great cormorant (*Phalacrocorax carbo*).

The diverse wetland types of the Kerang Lakes in Victoria make them important for waterbirds; over 50 species have been spotted. There is a breeding colony of 100,000 straw-necked ibises on Middle Lake. Other lakes support from 40-100,000 birds with Eurasian coot (*Fulica atra*) and grey teal (*Anas gibberifrons*) being plentiful. Other common birds include black swans, little pied cormorants (*Phalacrocorax melanoleucos*) and great crested grebes

At least 100,000 banded stilts were discovered on Lake Torrens in South Australia during 1990 after extensive inland floods.

(*Podiceps cristatus*). Many birds disperse during winter and spring to the flooded lakes and leave only when the water salinity becomes intolerable. As water levels decline the water becomes hypersaline and only red-capped dotterels (*Charadrius ruficapillus*) remain.

The freshwater lakes have a higher diversity of invertebrates than the saline lakes. However, the diversity of species living at the bottom of freshwater lakes is low compared to lakes elsewhere in the world. Zooplankton species are also less diverse.

The salt lakes have an invertebrate fauna that differs from that of salt lakes elsewhere in the world. There are many endemic species (such as the brine shrimp *Paratemia*). Some lakes in Tasmania contain finely separated communities of micro-organisms, including pigmented and non-pigmented sulphur bacteria, cyanobacteria and eukaryotic algae.

River and Creek Channels

Only the Murray-Darling Basin in Australia includes large permanent rivers. Many permanent small streams flow through Tasmania and New Zealand. Destruction of the freshwater margins and vegetation along the large permanent rivers has degraded much of the wetland habitat. In New Zealand many slow-flowing streams have been straightened.

Billabongs along the Australian riverine floodplains are joined to the rivers during floods. They can be important refuges for fish and invertebrate species from the rivers.

Towards their sources the large Australian inland rivers are lined with *Casuarina cunninghamiana* trees and support submerged aquatic plant species such as *Vallisneria gigantea* or *Potamogeton*. Emergents, including cumbungi, reed, *Triglochin procera* and *Eleocharis* grow in protected sites. Across the plains the rivers are characteristically lined with the majestic white-stemmed river red gums as well as scattered *Acacia stenophylla*, coolibah and black box. The water is usually very turbid and few submerged plants grow in the channels.

The phytoplankton in the Murray-Darling Basin is greatly influenced by the sediment carried in the rivers. In the River Murray the phytoplankton is more diverse than in the Darling which carries more sediment. In the Murray the phytoplankton species vary with changes in the flow regime. After floods, algae flushed from reservoirs and dams and surrounding wetlands predominate; in winter, diatom species dominate, whereas in the low flows of summer cyanobacteria, green algae and chrysophytes can form thick, unsightly and even toxic blooms.

Billabongs of inland rivers are, in fact, oxbow lakes. They are usually deep and retain water after floods. The vegetation is similar to that in the rivers - except that emergent species are more common - with

BARMAH FOREST, AUSTRALIA

The Barmah Forest is a 28,500 hectare (70,400 acre) river red gum forest located along the River Murray between Barmah and Tocumwal in northern Victoria.

Under natural conditions the forest used to flood, during spring, four out of every five years. Since construction of the Hume Weir in 1934, spring floods have become less frequent and summer floods more common. With the completion of the Dartmouth Reservoir in 1983 effective spring flooding now occurs in two out of every five years. During prolonged drought this could be reduced to a 10-year interval.

The wetland supports a large stand of river red gum trees with rushes and grasses in non-wooded areas. After periods of flood it supports large breeding colonies of sacred ibis (*Threskiornis aethiopica*), straw-necked ibis and yellow-billed spoonbill. The forest is also managed for timber production; waterbird hunting is permitted during set seasons.

Regulation of the river floods and a reduction in the frequency of spring floods threatens regeneration of the river red gum trees. Grazing by stock and rabbits has also contributed to changes in the grass and herb composition of the wetland floor. In December 1987, 7,000 hectares (17,000 acres) of the forest was designated a state park. A management plan prepared in 1990 has placed greater emphasis on nature conservation and recreation.

The Barmah Forest is a large and important river red gum forest along the River Murray. The flooding regime has been considerably altered by dams and weirs and great concern has been expressed over the effect this is having on the survival of the forest.

Lake Ellesmere, New Zealand, contains swampy places suitable for the pukeko (Porphyrio melanotus), *a very conspicuous rail.*

lignum growing on the banks; *Ottelia ovalifolia* and *Potamogeton tricarinatus* are common in shallow water.

The slow-flowing and usually short rivers of lowland areas in Tasmania and New Zealand contain a number of aquatic plants with rushes, reeds and sedges along the banks. The faster flowing highland rivers contain very few plants.

Large numbers of waterbirds inhabit the wetland habitats along the rivers and creeks. Australian shelduck (*Tadorna tadornoides*), pink-eared duck (*Malacorhynchus membranaceus*), grey teal, Pacific black duck and wood duck (*Chenonetta jubata*) inhabit river red gum forests. Black swans prefer wetter parts of the rivers.

The Barmah Forest in Victoria, along the River Murray, is an important area for waterbirds. Flow regulation may have eliminated some gastropod species from riverine wetlands. In the Murray, bivalves include the common genera *Sphaerium* and *Pisidium* and the basket shell (*Corbiculina australis*). The freshwater mussel *Velessunio ambiguus* is a floodplain species and appears to have survived weir construction better than the riverine *Alathyria jacksonia* and *Alathyria candola*. Crustaceans include the yabbie (*Chelax destructor*) and Murray crayfish (*Euastacus armatus*). The latter has declined following weir construction.

The more heavily vegetated lakes in New Zealand contain large numbers of eels and fishes. The big long-finned eels (*Anguilla dieffenbachii*) are usually found in streams, while the short-finned eels (*Anguilla australis*) live in the lakes and swamps. The eels eventually migrate down the rivers to the sea to breed.

A number of fish species occur in the Australian inland rivers and streams. Some 30 species are known in the Murray-Darling Basin alone. Many of these species are in decline, however. The Murray cod (*Maccullochella peeli*) is the largest species, reaching 1.8 m (6 ft) and 110 kg (240 lb). Once widespread throughout the Murray-Darling Basin, it has suffered severe decline over the last 50 years. It feeds on many animals, including the introduced carp (*Cyprinus carpio*). Other species include the silver perch (*Bidyanus bidyanus*), which is carnivorous and travels long distances upstream during floods, as does the golden perch (*Macquaria ambigua*). Dams and weirs interrupt the migration of many of these fish species.

Two mammals, the platypus (*Ornithorhynchus anatinus*) and water rat (*Hydromys chrysogaster*), live in the temperate inland rivers. The platypus was thought to be a hoax by naturalists in Europe when first described to them. It is a monotreme and therefore lays eggs, yet provides milk to its young. Furthermore, it has a duck-like bill, webbed feet and the male has poisonous spurs on its rear legs. It is carnivorous, feeding on insects, crustaceans and

Spotless crake, Porzana tabuensis, *in a taupo,* Typha orientalis, *swamp. This crake is a secretive inhabitant of fresh and saline wetlands in New Zealand. It is also found in Australia.*

high rainfall area in the west of the South Island, New Zealand. These are wet and ill-drained areas. Lowland bog forests in New Zealand are found as pockets within ordinary forests in high rainfall areas and are dominated by either podocarp (*Dacrydium intermedium* or *Dacrydium colensoi*) or mountain beech (*Nothofagus solandri*) trees. *Sphagnum* moss or bryophytes cover the soil. Manuka shrub, *Leptospermum scoparium*, grows in less fertile bogs. Other bog plants are often co-dominant with manuka.

There is a great variety of bogs in New Zealand. Raised bogs are well-developed in South Auckland, ranging in size from 300 to 23,000 hectares (740 to 57,000 acres), and with deep peat deposits. The locally called *awarua* bogs in parts of the delta plain of Southland (on the South Island) once covered some 40,000 hectares (99,000 acres). The peat in them is sometimes as much as 2 m (6 1/2 ft) deep, although there is often no more than a very thin surface layer. The largest remaining portion of these bogs now covers only 5,200 hectares (12,800 acres).

Cushion bogs in New Zealand are found on exposed sites that are either flat or gently sloping; they typically do not contain *Sphagnum*. Instead, they consist of cushions or mounds of tightly packed plant material raised above the surrounding water. Cushion-forming plants include *Donatia novaezelandiae* and *Phyllachne colensoi*. This community is well-developed on the summit plateaus of Otago in Southland and of Stewart Island and descends to sea level in the south of the South Island.

Buttongrass (*Gymnoschoenus sphaerocephalus*) covers extensive areas in the high rainfall zones of southwestern Tasmania. It is a tussock sedge with a firm fibrous base, narrow leaves 1-2 m (3-6 1/2 ft) long, and flowers and fruit that cluster into button-shaped heads. Herbs and sedges occupy depressions in between the tussocks. The bright yellow flowering *Xyris* species and the mauve *Patersonia fragilis* are conspicuous in summer.

Wet heath is widespread, but not extensive in any one area, in the Australian highlands. Tussock-grass

molluscs in the river sediment. It can be found in the River Murray and also in streams in the mountains of eastern Australia and Tasmania. The water rat is a rodent and is common in irrigation areas where it preys on fish and benthic invertebrates - that is, invertebrates from the lower depths of the waters.

Bogs

Bogs occur not only in highlands, but also in well-watered lowland areas. Many are dominated by *Sphagnum* moss. They are best developed in the alpine regions of southeastern Australia and Tasmania and in New Zealand. Extensive bogs include 30,000 hectares (74,000 acres) of the so-called *pakihi* in the

WHANGAMARINO WETLAND, NEW ZEALAND

The Whangamarino wetland is a 5690 hectare (14,060 acre) complex of peat bogs, swamps, fens, open water and river stretches in the Lower Waikato, 65 km (40 miles) from Auckland, North Island. It supports a number of threatened plant species, including the threatened black mudfish (*Neochanna diversus*) and the Australasian bittern (*Botaurus stellaris poiciloptilus*). Some

30-50,000 waterbirds, including black swans, mallard (*Anas platyrhynchos*) and Australasian shoveller have been counted on this site, although numbers may now be falling. Many of the wetlands have been degraded or destroyed.

There is a continuing problem of increasing eutrophication of peat bog margins by drainage from surrounding

farmland. More insidiously, the peat bogs are drying out as a result of drainage in the catchment. Plans have been made to increase, or at least maintain, the current water levels. Drainage of parts of the wetland was recently blocked by a court decision.

Further effort is needed to prevent water levels falling as a result of drainage elsewhere in the catchment.

wetlands, distinguished by *Empodisma minus* in the Eastern Highlands and *Poa gunnii* in Tasmania, occur on slope terraces. The sedge *Carex gaudichaudiana* is characteristic of alpine areas in the Eastern Highlands. Moss beds are well-represented in the sub-alpine belt. Cushion bog mounds also occur. The mounds are formed by the sedge *Oreobolus pumilio* in the Eastern Highlands, and *Phyllachne colensoi* and other species in Tasmania.

Birds comprise the main animal life in the lowland bogs of New Zealand. The most colourful is the swamp hen (*Porphyrio porphyrio*). Less conspicuous are the brown bittern (*Botaurus poiciloptilus*) and four species that rarely fly: the fern bird (*Bowdleria punctata*), the banded rail (*Rallus philippensis*), the marsh crake (*Porzana pusilla affinis*) and the spotless crake (*Porzana tabuensis plumbea*).

Introduced hares (*Lepus europeus*), thar (*Hemitragus jemlahicus*) and chamois (*Rupicapra rupicapra*) graze and trample the highland vegetation in New Zealand. On the swampy floors of valleys, red deer (*Cervus elaphus*) graze selectively on species of *Carex*.

Frogs that have been introduced from Australian to New Zealand bogs include the green and gold tree frog (*Litoria aurea*) and the nocturnal brown tree frog (*Litoria ewingi*). Galaxiid fish, *Neochanna* species, are endemic to the New Zealand bogs. Eels also inhabit many swamps.

The Eastern Highlands in Australia support at least six species of lizard and two species of snake that live above 1,500 m (4,900 ft) and hibernate in the peaty soil. The corroboree frog (*Pseudophyrne corroboree*) lives above 1,375 m (4,500 ft) in *Sphagnum* bogs that are covered by snow for several months a year.

In Tasmania the buttongrass is a poor habitat for animals. Grazing marsupials visit these areas only occasionally. Birds are also usually casual visitors. The exceptions are the ground parrot (*Pezoporus wallicus*) and emu wren (*Stipiturus malachurus*), which are permanent residents. They live and feed almost exclusively at ground level, very rarely resorting to flight.

New Guinea Freshwater Wetlands

The wide meandering rivers of the New Guinean lowlands are surrounded by a mosaic of different wetland types which are intricately connected and often impenetrable. Oxbow lakes abound along the rivers. In the river basins and coastal plains, lowland freshwater wetlands form fringes, sometimes more than 5 km (3 miles) wide.

Water depth and the flooding and drainage regime determine the shape and size of the wetlands and the mix of plants. The vegetation varies from submerged plant communities in the oxbow lakes to tall swamp forests.

Free-floating, floating-leaved and submerged plants are either mixed together or in distinct zones in the open water. At times, the shallow lakes are completely covered by aquatic plants. The deeper, stagnant permanent swamps are dominated by sedges, herbs and ferns, such as *Scleria* and *Hanguana* species and the fern *Cyclosorus interruptus*.

Lake Daviumba is part of the species-rich wetland system of the Fly-Strickland Rivers in Papua New Guinea.

Reeds and grasses are common in poorly drained and intermittently dry swamps. Grasses grow profusely on permanently swampy river plains and can tolerate flooding to a depth of 3 m (10 ft). On Lake Tebera large floating islands of *Leersia hexandra* support a 'sudd-type' community of grasses and herbs. In the southwest *Pseudoraphis spinescens* forms extensive mats on seasonally dry floodplains.

The ubiquitous tropical wetland weeds *Salvinia molesta* and *Eichhornia crassipes* (water hyacinth) are now widespread in the New Guinean wetlands. *Salvinia* was probably introduced to the Sepik River in 1971; by 1979 it had exploded to cover more than 25,000 hectares (62,000 acres) before biological control was introduced to deal with the problem. Water hyacinth is widespread in lowland areas and for this there is, so far, no effective control.

Permanent swamps contain a mixture of tree species. Palms and pandans form very dense stands under the trees. The sago palm (*Metroxylon sagu*) is common throughout the swampy woodland. The zone in between permanent stagnant swamps and seasonal swamps is characterized by a mosaic of herb and tree species. The herbs are overshadowed by tall *Melaleuca*, *Campnosperma* and *Syzygium* trees.

Sedge- and grass-dominated communities occur in wetlands above an altitude of 1,800 m (5,900 ft). Characteristic grasses are the *Arundinella furva*, *Isachne* and *Dimeria* species. *Phragmites karka* forms pure stands in seepage areas on slopes and valley flats up to 2,500 m (8,200 ft). Lakes on Mount Giluwe in the Southern Highlands contain pure stands of *Miscanthus floridulus* at the high-water mark and *Eleocharis sphacelata* or other sedges near the low-water level.

There are more than 115 waterbird species in the freshwater swamps. Endemic wetland species are the forest bittern (*Zonerodius heliosylus*) which frequents pools and swamps, Salvadori's duck (*Anas waigiuensis*) which inhabits river-edge bamboo thickets (and mangroves), and the New Guinea flightless rail (*Megacrex inepta*) which is restricted to highland areas up to about 3,900 m (12,800 ft). Migrating birds come from Asia and Australia, including waders, pelicans, straw-necked ibises, glossy ibises (*Plegadis falcinellus*) and royal spoonbills (*Platalea regia*).

Flocks of 100,000 magpie geese visit the shallow Suki Lagoon in Western Province, Papua New Guinea. New Guinea is also part of the East Asian-Australasian flyway which is used by 4-6 million or more shorebirds and an unknown number of herons, ducks, geese and other waterbirds.

Two crocodile species are found in New Guinea.

The New Guinea or freshwater crocodile (*Crocodylus novaeguineae*) is endemic and found in freshwater. By day it hides in thick grass or under fallen trees and moves into deep water at night. The larger and more dangerous estuarine crocodile often moves well inland. File snakes and a number of water snakes inhabit the wetlands. The pit-shelled turtle (*Carettochelys insculpta*) and the soft-shelled turtle (*Pelochelys bibroni*) are found in freshwaters south of the cordillera. Five tortoise species occur; three of them are endemic.

The fish of the New Guinean wetlands can be divided into two regional groups - those from the south and those from the north of the central cordillera. The southern rivers - for example, the Fly which has 103 species - contain more species than the northern and highland rivers. Fish in the Sepik River, north of the cordillera, are less diverse, though many are endemic. The native fishes are often small; the introduced tilapia (*Oreochromis mossambicus*) and carp (*Cyprinus carpio*) are more productive. The silver barramundi is a large species, however, that is favoured as a food.

Mangroves are well-developed in New Guinea around the mouths of most large rivers. These forests are large, species-rich and, in places, an important source of food, firewood and building materials for local people.

SEPIK AND RAMU FLOODPLAINS, PAPUA NEW GUINEA

The weed Salvinia molesta *formerly spread out over large parts of the Sepik River in Papua New Guinea and made food gathering and travel along the river extremely difficult. It was eventually controlled by biological means.*

These floodplains cover 1.2 million hectares (3 million acres) from the Irian Jaya border in the west to the upper Ramu valley southwest of Madang in the east. They include the 21,600 hectare (53,400 acre) Chambri Lake. Mangroves, mudflats and coastal lagoons and marshes abound, but the area is primarily freshwater marsh: grassland and forested wetlands associated with the rivers, oxbow lakes and floodplains.

The Sepik is about 1,100 km (680 miles) long and has a catchment area of 78,000 km² (30,000 sq miles). The floodplain of the lower and middle Sepik has a width of 30-70 km (roughly 20-45 miles), covers 780,000 hectares (1.9 million acres) and is inundated for at least five months of the year. The Ramu River is 720 km (450 miles) long and flows through very flat terrain in the lower reaches. During floods much of the area near the mouths of both rivers is flooded. There are about 1,500 oxbow and other lakes in the Sepik floodplain. The largest is the 4 m (13 ft) deep Chambri Lake. Some oxbows in the lower reaches of the river are 40 m (131 ft) deep. The river discharges to the sea through a single channel and a freshwater plume can extend 35 km (22 miles) offshore.

Many people are dependent on subsistence fisheries in these wetlands, catching especially the introduced common carp and tilapia. On the floodplain the sago palm is harvested for subsistence purposes. A hydroelectric scheme is located close to where the river leaves the Central Highlands. The wetlands are important for a variety of waterbirds, but quantitative data are not available. The area is also an important habitat for both of Papua New Guinea's species of crocodile.

The floating weed *Salvinia molesta* in the Sepik River caused great disruption to the daily lives of the local populace. However, following biological control it is no longer a serious problem. The presence of water hyacinth is a continuing threat.

The introduced deer *Cervus timorensis* grazes in large numbers in wetlands near Port Moresby, often with its head submerged.

The invertebrates are poorly known, except that, as in many tropical wetlands, insects are abundant.

VALUES AND USES OF WETLANDS

Wetlands in Australia are still used for subsistence by groups of Aboriginal people, especially in northern areas. In the Alligator Rivers Region, for example, the freshwater wetlands are a bountiful source of plant foods, such as sedge and lily bulbs and corms. Animal foods include magpie geese, turtles, file snakes, mussels and several fish species. Mangrove creeks are also important for fish and at low tide the large mud crabs are sought.

In New Guinea subsistence fishing in freshwater wetlands is very important. However, of 29 fish species recorded in the Sepik River only two, the introduced carp and tilapia, are important for subsistence. A commercial tilapia fishing enterprise operates in the Sepik. In southern rivers, barramundi fishing is of more commercial significance.

Rivers are vital for transport and travel throughout New Guinea, as was vividly brought home when the introduced weed *Salvinia molesta* choked the Sepik River and oxbow lakes. Villagers were unable to reach markets to sell produce; children were prevented from attending school, and there were declines in fish catches, crocodile hunting and sago collection.

The extensive mangrove stands are important resources, especially in New Guinea and to a lesser extent in the Oceanic islands. Firewood, building material for houses and canoes, as well as raw materials for clothing, tools, dyes, tanning agents and traditional medicines are extracted from the mangroves. Mud crabs, bivalves and the common cockle are important food sources.

Crocodiles are heavily exploited for hides and meat. Crocodile farming and the purchase and export of hides is now under government control in Papua New Guinea. However, both crocodile species are still endangered in Papua New Guinea.

Wetlands are of cultural and spiritual significance to the Maori people of New Zealand. They have traditionally provided a supply of food (fish, birds and shellfish) and weaving material (New Zealand flax and raupo). To the Maori people, water is the essential ingredient of life and their traditional harvesting rights are still maintained. A Maori proverb *Huutia te rito o te harakeke kei hea te koomako e koo* ('Pull out the young shoot of the flax and where will the bellbird sing') illustrates the value placed on wetlands.

Since the arrival of Europeans in New Zealand, wetlands have been valued more for their potential as 'reclaimed' farm lands and as a source of flax. Thus they have been widely destroyed rather than conserved. However, attempts to ensure the survival of *Galaxias* (whitebait) and other native fishes without banning fishing are a case where conservation and economic values have both been considered.

Commercial exploitation of coastal wetland animals is well known. The prawn, crab and fishing industries are well developed in Australia and large hauls are taken. In addition, attempts are being made to develop commercial crocodile and turtle farms in Australia and New Guinea.

Economic values can be placed on these industries. The New South Wales commercial fishing industry is currently worth about Aus$100 million (roughly US$80 million) for landed products (wholesale products). In Queensland the landed value is about Aus$290 million (US$230 million) with a retail value of Aus$580 million (US$470 million). Many

commercial fish species are, at some stage of their life, dependent on estuarine wetlands. Commercial food resources are valued, but often the wetland ecosystem is not valued. This can all too often lead to over-exploitation and a severe decline in commercial returns: a problem that plagues all the countries of Australasia and Oceania.

Recreational waterbird hunting and fishing are activities that involve many people. In Victoria there were an estimated 60,000 waterbird hunters some years ago. This has fallen to 24,000 following the introduction of bird identification tests for hunters in recent years. Amateur fishing for barramundi in the Northern Territory now takes precedence over commercial fishing. The barramundi and the Murray cod are important commercial and recreational fish species. In New South Wales the recreational value of estuarine fishing is at least equivalent to the commercial return. This gives a combined value that could reach Aus$300 million (roughly US$240 million). In Queensland the combined commercial, recreational and sport fishing industries have a recurring resource value of Aus$2,000 million (US$1,590 million). The value of mangroves for fisheries in Moreton Bay has been estimated at Aus$8,380 (US$6,640) per hectare - Aus$3,390 (US$2,690) per acre.

People in New Guinea make great use of wetland products, often at a subsistence level. The vast wetlands of New Guinea are probably the most pristine of all those in Australasia and Oceania. Every effort should be made to ensure that this valuable biological resource is not lost.

The Australian crake (Porzana fluminea) *frequents swamps, lagoons and streams, particularly in coastal areas.*

The sharp-tailed sandpiper (Calidris acuminata) *is a common migrant to Australasia from its Arctic breeding areas.*

In much of the seasonally dry country in Australia, cattle rely on wetlands for dry season food and water. The Channel Country of Queensland forms a remarkable natural fattening paddock when wet. However, it can, like many other regions, suffer a succession of devastating drought years.

Wetlands also have a major biological conservation value. From a purely ethical standpoint these areas should be conserved. The aesthetic appeal of many wetlands should not be underestimated, especially where the wetlands lie near large urban centres. Recreational activities, such as walking, camping, boating and bird-watching in wetlands have an immense but unquantifiable value. Furthermore, the cultural and anthropological significance of wetlands in the Murray Valley and Alligator Rivers Region, for example, is very high.

The tourism value of many of the South Pacific islands in particular is enormous, and wetlands could play a major part in this. However, experience elsewhere has already shown that the development of tourist facilities is often to the detriment of coastal habitats such as mangroves, salt marshes and brackish lagoons. Thus the expansion of tourism can be a two-edged sword.

The value of wetlands extends far beyond their importance to the obvious commercial industries. There are many qualities that are difficult to price and if care is not exercised these will be degraded, if not destroyed, by the time their true importance is realized. In Australia and New Zealand this has already too often been the case.

THREATS TO THE WETLANDS

The extent to which the countries in Australasia and Oceania differ has already been pointed out. However, they have one common, not very flattering, feature: over the last 100 years wetlands in these countries have been destroyed at a breakneck speed. This has been in response to short-term demands for industrial and agricultural growth. Wetland loss and degradation, particularly in Australia and New Zealand, has continued almost unabated, often subsidized by governments. Only now is the plundering of wetlands being restricted; it is now time to be active in reversing this loss.

Changing this awareness and approach is all the more important now we face the prospect of a rise in sea levels in the wake of global warming. The implications in Australia and New Zealand may be immense, or even catastrophic in some areas, but what about the many tiny island states of the South Pacific? What will happen to them? At present it is impossible to answer this question, but it must not be conveniently forgotten.

River Regulation and Drainage

Impounding of rivers into reservoirs and dams has destroyed many Australian wetlands (such as Lake Pedder in Tasmania) and fundamentally altered much of the remainder. Large dams on inland rivers have permanently submerged many floodplain wetlands and prevented substantial or regular flooding of others. Weirs create static ponds along river courses and make many permanent connections from the rivers

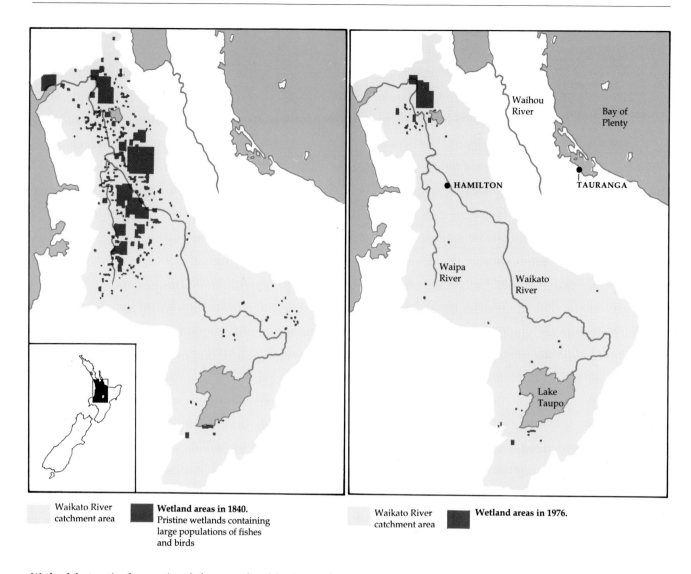

| Waikato River catchment area | | Wetland areas in 1840. Pristine wetlands containing large populations of fishes and birds | | Waikato River catchment area | | Wetland areas in 1976. |

Wetland destruction has continued almost unabated in New Zealand over the past 100 or so years. The Waikato Basin, taking in Hamilton on the North Island, is a prime example; the 161,400 hectare (398,820 acre) wetland that existed in 1840 was reduced to 26,200 hectares (64,740 acres) in 1976. Today only a small proportion of the remainder is in pristine condition.

to lagoons and billabongs that were once connected to them only during floods. Nearly 37,000 hectares (90,000 acres) of wetlands along the Murray floodplain are now permanently flooded. Numerous inland wetlands now hold water permanently (for example, Menindee Lakes in New South Wales). Many reservoirs have been constructed in New Zealand to provide water for electricity generation, a process that involves rapid changes in water depth and sudden releases of water downstream from the reservoir.

The ecological results of these changes can be catastrophic, and much remains to be learnt about them: flood suppression, for example, stops fish spawning; premature drops in water levels are disastrous for waterbird breeding; and the lack of periodic flooding prevents the regeneration of river red gum forests. In only a few cases are water releases made to maintain wetland habitats - the Macquarie Marshes are one spectacular example.

River regulation can be used advantageously for wildlife, but careful management is needed - to take

one instance, releases of cold and deoxygenated water can prevent migration and spawning of fish. Fish-ladders are required. Extreme care is needed to ensure that they are well placed and designed to encourage their use by as many fish as possible. Both inland and estuarine migratory fishes have suffered in Australia and New Zealand as a result of weirs blocking their migratory routes.

Drainage of coastal floodplains is another threat to wetlands. The draining of such plains in Australia, above all, has been extremely detrimental for waterbird breeding. Some 60 per cent of wetlands of high value for waterbirds in coastal New South Wales have been drained for flood mitigation. On the Hunter, Clarence and Macleay floodplains 29,000 hectares (72,000 acres) - that is, 91 per cent of the total area - have been affected by drainage.

In Victoria, wetland drainage has occurred on a large scale with, for example, the 25,000 hectare (62,000 acre) Carrum Swamp being reduced to 500 hectares (1,200 acres) and the 40,000 hectare (99,000 acre) Koo-wee-rup Swamp almost completely drained. Agriculture, flood mitigation, water supply, salinity control and sewerage developments have all contributed to wetland drainage. Port, industrial and urban development has also occurred on drained wetlands, particularly former mangrove forests. Floodgates have been installed in many coastal areas to prevent refilling of drained wetlands. A variety of flood-control structures on tidal wetlands have also prevented tidal water movements that are so necessary for the survival of mangroves.

Wetlands in New Zealand are now recognized as valuable resources to be conserved. Unfortunately, over the past 150 years 90 per cent have been lost through drainage and other development. In 1987, government subsidies for draining wetlands were belatedly removed. Diversion of water from wetlands, as has happened on the Kaituna River, has destroyed freshwater wetlands and degraded salt marshes in the Bay of Plenty. Erosion and the accumulation of silt have further threatened the Maketu Estuary in the bay.

Many wetland drainage schemes were funded by government agencies convinced that wasteland was being converted to more profitable uses. This attitude has not entirely disappeared. Wetlands fringing rivers have been used for rubbish disposal and then converted to ovals, roadways and building sites. For example, the Perth casino, where, ironically, the World Conservation Union (IUCN) recently debated the concepts of sustainable use and management of wetlands, is built on wetland reclaimed from the Swan River. On the Swan Coastal Plain 75 per cent of wetlands have been either filled or drained.

Land Clearing, Grazing and Pollution

Increased erosion and accumulation of sediment in wetlands have followed extensive clearing of land for agricultural purposes; rising water tables have caused waterlogging and salinization of ephemeral wetlands. Lignum clearing has been extensive and is still occurring. In Tasmania and New South Wales, highland wetlands have been destroyed by widespread cattle grazing.

Problems of waterlogging and salinization in the ephemeral wetlands are well known in Western Australia, following excessive clearing of land for agriculture. Sedimentation represents an insidious and almost irreversible infilling of wetlands. Land clearing (and wetland drainage) was invariably undertaken for purely economic reasons and often with the active participation of government agencies. Many New Zealand peatlands have been cleared and converted to grazing pastures. In the South Pacific islands large areas of mangroves were destroyed in the nineteenth century for coconut plantations.

Grazing is probably the most common way in which wetlands have been degraded in order to use the land for other purposes in Australia and New Zealand. It has occurred on virtually all coastal wetlands and inland floodplains and swamps. In some instances the natural vegetation has disappeared. Many stream banks are slumped and eroded as stock have grazed or trampled the vegetation that would have stabilized them. Such widescale erosion is now recognized as a national disaster in Australia. However, the basic cause of the problem has yet to be addressed: agricultural

Many wetlands near towns and cities were used as convenient rubbish dumps before being covered and converted into playing fields and urban parkland.

The Ranger uranium mine is situated in a mining lease area completely surrounded by the World Heritage and Ramsar-listed Kakadu National Park. The existence of this mine has been the centre of much controversy over the last 15 years.

Waigani Lake near Port Moresby has undergone extensive change as a result of nutrient seepage from nearby sewage ponds. It contains a productive carp and tilapia fishery, but the natural vegetation has been completely altered with emergent plants now dominant.

practices need to change now; inappropriate cropping and stocking should be stopped, and remedial land-care measures taken. Sustainable use of natural resources is needed. It is to be hoped that this is what is meant by 'conservation farming', a concept being embraced by a number of agricultural agencies.

Pollution of estuarine wetlands can be very obvious, such as the destruction of the mangroves in Botany Bay by oil spills. Many other estuaries, bays and inlets suffer from oil spills. Similarly, pesticide and heavy metal pollution are obvious threats to coastal wetlands. Unfortunately pollution often arises from multiple or many small and widespread (that is, diffuse) sources. Diffuse nutrient sources may be more

of a problem in wetlands than nutrients originating from single or point sources and are notoriously difficult to control. Massive algal blooms can occur following increased nutrient loadings. Nutrient enrichment in Cockburn Sound in Western Australia has led to increased growth of epiphytes on seagrasses and so to the decline of the seagrasses. In the nearby Peel Inlet and Harvey Estuary massive growths of macroalgae and blue-green algal blooms have reduced recreational values and fish populations respectively.

The spectacular and devastating examples of zinc pollution from the Captain's Flat mine in New South Wales and copper pollution from the Rum Jungle mine in the Northern Territory have awakened concern over point-source pollution. Consequently, the uranium mines in the Northern Territory, located near the wetlands of Kakadu National Park, are closely regulated. However, there is still a need for diligence as the long-term effects of uranium waste containment are not well-known. Further mining developments within Kakadu are being sought by an extremely aggressive mining industry. There is currently much debate over whether or not to allow mining at Coronation Hill and there could be even more debate over further uranium-mining proposals elsewhere within Kakadu.

The enormous Fly and Strickland Rivers in Papua New Guinea are potentially threatened by pollution from the Ok Tedi and Porgera mines. The Ok Tedi mine is now one of the largest open-cut copper and gold mines in the world. Rock and other wastes (tailings) are dumped into the river. The increased sediment loads could lead to increased siltation and higher concentrations of heavy metals in the waters and sediments of the river tributaries. The Porgera copper and silver mine could have similar effects, with the complication of having high concentrations of mercury in the tailings. Needless to say, these effects are being closely monitored by the mining companies in line with government requirements.

Sewage disposal in wetlands can be beneficial as a cheap treatment process. However, the very nature of the wetland can be degraded if nutrient loading is excessive. Disposal of wastes in wetlands as part of land reclamation has been widespread near large urban centres. Estuarine and riverine swamps have been the most severely affected. In Botany Bay 980 hectares (2,400 acres) of the original 2,400 hectares (5,900 acres) of wetlands have been lost in this manner. Leaching of nutrients and toxic substances from these buried waste dumps is now a serious problem.

Waigani Swamp (in effect a number of small, shallow lakes) near Port Moresby demonstrates some of the problems that face Papua New Guinean wetlands near urban centres. The main Waigani Lake is less than 2 m (6 ¹/₂ ft) deep, surrounded by emergent plants and heavily fished for carp and tilapia. Since 1965 nearby ponds have been used to treat sewage from Port Moresby and large amounts of effluent now enter the swamp. Simultaneously, the vegetation has undergone major change. The floating-leaved plants have been completely lost and the emergent species have declined. Nutrients in the effluent are held responsible.

Disposal of water from irrigation systems along the River Murray in Australia also pollutes wetlands. Many wetlands below the Hume Dam receive saline water from neighbouring irrigation systems. Irrigation has resulted in serious salinization problems; this is a major threat to rivers, swamps and lakes in much of southern Australia. It has hit the Murray-Darling area the hardest. Not only have inappropriate irrigationtechniques caused salinization

The 'noxious beauty' or water hyacinth is one of a number of introduced weeds that have invaded many Australian and New Guinean wetlands. Attempts to control this species using biological means have been undertaken.

of farming lands, but there is a great need to dispose of saline waste-water from the farms. Some of this is being dumped into existing wetlands. Increased salt levels and rising water tables have killed many trees and altered the floodplain soil structures.

Introduced Plants and Animals
Introduced plants have changed the character of many wetlands. Probably the worst weeds are *Salvinia molesta*, water hyacinth and *Mimosa pigra*. These species can occupy large areas of wetland and completely blanket the native vegetation and impede water flow. Water hyacinth was partly responsible for a massive diversion of water along the Gwydir River in New South Wales in the 1970s. A current and uncontrolled weed problem is the *Salvinia molesta* infestation in Kakadu National Park, but even this is dwarfed by the 45,000 hectares (111,000 acres) infested by *Mimosa pigra* on the floodplains in the Northern Territory. Farther south, alligator weed, *Alternanthera philoxeroides* and willows, *Salix* species, have also aggressively invaded wetlands.

Exotic plants threaten many wetlands in New Guinea. Whilst *Salvinia molesta* is under control in Papua New Guinea, water hyacinth is not and could cause major problems.

Feral animals also cause major problems. The buffalo problem in the Northern Territory has already been mentioned. More widespread and even more difficult to control is the feral pig which is particularly common in inland wetlands in Australia. Pigs disturb the soil and vegetation and affect native animals by competing for food, destroying habitats and direct predation.

The cane toad is regarded as a serious pest in northern Australia as it has a destructive effect on the native fauna; it eats some and is poisonous to many other potential predators. Introduced fish, especially the mosquito fish (*Gambusia affinis*), have become established in many wetlands and can deleteriously affect native fish populations.

In Papua New Guinea, distinctive river basin fish are threatened by fish introductions from other basins and from outside the archipelago. Unfortunately, it has proved extremely difficult and expensive to control feral animal populations, especially in the more inaccessible wetlands.

Tourism and Recreation
Tourism and recreational activities pose an increasing threat to wetlands in both heavily and sparsely populated areas. Tourist facilities, such as holiday resorts and marinas, are developed at the expense of wetland habitats, and wetland resources can be over-utilized. For example, excessive fishing of the silver

barramundi has had disastrous effects on the commercial and recreational fishing industries in Queensland. Throughout Australasia and Oceania recreational and sport fishing are immensely important. Fish habitats must be protected to conserve stocks. Too often this has not been done. This is the case with the Murray cod in the Murray-Darling Basin in southeastern Australia.

Much recreational activity is incompatible with the use of wetlands by birds, and yet birds are a major attraction in themselves. The region of the Gippsland Lakes in Victoria is one area where rapid expansion of recreational facilities has taken place. Similarly, the eastern coast of Queensland has seen a plethora of tourist developments. Off-road vehicles used by developers and tourists cause immense localized damage to wetlands and can destroy the resource that originally attracted the tourists.

On many Oceanic islands the remaining mangroves are still not safe from destruction. In particular, they are constantly threatened by tourist developments. Too often these developments pay little regard to the natural values of the mangroves and are accompanied by extensive road and public amenity infrastructures. As these economies become more and more dependent on the tourist industry for survival there is an ever-increasing risk of further wetland destruction.

WETLAND MANAGEMENT AND CONSERVATION
Wetland management and conservation in Australia are matters for the states and territories. National and international activities are coordinated through a council (CONCOM) comprising representatives from conservation departments in all states and territories. New Zealand and Papua New Guinea have observer status on this council.

The federal government of Australia is a signatory to the World Heritage Convention and in 1974 was the first signatory to the Ramsar Convention on Wetlands of International Importance. Moves are under way for Australia to join the Bonn Convention on Migratory Species. Two bilateral migratory bird agreements have been signed, with Japan (JAMBA) and China (CAMBA), and there is hope of a similar agreement being signed with the USSR.

Within each state or territory, national parks and wildlife services as well as conservation departments are responsible for direct conservation of wetlands. Therefore, whilst the federal government liaises with the Ramsar Bureau, for example, the states and territories are responsible for nominating and managing Ramsar sites - these currently number 40 and cover 4.48 million hectares (11 million acres). The establishment of a commission responsible for the Murray-Darling Basin is an attempt to integrate management activities in this important area. The commission currently incorporates three states and the federal government. In Queensland a series of coastal fisheries reserves has also been established, under the responsibility of the State Department of Primary Industries.

Governmental initiatives have recently expanded and considerable sums of money have been raised for wetland conservation through a duck stamp issue. Support has also been given to waterfowl and shorebird counts and education initiatives such as the Shortlands Wetland Centre in Newcastle.

Non-governmental organizations (NGOs) are now very active in wetland conservation issues. This includes an array of hunting associations seeking to reduce the controversy over annual duck hunting seasons and to improve the image of duck hunters. Conversely, an alliance of conservationists and animal liberationists is seeking to limit, if not totally ban, all duck hunting. Other NGOs have actively campaigned to further protect the wetlands of Kakadu National Park and have received considerable public backing. Special mention must be made of the Australian Littoral Society in Queensland that has been actively engaged in protecting coastal and marine wetlands for several decades, often in the face of determined offical and industrial or developmental opposition.

There is no specific legislation for wetland conservation in Papua New Guinea. Legislation directed towards general conservation, environmental planning and public water supply objectives does cover wetland areas. In Indonesia and hence in Irian Jaya the commercial harvesting of mangroves is regulated; undisturbed zones, 50 m (164 ft) wide along the seaward margin and 10 m (33 ft) wide along the rivers, are left. Subsistence use of mangroves is not regulated. Neither Papua New Guinea nor Indonesia is a member of the Ramsar or World Heritage Conventions.

New Zealand is a signatory to the World Heritage and Ramsar Conventions. Wetland conservation now comes fully within the remit of the Department of Conservation. Besides monitoring wetlands the department actively advocates protection of wetlands with landowners and developers. This can mean balancing economic activities with conservation goals rather than simply establishing areas solely for nature protection. Increased public awareness and education and involvement in conservation play a major role in promoting wetland conservation on both private and public land. NGOs are also active in waterfowl and wetland conservation and are attempting, as in Australia, to raise their public profile in order to further wetland conservation.

208

Glossary

Acid(ic) see **pH**

Acidification The process of becoming more acid

Algae Collective name of a large group of chlorophyll-containing plants, comprising the seaweeds and various freshwater forms, ranging in size from single cells to long stems

Algal Bloom Dramatic increase in algal growth resulting from high levels of nutrients or pollutants

Alkali Wetlands see **pH**

Alkaline see **pH**

Alluvial Formed by river flow processes e.g. alluvial plain

Alluvium Sediment deposited by flowing water

Anadromous Fish Fish that migrate from the sea into rivers or into coastal waters to spawn

Anaerobic (also Anoxic) Lacking oxygen; anaerobic organisms need an environment without oxygen

Anoxic see **Anaerobic**

Anthropogenic Of human origin; or relating to man

Aquaculture Fish or seafood farming

Aquatic plants:
  Emergent Plants, such as sedges, reeds and rushes, rooted in the sediment and protruding above the water surface
  Free-Floating Plants, such as water fern, floating at the water surface
  Floating-Leaved Plants, such as waterlilies, rooted in the sediment with leaves floating on the water surface
  Submerged Plants, such as najas, growing below the water surface

Aquifer An underground layer of rock, sand or gravel which holds water and allows water to percolate through

Bedrock Unbroken solid rock, usually overlaid by rock fragments or soil

Benthic Organisms Organisms attached to or rooted in the substratum at the bottom of a water body

Billabongs An Australian term for pools associated with a river channel which is isolated from the river in the dry season. Strictly the term refers to **Oxbow Lakes**

Biogeographical Region A region characterized by distinctive flora and fauna

Biological Control Control of pests using biological means, such as natural enemies

Biomass The amount (weight) of living material (plants or animals)

Biosphere Reserves A global network of reserves coordinated through UNESCO's 'Man and the Biosphere' programme to conserve the diversity and integrity of natural ecosystems; and to provide areas for environmental research, and for education and training

Biota Animal and plant life

Bivalves Invertebrates such as oyster, clam or mussel that have two shells hinged together

Blue-Green Algae see **Cyanobacteria**

Bonn Convention An international treaty for the conservation of migratory species

Boreal The Boreal climatic region lies below the Arctic region and is characterized by a vast belt of coniferous forest such as the taiga in the Soviet Union. (*Boreas* is the Latin word for north wind).

Brackish Slightly salty

Braided Rivers Rivers with mid-channel bars, exposed as islands at low flow, with a network of channels between them

Bryophytes A group of plants comprising mosses and liverworts

Calcareous Chalky

Capillary Streams Numerous small streams that feed into a larger stream, or that connect between two parts of a larger stream

Catchment see **Drainage Basin**

Cetaceans A group of mainly marine mammals including whales, dolphins and porpoises (belonging to the order Cetacea)

Chrysophytes Single-celled algae, of the Chrysophyta division, commonly called golden algae. Those with silica in their cell walls are called **diatoms**

Cyanobacteria Single-cell or filamentous organisms, also known as **blue-green algae** that are able to convert atmospheric nitrogen into forms that can be utilized for plant growth

Cyprinid Fish belonging to the family Cyprinidae, such as the carp

Dambo African term for seasonal rain-fed wetlands in impervious depressions

Deoxygenation Depletion of oxygen

Diatoms Single-celled algae found in most waters. Each cell is surrounded by two overlapping silica plates which show characteristic patterns. Diatoms are very important in food chains and are extremely productive (see also **Chrysophytes**)

Dissolved Oxygen Amount of oxygen in water

Drainage Basin In the context of this book: the area drained by a river and all its tributaries; also referred to as **Catchment** or, in North America, as **Watershed**

Ecotone Transitional zone between two plant communities, such as grassland and forest, or tundra and taiga. Ecotones are often species-rich as they receive immigrants from both sides.

Endemic Species Species that are unique to one region, i.e. they are found nowhere else in the world

Endoreic Drainage basins with no outlet to the sea

Ephemeral Waterbodies Hold water for very short periods only

Epiphytes Plants or animals that grow on plants. The host plants are used only as support, not as a source for nutrients

Eukaryotic Organisms, either single-celled or muticellular, whose cells contain a nucleus with a surrounding membrane. Their cells also contain other organelles, and their genetic information is organized in chromosomes (see also **Prokaryotic**)

Eutrophic see **Trophic Status**

Eutrophication Nutrient (mainly nitrogen and phosphorus) enrichment of a water body

Evaporation Loss of water from a free water surface or from the soil surface by vaporization

Evapotranspiration The combined loss of water by **Evaporation** and **Transpiration**

Exoreic Drainage basin with an outlet to coastal water

Fans Fan-shaped deposits. Alluvial fans are formed when the flow velocity of streams is suddenly decreased, for example at the mouth of ravines or at the foot of mountains

Fjord Narrow bay bordered by steep mountains

Flagellates Microscopic organisms (bacteria or **Algae**) that use whip-like filaments, called flagellae, to move around

Fluviatile Influenced or characterized by rivers; or found in or near rivers

Flyway Major route used by migratory birds

Fossil Water Water that has been in the aquifer since prehistoric times

Galaxiid Fish Australian freshwater fish of the genus *Galaxias* sometimes referred to as 'native trout'

Gallery Forest Tropical forest growing on **Levees** of rivers

Halobacteria Bacteria adapted to saline conditions

Herbaceous Plants Herb-like plants (as opposed to grasses)

Herbivorous Feeding on plants

Holarctic Realm See **Palearctic Realm**

Hummocky Moraines Glacial deposits with rounded conical hills and depressions formed under stagnating ice sheets

Hydrology The study of the cycle of water movement on, over and through the surface of the earth

Hydrosere Collective term for all stages in a succession beginning in water or wet habitats. It refers to a serial progression of plant communities and soils resulting from basin infilling or drying to a terrestrial community.

Hypersaline Containing high concentrations of salt. Hypersaline lakes, for example, are saltier than sea water

Insectivorous Feeding on insects

Inter-tidal The area between the high and low water marks which is exposed at low tide

Invertebrates Animals without back bones, such as insects and crustaceans

Lacustrine Living or occurring on or in lakes; also: of a lake, as is lacustrine floodplain

Leaching The process of nutrients being washed down through the soil into the groundwater

Littoral Zone The area extending from the high water mark into the water as far as the limit of the zone where **Photosynthesis** exceeds **Respiration**

Levee Raised bank along a river or **Riverine** floodplain

Macroalgae Literally 'big algae'. The term is used to differentiate these from small algae that have to be studied under the microscope

Macrophytes Literally 'big plants', used to describe water plants other than microscopic algae

Meandering Winding or bending in river beds; usually erosion occurs on the outer bend, while sediment is deposited on the inner bend. This can lead to the meander being cut off and the river changing its channel

Mesolithic Characteristic for a certain period during the Stone Age (c. 8500 BC)

Mesotrophic see **Trophic Status**

Microbial Respiration See **Respiration**

Microclimate The climate of a very small or confined area, influenced by local conditions

Monoculture Cultivation of the same crop in the same area year after year

Monospecific Stands Stands of one plant species only

Moraine A ridge or mound formed by a glacier

Nearctic Realm see **Palearctic Realm**

Nutrient Loading The amount of nutrients available over a time period

Oligotrophic see **Trophic Status**

Ombrotrophic Literally 'fed by rain'. The term applies to areas such as bogs that are entirely dependent on rain for their nutrient supply

Omnivorous Eating all kinds of food

Oxbow Lakes (Oxbows) Lakes formed in former river beds, when a bend in a **Meandering** river is cut off from the main stream

Oxidation Release of electrons or hydrogen ions. This reaction releases energy

Palearctic Realm A biogeographical region comprising Europe, northern Asia and North Africa. Together with the **Nearctic Realm**, that is temperate and arctic North America and also Greenland, it forms the **Holarctic Realm**

Pan Depression containing water, mud or mineral salts

Passerines Birds belonging to the large order of Passeriformes which embraces more than half of all birds. Also called songbirds or perching birds. They include finches, larks, sparrows, thrushes, crows, etc.

PCBs (Polychlorinated biphenyls) A class of chemicals used as electrical insulators. PCBs persist in the environment and accumulate through the foodchain.

Peat Dead plant material that has accumulated for a long time. It forms where the natural cycle of plant production and decomposition is disrupted under waterlogged conditions.

Periphyton Plants that grow attached to a solid, non-living substrate, such as rock or plastic

pH A measure of acidity of water, in which pH7 is neutral, values above 7 are alkaline and values below 7 acid. The ocean has a pH of about 8, an alkaline lake might be pH 10, and an acid bog pH 3.5

Photosynthesis The complex process carried out by plants and some bacteria in which light energy absorbed by the pigment chlorophyll is used to convert water and carbon dioxide into sugar (carbohydrates); oxygen is released

Phytoplankton The plant component of **Plankton**

Plankton Small organisms suspended in the water column. The plants are called **Phytoplankton**, the animals **Zooplankton**

Pleistocene The last ice age from 1.5 million to c.10,000 years ago

Podocarp Any tree from the coniferous Podocarpaceae family, which mainly occurs in the southern hemisphere

Polychaetes Group of animals (Polychaeta) including most of the common marine worms

Prokaryotic Primitive organisms whose cells do not contain nuclei or cell organelles, and whose genetic information is not organised into chromosomes (see also **Eukaryotic**)

Prop Roots Roots that grow from the tree trunk down to the soil or substrate as in some mangrove species

Reduction Uptake of electrons or hydrogen ions. This process consumes energy

Respiration The process by which the energy of organic material is made available to drive energy-consuming processes in the cell, such as the formation of cell walls, proteins, or cell movement. Carried out by plants (phyto-), animals (zoo-) and bacteria (microbial respiration), it can be aerobic in which case oxygen is consumed, or **Anaerobic**. In both cases carbon dioxide is given off

Riverine Situated beside a river; or of a river

Run-Off Overland flow of water following rain or irrigation events

Salmonid Fish A member of the salmon family, Salmonidae

Saltpan Dry bed of a salt lake after all water has evaporated; also: artificial basin created for evaporating sea water to collect salt

Salt Water Intrusion The inflow of salt water into fresh water habitats or aquifers, usually caused by a disruption of natural systems.

Sheet-Flow Slow overland flow of water across wide areas

Shell Middens A mound consisting of shells of edible molluscs (snails, mussels, clams, etc.), indicating a site of prehistoric occupation

Shoals Exposed sandbanks

Siltation The filling up of a wetland with water-borne sediment

Slash-and-Burn Farming A type of agriculture maintained by natives in tropical rain forest regions in which a patch of forest is cut and burned; crops are grown in the clearing until the soil is exhausted. The people then move on to another area and leave these fields to regenerate

Spit A narrow point of land projecting into the water

Sudd A mass of floating vegetation. The term originated from floating islands of papyrus on the White Nile

Terrapin Edible turtles or tortoises of the Emydidae family

Transhumant Characteristic of the seasonal migration of livestock and their herders between lowlands and adjacent mountains

Transpiration The loss of water from the leaves of plants through small pores (stomata) which close over night or under water stress (drought) conditions

Trophic Status Trophic comes from the Greek word for feeding. There are generally three classes distinguished:
1. eutrophic (well-fed) means nutrient-rich and is usually associated with low oxygen levels;
2. mesotrophic (medium);
3. oligotophic (little-fed), nutrient-poor except for oxygen.
The trophic status for any one wetland is a condition determined by the surrounding catchment, landform and geology

Viviparous Giving birth to live young

Wadi Arabian term for the channel of a watercourse that is dry except during period of rainfall

Wet Meadows Grazing land adjacent to wetlands that is flooded at peak water levels

World Heritage UNESCO international treaty for the conservation of cultural and national heritage

Zooplankton The animal component of **Plankton**

Ramsar Sites

Designated by the Contracting Parties -
Convention on Wetlands of International
Importance especially as Waterfowl Habitat
Ramsar, 1971

ALGERIA
Designated 4 November 1983
Lac Oubeïra — 2,200ha
Lac Tonga — 2,700ha

AUSTRALIA
Designated 8 May 1974
Cobourg Peninsula — 191,660ha
Designated 12 June 1980
Kakadu (Stage I) — 667,000ha
Designated 16 November 1982
Moulting Lagoon — 3,930ha
Logan Lagoon — 2,320ha
Sea Elephant Conservation Area — 1,730ha
Pittwater-Orielton Lagoon — 2,920ha
Apsley Marshes — 940ha
Cape Barren Island,
   east coast lagoons — 4,230ha
Lower Ringarooma River — 1,650ha
Jocks Lagoon — 70ha
Lake Crescent — 270ha
Little Waterhouse Lake — 90ha
Designated 15 December 1982
Corner Inlet — 51,500ha
Barmah Forest — 28,500ha
Gunbower Forest — 19,450ha
Hattah-Kulkyne Lakes — 1,018ha
Kerang Wetlands — 9,172ha
Port Phillip Bay & Bellarine
   Peninsula — 7,000ha
Western Port — 52,325ha
Western District Lakes — 30,182ha
Gippsland Lakes — 43,046ha
Lake Albacutya — 10,700ha
Designated 21 February 1984
Towra Point — 281ha
Kooragang — 2,206ha
Designated 1 November 1985
The Coorong and Lakes
   Alexandrina & Albert — 140,500ha
Bool and Hacks Lagoons — 3,200ha
Designated 1 August 1986
Macquarie Marshes — 18,200ha
Designated 15 June 1987
Coongie Lakes — 1,980,000ha
Designated 23 September 1987
Riverland — 30,600ha
Designated 15 September 1989
Kakadu (Stage II) — 692,940ha
Designated 25 January 1990
Ord River floodplain — 130,000ha
Lakes Argyle and Kununurra — 150,000ha
Roebuck Bay — 50,000ha
Eighty-mile Beach — 125,000ha

Forrestdale and Thomsons Lakes — 754ha
Peel-Yalgorup system — 21,000ha
Lake Toolibin — 437ha
Vasse-Wonnerup system — 740ha
Lake Warden system — 2,300ha

AUSTRALIA (CHRISTMAS ISLAND)
Designated 11 December 1990
Hosnie's Spring — 1ha

AUSTRIA
Designated 16 December 1982
Neusiedlersee — 60,000ha
Donau-March-Auen — 38,500ha
Untere Lobau — 1,039ha
Stauseen am Unteren Inn — 870ha
Rheindelta, Bodensee — 1,960ha

BELGIUM
Designated 4 March 1986
Vlaamse Banken — 1,900ha
Schorren van de Schelde — 417ha
Zwin — 550ha
IJzerbroeken — 2,160ha
Kalmthoutse Heide — 4,045ha
Marais d'Harchies — 535ha

BOLIVIA
Designated 27 June 1990
Laguna Colorada — 5,240ha

BULGARIA
Designated 24 September 1975
Srébarna — 600ha
Arkoutino — 97ha
Designated 28 November 1984
Atanassovo Lake — 1,050ha
Durankulak Lake — 350ha

BURKINA FASO
Designated 27 June 1990
La Mare d'Oursi — 45,000ha
La Mare aux hippopotames — 16,300ha
Parc national du "W" — 235,000ha

CANADA
Designated 15 January 1981
Cap Tourmente — 2,200ha
Designated 24 May 1982
Mary's Point — 1,200ha
Long Point — 13,730ha
Delta Marsh — 23,000ha
Last Mountain Lake — 15,600ha
Whooping Crane Summer Range — 1,689,500ha
Peace-Athabasca Delta — 321,300ha
Hay-Zama Lakes — 50,000ha
Alaksen — 520ha
Old Crow Flats — 617,000ha
Polar Bear Pass — 262,400ha

Queen Maud Gulf — 6,200,000ha
Rasmussen Lowlands — 300,000ha
McConnell River — 32,800ha
Dewey Soper Migratory
   Bird Sanctuary — 815,900ha
Designated 16 October 1985
St. Clair — 244ha
Chignecto — 1,020ha
Designated 27 May 1987
Polar Bear Provincial Park — 2,408,700ha
Lac Saint-François — 2,214ha
Baie de l'Isle-Verte — 1,927ha
Shepody Bay — 12,200ha
Grand Codroy Estuary — 925ha
Quill Lakes — 63,500ha
Oak Hammock Marsh — 3,600ha
Southern James Bay (Moose
   River & Hannah Bay) — 25,290ha
Point Pelee — 1,564ha
Musquodoboit Harbour — 1,925ha
Beaverhill Lake — 18,050ha
Designated 5 November 1987
Southern Bight-Minas Basin — 26,800ha
Designated 28 April 1988
Malpeque Bay — 24,440ha

CHAD
Designated 13 June 1990
Lac Fitri — 195,000ha

CHILE
Designated 27 July 1981
Carlos Anwandter Sanctuary — 4,877ha

CZECH AND SLOVAK FEDERAL REPUBLIC
Designated 2 July 1990
Modravské slate — 3,615ha
Trebonské rybníky — 10,165ha
Novozámecky a Brehynsky rybník — 923ha
Lednické rybníky — 553ha
Súr — 984ha
Parízské mociare — 141ha
Cicovské mrtve rameno — 135ha
Senné - rybníky — 442ha

DENMARK
Designated 2 September 1977
Fiilso — 4,320ha
Ringkobing Fjord — 27,520ha
Stadil and Veststadil Fjords — 7,184ha
Nissum Fjord — 11,600ha
Nissum Bredning with Harboore
   and Agger Peninsulas — 13,280ha
Vejlerne and Logstor Bredning — 45,280ha
Ulvedybet and Nibe Bredning — 20,304ha
Hirsholmene — 480ha
Nordre Ronner — 2,923ha
Læso — 67,840ha
Randers and Mariager Fjords (part) — 41,440ha

Anholt Island sea area	12,720ha	Wongha-Wonghé	380,000ha	Velence - Dinnyés	965ha
Horsens Fjord and Endelave	43,200ha	Petit Loango	480,000ha	Kardoskút	488ha
Stavns Fjord and adjacent waters	16,320ha	Setté Cama	220,000ha	Kisbalaton	14,745ha
Lillebælt	37,330ha			Mártély	2,232ha
Nærå Coast and Æbelo area	13,800ha	**GERMANY**		Kiskunság	3,903ha
South Funen Archipelago	39,200ha	*Designated 26 February 1976*		Pusztaszer	5,000ha
Sejero Bugt	42,560ha	Wattenmeer, Elbe - Weser - Dreieck	38,460ha	Hortobágy	15,000ha
Waters off Skælskor Nor and Glæno	17,120ha	Wattenmeer, Jadebusen &		*Designated 17 March 1989*	
Karrebæk, Dybso and Avno Fjords	19,200ha	westliche Wesermündung	49,490ha	Ocsa	1,078ha
Waters south-east of Fejo		Ostfriesisches Wattenmeer		Tata, Old Lake	269ha
and Femo Isles	32,640ha	& Dollart	121,620ha	Lake Fertö	2,870ha
Præsto Fjord, Jungshoved		Niederelbe, Elbaussendeichsgelände		Lake Balaton	59,800ha
Nor, Ulfshale and Nyord	25,960ha	Ostemündung bis Freiburg	11,760ha	Bodrogzug	3,782ha
Nakskov Fjord and Inner Fjord	8,960ha	Elbaue, Schnackenburg - Lauenburg	7,560ha		
Maribo Lakes	4,400ha	Dümmersee	3,600ha	**ICELAND**	
Waters between Lolland and		Diepholzer Moorniederung	15,060ha	*Designated 2 December 1977*	
Falster (incl. Rodsand etc.)	36,800ha	Steinhuder Meer	5,730ha	Myvatn-Laxá region (part)	20,000ha
Ertholmene Islands east of Bornholm	1,257ha	Rhein, Eltville - Bingen	475ha	*Designated 20 March 1990*	
Designated 14 May 1987		Bodensee	1,077ha	Thjórsárver	37,500ha
Vadehavet	140,830ha	Donauauen & Donaumoos	8,000ha		
		Lech - Donau - Winkel	230ha	**INDIA**	
DENMARK (GREENLAND)		Ismaninger Speichersee &		*Designated 1 October 1981*	
Designated 27 January 1988		Fischteichen	900ha	Chilka Lake	116,500ha
Aqajarua-Sullorsuaq	30,000ha	Ammersee	6,517ha	Keoladeo National Park	2,873ha
Qinguata Marraa-Kuussuaq	6,000ha	Starnberger See	5,720ha	*Designated 23 March 1990*	
Kuannersuit Kuussuat	4,500ha	Chiemsee	8,660ha	Wular Lake	18,900ha
Kitsissunnguit	16,000ha	Unterer Inn, Haiming - Neuhaus	1,955ha	Harike Lake	4,100ha
Naternaq	150,000ha	*Designated 31 July 1978*		Loktak Lake	26,600ha
Eqalummiut Nunaat-		Rügen/Hiddensee	25,800ha	Sambhar Lake	24,000ha
Nassuttuup Nunaa	500,000ha	Krakower Obersee	870ha		
Ikkattoq	35,000ha	Müritz See	4,830ha	**IRAN, ISLAMIC REUPBLIC OF**	
Ydre Kitsissut	8,000ha	Unterer Havel & Gülper See	5,792ha	*Designated 23 June 1975*	
Heden	125,000ha	Odertal, Schwedt	5,400ha	Miankaleh Peninsula, Gorgan Bay and	
Hochstetter Forland	140,000ha	Peitz Teichgebiete	1,060ha	Lapoo-Zaghmarz Ab-bandan	40,000ha
Kilen	30,000ha	Stausee Berga-Kelbra	1,360ha	Lake Parishan and Dasht-e-Arjan	6,600ha
		Galenbecker See	1,015ha	Lake Oroomiyeh (Rezaiyeh)	483,000ha
ECUADOR		*Designated 28 October 1983*		Neiriz Lake & Kamjan Marshes	108,000ha
Designated 7 September 1990		Rieselfelder Münster	233ha	Anzali Mordab (Talab) complex	15,000ha
Manglares-Churute	35,000ha	Weserstaustufe Schlüsselburg	1,550ha	Shadegan Marshes & mudflats of	
Machalilla	55,000ha	Unterer Niederrhein	25,000ha	Khor-al Amaya & Khor Musa	190,000ha
		Designated 1 August 1990		Hamoun-e-Saberi &	
EGYPT		Hamburgisches Wattenmeer	1,170ha	Hamoun-e-Helmand	50,000ha
Designated 9 September 1988				Lake Kobi	1,200ha
Lake Bardawil	59,500ha	**GHANA**		Hamoun-e-Puzak, south end	10,000ha
Lake Burullus	46,200ha	*Designated 22 February 1988*		Shurgol & Dorgeh Sangi Lakes	2,500ha
		Owabi	7,260ha	Bandar Kiashahr Lagoon	
FINLAND				and mouth of Sefid Rud	500ha
Designated 28 May 1974		**GREECE**		Amirkelayeh Lake	1,230ha
Aspskär	369ha	*Designated 21 August 1975*		Lake Gori	120ha
Söderskär and Långören	9,632ha	Evros Delta	10,000ha	Alagol, Ulmagol and Ajigol Lakes	1,400ha
Björkör and Lågskär	5,760ha	Lake Vistonis and Porto		Khuran Straits	100,000ha
Signilskär	11,600ha	Lagos Lagoons	10,000ha	Deltas of Rud-e-Shur, Rud-e-	
Valassaaret and Björkögrunden	17,700ha	Lake Mitrikou & adjoining lagoons	3,800ha	Shirin and Rud-e-Minab	20,000ha
Krunnit	4,600ha	Nestos Delta and		Deltas of Rud-e-Gaz and	
Ruskis	235ha	Gumburnou Lagoon	10,600ha	Rud-e-Hara	15,000ha
Viikki	247ha	Lakes Volvi and Langada (Koronia)	2,400ha	Gavkhouni Lake and marshes	
Suomujärvi - Patvinsuo	9,400ha	Kerkini reservoir	9,000ha	of the lower Zaindeh Rud	43,000ha
Martimoaapa - Lumiaapa	7,400ha	Axios - Loudias - Aliakmon Delta	11,000ha		
Koitilaiskaira	34,400ha	Lakes Mikri Prespa &		**IRELAND**	
		Megali Prespa	8,000ha	*Designated 15 November 1984*	
FRANCE		Amvrakikos Gulf	25,000ha	Wexford	194ha
Designated 1 October 1986		Messolonghi Lagoons	13,900ha	*Designated 31 July 1986*	
Camargue	85,000ha	Kotichi Lagoon	3,700ha	The Raven	589ha
Designated 8 April 1991				Pettigo Plateau	900ha
Etangs de la Champagne humide	135,000ha	**GUATEMALA**		Slieve Bloom Mountains	2,230ha
Etangs de la Petite Woëvre	5,300ha	*Designated 26 June 1990*		Owenduff catchment	1,382ha
Marais du Cotentin et		Laguna del Tigre	45,000ha	*Designated 1 June 1987*	
du Bessin, Baie des Veys	32,500ha			Owenboy	397ha
Golfe du Morbihan	20,000ha	**GUINEA-BISSAU**		Knockmoyle/Sheskin	732ha
La Brenne	140,000ha	*Designated 14 May 1990*		Lough Barra Bog	176ha
Rives du Lac Léman	3,335ha	Lagoa de Cufada	39,098ha	*Designated 6 September 1988*	
Etang de Biguglia	1,450ha			North Bull Island	1,436ha
		HUNGARY		*Designated 25 October 1988*	
GABON		*Designated 11 April 1979*		Rogerstown Estuary	195ha
Designated 30 December 1986		Szaporca	257ha	Baldoyle Estuary	203ha

Designated 6 December 1988
Clara Bog	460ha
Mongan Bog	127ha
Raheenmore Bog	162ha

Designated 10 July 1989
Tralee Bay	861ha

Designated 30 May 1990
Castlemaine Harbour	923ha
Easkey Bog	607ha
The Gearagh	300ha
Coole/Garryland	364ha
Pollardstown Fen	130ha
Meenachullion Bog	194ha

ITALY
Designated 14 December 1976
Pian di Spagna - Lago di Mezzola	1,740ha
Vincheto di Cellarda	99ha
Sacca di Bellocchio	223ha
Valle Santa	261ha
Punte Alberete	480ha
Palude di Colfiorito	157ha
Padule di Bolgheri	562ha
Laguna di Orbetello	887ha
Lago di Burano	410ha
Lago di Nazzano	265ha
Lago di Fogliano	395ha
Lago dei Monaci	94ha
Lago di Caprolace	229ha
Lago di Sabaudia	1,474ha
Lago di Barrea	303ha
Stagno di S'Ena Arrubia	300ha
Stagno di Molentargius	1,401ha
Stagno di Cagliari	3,466ha

Designated 6 December 1977
Le Cesine	620ha

Designated 10 March 1978
Valle Cavanata	243ha

Designated 28 March 1979
Stagno di Cabras	3,575ha
Stagno di Corru S'Ittiri e Stagno di San Giovanni e Marceddì	2,610ha
Stagno di Pauli Maiori	287ha
Valle Campotto e Bassarone	1,363ha

Designated 14 May 1979
Marano Lagunare - Foci dello Stella	1,400ha

Designated 2 August 1979
Saline di Margherita di Savoia	3,871ha

Designated 19 September 1980
Lago di Tovel	37ha

Designated 21 July 1981
Torre Guaceto	940ha

Designated 4 September 1981
Valle di Gorino	1,330ha
Valle Bertuzzi	3,100ha
Valli residue del Comprensorio di Comacchio	13,500ha
Piallassa della Baiona e Risega	1,630ha
Ortazzo e Ortazzino	440ha
Saline di Cervia	785ha

Designated 3 May 1982
Stagno di Sale Porcus	324ha
Stagno di Mistras	680ha

Designated 5 December 1984
Valli del Mincio	1,081ha
Torbiere d'Iseo	324ha
Palude Brabbia	459ha
Palude di Ostiglia	123ha

Designated 12 April 1988
Biviere di Gela	256ha

Designated 11 April 1989
Laguna di Venezia: Valle Averto	200ha
Vendicari	1,450ha
Isola Boscone	201ha
Bacino dell'Angitola	875ha

Designated 22 May 1991
Diaccia Botrona	2,500ha

JAPAN
Designated 17 June 1980
Kushiro-shitsugen	7,726ha

Designated 13 September 1985
Izu-numa and Uchi-numa	559ha

Designated 6 July 1989
Kutcharo-ko	1,607ha

JORDAN
Designated 10 January 1977
Azraq Oasis	7,372ha

KENYA
Designated 5 June 1990
Lake Nakuru	18,800ha

MALI
Designated 25 May 1987
Walado Debo/Lac Debo	103,100ha
Séri	40,000ha
Lac Horo	18,900ha

MALTA
Designated 30 September 1988
Ghadira	11ha

MAURITANIA
Designated 22 October 1982
Banc d'Arguin	1,173,000ha

MEXICO
Designated 4 July 1986
Ría Lagartos	47,480ha

MOROCCO
Designated 20 June 1980
Merja Zerga	3,500ha
Merja Sidi Bourhaba	200ha
Lac d'Affennourir	380ha
Baie de Khnifiss	6,500ha

NEPAL
Designated 17 December 1987
Koshi Toppu	17,500ha

NETHERLANDS
Designated 23 May 1980
De Groote Peel	900ha
De Weerribben	3,400ha
Het Naardermeer	752ha
De Boschplaat	4,400ha
De Griend	23ha
De Biesbosch (part)	1,700ha

Designated 2 May 1984
Waddenzee	249,998ha

Designated 3 April 1987
Oosterschelde	38,000ha

Designated 15 June 1988
Zwanenwater	600ha

Designated 2 June 1989
Oostvaardersplassen	5,600ha
Engbertsdijksvenen	975ha

NETHERLANDS (NETHERLANDS ANTILLES)
Designated 23 May 1980
Het Lac	700ha
Het Pekelmeer	400ha
Klein Bonaire Island and adjacent sea	600ha
Het Gotomeer	150ha
De Slagbaai	90ha
Het Spaans Lagoen	70ha

NEW ZEALAND
Designated 13 August 1976
Waituna Lagoon	3,556ha
Farewell Spit	11,388ha

Designated 4 December 1989
Whangamarino	5,690ha
Kopuatai Peat Dome	9,665ha

Designated 29 January 1990
Firth of Thames	7,800ha

NIGER
Designated 30 April 1987
Parc national du "W"	220,000ha

NORWAY
Designated 9 July 1974
Åkersvika	415ha

Designated 24 July 1985
Ora	1,560ha
Kurefjorden	400ha
Nordre Oyeren	6,260ha
Ilene and Presterodkilen	177ha
Jaeren	400ha
Orlandet	2,920ha
Tautra and Svaet	2,054ha
Stabbursneset	1,620ha

NORWAY (SPITZBERGEN)
Designated 25 July 1985
Forlandsoyane	60ha
Dunoyane	120ha
Kongsfjorden	140ha
Isoyane	30ha
Gåsoyane	100ha

PAKISTAN
Designated 23 July 1976
Thanedar Wala	4,047ha
Malugul Dhand	405ha
Kandar Dam	251ha
Tanda Dam	405ha
Kheshki Reservoir	263ha
Khabbaki Lake	283ha
Kinjhar (Kalri) Lake	13,468ha
Drigh Lake	164ha
Haleji Lake	1,704ha

PANAMA
Designated 26 November 1990
Golfo de Montijo	80,765ha

POLAND
Designated 22 November 1977
Luknajno Lake	710ha

Designated 3 January 1984
Slonsk	4,166ha
Swidwie Lake	382ha
Karas Lake	816ha
Siedem Wysp	1,016ha

PORTUGAL
Designated 24 November 1980
Estuário do Tejo	14,563ha
Ria Formosa	16,000ha

ROMANIA
Designated 21 May 1991
Danube Delta	647,000ha

SENEGAL
Designated 11 July 1977
Djoudj	16,000ha
Bassin du Ndiaël	10,000ha

Designated 3 April 1984
Delta du Saloum	73,000ha

Designated 29 September 1986
Gueumbeul 720ha

SOUTH AFRICA
Designated 12 March 1975
De Hoop Vlei 750ha
Barberspan 3,118ha
Designated 2 October 1986
De Mond (Heuningnes Estuary) 1,318ha
Blesbokspruit 1,858ha
Turtle Beaches/Coral Reefs
    of Tongaland 39,500ha
St. Lucia System 155,500ha
Designated 25 April 1988
Langebaan 6,000ha

SPAIN
Designated 4 May 1982
Doñana 49,225ha
Las Tablas de Daimiel 1,812ha
Designated 8 August 1983
Laguna de Fuentepiedra 1,355ha
Designated 5 December 1989
Lagunas de Cádiz
    (Medina y Salada del Puerto) 158ha
Lagunas del Sur de Córdoba
    (Zóñar, Amarga, Rincón) 86ha
Marismas del Odiel 7,185ha
Salinas del Cabo de Gata 300ha
S'Albufera de Mallorca 1,700ha
Laguna de la Vega (o del Pueblo) 34ha
Lagunas de Villafáfila 2,854ha
Umia-Grove, La Lanzada, Punta
    Carreiron y Lagoa Bodeira 2,561ha
Ria de Ortigueira y Ladrido 2,920ha
La Albufera 21,000ha
El Hondo 2,337ha
Salinas de la Mata y Torrevieja 2,100ha
Salinas de Santa Pola 2,400ha
Prat de Cabanes - Torreblanca 860ha

SRI LANKA
Designated 15 June 1990
Bundala 6,216ha

SURINAME
Designated 18 March 1985
Coppename Rivermouth 12,000ha

SWEDEN
Designated 5 December 1974
Falsterbo - Foteviken 7,530ha
Klingavälsån - Krankesjön 3,970ha
Helgeån 5,480ha
Ottenby 1,610ha
Öland, east coast 8,460ha
Getterön 340ha
Kävsjön - Store Mosse 7,580ha
Gotland, east coast 4,220ha
Hornborgasjön 6,370ha
Tåkern 5,650ha
Kvismaren 780ha
Hjälstaviken 770ha
Ånnsjön 11,000ha
Gammelstadsviken 430ha
Persöfjärden 3,320ha
Tärnasjön 11,800ha
Tjålmejaure - Laisdalen 21,400ha
Laidaure 4,150ha
Sjaunja 188,600ha
Tavvavuoma 28,700ha
Designated 12 June 1989
Åsnen 16,800ha
Träslövsläge - Morups Tånge 1,990ha
Stigfjorden 5,180ha

Dättern 3,920ha
Östen 1,010ha
Kilsviken 8,910ha
Stockholm, outer archipelago 15,000ha
Svartåområdet 1,990ha
Hovranområdet 4,750ha
Umeälvens delta 1,040ha

SWITZERLAND
Designated 16 January 1976
Baie de Fanel & le Chablais 1,155ha
Designated 18 February 1982
Bolle di Magadino 661ha
Designated 9 November 1990
Les Grangettes 330ha
Rive sud du lac de Neuchâtel 3,063ha
Rade de Genève et Rhône
    en aval de Genève 1,032ha
Lac artificiel de Klingnau 355ha
Lac artificiel de Niederried 303ha
Kaltbrunner Riet 150ha

TUNISIA
Designated 24 November 1990
Ichkeul 12,600ha

UGANDA
Designated 4 March 1988
Lake George 15,000ha

UNION OF SOVIET SOCIALIST REPUBLICS
Designated 11 October 1976
Kandalaksha Bay 208,000ha
Matsalu Bay 48,634ha
Volga Delta 650,000ha
Kirov Bays 132,500ha
Krasnovodsk and
    North-Cheleken Bays 188,700ha
Sivash Bay 45,700ha
Karkinitski Bay 37,300ha
Dounai and Yagorlits &
    Tendrov Bays 128,051ha
Kourgaldzhin and Tengiz Lakes 260,500ha
Lakes of the lower Turgay
    and Irgiz 348,000ha
Issyk-kul Lake 629,800ha
Lake Khanka 310,000ha

UNITED KINGDOM
Designated 5 January 1976
Cors Fochno and Dyfi 2,497ha
Bridgwater Bay 2,703ha
Bure Marshes 412ha
Hickling Broad and Horsey Mere 892ha
Lindisfarne 3,123ha
Lochs Druidibeg, a'Machair
    and Stilligary 1,780ha
Loch Leven 1,597ha
Loch Lomond 253ha
Lough Neagh and Lough Beg 39,500ha
Minsmere - Walberswick 1,697ha
North Norfolk Coast 7,700ha
Ouse Washes 2,276ha
Rannoch Moor 1,499ha
Designated 24 July 1981
Cairngorm Lochs 179ha
Loch of Lintrathen 218ha
Claish Moss 563ha
Silver Flowe 608ha
Abberton Reservoir 1,228ha
Rostherne Mere 79ha
Designated 17 July 1985
Dee Estuary 13,055ha
The Swale 5,790ha
Chesil Beach and The Fleet 763ha

Derwent Ings 783ha
Holburn Moss 22ha
Irtinghead Mires 608ha
Designated 28 November 1985
Leighton Moss 125ha
Martin Mere 119ha
Alt Estuary 1,160ha
Designated 25 September 1986
Loch of Skene 125ha
Loch Eye 195ha
Rockcliffe Marshes 1,897ha
Designated 4 November 1987
Chichester and Langstone Harbours 5,749ha
Designated 5 February 1988
Upper Severn Estuary 1,437ha
Designated 30 March 1988
The Wash 63,124ha
Pagham Harbour 616ha
Designated 14 July 1988
Gruinart Flats 3,170ha
Eilean Na Muice Duibhe (Duich Moss) 574ha
Bridgend Flats 331ha
Gladhouse Reservoir 186ha
Din Moss - Hoselaw Loch 46ha
Designated 25 April 1990
Fala Flow 323ha
Glac-na-Criche 265ha
Feur Lochain 384ha
Loch-an-Duin 3,606ha
Designated 15 February 1991
Redgrave and South Lopham Fens 125ha

**UNITED KINGDOM (TURKS AND CAICOS
ISLANDS)**
Designated 27 June 1990
North, Middle & East Caicos Islands 37,270ha

UNITED STATES OF AMERICA
Designated 18 December 1986
Ash Meadows 9,509ha
Edwin B Forsythe NWR 13,080ha
Izembek 168,433ha
Okefenokee 159,889ha
Designated 4 June 1987
Everglades 566,143ha
Chesapeake Bay 45,000ha
Designated 19 October 1988
Cheyenne Bottoms 8,036ha
Designated 21 November 1989
Cache-Lower White Rivers 145,690ha
Designated 4 December 1990
Horicon Marsh 12,911ha

URUGUAY
Designated 22 May 1984
Bañados del Este y Franja Costera 200,000ha

VENEZUELA
Designated 23 November 1988
Cuare 9,968ha

VIETNAM
Designated 20 September 1988
Red River Estuary 12,000ha

YUGOSLAVIA
Designated 28 March 1977
Obedska Bara 17,501ha
Ludasko Lake 593ha

Number of Contracting Parties: 62
Number of sites designated: 527
Total area of designated sites: 31,933,543ha
Information taken from the Ramsar
Database 17 June 1991

Further Reading

B.J.E Awachie, 1976. 'On Fishing and Fisheries Management in Large Tropical African Rivers with Particular Reference to Nigeria', pp 37-45 in R. Welcomme, editor, *Fisheries Management in Large Rivers*. FAO Technical Report No.94, Rome, Italy.

M.J. Burgis and J.J. Symoens, editors, 1987. *African Wetlands and Shallow water bodies*. ORSTOM, Paris.

E. Carp, 1980. *Directory of Wetlands of International Importance in the Western Palearctic*. IUCN, Gland, Switzerland. 506 pp.

R.A. Chabreck, 1988. *Coastal Marshes, Ecology and Wildlife Management*. University of Minnesota Press. 138 pp.

J.R. Clark and J. Benforado, editors, 1981. *Wetlands of Bottomland Hardwoods*. Elsevier Scientific Publishing Co., N.Y., U.S.A. 401 pp.

B. Coles and J. Coles, 1989. *People of the wetlands. Bogs, bodies and lake dwellers*. Thames and Hudson, London.

N.J. Collar & P. Andrew, 1988. 'Birds to Watch. The ICBP World Checklist of Threatened Birds'. *ICBP Technical Publication No.8*. ICBP, Cambridge, U.K.

Conservation Foundation, 1988. *Protecting America's Wetlands: An Action Agenda*. The Final Report of the National Wetlands Policy Forum. The Conservation Foundation, Washington, D.C. 69 pp.

S. Cowling and D. Savin, 1989. *Wetlands wildlife: The nature of wetlands in southern Australia*, Gould League of Victoria Inc., Prahan, Australia. 56 pp.

CWS, 1986. *North American Waterfowl Management Plan: A Strategy for Cooperation*. Canadian Wildlife Service, Ottawa. 19 pp.

P. Denny, 1985. *The Ecology and Management of African Wetland Vegetation*. Kluwer Academic Publishers.

P.J. Dugan, editor, 1990. *Wetland Conservation: A review of current issues and required action*. World Conservation Union (IUCN), Gland, Switzerland.

W.S. Ellis, 1990. 'A Soviet Sea Lies Dying'. *National Geographic* 177(2): 73-92.

FAO, 1982. *Management and Utilization of Mangroves in Asia and the Pacific*. Environment Paper No.3. Rome, Italy. 160 pp.

R.F.A. Grimmett and T.A. Jones, 1989. *Important Bird Areas in Europe*. ICBP and IWRB, Cambridge, UK. 888 pp.

P. Hutchings and P. Saenger, 1987. *Ecology of Mangroves*. University of Queensland Press, St Lucia, Australia. 388 pp.

P.A. Johnsgard, 1975. *Waterfowl of North America*. Indiana University Press. 575 pages.

A.W.D. Larkum, A.J. McComb and S.A. Shepherd, 1989. *Biology of Seagrasses*. Elsevier, Amsterdam. 841 pp.

A.J. McComb and P.S. Lake, 1988. *The Conservation of Australian Wetlands*. Surrey Beatty & Sons Pty Limited, Sydney. 196 pp.

A.J. McComb and P.S. Lake, 1990. *Australian Wetlands*. Collins/Angus & Robertson Publishers Australia, North Ryde. 258 pp.

J. McCormick, 1985. *Acid Earth: the global threat of acid pollution*. Earthscan. London, UK. 191 pp.

E. Maltby, 1986. *Waterlogged Wealth. Why waste the world's wet places?* Earthscan, London. 200 pp.

G.V.T. Matthews, editor, 1990. 'Managing Waterfowl Populations, Proceedings of an IWRB Symposium, Astrakhan, USSR, 2-5 October 1989'. *IWRB Special Publication* No.12. Slimbridge, UK. 230 pp.

R.H. Mepham and S. Mepham, in press. *A Directory of African Wetlands of International Importance*. IUCN, Gland, Switzerland.

W.J. Mitsch and J. G. Gosselink, 1986. *Wetlands*. Van Nostrand Reinhold Co., New York. 539 p.

B. Moss, 1980. *Ecology of Fresh Waters*. Blackwell Scientific Publications, London. 332 pp.

B. Moss, 1988. *Ecology of Freshwaters, Man and Medium*. Blackwells, London.

D.S. Mitchell, 1977. *Aquatic Weeds in Australian Inland Waters*. AGPS, Canberra. 189 pp.

J.P. Myers, R.I.G. Morrison, P.Z. Antas, B.A. Harrington, T.E. Lovejoy, M. Sallaberry, S.E. Senner and A. Tarak, 1987. 'Conservation Strategies for Migratory Species'. *American Scientist* 75: 19-26.

R.L. Myers and J.J. Ewel, editors, 1990. *Ecosystems of Florida*. University of Florida Press, Gainesville.

W.A. Niering, 1985. *Wetlands: National Audubon Society Nature Guide*. A.A. Knopf Inc., New York.

A.I. Payne, 1986. *The Ecology of Tropical Lakes*. John Wiley and Son. Kluwer Academic Publishers.

Ramsar, 1990. *Directory of Wetlands of International Importance*. Ramsar Convention Bureau, Gland, Switzerland.

C.J. Richardson, 1981. *Pocosin Wetlands*. Hutchinson Ross Publishing Co., Stoudsburg, Pa. 364 pp.

D.A. Scott, editor, 1989. *A Directory of Asian Wetlands*. IUCN, Gland, Switzerland and Cambridge, UK. 1181 pp.

D.A. Scott and M. Carbonell, editors, 1986. *A Directory of Neotropical Wetlands*. IUCN, Cambridge, and IWRB, Slimbridge, U.K.

D.A. Scott and C.M. Poole, 1989. *A Status Overview of Asian Wetlands*. Asian Wetland Bureau, Kuala Lumpur, Malaysia.

C.J. Tait, 1965. *Bangweulu: The Fish and Fisheries of Zambia*. Falcon Press, Ndola, Zambia.

J. Teal and M. Teal, 1969. *Life and Death of the Salt Marsh*. Audubon/Ballantine Books, New York. 274 pp.

A. Van der Valk, editor, 1989. *Northern Prairie Wetlands*. Iowa State University Press, Ames. 400 pp.

M.W. Weller, 1981. *Freshwater Marshes, Ecology and Wildlife Management*. University of Minnesota Press. 137 pp.

M. Williams, editor, 1990. *Wetlands: a threatened landscape*. Blackwells.

World Commission on Environment and Development, 1987. *Our Common Future*. Oxford University Press, Oxford, UK, 400 pp.

J. Zelazny and J.S. Feierabend, editors, 1988. *Proceedings of a Conference: Increasing Our Wetland Resources*. National Wildlife Federation, Washington, D.C. 363 pp.

Index

GEOGRAPHICAL INDEX

INDEX COMPILED BY
MICHAEL ALLABY

Picture Credits

Maps by ML Design

Diagram drawings by Carl Meek

Photographs:
Title page R. May
10 E. Maltby
11 E. Maltby
13 E. Maltby
15 E. Maltby
16 E. Maltby
17 E. Maltby
20 E. Maltby
21 E. Maltby
22 E. Maltby
23 E. Maltby
24 E. Maltby
29 E. Maltby
31 P. Uhd Jepsen
33 K.G. Preston-Mafham/Premaphotos
Wildlife
36 M. Moser
38 T. Jones
39 top P. Uhd Jepsen
bottom T. Jones
41 left T. Jones
right K.G. Preston-Mafham/Premaphotos
Wildlife
42 left K.G. Preston-Mafham/Premaphotos
Wildlife
right T. Jones
43 K.G. Preston-Mafham/Premaphotos
Wildlife
44 K.G. Preston-Mafham/Premaphotos
Wildlife
45 top J. Hale
bottom M. Moser
46 P. Uhd Jepsen
48 T. Jones
49 J. Stewart-Smith
51 P. Uhd Jepsen
52 left T. Jones
right T. Jones
53 T. Jones
55 M. Moser
60 R.B. Newton
61 M. Moser
62 R.B. Newton
63 J.S. Larson
64 J. Green
65 J. Green
67 J. Green
68 US Fish and Wildlife Service
69 J.S. Larson
70 J.S. Larson
71 J. Green
72 J. Green
73 US Fish and Wildlife Service
74 US Fish and Wildlife Service
75 M. Moser
76 J. Stewart-Smith
77 US Fish and Wildlife Service
78 R.B. Newton
79 J. Blossom/Wildfowl and Wetlands
Trust
80 J. Green

81 top R.B. Newton
bottom J.S. Larson
82 J.S. Larson
83 R.B. Newton
88 D.A. Scott
89 D.A. Scott
90 top D.A. Scott
bottom D.A. Scott
91 D.A. Scott
92 D.A. Scott
93 D.A. Scott
94 D.A. Scott
95 D.A. Scott
96 M. Moser
98 D.A. Scott
99 D.A. Scott
101 D.A. Scott
102 D.A. Scott
103 top D.A. Scott
bottom D.A. Scott
104 K.G. Preston-Mafham/Premaphotos
Wildlife
105 D.A. Scott
106 top left K.G. Preston-Mafham/
Premaphotos Wildlife
top right D.A. Scott
bottom K.G. Preston-Mafham/
Premaphotos Wildlife
107 D.A. Scott
108 top D.A. Scott
bottom D.A. Scott
109 D.A. Scott
111 D.A. Scott
112 D.A. Scott
113 D.A. Scott
119 P. Denny
120 P. Denny
121 P. Denny
122 C. Perennou
123 top P. Denny
bottom J. Skinner
124 J. Skinner
125 J. Skinner
126 P. Denny
127 P. Denny
128 P. Denny
129 P. Denny
130 P. Denny
131 P. Denny
132 J. Duckett
134 P. Denny
135 K.G. Preston-Mafham/Premaphotos
Wildlife
136 Anthony Bannister/NHPA
137 K.G. Preston-Mafham/Premaphotos
Wildlife
138 top P. Denny
bottom P. Denny
139 J. Skinner
140 P. Denny
141 P. Denny
142 J. Skinner
143 P. Denny
144 top P. Denny
bottom P. Denny
145 P. Denny

146 P. Denny
147 P. Denny
153 M. Moser
154 D.A. Scott
155 top D.A. Scott
bottom D.A. Scott
156 D.A. Scott
157 D.A. Scott
159 J.S. Larson
160 C. Perennou
161 top D.A. Scott
bottom D.A. Scott
162 D.A. Scott
163 D.A. Scott
164 top D.A. Scott
bottom C. Prentice
165 D.A. Scott
166 D.A. Scott
167 D.A. Scott
168 C. Prentice
169 D.A. Scott
170 C. Perennou
171 C. Perennou
172 D.A. Scott
173 top D.A. Scott
bottom D.A. Scott
174 J. Stewart-Smith
175 D.A. Scott
177 D.A. Scott
182 S. Jacobs
183 C.M. Finlayson
186 left I. von Oertzen
right I. von Oertzen
187 C.M. Finlayson
188 top M. Armstrong
bottom C.M. Finlayson
190 top C.M. Finlayson
bottom K. Brennan
191 P. Wettin
192 C.M. Finlayson
193 A.G. Wells
194 C.M. Finlayson
195 top C.M. Finlayson
bottom A.G. Wells
196 M. Beilharz
197 P. Morrison/Department of
Conservation, New Zealand
198 P. Moore/Department of Conservation,
New Zealand
199 P. Osborne
200 P. Osborne
201 C.M. Finlayson
202 D. Mitchell
203 left A.G. Wells
right A.G. Wells
205 C.M. Finlayson
206 top C.M. Finlayson
bottom P. Osborne
207 C.M. Finlayson